A NOT-SO-DISMAL SCIENCE

A Broader View of Economies and Societies

Edited by

Mancur Olson
Satu Kähkönen

OXFORD
UNIVERSITY PRESS

OXFORD

UNIVERSITY PRESS

Great Clarendon Street, Oxford OX2 6DP

Oxford University Press is a department of the University of Oxford.
It furthers the University's objective of excellence in research, scholarship,
and education by publishing worldwide in

Oxford New York

Athens Auckland Bangkok Bogotá Buenos Aires Calcutta
Cape Town Chennai Dar es Salaam Delhi Florence Hong Kong Istanbul
Karachi Kuala Lumpur Madrid Melbourne Mexico City Mumbai
Nairobi Paris São Paulo Singapore Taipei Tokyo Toronto Warsaw

with associated companies in Berlin Ibadan

Oxford is a registered trade mark of Oxford University Press
in the UK and in certain other countries

Published in the United States
by Oxford University Press Inc., New York

British Library Cataloguing in Publication Data

Data available

Library of Congress Cataloging in Publication Data

A not-so-dismal science : a broader view of economies and societies /
edited by Mancur Olson and Satu Kähkönen.
p. cm.
Includes bibliographical references (p.).
1. Institutional economics.   2. Economics.   3. Social sciences.
I. Olson, Mancur.   II. Kähkönen, Satu.
HB99.5.N68   2000
330—dc21   98–33705
ISBN 0-19-829369-0 (hbk)
ISBN 0-19-829490-5 (pbk)

1 3 5 7 9 10 8 6 4 2

Typeset in 11 / 12.5 Dante
by Footnote Graphics, Warminster, Wilts
Printed in Great Britain on acid-free paper by
T. J. International Ltd, Padstow, Cornwall

To our colleagues at IRIS

Preface

We are all familiar with metropolitan areas in which the central city, while gaining some high-rise buildings, has a stagnant population and an increasing proportion of poor people at the same time that the suburbs are growing and prosperous. To a degree, modern economics is like such a metropolitan area. Magnificent as we believe the skyscrapers at the center of economics are, in most American universities the number of economics majors has declined, the proportion of economics majors who go on to graduate work in the discipline has fallen, and the job market for those who have earned a doctorate in economics has tightened. In macroeconomics, no single paradigm has generated the professional consensus that characterizes successful science. In most parts of economics, contrary to popular belief, economists usually agree. Economic quackery nonetheless often commands more attention from the press and the politicians than the best economics, and governments often choose public policies that economists know to be absurd.

At the same time, the suburbs of economics are expanding rapidly in all directions. In the study of politics, economists and political scientists using economics-type methods have had an extraordinary influence. They have created the substantial and growing field variously called collective (or public or social) choice, neoclassical political economy, or positive political theory. In the study of law, ideas from economics have been the single most important source of intellectual change and "law and economics" has become a major field. In economic history, the quantitative and theory-inspired approach of economics has, partly through "cliometrics," had a profound influence. In sociology, economics has had a smaller but growing influence through "rational choice sociology" and economists' studies of demography, the family, and crime. Some economists have begun to study not only the prices, quantities, and fluctuations that they have traditionally studied, but also the governance structures and dispute-resolution mechanisms of societies. The label "New Institutional Economics" is sometimes applied to this last type of study and (for lack of any agreed-upon label) sometimes to the suburbanization of economics as a whole. The influence in other social sciences of the economist's deductive style of thinking and sensitivity to quantities has been so fundamental and wide ranging that we are beginning to see a theoretical integration of the social sciences under one overarching paradigm.

Some supporters of this intellectual unification call it "economic imperialism." This is a label that, for several reasons, we reject. An empire is held together by the armed forces of the government that controls it, but the intellectual integration that we observe comes from voluntary interaction and free choice. The empires of recent centuries have mainly involved European domination of other peoples, but the intellectual integration that this book describes has no racial or ethnic dimension. Imperial countries often have higher incomes and rates of advance than the areas they colonize, but no such relationship holds for the economics of the central city and the suburbs. Thus, the analogy with imperialism is inapt. The essays in this volume show that, just as the outward expansion of metropolitan areas is due mainly to advances in technologies for transportation and communication, so the widening ambit of economics and the increasing integration of the social sciences are due mainly to intellectual advances that extend the reach of our minds.

The chapters in this book illustrate the intellectual advances that are broadening economics and integrating the social sciences. They illustrate these advances in almost all of the fields in which they are occurring. This book was inspired in part by the belief that just such a book on the broader economics or integrated social science was needed—and that it would take a number of experts in different fields to illustrate the wide range of work being done.

This book was also inspired in part by accidental developments that contribute to the book's unity and account for an idiosyncratic feature that should not be concealed from prospective readers. The fortuitous developments began when Mancur Olson presented some lectures and seminars at various economics departments and research institutes in India. In these presentations Olson set out his own version of the not-so-dismal science. India was a lucky setting. The sad reality that there are literally hundreds of millions of impoverished people in that country can give debates there about economics an urgent practical focus that they do not always have elsewhere. At the same time, the customary focus on India's overpopulation and on its shortages of capital and other resources—and the harshness of the tradeoffs that appear to be inherent in any allocation of such scarce resources—can sometimes give economic discussions a dismal aspect.

Now consider shifting the focus from capital and other resources—usually taken to be more or less given in quantity—toward the quality of governance. In the suburbs of economics, governance is a focus, but not in the city center. The world has trillions of dollars of capital whose owners would dearly like to receive the higher returns that are attainable, if governance is good, where capital is scarce. It is the shortcomings of the economic policies and institutions of the capital-short countries of the world that keep investors and portfolio managers from putting much capital there. As we shall later see, these shortcomings also blight the productivity of the indigenous resources of the poor countries. Olson argued in India (as in Chapter 1 of this book) that governance is a decisive determinant of economic performance, and that, with the right economic policies and institutions, countries as poor as India could grow at very rapid rates and become developed nations far sooner than is usually supposed.

This is a far-from-dismal possibility. For some, it was also a startling possibility. It provoked some lively debates in India. The quality of the Indian comments on Olson's arguments was usually very high, both when they were supportive and when they were negative.

The Indian commentaries and debates helped persuade the US Agency for International Development (USAID) Mission in New Delhi to make an agreement with an organization—IRIS—that had recently been established at the University of Maryland. (IRIS is an acronym for the Center on "Institutional Reform and the Informal Sector," which does economic research and provides policy advice and technical assistance in formerly communist or Third World countries.) Under this agreement, USAID provided resources that IRIS could use to fund economic research in India and to bring American and other Western economists to India. Dr Satu Kähkönen of IRIS directed the program.

The relevant USAID program officer, Jonathan O'Rourke, naturally did not want to emphasize ideas that were already commonplace in India. Nor did he and his colleagues want studies so specialized that they would have no impact on policy debates and policy choices. They wanted to promote intellectual interchange between Indian economists and policy-makers and economists and others researchers from the West who would introduce exotic new ideas. They wanted more debate and discussion of the kind that had grown out of Olson's presentations in India.

IRIS brought each of the authors of the papers in this volume, plus a substantial number of other Indian and Western scholars and policy makers, to its conferences in India. The focus of these conferences was the Indian scene and India's policy choices. Most participants were economists with expertise about India or leading policy makers and opinion-leaders in India. Both the foreign and the Indian contributions to the conferences were widely discussed in the Indian press. (Most of these India-specific presentations at the conferences are being separately published, along with the present chapters, in India.)

What most distinguished these conferences were the ideas that have driven the expansion of economics—the variously named collective choice, new institutionalist, or neoclassical political economy ideas. These ideas also helped to account for some of the attention the conferences received. After people hear new ideas, they often see policy choices in a different way.

It is the subset of these papers that illustrate the broadening of economics and the emergence of an integrated approach to social science that make up this book. These papers focus not on problems that are peculiar to India, but on issues that are fundamental and important in any country.

Each of the authors that we have persuaded to contribute to this volume conducts distinctive and original research, and many of them are among the best known scholars in their fields. The broad range of subjects that they have analyzed reaches across most of economics and much of the rest of social science as well. The book is nonetheless unified, albeit by the preconceptions of the editors and its idiosyncratic origins. The contributors are to us inspiring partly because they all, independently, approach their research in much the same way that we ourselves do—or aspire to do. This means that, in spite of disagreements about policy and politics, all the contributors exemplify a single approach, and apply this approach, at least partly in the suburbs of economics.

The chapters that follow are exemplary in part because they resonate with the ideas propounded in the talks in India that gave rise to this book—and therefore also with each other.

College Park, Maryland   M. O.
                                                                           S. K.

Contents

Contributors

Pranab Bardhan	Professor of Economics, University of California, Berkeley
Robert D. Cooter	Herman F. Selvin Professor of Law, University of California, Berkeley
J. Bradford De Long	Associate Professor of Economics, University of California, Berkeley
Russell Hardin	Professor and Chair, Department of Politics, New York University
Satu Kähkönen	Associate Director, Center for Institutional Reform and the Informal Sector (IRIS), University of Maryland
Erik Moberg	Free-lance Political Scientist, Sweden
Joel Mokyr	Robert H. Strotz Professor of Arts and Sciences; Professor of Economics and History, Northwestern University
Edward Montgomery	Professor of Economics, University of Maryland; Chief Economist, US Department of Labor
Mancur Olson	Distinguished University Professor of Economics, University of Maryland; Principal Investigator of IRIS
Oliver E. Williamson	Edgar F. Kaiser Professor of Business Administration; Professor of Economics; Professor of Law, University of California, Berkeley

Introduction: The Broader View

Mancur Olson and Satu Kähkönen[1]

1 Background

Why did economics expand into the suburbs? One reason becomes evident when we think about the most basic assumptions, explicit and implicit, in economic theorizing. It is not much of an exaggeration to say that most economic thought is constructed out of four "primitives": four concepts so basic that they are the building blocks with which economic thought is constructed.

One of these primitives is that the individuals in any society have preferences, purposes, or utility functions. Another is that they have various resources or endowments (natural, human, and man-made) that are useful in producing the goods and services that satisfy these preferences. The third is that there is a technology (susceptible to improvement through research, development, and innovation) that explains how much resources are needed to satisfy given preferences: that is, a stock of knowledge that determines the frontiers of the "production functions" by which resources or inputs are transformed into goods and services. The extent to which the individuals in any society can satisfy their preferences, i.e. their real incomes, are limited by the resources available to it and the level of technology: to increase per capita incomes, a society must either accumulate more capital or other resources or else discover more productive technologies. As Milton Friedman pithily put it, there are no free lunches.

The fourth primitive of economic thought—and of most lay thinking on economics—is so elemental and natural that it is usually not even stated explicitly or introduced as an axiom in formal theorizing. It is the half-conscious

[1] We are deeply grateful to Kimberly Brickell, Brian Steinhardt, and especially Maria Coppola for help in organizing this volume and the conferences out of which they grew.

assumption that markets are natural entities that emerge spontaneously, not artificial contrivances or creatures of governments. The markets that a society needs, unless prohibited or repressed by government, may be taken for granted. Economists recognize that the transaction costs of some trades would exceed the gains, and that these trades do not take place. But such trades would not be consistent with economic efficiency anyhow. The tacit notion that the markets needed for a thriving economy will, if governments do not block their appearance, automatically be there is fundamental for almost everyone. Nevertheless, as we shall see, this assumption is wrong. Moreover, there was no way that economists could correct the error without going outside the city center.

Though the migration to the suburbs went in all directions, there were two boundaries where the growth of the discipline could be crossed only by moving into fields that other disciplines had already cultivated. One was the boundary that marked goods and services that, though important for well being, are not for sale in the stores. Some goods are not available through the market because they are indivisible: if they are obtained or consumed by any individual in some group or category, they are also available to the other individuals in that group or category. Such goods are, of course, *public goods* or *externalities*. If a levee protects anyone in a flood plain from a flood, it protects others in the flood plain as well; if anyone obtains cleaner air when the external diseconomy from air pollution is curbed by an effluent fee, everyone in the airshed can breathe more freely. Economists call the most basic or essential services provided by governments, including law and order, *public* or *collective goods*.

For reasons by now well known, large groups, such as the populations of nations, cannot obtain public goods or deal efficiently with externalities through voluntary action in the marketplace. Because the benefits of these goods go to everyone in some area or category—whether an individual has borne any of their costs or not—there is no incentive for individuals voluntarily to purchase or help to pay for them. Thus, it is typically in the government's power to impose compulsory taxation rather than voluntary market mechanisms that normally account for their provision. To deal with goods that are important for income and welfare, but cannot be provided to large groups through voluntary or market mechanisms, economists have had no choice but to extend their theory to cover the exercise of governmental power.

The second boundary that had to be crossed marked the many situations where the incomes of individuals and groups in a society depended not only on their endowments of productive resources and their productivity, but also on the use of power. Goods may be obtained by making them—and by taking them. They may sometimes be taken by individuals acting alone, as when one individual seizes the goods of another in a Hobbesian anarchy or in modern street crime. They may also be taken through the same power that typically accounts for the provision of public goods: the power of government.

The more that is taken, the less is the incentive to make. The use of power affects the level and rate of growth of income as well as its distribution. Thus, the economist who wants to explain how much income is produced—or who gets it—has no choice but to take government, law, and politics into account.

2 The Array of Markets

Economists did not usually notice the dramatic differences in the provision of public goods across different types of society until they began to study societies that were very different from those in which most of them did their work. Until recently, almost all of economics was done in Western Europe, the United States, or comparable First World countries. Only after World War II did many economists begin to study what we now call the Third World, and only after the collapse of communism could they study the unprecedented transitions in the societies of the Second World. Though often neglected, the differences between the public good provision in the First World, on the one hand, and in the Second and Third Worlds, on the other, are extraordinarily important. Paradoxically, the magnitude and importance of these differences in public good provision can best be seen by examining markets in different types of countries.

Remarkably, markets are commonplace in poor as well as rich societies. Why? Because many trades—such as those that can be consummated on the spot—are self-enforcing. The gain that some trades can bring to both parties (and the mother wit of the parties concerned) is all that is needed for the trades to take place. Such self-enforcing trades give a society some gains from specialization in production and mainly account for such sustenance as the poor societies afford. The standard assumption that the markets needed to realize the gains from trade will spring up automatically is true when transactions are self-enforcing.

But there are other trades where the *quid* is provided at one time or place and the *quo* at another, so the gains from trade will not be realized unless there is third-party enforcement of agreements. The transactions in insurance and futures markets are generally not self-enforcing. Neither are those between lenders and borrowers: would-be borrowers can persuade others to lend them the money only if they can credibly commit to paying it back with interest, and this usually requires third-party enforcement of the loan contract. Similarly, when equity investors seek the gains from pooling their capital in a joint-stock company, they can generally succeed only if outside enforcement of company laws prohibits corporate management from siphoning off the capital entrusted to them.

The markets required to obtain the gains from the foregoing types of trade do not emerge automatically, but normally are the product of social and especially governmental contrivance. They are typically a product of the legal institutions that enforce contracts and corporate law—and that protect property rights so that borrowers can obtain loans that are secured by the borrower's assets. These institutions are public goods that cannot be provided by market mechanisms, but arise only from what we call "market-augmenting government."

In the best-governed societies, lending even for long terms is commonplace, and widely held joint-stock companies account for a large part of total production. In the countries without appropriate governance—most of those in the Second and Third Worlds—there is little or no private long-term lending (except in families and similar social groups), little or no private capital-intensive production, and few if any large corporations.[2]

So, the familiar tacit assumption—that the range of markets that are needed to reap the gains from trade are (in the absence of government interference) automatically available—is wrong. While self-enforcing transactions take place spontaneously, there is no automatic process that creates the full range of markets needed for an efficient and prosperous economy. Until recently, many believed that all the communist countries needed to do to obtain a thriving market economy was to "let capitalism happen." Most economic textbooks (and lay writing on economics) said little or nothing that would lead the reader to expect that a country that repudiated communism and looked forward to capitalism would not naturally or spontaneously obtain many of the markets and gains from trade that are usually taken for granted in the First World.

2.1 *The Two-Edged Sword*

Thus, voluntary market mechanisms are not sufficient to provide for the enforcement of contracts, the prevention of anarchy, and the provision of other

[2] Though Thomas Hobbes pointed out in *Leviathan* in 1651 that, in the state of nature, "he that performs first has no assurance that the other will perform after," few writers notice the dependence of many markets on third-party enforcement of contracts or distinguish these markets from those with self-enforcing transactions. The economic historian Douglass North, by contrast, has explicitly distinguished self-enforcing transactions from those that require third-party enforcement; see his *Institutions, Institutional Change, and Economic Performance* (Cambridge University Press, 1990). There is a full analysis of this distinction and an array of econometric tests showing that it is extraordinarily important for the structure of economies, investment, and economic growth in Christopher Clague, Philip Keefer, Stephen Knack, and Mancur Olson, "Contract-Intensive Money: Contract Enforcement, Property Rights, and Economic Performance," IRIS Working Paper no. 151, 1995.

public goods: the coercive power of government is also necessary. But this coercive power is a two-edged sword. It takes us back to the second basic idea that helps account for the broadening of economics. Goods may be obtained, we recall, not only by making, but also by taking. The same governmental compulsion that is required even to obtain the full range of gains from trade can be—and often is—used simply for taking.

Taking, as we know, reduces the incentive for making, and there is often a lot of taking. Some countries' governments are kleptocracies: the leaders or their corrupt subordinates are mainly in the business of taking. In many developing and once-communist countries, and often also in the history of the West, this predation has been extraordinary (as parts of this book show), and has generated deadweight losses that are large in relation to the meager production of the societies concerned.

As is evident from some chapters of this book and from other writings, there is a lot of taking even in relatively well-governed and prosperous countries. Much of it is not recognized for what it is because it involves an *implicit* rather than an *explicit* redistribution of income. Typically, when a lobby wins a tariff, a subsidy, a tax loophole, or a regulation that limits the competition it faces, this takes some income from society and shifts it in the direction of the group with the successful lobby. In general, the incentive to produce and to engage in mutually advantageous trade is distorted, and society's income is normally made lower than it would otherwise be. For reasons elaborated elsewhere and not spelled out here, implicit taking often makes societies poorer *and* more unequal.[3] The social losses from special-interest lobbying and cartelization are sometimes so large that they can account for substantial differences in the growth rates and income levels across countries. For reasons inherent in the logic of collective action, the interests that have the capacity for collective action needed to obtain redistributions through government have, more often than not, above-average and sometimes very high incomes. This tends to make implicit taking increase inequalities.

There is also some taking that is, on balance, desirable or even essential, even though it interferes with making. We have seen that populations can obtain public goods only through taxation—through taking. When calculating the social cost of public goods, we must therefore think not only of their direct monetary costs, but also of the social costs of any extra taxation needed to raise the money. Taking for redistribution can also be, on balance, desirable. When the non-poor decide to tax themselves to aid the poor, they presumably do this because they (not unreasonably) believe that the poor need the money more

---

[3] The justifications for this assertion and for many of those in prior paragraphs are given in Mancur Olson, *The Logic of Collective Action* (Cambridge, Mass.: Harvard University Press, 1965), *The Rise and Decline of Nations* (New Haven: Yale University Press, 1982), and "The Varieties of Eurosclerosis", in *Economic Growth in Europe since 1945*, ed. Nicholas Crafts and Gianni Toniolo (Cambridge: Cambridge University Press, 1966), pp. 73–94.

than they do, so that the redistribution should increase social welfare. This can be true even though the taking for transfer to the poor also, as is widely known, distorts incentives. The required taxation increases the wedge between the social and private return to work and investment by taxpayers, and the transfers to the poor attenuate recipients' incentives to work.

Since taking—both when appropriate and when not—affects the incentive to make, and thus the level of income, there is no way that economics can leave it out of account. In other words, any logically complete economic analysis of the incentives to produce and engage in mutually beneficial trade cannot ignore the use of power. The use of political and governmental power is, of course, a long-standing concern of political science and the law. As later chapters of this book show, the generation of power is linked in previously unrecognized ways with social groups and with the ethnic conflicts, social selection, and discrimination that characterizes many social groups.

2.2 *Purposeful Life-plans and Self-interest*

Critics may concede that the economist should understand more than the market, but they argue that the methods used to study behavior in the market won't work when behavior in government, politics, and social life is at issue. Standard neoclassical economic theory, according to some critics, necessarily assumes that all behavior is self-interested and that—though this assumption may not be so far off the mark for the analysis of behavior in business and the marketplace—it is preposterously wrong when behavior in government, politics, and social life generally is at issue. This criticism is twice wrong.

First, nothing in economic theory excludes individual preferences where the individual has a concern for the welfare of others. The economist's type of thinking is not useful when individual preferences have no consistency or stability, but it does not require that individuals care only about themselves. Admittedly, economists (in this book as elsewhere) very often abstract from the extraordinary complexity of human motivation by assuming self-interest and are thereby able to make problems analytically tractable. The conclusions of their analyses are usually robust—that is, not sensitive to the degree of error in their simplifying assumptions. But to say that an assumption is usually useful is not to say that it is indispensable—or always appropriate.

We economists are, however, guilty of neglecting one important class of cases where this assumption is especially inappropriate. There are some choices that are crucial for a market economy, yet self-interest plays no role and it is principles and morals that mainly determines outcomes. Disputes about private property rights and about the enforcement of contracts are adjudicated by individuals who have no personal stake in the matters to be decided—and who therefore cannot make self-interested choices. The most prosperous societies, at least, leave these and many other important decisions to judges or jurors who, by virtue of governmental contrivance, can obtain no profit from deciding one way or another. If we did not expect that most people, when they had nothing personally at stake, would decide issues on the basis of principle, we would not want any decisions to be made by judges or juries.

The second problem with the twice-wrong criticism is that it forgets that it is generally the same people who make decisions in the market and in political and social spheres. Most of these people derive their choices in part from a more-or-less integrated life-plan and make tradeoffs across different spheres of life. Consumers, investors, employers, and employees in the market are also consumers, voters, neighbors, and members of families. Though there are exceptions, such as some directionless young adults that have not yet "found themselves," most people work out coherent goals for their lives and make integrated decisions about "economic," "social," and "political" objectives. The woman who values both a traditional mother's role and a career may have to make anguished choices, but that does not mean she makes them randomly or irrationally. When families choose where to live, they typically consider how good the neighborhood is for educating and bringing up children and also commuting times and housing prices. Sometimes it is different people who are working in different spheres, as with those who are leaders in business and in politics. Yet there is no reason to assume that personal ambition or rational calculation vary much between them.

It follows that an integrated conception of economics and social science is not only possible: it is indispensable. There is no other way to do justice to the integrated lives of individuals and their choices in trading off objectives in the traditional domains of different disciplines. There is no other way to understand all the options for—and implications of—human ambition. A logically complete analysis requires the integrated and conceptually comprehensive type of thinking that is advocated here. Reality cannot be divided into departments the way universities are.

3 Dismal and Not-so-dismal Sciences

It was Thomas Carlyle, in his "Occasional Discourse on the Negro Question" of 1849, who first named economics the "dismal science."[4] He disliked

[4] *Works of Thomas Carlyle*, (New York: Charles Scribner & Sons, 1904), vol. 29, pp. 348–83. Our account is inspired by and draws heavily upon Joseph Persky's "A Dismal Romantic," *Journal of Economic Perspectives*, 4 (Fall 1990): 165–72.

Malthus's theory of population, with its pessimistic prediction that population pressure would keep the mass of humanity at the margin of subsistence. In part this was because he believed the population problem could be solved by more European imperialism and overseas settlement.

But Carlyle found political economy (as it was then called) dismal for much more fundamental reasons as well. To him, the defining sin of economics was that it "reduces the duty of human governors to that of letting men alone." An apologist for slavery, Carlyle found the free black population of the West Indies indolent, and said that a marriage of philanthropy and the "dismal science" was to blame. What men everywhere needed was strong leadership and paternalism. Thus, he disliked the "ballot boxes" of representative government as well as free markets, and he admired feudal lords and British imperialism. A leader of the romantic movement, Carlyle's style of reasoning had nothing in common with the method of economics, and he ridiculed appeals to "statistics" and other "Fool Gospels."

It is time for disclaimers. First, this focus on Carlyle's writings about economics may create a misleading impression of his work as a whole, and it certainly does not convey the brilliance of his prose style. Second, those who today find economics—or this book—dismal are *not* in any way guilty by association with those opinions of Carlyle's that are today so extraordinarily offensive (and that offended the economist John Stuart Mill in Carlyle's own time). Carlyle is relevant here because he named economics the "dismal science."

He is also relevant because his complaint about Malthus's excessively pessimistic predictions applies to some unnecessarily discouraging formulations of modern economics. When our perspective includes the suburbs as well as the city center, we have a brighter as well as a broader view.

The needlessly dismal formulation of modern economics grows out of two of its primitive concepts: that a society has fixed endowments of productive resources, and that the amount of income or preference satisfaction obtainable from these resources is limited by the level of technology or productive knowledge. These primitives are often taken to imply that the only options we have are tradeoffs. A society cannot have more income, with present-day technology, than can be generated from its endowments of tangible and human resources. So, society cannot have more of this without less of that. Neither can an individual. There is, we recall, no free lunch.

This somewhat dismal conclusion is reinforced by the theory of "efficient markets." If some corporation has credibly announced that it will introduce a new product that promises it huge profits, it does not follow that we can make exceptional profits by buying its stock. Since the bright prospects of the company are public knowledge, others will have acted on that knowledge, and the price of the company's stock will already have been bid up to a level that takes account of the discounted present value of the future prospects. More generally, the efficient markets hypothesis holds that it is not possible to make more than normal returns from publicly available information, and that professionally chosen portfolios will, on average, do no better than randomly chosen investments.

The theory of efficient markets contains a lot of truth; for example, professionally managed mutual funds, on average, fall short of returning as much as market averages and index funds by about the amount of their extra fees and expenses. Thus, most students of finance conclude that no investment formula assures more than normal returns. Just as the wit and self-regard of those who precede us implies that we cannot expect to find big bills left on the sidewalk, so the enterprise of other investors keeps us from obtaining free returns in the capital markets.

This point holds not only in the financial markets but in the market economy as a whole. Just as any bills left on the sidewalk are picked up very quickly, so the rationality and enterprise of the actors in the economy implies that no industries, occupations, business strategies, or patterns of behavior will earn individuals or firms larger returns in long-run equilibrium than are normal for the value of the tangible and human capital they possess. If an activity or strategy earns returns out of proportion to the value of the resources employed, more resources will be devoted to that activity or strategy until it offers no more than normal returns. When every kind of human and tangible capital earns its normal return, the economy tends to be efficient.[5] In other words, the same elemental force that explains why we don't normally see big bills on the sidewalks also tends to make economies efficient—to ensure that neither individuals nor societies can obtain more of this without less of that. The idea that there are no free lunches has an even stronger justification than it initially appears to have.

Thus, Carlyle's complaint that economics is erroneously pessimistic still applies to many expositions of the subject. Though the dismal logic that there are no free lunches applies everywhere, its application to the poor countries of the world is especially important. It implies that the poor countries are poor because they are poorly endowed: because they lack the natural, human, or man-made resources needed to produce high incomes. The poor countries are overpopulated, so they have do not have enough land and natural resources for their populations, and they do not have and cannot freely obtain the tangible

[5] To set out the complete logic behind this sentence and the many major qualifications it requires would take us into some complex, lengthy, and fascinating issues that do not have that much to do with our criticism of the no-free-lunch theory. In part, the sentence is supported by one of the two basic theorems of welfare economics, which demonstrates that, if a competitive equilibrium exists, it is Pareto-efficient. In part, the assertion is misleading because it assumes away not only the public goods, externalities, and missing markets that we have already discussed, but also some problems that arise from economies of scale, asymmetric information, and the theory of the second best.

and human capital needed to generate high incomes. So, the abject poverty of many hundreds of millions of people can be overcome only when poor countries accumulate—or, improbably, are given—much more resources. The poor peoples of the world are, as the neoclassical theory of economic growth and standard econometric practice supposes, on the frontiers of their "aggregate production functions." In short, there are not any big bills left to pick up on the footpaths of poor countries either.

3.1 *Broader is Brighter*

This somewhat dismal conclusion depends on three implicit and often unnoticed assumptions. Two of these assumptions become evident when we look back at the logic that forced economics to create suburbs. First, the theory that there are tradeoffs but no free lunches applies only to societies in which there is no socially gratuitous taking. Though some taking is needed to finance public goods and to aid the poor, a very large part of the taking that goes on, as we pointed out earlier, serves no such social purpose. Since taking reduces the incentive to make, a society can increase its output without obtaining any additional resources when it curtails taking.

Second, the no-free-lunch theory also overlooks the many missing markets, especially in the developing and the lately communist parts of the world. We know that the countries of the Second and Third Worlds do not usually obtain the gains from trade that require third-party enforcement. They do not, for example, now usually reap the gains from production with modern capital-intensive techniques or from mobilizing capital in large private enterprises. If they impartially enforced contracts, they could obtain vast gains from trade from an array of new markets. By continually and impartially enforcing contracts with foreign as well as domestic investors and firms, the developing and transitional countries could tap the trillions of dollars of mobile capital in the developed countries—and continue to do so until the return at the margin to capital became the same as in the First World. (At this point they would have as much capital in relation to their endowments of labor and natural resources as the First World.) If the poor countries were to do this, their gains from trade in capital markets would buy more free lunches than anyone could count.

Third, the no-free-lunch theory overlooks the many economic policies that are simply stupid—that is, policies that may have no predatory purpose or involve no missing markets, yet are socially inefficient. If these policies were eliminated, the resulting boost in output would be enough to compensate those who gained from them and still leave something left over for others. Usually, a wider mastery of the economics of the central city is all that is required to remedy these stupidities, so it would take us far afield to go into them here.

Though the economics of the central city has many sins of omission, it has very few sins of commission. If it were more widely understood, there would not be nearly so many irrational policies, and we would all be better off. Thus, the idea that there are no free lunches is not entirely consistent with the theory from which it is derived: it overlooks the extra lunches societies could buy if they were to wise up.

What is the evidence for the quantitative importance of the foregoing argument? How could we determine whether the societies of the Second and Third Worlds have low incomes mainly because they have poor endowments, or mainly because they suffer more than the rich countries do from socially gratuitous taking, from missing markets, and from stupid economic policies? As it turns out, clear and startling answers to these questions emerge the moment that we look at the borders of countries and at the flows of labor and capital that cross them. The boundaries of countries delineate areas of different types and qualities of governance—of different economic policies and institutions, and thus different structures of incentives. We can learn a lot from the directions and magnitudes of movements of labor and capital across these borders. We can learn a lot from the changes in the productivity of workers that arise when workers migrate from poor to rich countries. And we can learn a lot from looking at the borders where rich and poor countries are adjacent to one another.

That, at least, is what is argued in the next chapter of this book, "Big Bills Left on the Sidewalk: Why Some Nations Are Rich, and Others Poor." It claims to show that the low-income countries of the Second and Third Worlds are poor mainly because they are much farther below their potential incomes than the rich countries are. If these countries improved their governance sufficiently, they would obtain colossal gains from foreign investment and advanced technologies. These gains are so large because the low-income countries of the Second and Third Worlds can enjoy exceptionally rapid "catch up" growth. They can grow, as some low-income countries have, at more than 7 percent per capita a year, and thus double their per capita incomes in a decade. By keeping this up for three decades, they could obtain an eight-fold increases in per capita income.

There is no great likelihood that most poor countries will soon come to understand what changes they need to make in their institutions and policies, much less be able to undertake collective action needed to make the appropriate changes. Therefore, our broader perspective does *not* by any means imply optimistic predictions. Given the ubiquity of bad governance and the tenacity with which even the worst governments hang onto power, ours is not an exceptionally encouraging perspective. But it is not so dismal either, because it does call our attention to a brighter *possibility*: that any country can become more prosperous by improving its governance, and that the poor countries of the world, if they substantially improve their economic policies and institutions, can escape poverty surprisingly quickly. This should be a source of hope for the poor peoples of this world. There are countless free lunches out there, even if misgovernment keeps many of the poor peoples from eating them.

3.2 Resistance to Innovation

The chapter immediately after "Big Bills . . ." provides additional reasons for concluding that the rate at which a country grows is not pre-determined by its endowments and depends much more on the extent to which it adopts superior technologies. This chapter, "Innovation and its Enemies: The Economic and Political Roots of Technological Inertia," is by Joel Mokyr, who is the author of, among other works, *The Lever of Riches*,[6] and thus has studied the Industrial Revolution and the revolutionary implications technical innovations can have.

Sometimes, Mokyr emphasizes, superior technologies are not adopted: "outright resistance to new technology is a widely observed historical phenomenon," and technological inertia and economic stagnation have been commonplace. This is obviously an issue of momentous importance. In studying it, Mokyr argues—in keeping with the broader approach of all of the essays in this book—that "artificial distinctions between the 'economic sphere' and the 'political sphere' are doomed," and that technological inertia is usually the result of rational behavior by utility-maximizing individuals.

The market, Mokyr points out, provides an aggregation of the gains and losses from an innovation. If the market alone determines whether innovations will be adopted, the innovations that provide a greater balance of market gains than market losses will be adopted. But the market is by no means the only way of aggregating the gains and losses from adopting an innovation: a variety of regulatory or political processes can be used to determine whether an innovation is to be adopted, and each will in general aggregate the gains and losses differently and thus will often come up with different answers about whether an innovation should be adopted.

Though Mokyr is mindful of concerns in many societies about social stability, and aware that the adoption of some innovations might inappropriately disrupt it, what is most striking are his many examples of organizations that have (surely harmfully) resisted the adoption of superior technologies. These include the artisanal guilds of pre-modern urban Europe, which "enforced and eventually froze the technological status quo," and similar organizations in China. While emphasizing the importance of other factors as

---

[6] Joel Mokyr, *The Lever of Riches* (New York: Oxford University Press, 1990).

well, he argues that differences in the power of guilds was one of the reasons why the Industrial Revolution occurred in Britain rather than on the European continent. He also offers other examples: shopkeepers in Germany in the late nineteenth century persuaded states to impose discriminatory taxes on large department stores; organized workers in Bombay in the 1920s and 1930s resisted technical and administrative rationalization; printers and other workers in London's Fleet Street frequently interrupted production and resisted innovation; unions in the European auto industry resisted flexible practices pioneered by Japanese auto manufacturers. (The social losses from such narrow or special interest groups come up repeatedly this volume.)

By contrast, Mokyr points to the many labor unions in such places as Sweden and Germany that have welcomed innovation, and notes that a union with an "encompassing interest"—one that represented such a large proportion of a nation's income earning capacity that it would obtain a significant share of the gains from a more efficient economy—has an incentive to accept superior technologies. (The argument that encompassing interests, because they have by definition a large stake in the productivity of society, tend to take its interests into account also recurs often in this volume.)

Taking all of Mokyr's examples together, we infer that the aggregation systems that most often resist superior innovations are those in which the separate groups of workers or firms that would lose from a given innovation have substantial influence. If this is true, the extent to which these interests are organized to lobby or to undertake industrial action is an important determinant of economic progress.

---

4 Broader Theories of the Firm and the State

If the two chapters discussed above are correct, it is the economic policies and organizational arrangements of a society that mainly determine how innovative and prosperous it is. Thus, ideas, such as those in the chapter we consider next, that can help to improve these arrangements are especially important. This chapter is by Oliver Williamson, author of (among many other works) *The Economic Institutions of Capitalism*.[7] In his chapter, "Economic Institutions and Development: A View from the Bottom," he sets out and summarizes some economic theorizing that is considerably broader than most economics has been. As in most of his other work, he focuses mostly on the firm, and especially the corporate hierarchy.

[7] Oliver Williamson, *The Economic Institutions of Capitalism* (New York: Free Press, 1985).

If any kind of organization has always been at the center of economic analysis, it is surely the firm. How, then, can we argue that this book is about the broadening or suburbanization of economics?

Williamson's analysis shows that a broader approach to economics than economists once thought appropriate is needed even for the study of the firm and industrial organization, and that the parallels between hierarchical firms and governments are startling. Williamson builds upon a point that Ronald Coase first made in the 1930s: the existence of the hierarchical firm cannot be explained except in terms of what can be called a "market failure." Market failure not in the sense that government rather than private enterprises should be producing the goods, but in the sense that, in a competitive economy, the survival of an unsubsidized firm hierarchy can be explained only by the disadvantages or costs of markets. If the time of each worker and the services of each unit of the other factors of production that cooperate in some productive process were always most efficiently coordinated through the market, the costly hierarchies of the typical modern corporate enterprise would not be sustainable. That is, the production that the firm hierarchy organizes would be coordinated at less cost by the market and there would be no reason to bear the costs of the firm hierarchy. As Williamson's chapter points out, markets and hierarchies are alternative ways of organizing production. We can see that in some circumstances firms choose to organize more activity through their hierarchies, as when they integrate vertically and one larger firm coordinates activity previously coordinated by a market relationship among firms; at other times firm hierarchies can coordinate less and the market more, as when a conglomerate breaks up or a firm contracts out for some work it previously did for itself. We cannot, in other words, understand what does and does not go on in the marketplace unless we include firm hierarchies as well as market relationships in our theory.

That Williamson's analysis is broader is also evident from his conception of the firm. Traditionally, economists have conceived of the firm in terms of one of the primitives or building blocks we considered earlier. That is, they have taken the firm to be a "production function": a relationship, given by the available stock of technological and other knowledge, between the resources or inputs that a firm uses and the goods or outputs that it produces. To Williamson, the firm is more usefully considered a "governance structure," more an organizational than a technological construction. The general organizational logic that is applicable, for example, to governments is also applicable to firms, and the organizational logic that is evident in the firm is applicable to governments and other non-business organizations.

For example, Williamson points out that the separation of ownership and control in the corporation has its parallel in government. Berle and Means pointed out long ago that the managers of widely held corporations did not have to focus exclusively on the returns to the stockholders for whom they are supposed to work.[8] Though neither Berle and Means nor Williamson put it just this way, the many dispersed stockholders have to overcome usually insurmountable difficulties of collective action in order to make their legal control over the management effective. So corporate managers may be able to keep their jobs even when they shirk, or to give themselves excessive perks, or to engage in unprofitable empire building. Even though managers of widely held corporations are also constrained by hostile takeovers and other features of the market for corporate control, these constraints are by no means always sufficient to ensure that widely held corporations are always run solely in the interests of the stockholders.

Williamson shows that the same thing happens in democratic governments. The electorate in a democracy, like the stockholders in a corporation, nominally has complete control. In practice, those who manage the government are often able to indulge their own preferences about government policy and other things. For this and other reasons, governments often fail, sometimes egregiously, to serve the interests of electorates. To put his point in our language, Williamson observes that goods and services can be obtained not only by making, but also by taking, and that taking makes societies less efficient.

Therefore, all mechanisms are imperfect and both markets and governments fail. Economists should not deplore any arrangement as irrational unless there is a remedy that can be implemented—some achievable alternative mechanism that will work better. Thus, Williamson, who has criticized many policies that have emerged from the political process, also counsels us to be "respectful of politics." This is presumably in part because he emphasizes that appropriate governance is needed to protect property and contract rights. But he also points out that some of the social losses that arise because political power is used for socially costly redistributions in favor of those who wield it are a cost of democracy. There is sometimes no remedy for such losses of efficiency resulting from redistribution—no way that you can always prevent them.

We agree that there is no universal remedy—and sometimes no remedy at all—for the losses that arise from the use of political power for taking. Some constitutional rules are better than others,[9] but surely no pages of parchment can hold back all the powerful political forces that can serve their interests

---

[8] Adolph Berle and G. C. Means, *The Modern Corporation and Private Property* (New York: Macmillan, 1932).

[9] Williamson's argument brings to mind the seminal and now-classic work on constitutions by James Buchanan and Gordon Tullock, *The Calculus of Consent* (Ann Arbor: University of Michigan Press, 1962). This book argued that restrictive constitutions that permitted action only when there was much-more-than-majority support would largely prevent such redistributions. Though Williamson does not discuss constitutions, his conclusion that sometimes there is no remedy may suggest that there are limits to what we can expect from constitutional reform. The same opportunism and other difficulties that make many other ostensibly attractive deals or contracts unworkable might also bedevil constitutional construction and interpretation.

by obtaining protection against imports, restrictions on competition, tax loopholes, or other types of implicit redistribution. That is one reason why the not-so-dismal science is not necessarily optimistic, much less utopian. Nonetheless, most special-interest lobbying serves the interests of small minorities, so this lobbying will not prevail if the public—or even the intellectuals—understand what is happening. This means that good economic research—and a wider dissemination of the research results and a better climate of opinion—can improve economic performance. Again, while the not-so-dismal science can offer no assurances, it does call attention to a brighter possibility.

4.1 *A Broader Economic Theory of the State*

Whereas Williamson proceeds "bottom up" from the firm to government and society, he agrees that it is also useful to proceed from the "top down": to look at the incentives facing leaders of governments in various circumstances and the patterns of policies that result from them, and then to note the implications of these policies for firms and for the private sector generally. This is what Chapters 4, 5, and 6 do. The first of these, "Dictatorship, Democracy, and Development," provides a version of one of Olson's presentations in India that helped give rise to this book. Because some of the subsequent contributions in this volume criticize, build upon, or go beyond it, we must provide a full summary of it.

The chapter is part of a series of writings that began with Olson's essay on "Autocracy, Democracy, and Prosperity," published in 1991.[10] It puts forth, in an intuitive and nontechnical way, a *part* of the theory that is set out with formal proofs and crucial additional results in Martin McGuire and Mancur Olson's "Economics of Autocracy and Majority Rule."[11] It analyzes the kings or dictators who control autocratic governments—and the oligarchies or majorities or other ruling interests that control other types of government—in just the way that economists analyze the behavior of firms, consumers, and workers. That is, it takes a broader approach to economics by applying the familiar assumption of rational self-interest to the autocrats or other ruling interests that control a government, and then finds what types of policy will best serve the ruling interest.

When this is done, it quickly becomes evident that a rational autocrat, even if he began as the leader of a gang of roving bandits and is solely interested

---

[10] Mancur Olson, "Autocracy, Democracy, and Prosperity," in Richard Zeckhauser, ed., *Strategy and Choice* (Cambridge, Mass.: MIT Press, 1991), pp. 131–57, which develops the argument about encompassing and narrow interests in Olson's previously cited *Rise and Decline of Nations*. There are very important early insights in this line of thinking in various unpublished drafts by Martin McGuire in the early and mid-1990s.

[11] Martin McGuire and Mancur Olson, "Economics of Autocracy and Majority Rule," *Journal of Economic Literature*, 34 (March 1996): 72–96.

in taking as much as possible from others, will take the interests of those he exploits into account whenever he has secure control that he expects will last for some time. His monopoly over taking, whether we call it theft or taxation, gives him an "encompassing interest"—that is, we recall, a large stake in the productivity of his domain. This makes him moderate his tax theft. He has an incentive to limit the rate of his tax theft because taxation reduces his subject's incentive to produce and thus also his tax base. If he took everything, he would eliminate the incentive to produce and would collect nothing. He maximizes his total tax collections by lowering his tax rate until what he gains at the margin from the resulting increase in the income of his domain, and thus his tax base, just equals what he loses from taking a smaller share of output. For instance, if his tax rate were 50 percent—and at that rate the last dollar he collected in taxes would reduce the national income by two dollars—he would be at his optimum.

An autocrat's encompassing interest also makes him use some resources that he could spend on his own purposes or consumption to provide public goods for those from whom he takes. If his optimal tax rate were 50 percent, he would obviously gain from spending his money on public goods up to the point where the national income increases by two dollars for each dollar spent, because he will receive one of these two dollars.

A majority or other ruling interest made up of people who earn income in the market will *necessarily* have a more encompassing interest than an autocrat. If such a ruling interest redistributed as much to itself as an optimizing autocrat would redistribute to himself, it would gain from reducing the redistributive tax rate. This increases not only the tax base, just as it does for the autocrat, but also the market incomes of those in the ruling interest. Majorities and other ruling interests that obtain a sufficiently large fraction of a society's income ("super-encompassing interests") will, as McGuire and Olson have proven, best serve their interests by redistributing nothing whatever from the minority to themselves. Majorities and oligarchies also provide more public goods than an autocrat would.[12]

Some aspects of economic policy in most societies are not, in fact, controlled by either an autocrat or a monolithic majority or oligarchy that rationally serves its collective interest. Most protectionism and other types of subsidy favoring individual industries or occupations arise because of pressure from organizations of firms, professions, or workers in that industry or occupation— from the influence of guilds, professional associations, trade associations, unions, or other special-interest groups. The firms or workers in any single

---

[12] This paradoxical possibility that self-interest could make a sufficiently encompassing ("super-encompassing") ruling interest avoid any redistribution to itself is demonstrated in the McGuire–Olson article cited above, but was not understood when the paper in this book was written and is not mentioned in it.

industry or occupation are by no means an encompassing interest: they are, on the contrary, a narrow or special interest. If an organized interest in a particular market earned, say, 1 percent of the total income earned in a country or city-state, it would not have any incentive to cease using its lobbying or cartel power to obtain redistributions for itself until the social income fell at the margin by 100 times as much as it obtained from redistribution; for it would, on average, bear only about 1 percent of the social loss from a less efficient economy. This logic suggests that countries that have a high density of narrow special-interest organizations will tend to grow less rapidly than otherwise comparable nations.

A country develops a dense network of special-interest lobbies and cartels only if it has enjoyed a long period of stability. This is because the benefits that lobbying or cartelization bring to the firms or workers in a market automatically go to all the firms or workers in the market, whether or not they have paid dues to the organization that organized the lobbying or cartelization. In other words, they must overcome the great difficulties of collective action by working out the complex agreements and "selective incentives" that make it rational for the firms and workers in a given market to pay the costs of collective action. It takes a long time to overcome these difficulties. That is why only long-stable societies normally have a high density of special-interest organizations and suffer the losses in efficiency and dynamism that they bring about.

This, along with international differences in ideology and in economic understanding, explains much of the variation in economic growth across the developed countries. Totalitarianism and foreign occupation destroyed most of the special-interest organizations in the Axis countries (or replaced them with relatively encompassing structures of allied or other postwar design). Accordingly, in the first quarter-century after World War II, West Germany, Japan, and Italy enjoyed "economic miracles." By contrast, the same Great Britain that invented modern economic growth with its Industrial Revolution (see the Mokyr and De Long chapters) suffered from the "British Disease" of slow growth. In long-stable and undefeated Britain and in the long-settled and always stable parts of the United States, dense networks of lobbying and cartelistic organizations had emerged. Thus, these places suffered large losses in efficiency and dynamism from narrow or special interests, and this mainly explained their slow growth. By contrast, the more recently settled western and "defeated" southern parts of the United States were not much afflicted by such narrow interests and grew relatively rapidly.

The one country with an exceptionally high level of membership in interest organizations that also had impressive growth in the 1950s and 1960s was Sweden. At that time, with not much more than one big labor union and one employers' federation, it had a uniquely encompassing interest-group structure. Why did this exceptionally encompassing and socially prudent structure emerge in Sweden? Why may it have devolved and deteriorated into a narrower set of special interests with the passage of time? Why ultimately did the Swedish economy head south and discredit the "Swedish model"? As we shall see from Eric Moberg's chapter and later discussion, the answers to these questions raise general theoretical issues and turn out to be important for all countries.

We have argued that autocrats have an encompassing stake in their domains that gives them some interest in their productivity, but that majorities in democracies have more encompassing interests and therefore a greater incentive to take account of the interests of society. Special-interest organizations, by contrast, face very different incentives. Except in the rare and unsustainable cases where they are encompassing, they represent only the firms or workers in a particular industry or market. These narrow interests give them little or no reason to take account of the social losses that their lobbying and cartelization bring about.[13]

In the long run, probably the most important difference between autocratic rule and representative government is in the degree to which they protect property rights and enforce contracts. Chapter 4 argues that, when an autocrat, because of uncertainty about his tenure or any other reason, takes a short-term view, it pays him to take any asset whose tax yield over the short planning horizon is less than its capital value. Thus, any autocrat with a sufficiently short time horizon becomes, in effect, a roving bandit and takes all of the readily confiscable fortunes and assets in his domain. In oligarchies or democracies in which power is shared, no single individual has the power unilaterally to confiscate the assets of others. Those who share power also have an incentive to make sure that no one, including the leader of the government, can become a dictator, so they limit the power of the government and its leader. The resulting limitations also make private property and contract rights more secure. Because of this and the frequency of succession crises in autocracies, property and contract rights are much more secure over the long run in representative governments, whether they have universal suffrage or oligarchic electorates.

4.2 The Broader Approach to the State and the Rise of the West

The importance of the incentives facing the leaders of governments—and the intimate connection between these incentives and property and contract

[13] Narrow special-interest groups have considerable influence in most autocratic societies. Guilds, for example, were important even under the absolutist monarchies in early modern Europe, and the Soviet-type societies in their later years were dense with insider lobbies. Still, dictatorships that are both new and strong may sometimes emerge, and they may repress special interests. This happened for a time in South Korea, Taiwan, and Chile.

rights—is evident from J. Bradford De Long's chapter, "Overstrong Against Thyself: War, the State, and Growth in Europe on the Eve of the Industrial Revolution." His historical analysis of early modern western Europe demonstrates that it was the interests of kings and the forms of government that mainly determined whether there was economic growth or stagnation—and even partly explained the source of our modern world, the Industrial Revolution. De Long's recent experience in the US government also suggests to him that the same principles that explained the far-from-encouraging relationship of political power and economic performance in early modern Europe also apply in late twentieth-century Washington.

De Long notes that northwestern Europe, over the long sweep of history, has mostly been a relatively backward area, and its status as the cradle of industrial life needs to be explained. He looks first at the cities of Europe and concludes that "city growth had a very strong allergy to the presence of strong, centralizing Princes who called themselves 'absolute' in the sense of being not subject to, but creators of the legal order, and a strong attraction to mercantile republics: city-states governed by representative or not-so-representative oligarchies of merchants." He draws on the quantitative evidence in his important article with Andrei Shleifer on "Princes and Merchants," which examined urban growth and decline century by century in nine different regions of Europe.[14] The De Long—Shleifer statistical analysis suggests that "each century that a west European region . . . was ruled by a strong 'absolutist' prince saw its urban population fall by roughly 180,000 people, and its number of cities with more than 30,000 people fall by roughly one and a half, relative to what the experience of *that* region in *that* era would have been in the absence of absolutist rule." After looking at some specific features of European military and political history, De Long can show that there is a causal arrow going from the nature of the rule to the growth of cities. For example, in the year 1000 southern Italy outstripped northern Italy in agricultural productivity, population, and urbanization. But then "Robert I d'Hauteville and his brothers win their wars to bring southern Italy under their control, and its city-states become part of the 'prototype absolutism' that was the Kingdom of Sicily in the first few centuries of the present millennium." After five centuries of absolutist rule, southern Italy had become quite backward in relation to the more urban and dynamic north.

In pre-industrial Europe, De Long argues, a city-state was typically controlled by an oligarchy of merchant burghers. When landlords or burghers with substantial private wealth have an important political role in representative assemblies, they take into account the impact of alternative public policies on their private wealth. When Lorenzo di Medici "the Magnificent" guided the

---

[14] J. Bradford De Long and Andrei Shleifer, "Princes and Merchants," *Journal of Law and Economics*, 36(2), (October 1993): 671–702.

government of Florence, his wealth depended as much on the revenues of the Medici bank as on the city's treasury.

De Long's results are completely consistent with his logical analysis and obviously also with the theory in Chapter 4 on "Dictatorship, Democracy, and Development." An oligarchy, majority, or other ruling interest that not only controls the fisc, but also earns income in the marketplace, is bound to have a more encompassing interest than an autocrat whose income depends only on his control of government. A ruling interest that earns income in the marketplace, we recall, will necessarily best serve its interests by redistributing less to itself than an autocrat who was earning no income in the market would have done.

The evidence gathered by De Long and De Long and Shleifer also shows that absolutist autocracies often lead to short time horizons and thus, in effect, to roving banditry. Taking the kings of England between 1066 and 1715 as an example, De Long and Shleifer show that something went wrong in 18 of the 31 royal successions. They found that "there was only a 13 percent chance that the legitimate heir who was grandson, granddaughter, grandnephew, or other relative of an English monarch would inherit the throne without disturbance in the line of succession." Though De Long does not go into this, one would suppose that in pre-industrial Europe the fortunes in cities were more readily confiscable than the widely scattered assets in rural areas. If so, the form of government probably had more impact on economic performance in urban industries than in agriculture.

De Long's accounts of Hapsburg Spain and Bourbon France illustrate how imperial ambition—manifested especially in high military expenditures— implied excessive taxation and economic blight. In defending itself in life-and-death wars, the Dutch Republic was driven not only to tax itself heavily but also to borrow huge sums. This implied taxation so oppressive and long-lasting that the Dutch economy ultimately stagnated. Somewhat later Britain was left with similar military exigencies and the high taxes and borrowing that go with them. De Long argues that an increased population with more taxpayers and other favorable breaks kept the British debt and taxation distortions from reaching ruinous levels, so that Britain was soon host to the Industrial Revolution.

5 The Structure of Incentives in the Modern Welfare State

The logic of narrow and encompassing interests and of different time horizons is no less pertinent to the democratic welfare states of the present day than it was to the societies of medieval and early modern Europe. In some ways, the prototypical or most advanced or extreme example of the modern democratic welfare state is Sweden—famous since before World War II for the "middle way" between capitalism and communism and for an exceptionally large and egalitarian welfare state.

Erik Moberg's chapter on Sweden (Chapter 6) partly extends and applies the concepts of encompassing and narrow or special interests set out above and in some of Olson's earlier publications. It also attacks part of Olson's analysis and offers an alternative and novel theory of Swedish developments. Moberg points out that, though the Swedish economy is performing very badly in the 1990s, Sweden was for a considerable period famous for achieving a very high per capita income while having an exceptionally generous welfare state. The high per capita income of Sweden in the 1950s and 1960s needs explanation, as does the more recent severe decline of the Swedish economy.

Moberg reviews the explanation of these developments that Olson, using the theory of encompassing and narrow interests, offered in two books.[15] He points out that Olson had, in the 1980s, asked two parallel questions: (1) Why wasn't Sweden's economy doing better? (2) Why wasn't Sweden's economy doing worse? Olson had said the answer to the first question was obvious and well known—it was because of the disincentives and distortions inherent in the exceptionally large Swedish welfare state—and that the real challenge was to answer the second question. Moberg emphasizes that on this formulation of the question the large size of the Swedish welfare state is taken as a given, but he is above all concerned to explain this.

Moberg and Olson agree that Sweden's economic growth has been slowed by the disincentives of exceptionally high welfare spending and taxation—and that it is also a long-stable country with an exceptionally high density of membership in labor unions and employers' organizations. So why had not Sweden performed worse and got into trouble sooner? As we have already seen, the relatively wealthy and rapidly growing Sweden of the 1950s and 1960s had an exceptionally encompassing structure of interest organizations, and (as the theory of encompassing and narrow interests predicted) the policies of these encompassing organizations showed a concern for the economic efficiency of the society that is not evident in narrow special-interest organizations. Though he had initially been agnostic about the very long-run effects of such groups, Olson argued, beginning in 1986,[16] that encompassing interest organizations tend to devolve over time into systems of smaller and

---

[15] Mancur Olson, *How Bright are the Northern Lights? Some Questions about Sweden* (Lund: Institute of Economic Research, Lund University Press, 1990), and the *Rise and Decline of Nations*.

[16] Mancur Olson, "A Theory of the Incentives Facing Political Organizations: Neo-Corporatism and the Hegemonic State," *International Political Science Review*, 7(2) (April 1986): 165–89; "The Devolution of the Nordic and Teutonic Economies," *AEA Papers and Proceedings*, 85(2) (May 1995): 22–7, and in the already cited "Varieties of Eurosclerosis."

narrower organizations and into interest organizations that, when large, are mainly shells or fronts for increasingly powerful and autonomous branches and other ostensibly subordinate units. The Norwegian rational choice theorist Gudmund Hernes has independently made a similar argument.[17]

Moberg agrees that Sweden had relatively encompassing interest organizations and also that they tended to display the prudent concern about the impact of their policies on the productivity of the society that the theory predicts. But he emphasizes the need for an adequate explanation of why Sweden came to have encompassing interest organizations in the first place. He argues that Olson's brief and tentative references to Sweden's homogeneity, small size, and special historical circumstances are *not* by themselves sufficient to explain why Sweden came to have encompassing organizations.

To provide a fuller and better explanation, Moberg notes that Sweden has a parliamentary government with proportional representation and shows that this makes for highly disciplined political parties. In a presidential system of the kind that prevails in the United States, the administration does not require majority support in the Congress for its continuance, so no crisis or change of government need occur when members of the president's party vote contrary to the administration's policy. Such a system can operate with weak and undisciplined political parties. In a parliamentary system, by contrast, the government cannot remain in office unless it continues to have sufficient support in the parliament, so it must have one or more disciplined parties that continue to support it: the government, indeed, is essentially an artifact of the party or parties out of which it is made. With proportional representation, moreover, members of the parliament owe their seats not to any plurality in a district, but to their place on a party list of candidates and the electoral fortunes of that party. The political fortunes of a politician depend on the party's fortunes and how high he or she ranks on the party list. So the politicians stay in line and the political party has discipline and coherence. Moberg also points out that the Social Democratic party that has controlled Sweden for most of the last sixty years is linked institutionally as well as ideologically with one large labor union.

Accordingly, Moberg says it is not so much Sweden's homogeneity, small size, and the other factors Olson had mentioned that explain how it came to have an encompassing interest group structure, but even more the country's constitutional system. His argument certainly applies to the left–labor side of the spectrum, for it generates disciplined political parties, and on the left there is one large party that is institutionally linked with a labor union. Though Moberg's argument may perhaps not help explain the encompassing character of the Swedish Employers' Federation that represents almost all Swedish

---

[17] Gudmund Hernes, "The Dilemmas of Social Democracies: the Case of Norway and Sweden," *Acta Sociologica*, 34(4) (December 1991): 239–60.

business, it must provide a large part of the explanation of why Sweden came to have one unusually encompassing organization in the form of the Social Democratic party linked with one large labor union. It is important to acknowledge that Moberg here repairs one flaw in some of Olson's writings on encompassing organizations.

Moberg also disagrees at least partly with Olson's contention that Sweden's initial success with encompassing organization helps to explain why it overconfidently went on to expand its welfare state redistribution beyond sustainable levels. He offers his own novel theory: that the Swedish constitutional structure was the most important factor in explaining the exceptional expansion of Sweden's welfare state. The disciplined political parties in Sweden lowered the transaction costs involved in putting together packages of redistributions that would command a majority. He contends that, by contrast, in presidential systems of the kind in the United States, it is much more difficult to work out the political deals needed to pass a package of redistributive measures. He argues, contrary to common opinion, that the US political system is not especially open to influence by lobbies.

Moberg in his debate with Olson has raised some issues that call for further research. In view of the fundamental importance of these issues, not only for Sweden but also for other countries (and for theoretical reasons as well), we must hope that a number of scholars will investigate these matters. Moberg's examination of the Swedish welfare state also demonstrates that the same tools of thought that are useful in analyzing the market, the corporation, and the kings and oligarchies of early modern times also illuminate the welfare state in a modern democracy. We cannot understand such an important feature of modern society as the welfare state without a broader economics or an integrated social science.

6 Ethnic Conflict, Discrimination, and Coordination in Social Groups

Chapters 7—Edward Montgomery's "Affirmative Action and Reservations in the American and Indian Labor Markets"—and 8—Russell Hardin's "Communities and Development"—turn to a different suburb of economics than those we have so far discussed. These two chapters examine the cultural, ethnic, racial, religious, linguistic, tribal, and caste groupings into which humanity is, to various degrees, divided. The consideration of such groupings raises what may be the best-known criticism of the economist's paradigm and the theoretically unified approach to social science.

This line of criticism correctly emphasizes that economic theory—and the rational-choice approaches to social science that are integrated with it—take the individual as a fundamental unit of analysis. It is wrong to identify the economic and rational-choice methodology with "individualism," much less "rugged individualism," as a social or political creed. This approach does, however, require *methodological* individualism. That is, it requires the kind of thinking that De Long brings out at the beginning of Chapter 5, where he reports his reaction to the White House functionary who said that "what you economists don't see, is that you are pushing for the public interest. But there are other interests that can be more important." De Long's immediate and outraged reaction that the public interest would have to be the sum of private interests, so that no interest could possibly be more important, is one aspect of methodological individualism. But another aspect is evident in De Long's next paragraph, where he takes account of the fact that kings or other political leaders may sometimes place their individual welfare above that of their subjects. If the King says "L'état, c'est moi" and has the power to act accordingly, then a methodologically individualistic account of government must give a great role to the individual who is king.

Critics of the methodological individualism that characterizes the broader economics and the integrated approach to social science emphasize that everyone is born into and is socialized by social groups of the kind the Montgomery and Hardin consider. No man is an island, and individuals are greatly influenced by their different patterns of socialization. Those socialized pick up different cultures with different attitudes toward work, saving, and leisure, different religions and languages, different tolerances and prejudices, and different group loyalties and hatreds. Accordingly, some argue, any method of analysis that begins with individuals is mistaken because it leaves out an even more fundamental reality: the groups and communities that mainly determine what individuals in different groups believe and thus what they choose. Some other holistic, communitarian, nationalistic, or group-based or class-centered method should supplant the methodologically individualistic economics and social science on display in this book. Though socialization matters, and there are often important differences in the ways that different groups have been brought up, we shall argue, drawing on the Montgomery and Hardin chapters, that the integrated approach to social science nonetheless generates bigger payoffs than any other single approach.

The case for theory that starts with the group rather than the individual is probably strongest with problems of the kind considered in Montgomery's chapter. He considers race and "affirmative action" in the United States and compares them with caste and the "reservations" of government jobs for "scheduled castes and tribes" in India. In these cases groups are exceptionally important. When there is discrimination against a race or caste—or a government program to assist or favor a race or caste—outcomes obviously cannot be explained only in terms of individual attributes: the race or caste an individual is identified with manifestly makes a difference. Yet no one who reads and understands Montgomery's chapter, and the rich literature he draws upon and extends, could deny that the methodologically individualistic method used by him and those he builds upon makes important contributions to our understanding.

To see why, consider a type of discrimination that, though probably not the most important, arises directly from individual choices. Suppose there is an attribute whose average value differs across groups and also among individuals within each group, and that it is impossible or costly to determine the value of this attribute for each individual. Adolescent and young adult males, for example, account for a disproportionate share of violent crimes, yet many of them would not commit a violent crime and many individuals in other demographic categories would. This means that a taxi driver in a high-crime area may rationally avoid picking up young males at the same time that law-abiding young males there reasonably resent the unjust discrimination that they suffer. As Montgomery shows, the assumption of rational behavior can not only help us understand the discrimination that arises from stereotyping, but also can illuminate the consequences of different policies for dealing with it.

A "taste" for discrimination (a desire to discriminate), like other tastes, cannot be explained by a theory of rational behavior, but economic theory can say a lot about the costs and consequences of such a taste when there are markets. The employer who indulges such tastes cannot usually obtain the best value when hiring labor and therefore pays a price for acting out of prejudice, as do workers and consumers who make discriminatory choices. Market forces make this type of discrimination less common than it would otherwise be. This logic helps to explain why governments, and extra-legal sources of coercion, were so heavily implicated in the Jim Crow system that used to prevail in the US South, and why the changes in US legislation, such as the civil rights and voting rights acts of the 1960s, brought about unexpectedly rapid and pacific racial integration of workforces in the South. Though Montgomery does not go into this history, he discusses "taste" models of discrimination and of affirmative action. He shows that government policies that give preferences to specified groups will, not surprisingly, usually be efficiency-increasing when they offset discrimination, but will usually be efficiency-reducing when they change what would otherwise have been a nondiscriminatory outcome in a competitive market.

The word "usually" need emphasis. Montgomery's chapter shows the richness and variety of the results that have been achieved in economists' studies of this subject. In reading it, one is struck especially by how sensitive the impacts of policies can be to such considerations as the existence of covered and uncovered sectors, and the numbers of individuals with pertinent skills in the groups that are favored or not by affirmative action programs. The economy is a general equilibrium system, and any discrimination or preferential policy in a covered sector of an economy changes prices and quantities of the goods that this sector buys and sells. This in turn makes it profitable for firms and consumers in the uncovered sector to choose different patterns of production and consumption than before, and this generally changes the relative demands in the uncovered sector for different sorts of labor. As a result of such forces, it is easily possible that a public policy can have a net effect that is the opposite of the expected effect. Thus, the methodologically individualistic method of economic theory alerts us, as no other theory has done, to important counter-intuitive possibilities that policy-making has to take into account if it is to deal in a socially rational way with legacies of segregation and other "group" problems.

6.1 *Social Structure and Collective Action*

Hardin's chapter—along with his books, *One for All* and *Collective Action*[18]—also helps us understand the origins of social groups and the patterns of exclusion and discrimination that they sometimes engage in. He emphasizes, building on the two just cited books and on Olson's *Logic of Collective Action*, that social groups cannot organize or act to achieve any group interest unless they can overcome the difficulties of collective action. If collective action, whether in the political system or in the marketplace, provides some benefit to a group, normally everyone in that group will benefit, whether or not they have borne any of the costs of the collective action. Collective action or organization by a group thus inherently involves an indivisibility of the kind described earlier in this chapter.

We recall that this means that the individuals in any large group do not have an automatic incentive to contribute to or act in the interest of their group, and large groups will be able to organize and act in their common interest only if they are able to work out "selective incentives," or punishments and rewards, that apply to individuals according to whether they do or do not share in the costs of organization and action on behalf of the group. Thus, the groups that act and play a role in society are not all those with some common interest or need for a collective good, but are those lucky enough to be in circumstances that make it possible for them to organize. Hardin points out that we should not take it for granted that this good fortune gives a group a moral claim on the rest of the society.

[18] Russell Hardin, *One for All* (Princeton: Princeton University Press, 1995) and Russell Hardin, *Collective Action* (Baltimore: The Johns Hopkins University Press, 1982).

Hardin has explained another aspect of this matter by considering co-ordination problems in game theory. Obviously there would be great problems if people in a country did not drive on the same side of the road. But they do, even in the absence of any laws requiring it. People rationally follow whatever convention emerges. Often such coordination leads to outcomes that are far inferior to alternatives that might have been chosen, but still much better than would occur without any coordination.

As Hardin has pointed out, there are many spontaneously successful coordination games, and they are typically the source of conventions followed in each social group. Many of the differences in convention across different social groups are arbitrary artifacts of the outcomes of initial coordination games. This means that some of the distinctive cultural practices of particular groups are often *not* the result of profound moral choices. Nor are they the only practices that could be workable and congenial for this group. Rather, they are artifacts of unimportant or even accidental factors in initial coordination games. Different outcomes of initial coordination games can also come to play a role in distinguishing and dividing different groups.

Some social groups and cultural practices, such as the Indian sub-caste or Jati, appear to have mainly different types of origin but are still amenable to a methodologically individualistic explanation. As Montgomery's chapter points out, most of the caste groupings take their names from occupations or crafts. Historically, given sub-castes had a monopoly of practising a given occupation in a given community. Though the Indian caste groups often go back to far earlier periods of history, they are in this respect like the guilds in Europe and many other parts of the world.

Consider the problem facing a group that has a monopoly over a given occupation and wishes to continue to enjoy the monopoly return and pass it on to their descendants. Though Montgomery and Hardin do not go into this, we can see that, to continue enjoying monopoly returns from a cartel, a group must continue to restrict the supply. If the members of such a group can not only pass membership in that monopoly on to their sons, but also offer dowries for their daughters in the form of rights of membership in the cartel to sons-in-law, then the number that practice that occupation in the next generation will double even in the absence of any growth of population.

That won't do for any cartelistic organization that obtains its gains by restricting the supply. Thus, endogamy—the rule that marriage must be only inside the group—is not only a universal feature of the caste system, but also something that enables caste-type groupings to persist for very long periods: it enables the members of a sub-caste to preserve the value of their monopoly control and to pass it on to their children.[19] In the same way, the traditional

---

[19] Olson, *Rise and Decline*, ch. 6.

resistance in European royalty to marriages to commoners was similarly necessary to preserve the full value of royal descent. Such practices as these are examples of the general proposition that those in a group that receive a redistribution, so long as they remain powerful enough to continue to receive the redistribution, will be better off the fewer they have to share the redistribution with. When redistribution is at issue, it is always best to be in a "minimum winning coalition."

The distinctive social customs of different groups that emerge from coordination games of the kind Hardin has explained can make collective action easier. To the extent that people can feel "at home" only with the customs that they have been acculturated to, they have a preference for companionship, marriage, and social interaction within their own group. They then particularly value the respect of those in their group and suffer social loss if they do not have access to social interaction with them. Thus, respect within and access to a group serves as a selective incentive that can motivate collective action by the group.

Though such collective action can be beneficent, Hardin has shown that it is also often exclusionary and harmful. It is, he points out, the mainspring of ethnic conflicts such as those in Bosnia, Northern Ireland, Rwanda, and Somalia. He also shows how "communitarian" ethical philosophies—which do not recognize the problematic nature of the collective action that creates the communal forces that we observe, or appreciate the arbitrary or accidental origins of communal customs—are erroneous.

When one takes Montgomery's and Hardin's work together and combines them with resonant work by others, we see the not-so-dismal science from a new perspective. Some argue, we know, that the methodological individualism that characterizes the not-so-dismal science is wrong because individuals are greatly influenced by socialization in the groups into which they are born, so that research should begin with groups that socialize individuals rather than with individuals.

But the groups that socialize individuals, we must not forget, are made up of individuals. Also, such groups had to emerge as a result of the interactions of individuals: they could not exist before the individuals who, purposely or inadvertently, formed them. So we can use the broader, integrated approach on display here to study groups and the influence that they have, through socialization, on individuals. The ultimate goal is a theory of general social equilibrium that simultaneously considers the individuals and groups in society and their interactions. Some rational-choice sociologists, such as James Coleman, have already explicitly endeavored to do this and have made significant progress.[20] If the chapters by Montgomery and Hardin and the

---

[20] James Samuel Coleman, *Foundations of Social Theory* (Cambridge, Mass.: Harvard University Press, 1990).

related work discussed above are right, a beginning has already been made to try to explain the origins and characteristics of some kinds of social groups.

7 The State versus the Market

The remaining two chapters, Robert Cooter's and Pranab Bardhan's, are also concerned with social norms and social groups. But they consider how these norms and groups should affect the respective roles of the private and the public sectors. In different ways, these two chapters bring us back to the long-standing debate between the right and the left about the proper roles of governments and markets. This is not just the question of how large or small the government should be, but also whether government should be viewed in substantial part as a body that strengthens and enforces norms that evolved first in the private sector—or as the only instrument that can overcome some entrenched impediments to progress in fragmented societies with dysfunctional institutions.

Cooter shows how private-market interaction can sometimes give rise to certain social norms that are better than those that would arise through an initiative from the central government, so that government at its best sometimes codifies, strengthens, and enforces a social norm emerging from a private sector which shares in the task of enforcing this norm. Bardhan points to impediments to economic development and social dysfunctions that market mechanisms cannot cure because the needed large-number collective action cannot emerge spontaneously. The difference in emphasis in each chapter may be due partly to differences in the societies and problems analyzed.

7.1 *The Spontaneous Emergence of Socially Useful Norms*

Cooter is inspired by successful advances in commercial law in relatively competitive and thriving economies. He starts in Chapter 9 with Judge Mansfield's modernization of English common law in the eighteenth century (that is, in the country and the century in which the Industrial Revolution began) and with Professor Llewellyn's effort to identify the best commercial practices in twentieth-century United States and to write them into the commercial code. Cooter finds that the state built on pre-existing social norms, so that, as in his title, there is "law from order." He argues that "in an environment of open competition, business practices tend to evolve rapidly towards efficiency. Without open competition, however, harmful business norms can create monopoly power or distort consumer information, and incomplete markets can impose external costs."

How can a desirable social norm emerge in the private sector? Though Cooter does not emphasize this, such a social norm is a public good. If the numbers involved are large, we should expect that the difficulties of collective action could not be overcome, so the social norm would not evolve under laissez-faire. Cooter considers cases where principals hire agents, but where in any period an agent can appropriate the principal's investment for himself and thereby obtain much more in that period than a cooperative agent would have earned. In future periods a principal would retain only agents who did not do this, so the offending agent has to seek other principals who might hire him and thus does not earn income in as many periods as a cooperative agent. Drawing on evolutionary game theory, Cooter makes it clear that, if there is an equilibrium in the society with both types of agent, the appropriators and cooperators must in this equilibrium earn the same average rate of return.

Since principals would never knowingly hire an agent that intended to appropriate from them, it pays all agents to claim emphatically that they are cooperators, even if they plan to appropriate. This uniform signaling means that the self-interest of the agents assures that the norm that agents should cooperate gets a lot of good free publicity!

Cooter also points out that many situations do not lead to uniform signaling. Hard bargainers, for example, may gain from a reputation that they won't give in, so even though society would presumably have lower transaction costs with a social norm that everyone should be a soft bargainer, there is no tendency for such a social norm to emerge.

Where there is uniform signaling, it not only affects speech and beliefs, but also leads, Cooter hypothesizes (through psychological processes that he leaves to the psychologists to analyze), to an internalization of some degree of willingness to act on and help to enforce the norm. Cooter is aware that, when an individual punishes someone who violates a norm, the benefits accrue mainly to others; but he assumes that, when a group has sufficient "coherence," individuals are sometimes motivated to enforce social norms. He assumes that, in groups with sufficient coherence, externalities of many kinds will at times be internalized, at least if the externalities are "symmetric" ones that leave most individuals as victims as well as perpetrators of the diseconomy.

These conclusions, and the principal–agent and commercial law contexts that Cooter emphasizes, leave the reader with the impression that he is thinking mostly of groups that are not very large. Though he does not go into the numbers issue explicitly, it is clear that if the numbers involved are sufficiently small his conclusions are beyond challenge. But if the numbers involved are sufficiently large, Cooter has no alternative but to rely on the psychologists to fill in the gap in rational behavior.

Here the contrast between Bardhan and Cooter is especially instructive. Bardhan explicitly emphasizes not only large numbers but also social fragmentation, and concludes that spontaneous market behavior does not prevent very bad outcomes. Cooter, by contrast, emphasizes contexts where numbers are probably small and finds that in the right circumstances, with uniform signaling and social coherence, useful social norms may emerge.

Still, even when conditions are favorable to the development of useful social norms and efficient business practices, Cooter finds that law and government should often be brought in. When a practice that runs against a social norm is outlawed, the government not only plays an important role in enforcement, but also strengthens private enforcement: individuals are more aggressive in criticizing and punishing violators of social norms when these violations are illegal. Cooter argues that the law works best when, as with the common law in eighteenth-century Britain or the Uniform Commercial Code in the twentieth-century USA, it reinforces and even follows social norms. By contrast, when the laws and social norms go in opposite directions, the results will probably be bad. Cooter's most basic point—that the law works best when it is consistent with the outcomes in competitive markets and the social norms of a coherent society—is surely valid.

7.2 Tenacious Institutional Impediments to Development

The last chapter in this collection, Pranab Bardhan's "The Nature of Institutional Impediments to Economic Development," like all of the others herein, goes beyond the classical analysis of preferences, resources, technology, and markets; it considers governance, institutions, and (especially) the difficulties of collective action as well, and their importance in determining whether there is stagnation or progress.

Bardhan not only illustrates the broader economics, but also takes us back to the substantive issues with which this introductory chapter began. There we challenged a tacit and almost unconscious assumption that characterized much economic (and lay) thinking, at least until fairly recently. This second-nature assumption was that, unless government intervention prevents it, the markets required for an efficient market economy will arise spontaneously and automatically: that markets are not an artifact of government. We have attempted to show that this assumption, though correct for self-enforcing transactions, was not true in general because many crucial transactions, such as most of those in the capital market, require third-party enforcement at least as a last resort.

Bardhan also emphasizes that there is no necessity for spontaneous or automatic processes in order to obtain socially efficient or desirable outcomes. Some economists have supposed that large changes in the proportions of the production factors make a relatively scarce factor more valuable, and this in turn motivates the development of better property rights for the more valuable factor. Bardhan points out that this need not necessarily happen. The difficulties of collective action could prevent the realization of the gains that better property rights or other institutional improvements would have brought about. The rationality of individuals need not, because of the infeasibility of collective action or other difficulties, bring about the elimination of even dramatically dysfunctional institutions, much less guarantee social efficiency. Bardhan's starting point is not English commercial law in the century of the Industrial Revolution or the propitious development of the Uniform Commercial Code in the United States: it is the poverty-stricken millions and social fragmentation in India.

In keeping with his argument that some serious impediments to development do not disappear spontaneously, Bardhan finds simplistic conceptions of the state—such as the theory of the state as simply a predator on the rest of society, or alternatively as just an instrument of domination for one social class over another—to be insufficient. He prefers a more nuanced view that recognizes not only predation and the exercise of dominance, but also (as at times in East Asia) relatively constructive action which promotes prosperity. In keeping with other analyses in this volume, he points out that such constructive action could arise from an encompassing interest.

Bardhan also finds that even the familiar tradeoff between efficiency and equity may in some cases be too simple. The mechanisms for third-party enforcement of contracts are often poor, so that those who would make productive use of working capital cannot borrow it unless they can provide lenders with very good collateral, such as equity in land. In such circumstances, a less unequal ownership of land could give more cultivators the capacity to borrow working capital, and thus perhaps increase both equity and efficiency.

Bardhan points out how the obstacles to collective action can not only keep spontaneous or market forces from automatically eliminating dysfunctional institutions, but also keep societies from obtaining adequate supplies of public goods. Social fragmentation can increase the difficulties of collective action, and that can mean that (notwithstanding a pre-existing government) the political and governmental processes do not work in ways that assure an adequate supply of public goods. Bardhan points out that in India there is considerable social fragmentation (and, of course, very large numbers), and that this sometimes keeps even local communities and governments from making adequate provision for such basic needs as elementary education. It is difficult to see how anyone could explain the continuing high rates of illiteracy in parts of India without taking account of Bardhan's argument.

....

8 Theory, Ideology, and Cumulative Research

The issue of what should be the proper roles of the government and the market brings up the insistent question of how the suburbanization of economics relates to the ideological struggles in society. The broader and the more general the ideas, the more often people ask how they relate to the ideologies of the time. So, many people ask: is the broadening of economics an outgrowth of an ideological agenda? Or is it a triumph for one side or the other in the ideological struggle? The opposite ideological implications of the final two chapters hint that the answer should be no. Yet some observers think that at least one of the answers should be yes. Since these questions keep coming up, we must deal with them.

If what we have said so far is correct, the not-so-dismal science cannot always favor one ideology or another. As we saw at the beginning, one source of the broader approach is the awareness that some goods cannot be provided, at least not to sufficiently large groups, by voluntary or market mechanisms. The need to accommodate public goods (or, more generally, to analyze market failure) is one of the two main sources of the broadening of economics. Therefore, at least in comparison with narrower or city-center economics, the not-so-dismal science is not single-mindedly focused only on markets. It begins with the difficulties of collective action and the need for governmental or other collective mechanisms.

The second main source of the broader economics is the recognition that, to understand the growth and distribution of income, the economist must also consider the other side of the coin of market failure: it is usually remedied only by the use of coercive power, and wherever there is power, there is the power to take, and often lots of taking. The proceeds of this taking usually go to those with the power to take, rather than to the relatively powerless poor. Obviously, behavior in markets, which is inherently voluntary, cannot lead to such bad outcomes as can occur from the power to take. In a particular transaction, an individual may be the victim of fraud, and thus be made worse off by the transaction. But rational individuals will never voluntarily participate in repeated fraudulent transactions—you can't sell anyone the Brooklyn Bridge twice. Any voluntary market interactions that continue to occur must make people better off.

Not so with the power to take: there is essentially no limit to the damage that this can do. Thus, there is government failure as well market failure, and the consequences of government failure are often incalculably more harmful than anything that can occur from voluntary interaction in a market, however imperfect the market.[21] However, since we cannot get along without governments with the power to coerce, the fact that governments have incomparably greater capacity to do harm than markets is not the whole story. As Oliver Williamson's chapter pointed out, we should not condemn a practice or institution as irrational unless we can find a remedy.

Accordingly, when we take the two sources of the suburbanization of economics together, we see that the logic that led to the broader economics is inherently two-sided and eminently suitable for analyzing both the contribution of markets and market failure: it emphasizes both the need for government and the prevalence of government failure. If devotees of any ideology or political tendency should find the results of good integrated social science work in conflict with their preconceptions, they should ask whether these preconceptions are valid and well balanced.

In any case, the question of whether the suburbanization of economics will favor this or that ideology is the wrong question. What we really need to know about any research results is how much truth, if any, they contain and whether they inseminate new and fruitful inquiries. The professor of theology at a seminary might have the responsibility of coming up with arguments that help the village priest out-argue the village atheist. But economists and other social scientists (unless they have sold themselves to some interest group or party) have no corresponding responsibility to any of the contending ideologies. Our task is rather to improve the understanding of the realities that individuals and societies confront and thereby to help them find means that are better adapted to achieving the ends that people seek. Many individual researchers do, of course, start with strong preconceptions growing out of one ideology or another, but if they find new and fruitful truths, these truths are not either poisoned or blessed by the creed that inspired them. They are, on the contrary, valuable to us all: they reduce the extent to which illusions govern choices.

8.1 Cumulative Knowledge

Some say that the truth of today is the error of tomorrow, and this is sometimes the case. But, as others before us have pointed out, in science and scholarship the truth of today is much more often the special case of the truth of tomorrow.

---

[21] The complete absence of government leads not to voluntary market interaction, but to the private taking of Hobbesian anarchy.

Science and scholarship, whenever they are making much progress, are inherently cumulative: later work generalizes, extends, amends, and improves what was done earlier. There are some lines of literature in the social sciences in which successive writings begin by demolishing or belittling what has gone before, but there is usually not much of value in them. By contrast, the suburbanization of economics and the emergence of an integrated social science are examples of decidedly cumulative science and scholarship: the truths of yesterday are indeed special cases of the truths of today.

The suburbanization of economics does not discredit or contradict anything in the city center. On the contrary, it suggests that the two-and-a-quarter centuries of cumulative work in economics, some of it by men of unquestioned genius, has an even greater value and wider potential than has usually been supposed. The modern economist can say, as Paul of Tarsus did (Acts, 21), that he comes from "no mean city."

1 Big Bills Left on the Sidewalk: Why Some Nations are Rich, and Others Poor

Mancur Olson[1]

1 Introduction

There is one metaphor that not only illuminates the idea behind many complex and seemingly disparate articles, but also helps to explain why many nations have remained poor while others have become rich. This metaphor grows out of debates about the "efficient markets hypothesis," that all pertinent publicly available information is taken into account in existing stock market prices, so that an investor can do as well by investing in randomly chosen stocks as by drawing on expert judgment. It is embodied in the familiar old joke about the assistant professor who, when walking with a full professor, suddenly reaches for the $100 bill he sees on the sidewalk; but he is held back by his senior colleague, who points out that, if the $100 bill were real, it would have been picked up already. This story epitomizes many articles showing that the optimization of the participants in the market typically eliminates opportunities for supra-normal returns: big bills aren't often dropped on the sidewalk, and if they are they are picked up very quickly.

Many developments in economics in the last quarter-century rest on the idea

[1] This article was previously published, under the same title, as the Distinguished Lecture on Economics in Government in the *Journal of Economic Perspectives*, 10(2) (Spring 1996), 3–24. It is reprinted with permission of the American Economic Association. I am grateful to the US Agency for International Development for supporting this research and many related inquiries through the IRIS Center at the University of Maryland. I am indebted to Alan Auerbach, Christopher Clague, David Landes, Wallace Oates, Robert Solow, Timothy Taylor, and especially to Alan Krueger for helpful criticisms, and to Nikolay Gueorguiev, Jac Heckelman, Young Park, and Robert Vigil for research assistance.

that any gains that can be obtained are in fact picked up. Though primitive early versions of Keynesian macroeconomics promised huge gains from activist fiscal and monetary policies, macroeconomics in the last quarter-century has more often than not argued that rational individual behavior eliminates the problems that activist policies were supposed to solve. If a disequilibrium wage is creating involuntary unemployment, that would mean that workers have time to sell what is worth less to them than to prospective employers, so a mutually advantageous employment contract will eliminate the involuntary unemployment. The market ensures that involuntarily unemployed labor is not left pacing the sidewalks.

Similarly, profit-maximizing firms have an incentive to enter exceptionally profitable industries and this reduces the social losses from monopoly power. Accordingly, a body of empirical research finds that the losses from monopoly in US industry are slight: Harberger triangles are small. In the same spirit, many economists find that the social losses from protectionism and other inefficient government policies are only a minuscule percentage of the GDP.

The literature growing out of the Coase theorem similarly suggests that, even when there are externalities, bargaining among those involved can generate socially efficient outcomes. As long as transactions costs are not too high, voluntary bargaining internalizes externalities, so there is a Pareto-efficient outcome whatever the initial distribution of legal rights among the parties. Again, this is the idea that bargainers leave no money on the table.

Some of the more recent literature on Coaseian bargains emphasizes that transactions costs use up real resources and that the value of these resources must be taken into account in defining the Pareto frontier. It follows that, if the bargaining costs of internalizing an externality exceed the resulting gains, things should be left alone. The fact that rational parties won't leave any money on the table automatically insures that laissez-faire generates Pareto efficiency.

More recently, Gary Becker[2] has emphasized that government programs with deadweight losses must be at a political disadvantage. Some economists have gone on to treat governments as institutions that reduce transaction costs and have applied the Coase theorem to politics. They argue, in essence, that rational actors in the polity have an incentive to bargain politically until all mutual gains have been realized, so that democratic government, though it affects the distribution of income, normally produces socially efficient results.[3] This is true even when the policy chosen runs counter to economist's

[2] Gary Becker, "A Theory of Competition among Pressure Groups for Political Influence," *Quarterly Journal of Economics*, 98 (August 1983), 371–400; Gary Becker, "Public Policies, Pressure Groups, and Dead Weight Costs," *Journal of Public Economics*, 28(3) (December 1985), 329–47.

[3] George J. Stigler, "The Theory of Economic Regulation," *Bell Journal of Economics and Management Science*, 2 (Spring 1971), 3–21; George J. Stigler, "Law or Economics?" *Journal of Law and Economics*, 35(2) (October 1992), 455–68; Donald Wittman, "Why Democracies Produce Efficient Results," *Journal of Political Economy*, 97(6) (December 1989), 1395–1424; Donald Wittman, *The Myth of Democratic Failure: Why Political Institutions Are Efficient* (Chicago: University of Chicago Press, 1995); Earl Thompson and Roger Faith, "A Pure Theory of Strategic Behavior and Social Institutions," *American Economic Review*, 71(3) (June 1981), 366–80; A. Breton, "Toward a Presumption of Efficiency in Politics," *Public Choice*, 77 (1993), 53–65.

prescriptions: if some alternative political bargain would have left the rational parties in the polity better off, they would have chosen it! Thus, the elemental idea that mutually advantageous bargaining will obtain all gains that are worth obtaining—that there are no bills left on the sidewalk—leads to the conclusion that, whether we observe laissez faire or rampant interventionism, we are already in the most efficient of all possible worlds.[4]

The idea that the economies we observe are socially efficient, at least to an approximation, is not only espoused by economists who follow their logic as far as it will go, but is also a staple assumption behind much of the best-known empirical work. In the familiar aggregate production function or growth-accounting empirical studies, it is assumed that economies are on the frontiers of their aggregate production functions. Profit-maximizing firms use capital and other factors of production up to the point where the value of the marginal product equals the price of the input, and it is assumed that the marginal private product of each factor equals its marginal social product. The econometrician can then calculate how much of the increase in social output is attributable to the accumulation of capital and other factors of production and can treat any increases in output beyond this—"the residual"—as due to the advance of knowledge. This procedure assumes that output is as great as it can be, given the available resources and the level of technological knowledge.

If the ideas evoked here are largely true, then the rational parties in the economy and the polity ensure that the economy cannot be that far from its potential, and the policy advice of economists cannot be especially valuable. Of course, even if economic advice increased the GDP by just 1 percent, that would pay our salaries several times over. Still, the implication of the foregoing ideas and empirical assumptions is that economics cannot save the world, but at best can only improve it a little. In the language of Keynes's comparison of professions, we are no more important for the future of society than dentists.

---

2 The Boundaries of Wealth and Poverty

How can we find empirical evidence to test the idea that the rationality of the individuals in societies makes them achieve their productive potential? This question seems empirically intractable. Yet there is one type of place where

---

[4] A fuller statement of this argument, with additional citations to the literature on "efficient redistribution," appears in my draft paper on "Transactions Costs and the Coase Theorem: Is This the Most Efficient of All Possible Worlds?" which is available on request. [This has been superseded by a joint paper with Avinash Dixit, also available on request. *Eds.*]

evidence abounds: the borders of countries. National borders delineate areas of different economic policies and institutions, and so—to the extent that variations in performance across countries cannot be explained by the differences in their endowments—they tell us something about the extent to which societies have attained their potentials.

Income levels differ dramatically across countries. According to the best available measures, per capita incomes in the richest countries are more than twenty times as high as in the poorest. Whatever the causes of high incomes may be, they are certainly present in some countries and absent in others. Though rich and poor countries do not usually share common borders, there are cases of vast differences of per capita income on opposites sides of the same boundary. Sometimes there are great differences in per capita income on opposite sides of a meandering river, like the Rio Grande, or where opposing armies happened to come to a stalemate, as between North and South Korea, or where arbitrary lines were drawn to divide a country, as not long ago in Germany.

At the highest level of aggregation, there are only two possible types of explanation of the great differences in per capita income across countries that can be taken seriously.

The first possibility is that, as the aggregate production function methodology and the foregoing theories suggest, national borders mark differences in the scarcity of productive resources per capita: the poor countries are poor because they are short of resources. They might be short of land and natural resources, or of human capital, or of equipment that embodies the latest technology, or of other types of resources. On this theory, the Coase theorem holds as much in poor societies as in rich ones: the rationality of individuals brings each society reasonably close to its potential, different as these potentials are. There are no big bills on the footpaths of the poor societies, either.

The second possibility is that national boundaries mark the borders of public policies and institutions that are not only different, but in some cases better and in other cases worse. Those countries with the best policies and institutions achieve most of their potential, while other countries achieve only a tiny fraction of their potential income. The individuals and firms in these societies may display rationality, and often even great ingenuity and perseverance, in eking out a living in extraordinarily difficult conditions, but this individual achievement does not generate anything remotely resembling a socially efficient outcome. There are hundreds of billions or even trillions of dollars that could be—but are not—earned each year from the natural and human resources of these countries. On this theory, the poorer countries do not have a structure of incentives that brings forth the productive cooperation that would pick up the big bills, and the reason they don't have it is that such structures do not emerge automatically as a consequence of individual rationality. The structure of incentives depends not only on what economic policies are chosen in each period, but also on the long-run or institutional arrangements: on the legal systems that enforce contracts and protect property rights and on political structures, constitutional provisions, and the extent of special-interest lobbies and cartels.

How important are each of the two foregoing possibilities in explaining economic performance? This is an extraordinarily important question. The answer must not only help us judge the theories under discussion, but also tell us about the main sources of economic growth and development.

I will attempt to assess the two possibilities by aggregating the productive factors in the same way as in a conventional aggregate production function or growth-accounting study and then consider each of the aggregate factors in turn. That is, I will separately consider the relative abundance or scarcity of "capital," of "land" (with land standing for all natural resources), and of "labor" (with labor including not only human capital, in the form of skills and education, but also culture). I will also consider the level of technology separately, and will find some considerations and evidence that support the familiar assumption from growth-accounting studies and Solow-type growth theory that the same level of technological knowledge is given exogenously to all countries.[5] With this conventional taxonomy, and the assumption that societies are on the frontiers of their aggregate neoclassical production functions, we can derive important findings with a few simple deductions from familiar facts.

The next section shows that there is strong support for the familiar assumption that the world's stock of knowledge is available at little or no cost to all the countries of the world. I next examine the degree to which the marginal productivity of labor changes with large migrations, and the evidence on population densities, and show that diminishing returns to land and other natural resources cannot explain much of the huge international differences in income. After that, I borrow some calculations from Robert Lucas on the implications of the huge differences across countries in capital intensity, and relate them to facts on the direction and magnitude of capital flows, to show that it is quite impossible that the countries of the world are anywhere near the frontiers of aggregate neoclassical production functions. I then examine some strangely neglected natural experiments with migrants from poor to rich countries to estimate the size of the differences in endowments of human capital between the poor and rich countries, and demonstrate that they are able to account for only a small part of the international differences in the marginal product of labor. Since neither differences in the endowments of any of the three classical aggregate factors of production nor differential access to technology explain much of the great variation in per capita incomes, we are left with the second of

---

[5] The different assumptions of endogenous growth theory are explored later.

the two (admittedly highly aggregative) possibilities set out above: that the most important explanation of the differences in income across countries is the difference in their economic policies and institutions. There will not be room here to set out many of the other types of evidence supporting this conclusion, or to offer any detailed analysis of what particular institutions and policies best promote economic growth. Nonetheless, by referring to other studies—and by returning to something that the theories with which we began overlook—we shall obtain some sense of why variations in institutions and policies are surely the main determinants of international differences in per capita incomes. We shall also obtain a faint glimpse of the broadest features of the institutions and policies that nations need in order to achieve the highest possible income levels.

3 The Access to Productive Knowledge

Is the world's technological knowledge generally accessible at little or no cost to all countries? To the extent that productive knowledge takes the form of unpatentable laws of nature and advances in basic science, it is a nonexcludable public good available to everyone without charge. Nonpurchasers can, however, be denied access to many discoveries (in countries where intellectual property rights are enforced) through patents or copyrights, or because the discoveries are embodied in machines or other marketable products. Perhaps most advances in basic science can be of use to a poor country only after they have been combined with or embodied in some product or process that must be purchased from firms in the rich countries. We must, therefore, ask whether most of the gains from using modern productive knowledge in a poor country are captured mainly by firms in the countries that discovered or developed this knowledge.

Since those third world countries that have been growing exceptionally rapidly must surely have been adopting modern technologies from the first world, I tried (with the help of Brendan Kennelly) to find out how much foreign technologies had cost some such countries. As it happens, there is a study[6] with some striking data for South Korea for the years 1973–1979. In Korea during these years, royalties and all other payments for disembodied technology were minuscule—often less than one-thousandth of GDP. Even if we treat all profits on foreign direct investment as solely a payment for knowledge and add

[6] Bohn-Young Koo, "New Forms of Foreign Direct Investment in Korea," Korean Development Institute Working Paper 82–02 (June 1982).

them to royalties, the total is still less than 1.5 percent of the *increase* in Korea's GDP over the period. Thus, the foreign owners of productive knowledge obtained less than a fiftieth of the gains from Korea's rapid economic growth.[7]

The South Korean case certainly supports the long familiar assumption that the world's productive knowledge is, for the most part, available to poor countries, and even at a relatively modest cost.[8] It would be very difficult to explain much of the differences in per capita incomes across countries in terms of differential access to the available stock of productive knowledge.[9]

....

4 Overpopulation and Diminishing Returns to Labor

Countries with access to the same global stock of knowledge may nonetheless have different endowments, which in turn might explain most of the differences in per capita income across countries. Accordingly, many people have supposed that the poverty in poor countries is due largely to overpopulation, that is, to a low ratio of land and other natural resources to population. Is this true?

There is some evidence that provides a surprisingly persuasive answer to this question. I came upon it when I learned through Bhagwati[10] of Hamilton and Whalley's[11] estimates about how much world income would change if more workers were shifted from low-income to high-income countries. The key is to examine how much migration from poorer to richer countries *changes* relative to wages and the marginal productivities of labor.

---

[7] My calculation leaves out that portion of the cost of new equipment that is an implicit charge for the new ideas embodied in it. We must also remember that by no means all of Korea's growth was due to knowledge discovered abroad.

[8] It is sometimes said that developing countries do not yet have the highly educated people needed to use modern technologies, and so the world's stock of knowledge is not in fact accessible to them. This argument overlooks the fact that the rewards to those with the missing skills, when other things are equal, would then be higher in the poor societies than in societies in which these skills were relatively plentiful. If difficulties of language and ignorance of the host country's markets can be overcome, individuals with the missing skills would then have an incentive to move (sometimes as employees of multinational firms) to those low-income countries in which they were most needed.

[9] We shall see, when we later consider a heretofore neglected aspect of the relationship between levels and rates of growth of per capita incomes, that the new or endogenous growth theory objection to this assumption need not concern us here.

[10] J. Bhagwati, "Incentives and Disincentives: International Migration," *Weltwirtschaftliches Archiv*, 120 (1984), 678–701.

[11] R. Hamilton and J. Whalley, "Efficiency and Distributional Implications of Global Restrictions on Labour Mobility: Calculations and Policy Implications," *Journal of Development Economics*, 14(1–2) (January–February 1984), 61–75.

For simplicity, suppose that the world is divided into only two regions: North and South, and stick with the conventional assumption that both are on the frontiers of their aggregate production functions. As we move left to right from the origin of Figure 1.1, we have an ever larger workforce in the North until, at the extreme right end of this axis, all of the world's labor force is there. Conversely, as we move right to left from the right-hand axis, we have an ever larger workforce in the South. The marginal product of labor or wage in the rich North is measured on the vertical axis at the left of the figure. The curve MPL_N gives the marginal product or wage of labor in the North, and of course, because of diminishing returns, it slopes downward as we move to the right. The larger the labor force in the South, the lower the marginal product of labor in the South, so MPL_S, measured on the right-hand vertical axis, slopes down as we move to the left. Each point on the horizontal axis will specify a distribution of the world's population between the North and the South. A point like S represents the status quo. At S, there is relatively little labor and population in relation to resources in the North, and so the Northern marginal product and wage is high. The marginal product and wage in the overpopulated South will be low, and the marginal product of labor in the North will exceed that in the South by a substantial multiple.

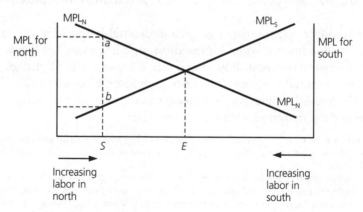

Fig. 1.1 Population Distribution and Relative Wages

This model tells us that, when workers migrate from the low-wage South to the high-wage North, world income goes up by the difference between the wage the migrant worker receives in the rich country and what that worker earned in the poor country, or by amount ab.

Clearly, the world as a whole is not on the frontier of its aggregate production, even if all of the countries in it are: some big bills have not been picked up on the routes that lead from poor to rich countries.[12] Of course, the argument that has just been made is extremely simple, and international migration involves many other considerations. We can best come to understand these considerations—as well as other matters—by staying with this simple factor proportions story a while longer.

....

5 The Surprising Results of Large Migrations

This elementary model reminds us that, if it is diminishing returns to land and other natural resources that mainly explain international differences in per capita incomes, then large migrations from poorer to richer societies will, if other things (like the stocks of capital) remain equal, necessarily reduce income differentials. Such migration obviously raises the resource–population ratio in the country of emigration and reduces it in the country of immigration, and if carried far enough will continue until wages are equalized, as at point E in Figure 1.1.

Now consider Ireland, the country that has experienced much the highest proportion of outmigration in Europe, if not the world. In the census of 1821, Ireland had a population of 5.4 million people and Great Britain 14.2 million.[13] Though the Irish have experienced the same rates of natural population increase that have characterized other European peoples since 1821, in 1986 Ireland had only 3.5 million people. By this time, the population of Great Britain had reached 55.1 million. In 1821, the population density of Ireland was greater than that of Great Britain; by 1986, it was only about a fifth as great.[14]

If the lack of "land" or overpopulation is decisive, Ireland ought to have enjoyed an exceptionally rapid growth of per capita income, at least in comparison with Great Britain, and the outmigration should eventually have ceased. Not so. Remarkably, the Irish level of per capita income is still only about five-eighths of the British level and less than half of the level in the United States, and the outmigration from Ireland is continuing. [*Note:* Since the

---

[12] In other words, there has not been a Coase-style bargain between rich and poor regions. Given that income increases by, say, tenfold when labor moves from the poor to the rich countries, there would be a continuing incentive for the poor to migrate to the rich countries even if the rich countries took, for example, half of this increase and kept it for their citizens. The transactions costs of such a deal would surely be minute in relation to the gains.

[13] At the time I wrote this I had not read Joel Mokyr's analysis of 19th-cent. Ireland: for a richer analysis of 19th-cent. Ireland see his *Why Ireland Starved: A Quantitative and Analytical History of the Irish Economy 1800–1850* (London and Boston: Allen & Unwin, 1983). After detailed quantitative studies, he concludes that "there is no evidence that pre-famine Ireland was overpopulated in any useful sense of the word" (p. 64).

[14] Northern Ireland is excluded from both Great Britain and Ireland. See Brian R. Mitchell and H. G. Jones, *Second Abstract of British Historical Statistics* (Cambridge: Cambridge University Press, 1971), Brian R. Mitchell, *Abstract of British Historical Studies* (Cambridge: Cambridge University Press, 1962), Ireland Central Statistical Office, *Annual Abstract of Statistics* (London: H.M.S.O., 1988), and Great Britain Central Statistical Office, *Annual Abstract of Statistics* (London: H.M.S.O., 1988).

research on this matter was carried out, Irish per capita incomes have grown faster than in most of Europe and outmigration has ceased. Irish economic policies have also changed substantially in recent decades. *Eds.*] As we shall see later, such large disparities in per capita income cannot normally be explained by differences in human capital, and it is clear that in the United States, Britain, and many other countries, immigrants from Ireland tend to earn as much as other peoples, and any differences in human capital could not explain the *increase* in wage that migrants receive when they go to a more productive country. Thus, we can be sure that it is not the ratio of land to labor that has mainly determined per capita income in Ireland.

Now let us look at the huge European immigration to the United States between the closing of the US frontier in about 1890 and the imposition of US immigration restrictions in the early 1920s. If diminishing returns to labor were a substantial part of the story of economic growth, this vast migration should have caused a gradual reduction of the per capita income differential between the United States and Europe. In fact, the United States had a bigger lead in per capita income over several European countries in 1910 and 1920 than it had in the nineteenth century. Although many European countries did *not* narrow the gap in per capita incomes with the United States in the nineteenth century when they experienced a large outmigration to that country, many of these same countries did nearly close that gap in the years after 1945, when they had relatively little emigration to the United States, and when their own incomes ought to have been lowered by a significant inflow of migrants and guest workers. Similarly, from the end of World War II until the construction of the Berlin wall, there was a considerable flow of population from East to West Germany, but this flow did not equalize income levels.

Consider also the irrepressible flow of documented and undocumented migration from Latin America to the United States. If diminishing returns to land and other natural resources was the main explanation of the difference in per capita incomes between Mexico and the United States, these differences should have diminished markedly at the times when this migration was greatest. They have not.

Several detailed empirical studies of relatively large immigration to isolated labor markets point to the same conclusion as the great migrations we have just considered. Card's[15] study of the Mariel boatlift's effect on the wages of natives of Miami, Hunt's[16] examination of the repatriation of Algerian French workers to southern France, and Carrington's and De Lima's[17] account of the repatriates

[15] David Card, "The Impact of the Mariel Boatlift on the Miami Labor Market," *Industrial and Labor Relations Review*, 43(2) (January 1990), 245–57.

[16] Jennifer Hunt, "The Impact of the 1962 Repatriates from Algeria on the French Labor Market," *Industrial and Labor Relations Review*, 45(3) (April 1992), 556–72.

[17] William J. Carrington and Pedro J. F. De Lima, "The Impact of 1970s Repatriates from Africa on the Portuguese Labor Market," *Industrial and Labor Relations Review*, 49(2) (January 1996), 330–47.

from Angola and Mozambique after Portugal lost its colonies, all suggest that the substantial inmigration did not depress the wages of natives.[18]

Perhaps in some cases the curves in Figure 1.1 would cross when there was little population left in a poor country. Or maybe they would not cross at all: maybe even that last person who turned the lights out as he left would obtain a higher wage after migrating.

6 Surprising Evidence on Density of Population

Let us now shift the focus from changes in land–labor ratios resulting from migration to the cross-sectional evidence at given points in time on ratios of land to labor. Ideally, one should have a good index of the natural resource endowments of each country. Such an index should be adjusted to take account of changes in international prices, so that the value of a nation's resources index would change when the prices of the resources with which it was relatively well endowed went up or down. For lack of such an index, we must here simply examine density of population. Fortunately, the number of countries on which we have data on population and area is so large that population density alone tells us something.

Many of the most densely settled countries have high per capita incomes and many poor countries are sparsely settled. Argentina, a country that fell from having one of the highest per capita incomes to third world status, has only 11 persons per square kilometer; Brazil has 16; Kenya, 25; and Zaire, 13. India, like most societies with a lot of irrigated agriculture, is more densely settled, with 233 people per square kilometer. But high-income West Germany, with 246 people per square kilometer, is even more densely settled; Belgium and Japan have half-again higher population density, with 322 and 325 people per square kilometer, and Holland has still greater density with 357. The population of Singapore is 4,185 per square kilometer; that of Hong Kong, over 5,000 persons per square kilometer;[19] these two densely settled little fragments of land also have per capita incomes ten times as high as the poorest countries—and as of this writing they continue, like many other densely settled countries, to absorb migrants, at least when the migrants can sneak through the controls.

The foregoing cases could be exceptions, so we need to take into account all countries for which data are available and summarily describe the overall relationship between population density and per capita income. If we remember that the purpose is description and are careful to avoid drawing causal

---

[18] I am grateful to Alan Krueger for bringing these studies to my attention.

[19] United Nations, *Demographic Yearbook* (1986).

inferences, we can describe the available data with a univariate regression in which the natural log of real per capita income is the left-hand variable and the natural log of population per square kilometer is the "explanatory" variable. Obviously, the per capita income of a country depends on many things, and any statistical test that does not take account of all important determinants is misspecified and thus must be used only for descriptive and heuristic purposes. It is nonetheless interesting—and for most people surprising—to find that there is a *positive* and even a statistically significant relationship between these two variables: the *greater* the number of people per square kilometer, the *higher* the per capita income.[20]

The law of diminishing returns is indisputably true: it would be absurd to suppose that a larger endowment of land makes a country poorer. This consideration by itself would, of course, call for a negative sign on population density. Thus, it is interesting to ask what might account for the "wrong" sign and to think of what statistical tests should ultimately be conducted. Clearly, there is a simultaneous two-way relationship between population density and per capita income: the level of per capita income affects population growth just as population, through diminishing returns to labor, affects per capita income.

The argument offered here suggests that perhaps countries with better economic policies and institutions come to have higher per capita incomes than countries with inferior policies and institutions, and that these higher incomes bring about a higher population growth through more immigration and lower death rates. In this way, the effect of better institutions and policies in raising per capita income swamps the tendency of diminishing returns to labor to reduce it. This hypothesis also may explain why many empirical studies have not been able to show a negative association between the rate of population growth and increases in per capita income.

One reason why the ratio of natural resources to population does not account for variations in per capita income is that most economic activity can now readily be separated from deposits of raw materials and arable land. Over time, transportation technologies have certainly improved, and products that have a value in relation to their weight, such as most services and manufactured goods like computers and airplanes, may have become more important. The Silicon Valley is not important for the manufacture of computers because of deposits of silicon, and London and Zurich are not great banking centers because of fertile land. Even casual observation suggests that most modern manufacturing and service exports are not closely tied to natural resources. Western Europe does not now have a high ratio of natural resources to population, but it is very important in the export of manufactures and services. Japan

---

[20] Specifically, the regression results are:

$$PER\ CAPITA\ GDP = 6.986 + 0.1746\ POPULATION\ DENSITY.$$

The $r^2 = 0.05$, and the t-statistic is 2.7.

has relatively little natural resources per capita, but it is a great exporter of manufacturers. Certainly the striking successes in manufactures of Hong Kong and Singapore cannot be explained by their natural resources.

....

7 Diminishing Returns to Capital

We have seen that large migrations of labor do not change the marginal productivities of labor the way that they would if societies were at the frontiers of aggregate neoclassical production functions, and that there is even evidence that labor is on average more highly paid where it is combined with less land. We shall now see that the allocation of capital across countries—and the patterns of investment and migration of capital across countries of high and low capital intensities—contradict the assumption that countries are on the frontiers of aggregate neoclassical production functions in an even more striking way.

This is immediately evident if we return to Figure 1.1 and relabel its coordinates and curves. If we replace the total world labor supply given along the horizontal axis of the figure with the total world stock of capital, and assume that the quantity of labor as well as natural resources in the North and South do not change, we can use the figure to analyze diminishing returns to capital in the same way we used it to consider diminishing returns to labor.

As everyone knows, the countries with high per capita incomes have incomparably higher capital intensities of production than do those with low incomes. The countries of the third world use relatively little capital and those of the first world are capital-rich: most of the world's stock of capital is "crowded" into North America, Western Europe, and Japan.

If the countries of the world were on the frontiers of neoclassical production functions, the marginal product of capital would therefore be many times higher in the low-income than in the high-income countries. Robert Lucas[21] has calculated, albeit in a somewhat different framework,[22] the marginal products of capital that should be expected in the United States and in India. He estimated that, if an Indian worker and an American worker supplied the same

---

[21] Robert Lucas, "Why Doesn't Capital Flow from Rich to Poor Countries?" *American Economic Review*, 80 (May 1990), 92–6.

[22] Lucas's calculations are set in the context of Solow's growth theory. To bring the contradiction between the assumption that societies are on the frontiers of aggregate neoclassical production functions and what is actually observed, most starkly and simply, I have focused on a single point in time and used the framework Solow put forth for empirical estimation. It would add little insight to the present argument to look at the growth paths of different countries.

quantity and quality of labor, the marginal product of capital in India should be 58 *times* as great as in the United States. Even when Lucas assumed that it took *five* Indian workers to supply as much labor as one US worker, the predicted return to capital in India would still be a multiple of the return in the United States.

With portfolio managers and multinational corporations searching for more profitable investments for their capital, such gigantic differences in return should generate huge migrations of capital from the high-income to the low-income countries. Capital should be struggling at least as hard to get into the third world as labor is struggling to migrate into the high-wage countries. Indeed, since rational owners of capital allocate their investment funds across countries so that the risk-adjusted return at the margin is the same across countries, capital should be equally plentiful in all countries. (As we know from the Heckscher–Ohlin–Stolper–Samuelson discovery, if all countries operate on the same aggregate production functions, free trade alone will equalize factor price ratios and thus factor intensities even in the absence of capital flows.)

Obviously, the dramatically uneven distribution of capital around the world contradicts the familiar assumption that all countries are on the frontiers of aggregate neoclassical production functions. A country could not be Pareto-efficient, and therefore could not be on the frontier of its aggregate production, unless it had equated the marginal product of capital in the country to the world price of capital.[23] If it were not meeting this law-of-one-price condition, it would be passing up the gains that could come from borrowing capital abroad at the world rate of interest, investing it at home to obtain the higher marginal product of capital, and pocketing the difference—it would be leaving large bills on the sidewalk. Accordingly, the strikingly unequal allocation of the world's stock of capital across the nations of the world proves that the poor countries of the world cannot be anywhere near the frontiers of their aggregate production functions.

Sometimes the shortcomings of the economic policies and institutions of the low-income countries keep capital in these countries from earning rates of return appropriate to its scarcity, as we may infer from Harberger's[24] findings and other evidence. Sometimes the shortcomings of the economic policies and institutions of poor countries make foreign investors and foreign firms unwelcome, or provoke the flight of locally owned capital, or make lending to these countries exceedingly risky. Whether the institutional and policy shortcomings of a country keep capital from having the productivity appropriate to its scarcity, or discourage the investments and lending that would equalize the

---

[23] Since each third world economy is small in relation to the world economy, it is reasonable to assume that no one of them could change the world price of capital, so that the marginal cost of capital to the country is equal to its price.

[24] Arnold Harberger, "Perspectives on Capital and Technology in Less Developed Countries," in *Contemporary Economic Analysis*, ed. M. Artis and A. Nobay (London: Croom Helm, 1978).

marginal product of capital across countries, they keep it from achieving its potential.

On top of all this, it is not rare for capital and labor to move *in the same direction*: both capital and labor are sometimes trying to move out of some countries and into some of the same countries. Of course, in a world where countries are on the frontiers of their aggregate production functions, capital and labor move in opposite directions.[25]

Given the extraordinarily uneven allocation of capital across the countries of the world and the strong relationship between capital mobility and the economic policies and institutions of countries, the stock of capital cannot be taken to be exogenous in any reasonable theory of economic development.

---

8 Distinguishing Private-Good and Public-Good Human Capital

The adjustment of the amount of human capital per worker in Lucas's foregoing calculation for India and the United States raises a general issue: can the great differences in per capita income be explained mainly by differences in the third aggregate factor, labor, i.e. by differences in the *human* capital per capita, broadly understood as including the cultural or other traits of different peoples as well as their skills? The average level of human capital in the form of occupational skills or education in a society can obviously influence the level of its per capita income.

Many people also argue that the high incomes in rich countries are due in part to cultural or racial traits that make the individuals in these countries adept at responding to economic opportunities: they have the "Protestant ethic" or other cultural or national traits that are supposed to make them hard workers, frugal savers, and imaginative entrepreneurs. Poor countries are alleged to be poor because they lack these traits.[26] The cultural traits that perpetuate poverty are, it is argued, the results of centuries of social accumulation and cannot be changed quickly.

Unfortunately, the argument that culture is important for economic development, though plausible, is also vague: the word "culture," even though it is widely used in diverse disciplines, has not been defined precisely or in a way

---

[25] In a neoclassical world with only capital and labor, they would necessarily move in opposite directions, but when there is a disequilibrium with respect to land or other natural resources, both capital and labor could move to correct this disequilibrium.

[26] In his Ely lecture, Landes made an argument along these lines; see Landes, "Why are We So Rich and They So Poor?", *American Economic Review*, 80 (May 1990): 1–13.

that permits comparison with other variables in an aggregate production function.

We can obtain conceptions of culture that are adequate for the present purpose by breaking culture down into two distinct types of human capital. Some types of human capital are obviously marketable: if a person has more skill, or a propensity to work harder, or a predilection to save more, or a more entrepreneurial personality, this will normally increase that individual's money income. Let us call these skills, propensities, or cultural traits that affect the quality or the quantity of productive inputs that an individual can sell in the marketplace "marketable human capital" or, synonymously, "personal culture." Max Weber's analysis of what he called the Protestant ethic was about marketable human capital or personal culture.

The second type of culture or human capital is evident when we think of knowledge that individuals may have about how they should vote: about what public policies will be successful. If enough voters acquire more knowledge about what the real consequences of different public policies will be, public policies will improve and thereby increase real incomes in the society. But this better knowledge of public policy is usually not marketable: in a society with *given* economic policies and institutions, the acquisition of such knowledge would not in general have any affect on an individual's wage or income. Knowledge about what public policy should be is a public good rather than a private or marketable good. Thus, this second kind of human capital is "public-good human capital" or "civic culture." Whereas marketable human capital or personal culture increases an individual's market income under given institutions and public policies, public-good human capital or civic culture is not normally marketable and affects incomes only by influencing public policies and institutions.

With the aid of the distinction between marketable and public-good human capital, we can gain important truths from some natural experiments.

....

9 Migration as an Experiment

As it happens, migration from poor to rich countries provides researchers with a marvelous (and so far strangely neglected) natural experiment. Typically, the number of individuals who immigrate to a country in any generation is too small to bring about any significant change in the electorate or public policies of the host country. But the migrant who arrives as an adult comes with the marketable human capital or personal culture of the country of origin; the Latin American who swims the Rio Grande is not thereby instantly baptized with the Protestant ethic. Though the migrant may in time acquire the culture of the host country, the whole idea behind the theories that emphasize the cultural or other characteristics of peoples is that it takes time to erase generations of socialization: if the cultural or other traits of a people could be changed overnight, they would not be significant barriers to development. Newly arrived immigrants therefore have approximately the same marketable human capital or personal culture they had before they migrated, but the institutions and public policies that determine the opportunities that they confront are those of the host country. In the case of migration to the United States, at least, the data about newly arrived migrants from poor countries are sufficient to permit some immediate conclusions.

Christopher Clague,[27] drawing on the work of Borjas,[28] has found that individuals who had just arrived in the United States from poor countries, in spite of the difficulties they must have had in adjusting to a new environment with a different language and conditions, earned about 55 percent as much as native Americans of the same age, sex, and years of schooling.[29,30] Profit-maximizing firms would not have hired these migrants if they did not have a marginal product at least as large as their wage. The migrant's labor is, of course, combined with more capital in the rich than the poor country, but it is not an accident that the owners of capital chose to invest it where they did: as the foregoing argument showed, the capital–labor ratio in a country is mainly determined by its institutions and policies.

Migrants might be more productive than their compatriots who did not migrate, so it might be supposed that the foregoing observations on immigrants are driven by selection bias. In fact, no tendency for the more productive people in poor countries to be more likely to emigrate could explain the huge increases in wages and marginal products of the *migrants themselves*. The migrant earns and produces much more in the rich country than in the poor country, so no tendency for migrants to be more productive than those who did not migrate

[27] Christopher Clague, "Relative Efficiency Self-Containment and Comparative Costs of Less Developed Countries," *Economic Development and Cultural Change*, 39(3) (April 1991), 507–30.

[28] G. Borjas, "Self-selection and the Earnings of Immigrants," *American Economic Review*, 77 (1987), 531–53.

[29] Clague takes the intercept of Borjas's regression about how the migrants' wages increase with time in the USA as the wage on arrival.

[30] Apparently somewhat similar patterns can be found when there is migration from areas of low income to other high-income countries. The increases in the wages that migrants from low-wage countries like Turkey or the German Democratic Republic have received in West Germany are well known and in accord with the argument I am making. As Krueger and Pischke show, after German unification, East German workers who now work in West Germany earn more than those who work in East Germany; see Alan Krueger and Jorn-Steffen Pischke, "A Comparison on East and West German Labor Markets Before and After Unification," in R. Freeman and L. Katz (eds), *Differences and Changes in Wage Structures* (Chicago: University of Chicago Press, 1995), pp. 405–45. By my reading of their numbers, the increase from this migration is less than it was before German unification. If Germany is succeeding in its efforts to create the same institutional and policy unification environment in East as in West Germany, the gains from East-to-West migration in Germany should diminish over time. The structures of incentives in East and West Germany are not yet by any means identical.

could explain the *increase* in the migrant's marginal product when he or she moves from the poor to the rich country.[31] In any event, developing countries often have much more unequal income distributions than developed nations, so the incentive to migrate from these countries is greatest in the least successful half of their income distributions, as is evidenced in studies of migrants to the United States.[32]

It is also instructive to examine the differences in productivity between migrants from poor countries and migrants from rich countries, and then to see how much of the difference in per capita incomes in the countries of origin is likely to be due to the differences in the marketable human capital or personal culture of their respective peoples. Compare, for example, migrants to the United States from Haiti, one of the world's least successful economies, with migrants from West Germany, one of the most successful. According to the 1980 US Census, self-employed immigrants from Haiti earned $18,900 per year, while those from West Germany earned $27,300; salaried immigrants from Haiti earned $10,900, those from West Germany, $21,900. Since the average Haitian immigrants earned only two-thirds or half as much as their West German counterparts in the same American environment, we may suspect that the Haitians had, on average, less marketable human capital than the West Germans.

So now let us perform the thought experiment of asking how much West Germans would have produced if they had the same institutions and economic policies as Haiti, or conversely how much Haitians would have produced had they had the same institutions and economic policies as West Germany. If we infer from the experience of migrants to the United States that West Germans have twice as much marketable capital as the Haitians, we can then suppose that Haiti, with its present institutions and economic policies but with West German levels of marketable human capital, would have about twice the per capita income that it has. But the actual level of Haitian per capita income is only about a tenth of the West German level, so Haiti would still, under our thought experiment, have less than one-fifth of the West German per capita income. Of course, if one imagines Haitian levels of marketable human capital operating with West German institutions and economic policies, one comes up with about half of the West German per capita income, which is again many times larger than Haiti's actual per capita income.

Obviously, one of the reasons for the great disparity implied by these thought experiments is the different amounts of tangible capital per worker in the two countries. Before taking this as given exogenously, however, readers

---

[31] To account for this result in terms of selection bias, one would have to argue that those workers who remained in the poor countries would not have a similar increase in marginal product had they migrated.

[32] G. Borjas, *Friends or Strangers: The Impact of Immigrants on the US Economy* (New York: Basic Books, 1990).

should consider investing their own money in each of these two countries. It is also possible that different selection biases for immigrants from different countries help account for the results of the foregoing thought experiments. Yet roughly the same results hold when one undertakes similar comparisons from migrants from Switzerland and Egypt, Japan and Guatemala, Norway and the Philippines, Sweden and Greece, the Netherlands and Panama, and so on.[33] If, in comparing the incomes of migrants to the United States from poor and rich countries, one supposes that selection bias leads to an underestimate of the differences in marketable human capital between the poor and rich countries, and then makes a larger estimate of this effect than anyone is likely to think plausible, one still ends up with the result that the rich countries have vastly larger leads over poor countries in per capita incomes than can possibly be explained by differences in the marketable human capital of their populations. Such differences in personal culture can explain only a small part of the huge differences in per capita income between the rich and the poor countries.

History has performed some other experiments that lead to the same conclusion. During most of the postwar period, China, Germany, and Korea have been divided by the accidents of history, so that different parts of nations with about the same culture and group traits have had different institutions and economic policies. The economic performances of Hong Kong and Taiwan, West Germany, and South Korea have been incomparably better than the performances of mainland China, East Germany, and North Korea. Such great differences in economic performance in areas of very similar cultural characteristics surely could not be explained by differences in the marketable human capital of the populations at issue.

It is important to remember that the foregoing experiments involving migration do not tell us anything about popular attitudes or prejudices in different countries regarding what public policy should be. That is, they do not tell us anything about the public-good human capital or civic cultures of different peoples. As we know, the migrants from poor to rich countries are normally tiny minorities in the countries to which they migrate, so they do not usually change the public policies or institutions of the host countries. The natural experiments that we have just considered do not tell us what would happen if the civic cultures of the poor countries were to come to dominate the rich countries. For example, if traditional Latin American or Middle Eastern beliefs about how societies should be organized came to dominate North America or western Europe, then institutions and economic policies—and presumably also economic performance—would change.

---

[33] I am thankful to Robert Vigil for help in studying the incomes of migrants from other countries to the USA.

10 The Overwhelming Importance of Institutions and Economic Policies

If what has been said so far is correct, then the large differences in per capita income across countries cannot be explained by differences in access to the world's stock of productive knowledge or to its capital markets, by differences in the ratio of population to land or natural resources, or by differences in the quality of marketable human capital or personal culture. Albeit at a high level of aggregation, this eliminates each of the factors of production as possible explanations of most of the international differences in per capita income. The only remaining plausible explanation is that the great differences in the wealth of nations are due mainly to differences in the quality of their institutions and economic policies.

The evidence from the national borders that delineate different institutions and economic policies not only contradicts the view that societies produce as much as their resource endowments permit, but also directly suggests that a country's institutions and economic policies are decisive for its economic performance. The very fact that the differences in per capita incomes across countries—the units with the different policies and institutions—are so large in relation to the differences in incomes across regions of the same country supports my argument. So does the fact that national borders sometimes sharply divide areas of quite different per capita incomes.

11 The Old Growth Theory, the New Growth Theory, and the Facts

The argument offered here also fits the relationships between levels of per capita income and rates of growth better than either the old or the new growth theories do. As has often been pointed out, the absence of any general tendency for the poor countries with their opportunities for catch-up growth to grow faster than the rich countries argues against the old growth theory. The new or endogenous growth models feature externalities that increase with the investment of stocks of human or tangible capital and can readily explain why countries with high per capita incomes can grow as fast or faster than low income countries.

But neither the old nor the new growth theories predict the relationship that is actually observed: *the fastest growing countries are never the countries with the highest per capita incomes, but always a subset of the lower-income countries.* At the same time that low-income countries as a whole fail to grow any faster than high-income countries, a subset of the lower-income countries grows far faster than *any* high-income country does. The argument offered here suggests that poor countries on average have poorer economic policies and institutions than rich countries and therefore, in spite of their opportunity for rapid catch-up growth, they need not grow faster on average than the rich countries.

But any poorer countries that adopt relatively good economic policies and institutions enjoy rapid catch-up growth: since they are far short of their potential, their per capita incomes can increase not only because of the technological and other advances that simultaneously bring growth to the richest countries, but also by narrowing the huge gap between their actual and potential income.[34] Countries with the highest per capita incomes do not have the same opportunity.

Thus, the argument here leads us to expect what is actually observed: no necessary connection between low per capita incomes and more rapid rates of growth, but much the highest rates of growth in a subset of low-income countries—the ones that adopt better economic policies and institutions. During the 1970s, the four countries that (apart from the oil-exporting countries) had the fastest rates of growth grew on average 6.9 percentage points faster than the United States—more than five times as fast. In the 1980s, the four fastest growers grew 5.3 percentage points faster than the United States—four times as fast. They outgrew the highest-income countries as a class by similarly large multiples. All four of the fastest growing countries in each decade were low-income countries.

In general, the endogenous growth models do not have anything in their structures that predicts that the most rapid growth will occur in a subset of low-income countries, and the old growth theory is contradicted by the absence of general convergence.

Note also that, as the gap in per capita incomes between the relatively poor and relatively rich countries has increased over time, poor countries have also fallen further behind their potential. Therefore, the argument offered here predicts that the maximum rate of growth that is possible for a poor country—and the rate at which it can gain on the highest per capita income countries—is increasing over time. This is also what has been observed. In the 1870s, the four continental European countries with the fastest growth of per capita incomes grew only 0.3 percent per annum faster than the United Kingdom; the top four such countries in the 1880s also had the same 0.3 percent gain over the UK. As

[34] Robert J. Barro, "Economic Growth in a Cross Section of Countries," *Quarterly Journal of Economics,* 106(2) (May 1991), 407–43.

we have seen, the top four countries in the 1970s grew 6.9 percentage points faster than the United States, and the top four in the 1980s 5.3 percentage points faster. Thus, the lead of the top four in the 1970s was *23 times* as great as the lead of the top four in the 1870s, and the lead of the top four in the 1980s was more than *17 times* as great as the lead of the top four a century before.[35]

Thus, neither the old nor the new growth theory leads us to expect either the observed overall relationship between the levels and rates of growth of per capita incomes or the way this relationship has changed as the absolute gap in per capita incomes has increased over time. The present theory, by contrast, suggests that there should be patterns like those we observe.

··

12   Picking Up the Big Bills

The best thing a society can do to increase its prosperity is to wise up. This means, in turn, that it is very important that economists, inside government and out, get things right. When we are wrong, we do a lot of harm. When we are right—and have the clarity needed to prevail against the special interests and the quacks—we make an extraordinary contribution to the amelioration of poverty and the progress of humanity. The sums lost because poor countries obtain only fraction of—and because even the richest countries do not reach—their economic potentials are measured in the trillions of dollars.

None of the familiar ideologies is sufficient to provide the needed wisdom. The familiar assumption that the quality of a nation's economic institutions and policies is given by the smallness, or the largeness, of its public sector—or by the size of its transfers to low-income people—does not fit the facts very well.[36]

[35] Germany was the fastest growing European country in the 1870s, but its borders changed with the Franco-Prussian war, and so the "1870s" growth rate used for Germany is 1872–82. Angus Maddison's estimates were used for the 19th cent. World Bank data for the 20th. The top four qualifying growth countries in each decade were: for the 1980s, Korea, China, Botswana, and Thailand; for the 1970s, Botswana, Malta, Singapore, and Korea; for the 1880s, Germany, Finland, Austria, and Denmark; for the 1870s, Germany, Belgium, the Netherlands, and Austria.

Those countries that still had open frontiers in the 19th cent. or in some cases even until World War I, or that were major oil exporting countries at the times of the oil shocks, are not apt countries for the comparisons at issue now. It would be going much too far to extend the argument here about the limited importance of land and natural resources to growth to countries that are in major disequilibrium because of open frontiers or huge changes in their terms of trade. That is why I excluded the oil exporting countries and compared the fastest growing continental European countries with Britain in order to analyze the speed of catch-up after the industrial revolution. I am thankful to Nikolay Gueorguiev for gathering and analyzing the data on this issue.

[36] Ross Levine and David Renelt, "A Sensitivity Analysis of Cross-Country Growth Regressions," *American Economic Review*, 82 (1992), 942–63; Richard Rubinson, "Dependency, Government Revenue, and Economic

But the hypothesis that economic performance is determined mostly by the *structure of incentives*—and that it is mainly national borders that mark the boundaries of different structures of incentives—has far more evidence in its favor. This paper has set out only one of the types of such evidence; there is also direct evidence of the linkage between better economic policies and institutions and better economic performance; though it is not feasible to set this out here, a lot of it is available in other writings.[37]

We can perhaps obtain a glimpse of another kind of logic and evidence in support of the argument here—and a hint about what kinds of institutions and economic policies generate better economic performance—by returning to the theories with which we began. These theories suggested that the rationality of the participants in an economy or the parties to a bargain implied that there would be no money left on the table. We know from the surprisingly good performance of migrants from poor countries in rich countries, as well as from other evidence, that there is a great deal of rationality, mother wit, and energy among the masses living in poor countries: individuals in these societies can pick up the bills on the sidewalk about as quickly as we can.

The problem is that the really big sums cannot be picked up through uncoordinated individual actions. They can be obtained only through the efficient cooperation of many millions of specialized workers and other inputs: in other words, they can be attained only if a vast array of gains from specialization and trade are realized. Though the low-income societies obtain most of the gains from self-enforcing trades, they do not realize many of the largest gains from specialization and trade. They do not have the institutions that enforce contracts impartially, and so they lose most of the gains from those transactions (like those in the capital market) that require impartial third-party enforcement. They do not have institutions that make property rights secure over the long run, so they lose most of the gains from capital-intensive production. Production and trade in these societies is further handicapped by misguided economic policies and by private and public predation. The intricate social cooperation that emerges when there is a sophisticated array of markets requires far better institutions and economic policies than most countries have. The effective correction of market failures is even more difficult.

The spontaneous individual optimization that drives the theories with which I began is important, but it is not enough by itself. If spontaneous Coase-style bargains, whether through laissez-faire or political bargaining and government, eliminated socially wasteful predation and obtained the institutions that are

Growth," *Studies in Comparative Institutional Development*, 12 (1977), 3–28; Mancur Olson, "Supply-Side Economics, Industrial Policy, and Rational Ignorance," in *The Politics of Industrial Policy*, ed. Claude E. Barfield and William A. Schambra (Washington: American Enterprise Institute for Public Policy Research, 1986), pp. 245–69.

[37] C. Clague, P. Keefer, S, Knack and M. Olson, "Contract-Intensive Money: Contract Enforcement, Property Rights, and Economic Performance," IRIS Working Paper no. 151 (University of Maryland, 1995).

needed for a thriving market economy, then there would not be so many grossly inefficient and poverty-stricken societies. The argument presented here shows that the bargains needed to create efficient societies are not, in fact, made. Though that is another story, I can show that in many cases such bargains are even logically inconsistent with rational individual behavior.[38] Some important trends in economic thinking, useful as they are, should not blind us to a sad and all-too-general reality: as the literature on collective action demonstrates,[39] individual rationality is very far indeed from being sufficient for social rationality.

[38] The logic at issue is set out in a preliminary way in the aforementioned Olson working paper, "Transactions Costs and the Coase Theorem" [This paper has been superseded by a joint paper with Avinash Dixit, available on request. *Eds.*]

[39] Mancur Olson, *The Logic of Collective Action* (Cambridge: Harvard University Press, 1965); Russell Hardin, *Collective Action* (Baltimore: Johns Hopkins University Press, 1982); Todd Sandler, *Collective Action* (Ann Arbor: University of Michigan Press, 1992).

2 Innovation and its Enemies: The Economic and Political Roots of Technological Inertia

Joel Mokyr

1 Introduction

Are the crucial decisions that determine economic growth, even in economies committed to free-enterprise economics, made primarily in the marketplace? Markets determine the allocation of existing resources and are believed by most economists to be better at this than any alternative. But how about technological change? The bulk of the economics of new technology is concerned with the generation of new knowledge and the problems of appropriability and incentives in the creation of new technology. It rarely asks when and how decisions to adopt new technology are made by firms.

Much as economists might deplore the fact, the acceptance of innovation is more than an economic phenomenon, and certainly far more than a pure advance in productive knowledge. The concept of competition remains central here, but it is not so much the neoclassical concept of price competition of firms in the marketplace as much as Schumpeter's concept of competition between different techniques struggling to be adopted by existing firms or between different final products slugging it out over the consumer's preferences. At times individual techniques may be identified with a firm, but often techniques struggle for adoption within a *single* organization. How are these decisions made? Why is it that, even when a new and superior technology is made available at zero marginal costs, the economy to which it is proposed may choose to reject it?

Economic analysis implicitly assumes that new techniques will be adopted if they pass some kind of "market test." That is, if they can out-compete existing techniques, by producing a more desirable product and/or producing it more cheaply, new technological ideas will be adopted. This is a simple but powerful Darwinian model of technological evolution, and, while many of its more Panglossian implications have been muted in recent years, the idea of the market as an arbiter of which techniques will be adopted is still powerful. Economists in the neoclassical tradition are convinced that, although it is theoretically possible for market selection to come up with non-optimal outcomes, such outcomes are in fact rare.

Non-economists are dissatisfied with this approach.[1] Technological progress, it is felt, is a social phenomenon, which changes almost every variable in society. In this paper I wish to focus on one particular issue: namely, that new technologies will fail to be implemented despite their ostensible economic superiority. For this class of problems, artificial distinctions between the "economic sphere" and the "political sphere" are doomed, and we will not even attempt them.

The idea that seemingly superior inventions are spurned or rejected is hardly new. In 1679, William Petty wrote that,

Although the inventor, often times drunk with the opinion of his own merit, thinks all the world will invade and incroach upon him, yet I have observed that the generality of men will scarce be hired to make use of new practices, which themselves have not been thoroughly tried . . . for as when a new invention is first propounded, in the beginning every man objects, and the poor inventor runs the gantloop of all petulant wits . . . not one [inventor] of a hundred outlives this torture . . . and moreover, this commonly is so long a doing that the poor inventor is either dead or disabled by the debts contracted to pursue his design.[2]

In this paper, I plan to pursue a somewhat different issue from the disbelief and friction Petty speaks of namely, the purposeful resistance to new technology. Without an understanding of the political economy of technological change, the historical development of economic growth will remain a mystery. The issue of the receptivity of society to new technological ideas is highly relevant to the experience of underdeveloped countries whose failure to adopt best-practice technologies is often regarded as an integral part of underdevelopment. In the very long run, technological progress in its widest sense remains indispensable to sustainable economic growth. Of course, the failure to adopt a new technology can have many reasons: new technology is often embodied in expensive capital goods; it often requires scarce complementary

---

[1] As are some economists. See especially Geoffrey M. Hodgson, *Economics and Evolution: Bringing Life Back into Economics* (Oxford: Polity Press, 1993), ch. 13.

[2] William Petty, *A Treatise of Taxes and Contributions* (London: Obadiah Blagrave, 1679), p. 53. I am indebted to Patrick O'Brien for bringing this text to my attention.

factors such as infrastructural capital or a highly skilled labor force. Yet outright resistance is a widely observed historical phenomenon.[3] The adoption of a wholly new technology is often the target of long debates and public discourse, unlike many other technical and economic choices. The role of persuasion and rhetoric in these decisions is something economists have paid scant attention to; hence they have not had much success in understanding why, for example, some economies have adopted nuclear power, or why some have allowed experimental drugs to be sold and others have not. Furthermore, not all resistance is purely social. There are instances in which the technological "system" resists a novel and improved component because it does not fit the operation of the whole.

In any event, technological inertia in many societies has often been ascribed to irrationality, technophobia, or a blind adherence to traditional but outmoded values and customs. In what follows, I hope to establish two basic propositions. One is that inertia is usually a characteristic widely observed in complex systems that follow an evolutionary dynamic. Second, technological inertia is usually the outcome of rational behavior by utility-maximizing individuals, and we do not have to fall back on differences in preferences to explain why some societies are more amenable to technological change than others.

2 Rules and Resistance

To simplify matters, define the adoption of a new technique as a binary process: either it is adopted or it is not. Each individual has a set of idiosyncratic exogenous variables (preferences, age, endowments, education, wealth, etc.) which lead him or her to either "support" or "object to" the innovation. To reach this decision, society follows what I will call an aggregation rule, which maps a vector of n individual preferences into a $<0,1>$ decision. This aggregation rule may be a market process (as would be the case in a pure private economy), but such a rule is a very special case. Any change in technology leads almost inevitably to an improvement in the welfare of some and a deterioration in that of others. To be sure, it is *possible* to think of changes in production technology that are Pareto-superior, but in practice such occurrences are extremely rare. The pure market outcome is equivalent to an aggregator that weights preferences by their income. The optimality of the outcome will vary with the income distribution even for the market

---

[3] For some historical detail, see Joel Mokyr, "Progress and Inertia in Technological Change," in J. James and M. Thomas eds, *Capitalism in Context: Essays in Honor of R. M. Hartwell* (Chicago: University of Chicago Press, 1994), pp. 230–54.

aggregator. Unless all individuals accept the "verdict" of the market outcome, the decision whether to adopt an innovation is likely to be resisted by losers through non-market mechanism and political activism.[4] Two recent books dealing with social response to technology, while totally different in tone and background, implore social scientists to pay more attention to the question of resistance to the seemingly inexorable march of new technology.[5]

One important distinction should be made between the introduction of a totally new invention in the economy in which it originates, and the transfer of existing technology into new places after it has already been practised and tried elsewhere. In both cases resistance may emerge, but its nature may differ substantially between the two. Either way, however, markets judge techniques by profitability and thus, as a first approximation, by economic efficiency.

How, then, does conflict occur? To start with, different groups in the economy favor different aggregation rules. In the terminology of the new Historical Institutional Analysis, an aggregator is an *institution*, that is, a non-technologically determined constraint on economic behavior.[6] If the market outcome rules in favor of one group, another might find it in its interest to circumvent the market process.

Suppose that a new technology T_1 is superior to the old T_0 for some individuals belonging to subset $S \in N$, but makes those belonging to $s \in N$ worse off. In general, then, $\exists$ some welfare aggregator G_S, so that $G_S(T_1) > G_S(T_0)$, and $\exists$ G_s such that $G_s(T_1) < G_S(T_0)$. If the members of S and s could form separate societies, one of these would adopt T_1 and the other would not. Because they cannot, resistance can be interpreted as the attempt of the members of the losing side (say, s) to abandon the dictates of the aggregation rule in place (for example the market) and to impose a different aggregator on the economy such as a regulating or licensing agency.[7] It is possible that the number of members in s is larger than that in its complement $\tilde{s}$. In that case there will be a difference between the market, in which "votes" are weighted by expenditures, and a democratic process, where each person has one vote.[8] In decisions about

---

[4] As one author has put it, "opposition to a technology is a special case of a broader class of political activities usually referred to as 'special interest' politics, as opposed to the politics of party identification or patronage." See Allan C. Mazur, "Controlling Technology," reprinted in Albert Teich, ed., *Technology and the Future* (New York: St Martin's Press, 1993), p. 217.

[5] Martin Bauer (ed.), *Resistance to New Technology* (Cambridge: Cambridge University Press/Kirkpatrick Sale, 1995), and *Rebels against the Future: the Luddites and their War on the Industrial Revolution* (Reading, Mass.: Addison Wesley, 1995).

[6] The terminology is borrowed from Avner Greif, "Micro Theory and the Study of Economic Institutions through Economic History," prepared for a symposium on economic history at the 7th World Congress of the Econometric Society, Tokyo, 1995.

[7] Joel Mokyr, "Technological Inertia in Economic History," *Journal of Economic History*, 52(2) (June 1992): 325–38; and "Progress and Inertia."

[8] It clearly is highly ironic to cite here a prominent Indian businessman, Titoo Ahluwalia, as saying that "the average Indian has two sides to him. There is one side that is a consumer and one that is a voter" (*Business Week*, Oct. 23, 1995, p. 50).

technology, at least, there could be a serious inconsistency between democracy and continuous innovation.[9] In other words, unlike the optimism of free-market advocates in the Friedman tradition, it may well be that democratic decision processes do not maximize the long-term economic welfare of economies.

This dilemma faced by democratic countries wishing to undergo rapid development has long been recognized.[10] Barbara Ward explained that uncontrolled market decisions will create intolerable gaps in income distribution and thus a resistance to new technology, and totalitarian dictatorships would implement technologies regardless of cost. "But in India," she adds, "a balance has always to be struck, the dilemma is never absent." Yet in her view this is precisely India's strength, since whatever modernization is introduced is usually based on a consensus and thus is unlikely to ignite political explosions.[11]

The reason why members of S and s prefer different aggregation rules needs some elaboration. One issue is that technology may appear *directly* in people's utility function. Such a concept may appear bizarre to economists, but not so to sociologists or psychologists.[12] For economists, moreover, it has been deemed traditionally uninteresting to ascribe differences in behavior to different utility functions. Historically, however, cultural and religious elements may have had a big influence on technological decision-making.[13] Technology is something profoundly unnatural, as Freud observed in his *Civilization and its Discontents* when he compared it to an artificial limb. Technology is regarded by many writers as something uncontrollable and incomprehensible and thus somehow evil in itself. The literature on this issue is rather large and cannot be done justice to here.[14] At this stage, I will assume identical utility functions and

[9] The notion that democracy endangers technological creativity was particularly embraced by 19th-cent. reactionary writers opposed to the extension of the franchise such as Sir Henry Maine, who argued that universal suffrage would have prevented most of the major technological breakthroughs of the Industrial Revolution. See Albert Hirschman, *The Rhetoric of Reaction* (Cambridge, Mass.: Harvard University Press, 1991), pp. 97–100, who adds that the argument was palpably absurd and immediately proven to be so. Yet it is not impossible that democracy could under certain circumstances be *less* hospitable than other political regimes to technological progress.

[10] For an interesting discussion which concludes firmly that "democracy entrenches economic freedoms, and in doing so underpins growth," see "Why Voting is Good for You," *The Economist* (Aug. 27 1994): 15–17.

[11] Barbara Ward, *India and the West* (New York: W. W. Norton, 1964) pp. 150–2. These words were written many years before the experience of the Shah of Iran confirmed her insight.

[12] In the psychological literature there is a great deal of emphasis on seemingly "irrational" phenomena such as fear of new technology. Psychological "diagnosis" of "cyberphobia," "technophobia," and even "neophobia" (fear of new things) is common. For a thoughtful debunking of this literature, see Martin Bauer, " 'Technophobia': a Misleading Conception of Resistance to New Technology," in Bauer, *Resistance to New Technology*, pp. 87–122.

[13] All technology, as it involves manipulation of nature, is inextricably mixed up with religion, and not just medical and biological research as in our time. For some introductory notes, see Joel Mokyr, *The Lever of Riches: Technological Creativity and Economic Progress* (New York: Oxford University Press, 1990), pp. 170–3, 200–6.

[14] For a historiographical introduction, see Langdon Winner, *Autonomous Technology* (Cambridge, Mass.: MIT Press, 1977), pp. 107–34.

attribute the differences in opinion to observable parameters such as differences in information, economic costs, and endowments. Proposed technological changes are expected to benefit one segment of society and harm another; the market may determine one outcome, which could be circumvented by another aggregator.

Formally, we may distinguish between the following decision rules. G_M, which is the pure market aggregator, means that the new technology will be adopted by profit-maximizing firms following exclusively the dictates of the market. G_D is a decision rule that designates an *authorized subset*, such as a representative parliament or a panel of technical experts, a violent mob, a court, or a single dictator, to decide whether to permit and/or support the new technology. G_V is a voting rule, say one-person–one-vote, in which a new technology is voted in or out by some kind of referendum. In most realistic situations, the actual decision rule or aggregator that maps individual preferences to the decision space $<0,1>$ is $G = \alpha G_M + \beta G_D + (1-\alpha-\beta)G_V$ where $\alpha + \beta \leq 1$. The pure market outcome occurs only when $\alpha = 1$.

The social decision process may thus be viewed as consisting of two stages. First, society determines the political rules of the game; that is, it sets α and β. Then, depending on the aggregator chosen, it determines whether or not the new technique will be adopted. An obvious elaboration of the simple model is that one decision-maker may delegate decisions to another: the authorized subset can decide to hand things over to a referendum or leave it up to the market. An election, on the other hand, can appoint a body of people delegated to make the decision or do nothing at all so that the decision to adopt is effectively left to the market. The interpretation of α and β as probabilities or proportions of the "cases" that are decided in one arena or another thus lends some intuitive meaning to G.

A great deal of political and social struggle involves not only the implementation of new technology, but the decision rules themselves, as it is reasonably believed that some decision rules favor one interest group more than another. Economists, in particular, are concerned by the size of α, that is, how much of the decision is left to the market and how much will be decided on by other aggregators. In part, the aggregator will be determined by the nature of the product—technological change in public goods and other areas of market failure will be obviously largely outside the market decision process— but there is a huge gray area of private goods where there is room for political action. It may be thought that societies will be more creative and technologically successful the larger is α, but this is by no means certain. It may well be that the free market, for reasons of its own, forgoes technological opportunities. For instance, the new technology may require unusually large capital spending or a coordination between existing firms that cannot be materialized without direct intervention. In that case, the government may step in to make up for the market failure. Pre-revolutionary France, especially, saw a great deal of government involvement in trying to encourage French entrepreneurs to accept British techniques.

When the aggregator has been decided upon, as long as $\alpha < 1$, so that—as is often the case—some non-market decision is necessary to approve the new technology, opposition occurs within given political structures, such as a courtroom or a parliamentary committee. Of course, many new technologies are too trifling to be the matter of public debate; one hears little of a public outcry over the switch, say, from spark-plugs to fuel injection or from dot-matrix to ink-jet printers. In those cases the decision will normally be delegated to the market. But when there are major technical choices that involve public expenditures, complementary or substitute relations with other technologies, or other types of spillover effects, they will end up being judged by non-market criteria.[15] Similarly, uncertainty of any nature regarding possible externalities, especially when these concern public health and safety, almost invariably lead to a reduction of the market component in the aggregator. In those cases, political lobbying about the new technology is natural. The usual rules of political economy and collective decision-making by interest groups apply, with the additional complications that the introduction of a new technology is by definition a highly uncertain event, involving known and unknown dangers that play no role in, say, political decisions about tariff policy or public work procurements. Moreover, the technical and scientific issues are often highly complex, and even a phrasing of the correct *questions* (let alone the answers) is often beyond the intellectual capability of decision-makers. Precisely for that reason, there is more reliance on the opinion of "experts" but also, paradoxically, a frequent appeal to emotions, fears, and religious and nationalist sentiments. As litigation becomes increasingly important, technological decisions are relegated to courts, and rhetorical imagery and other persuasive tools, from TV ads to neighborhood rallies, become a means by which techno-logical decisions are made. Reliance on technical expertise, a long-standing practice in the West, is weakened by disagreements among experts and even disagreements as to *who* is an expert to begin with.[16]

An anti-technological and conservative bias can be built into a culture, so that the decision-making body becomes technologically reactionary. In this fashion, the technological status quo does not have to fight battles against hopeful innovations over and over again. This cultural bias can be introduced through

[15] The adoption of fluoridation of drinking water in the USA, the use of insecticide in mosquito abatement, and all matters pertaining to military technology are prime examples of such public technical choices.

[16] Dorothy Nelkin has pointed out that the very fact that experts disagree—more even than the substance of their disagreement—leads to protests and demands for more public participation. See Dorothy Nelkin, "Science, Technology and Political Conflict," in Dorothy Nelkin, ed., *Controversy: Politics of Technical Decisions* (3rd edn, London: Sage, 1992).

an education system that fosters conformist values in which traditions are held up in respect and deviancy and rebellion made highly risky.[17] Morris lists the sources of technological reaction in traditional India: there was no organization for the propagation or dissemination of knowledge, and an unbridgeable social barrier between theorists and craftsmen.[18] Eric L. Jones has argued that the Indian caste system was a deeply conservative and rigidified institution in which ascriptiveness is pervasive and personal achievement "is excluded in principle." Jones realizes that a caste system, too, could never be an *absolute* constraint on economic growth—it "may constitute an infuriating brake, yet it will not be able to switch off a motor located somewhere else in society."[19] The argument made here is exactly about such brakes; societies with such brakes would develop much more slowly than those without. Perhaps that is as much as we will ever be able to say about economic growth.

All cases of resistance to technological change can be reduced to those two main typologies: a struggle *over* the decision rules, and (if $\alpha < 1$) a struggle *within* them. The political battles over technology have profound implications for economic history. One is, as I have emphasized elsewhere, that technological progress in a given society is by and large a temporary and vulnerable process, with many powerful enemies whose vested interest in the status quo or aversion to change of any kind continuously threatens it.[20] The net result is that changes in technology, the mainspring of economic progress, have been rare, and that *stasis* or change at very slow rates has been the rule rather than the exception. It is our own age, and especially the rapid technological change in the Western world, that is the historical aberration.

Another implication is that most underdeveloped countries cannot take technology transfer for granted. Even when capital is available and complementary inputs such as skilled labor and infrastructure are present, attempts to transplant technology from one society to another are likely to run into social barriers that economists may find difficult to understand. Before we can delve into the economic and social causes of resistance, we need to place its importance in a theoretical framework.

[17] Bernard Lewis has pointed out that in the Islamic tradition the term *Bidaa* (innovation) eventually acquired a seriously negative connotation, much like "heresy" in the West, and that such subtle cultural changes account for much of the technological slow-down of the Islamic Middle East after 1400. Cf. Bernard Lewis, *The Muslim Discovery of Europe* (New York: W. W. Norton, 1982), pp. 229–30. This is not to argue that *any* religion is inherently anti-technological, even in a relative sense. Yet there are many subtle ways in which an entrenched elite can manipulate institutions and culture in order to make any contemplated challenge to their dominance more difficult.

[18] Morris D. Morris, "The Growth of Large-scale Industry till 1947", in Dharma Kumar, ed., *The Cambridge Economic History of India*, Vol. 2 (Cambridge: Cambridge University Press, 1983), p. 563.

[19] Eric L. Jones, *Growth Recurring* (Oxford: Oxford University Press, 1988), pp. 103–6.

[20] Joel Mokyr, "Cardwell's Law and the Political Economy of Technological Progress," *Research Policy*, 23 (1994): 561–74.

3 Inertia and Evolution

Many scholars have recognized that new techniques emerge in a manner that is in some ways analogous to the emergence of new species and variations on existing ones in the evolution of living beings.[21] The choice of techniques is akin to the process of natural selection; natural selection is really a metaphor for an impersonal process in which no concrete entity actually does the selecting. New technologies are similarly selected (although here at least in some cases the selecting is done by conscious individuals making deliberate choices). The market is of course one arena in which this selection takes place; the political sphere is another.

Despite the seemingly unbelievable diversity of life forms, actual phenotypical change is quite unusual and encounters many barriers. The understanding that natural selection is inherently a *conservative* process was first emphasized by Alfred Russel Wallace, who likened natural selection to a governor on a steam engine, i.e. essentially a device to correct deviations automatically. The eminent biologist Gregory Bateson, who points this out, notes that the rate of evolution is limited by the barrier between phenotypic and genotypic change, so that acquired characteristics are not passed on to future generations; by sexual reproduction, which guarantees that the DNA blueprint of the new does not conflict too much with that of the old; and by the inherent conservatism of the developing embryo, which necessarily involves a convergent process that Bateson calls epigenesis.[22] System externalities have an equivalent in biology known as "structural constraints." Genetic material is transmitted in "packages" and thus sticks together. The information transmitted from generation to generation does not consist of independent and separately optimizable pieces. A "little understood principle of correlated development" (as Darwin called it) implies that certain features develop not because they increase fitness but because they are correlated with other developments. We now know why this is so: genetic linkage causes genes that are located in close proximity on the chromosome to be inherited. At the same time, evolution tends to be localized and cannot change too much at once. As François Jacob put it in a famous paper, evolution does not so much create as tinker: it works with what is available, odds and ends, and much of it involves therefore minor variations on existing structures.[23] Selection could also misfire

---

[21] For a recent summary see Joel Mokyr, "Evolution and Technological Change: a New Metaphor for Economic History?" in Robert Fox, ed., *Technological Change* (London: Harwood, 1996), pp. 63–83.

[22] Gregory Bateson, *Mind and Nature: a Necessary Unity* (New York: Dutton, 1979), pp. 175–6.

[23] See François Jacob, "Evolution and Tinkering," *Science*, 196 (4295) (June 1977), p. 1165. Such "minor" variations, however, can have huge consequences on the phenotype. As Jacob notes, "small changes modifying the distribution in time and space of the same structures are sufficient to affect deeply the form, the

when a trait leads to what is called "positive feedback traps," that is, when a trait is selected because of its success in satisfying the fitness criterion but is trapped by it at a low level of fitness.[24]

Furthermore, the emergence of new species (speciation), analogous to the emergence of new techniques, is both rare and poorly understood. Although the resistance to change in natural systems is of an entirely different nature than that in technological systems, it too implies a cohesive force that limits the amount and rate of change. As Mayr has recently explained,

Just exactly what controls this cohesion is still largely unknown, but its existence is abundantly documented ... during the pre-Cambrian period, when the cohesion of eukaryote genotype was still very loose, seventy or more morphological types (phyla) formed. Throughout evolution there has been a tendency for a progressive "congealing" of the genotype so that deviation from a long-established morphological type has become more and more difficult.

While such genetic cohesion has of course not precluded the well-known adaptive radiations that created different species, these explosions of variety are little more than ad hoc variations on a *bauplan* or structural type.[25] This cohesion, as Mayr emphasizes, while not wholly understood, is essential to the development of the world of living species: the key to success is to strike a compromise between excessive conservatism and excessive malleability. Evolutionary systems, whether biological or other, that are too conservative will end up in complete stasis; too much receptivity to change will result in chaos.[26]

In the economic history of technology, we may have been more fortunate. Radically new technological ideas, from antibiotics to nuclear power to telegraphy, have emerged time and again despite the odds against them. Yet the dynamic may be similar: a system that struggles to change against built-in inertia is more likely to change in sudden bursts than in slow, continuous fashion. The idea of "punctuated equilibria" in evolutionary change can be

---

functioning and behavior of the final product" p. 1165). For a similar view see Stephen Jay Gould, "Is a New and General Theory of Evolution Emerging?" *Paleobiology*, 6(1) (1980): 127.

[24] Peter M. Allen and M. Lesser, "Evolutionary Human Systems: Learning, Ignorance and Subjectivity," in P. P. Saviotti and J. S. Metcalfe, eds., *Evolutionary Theories of Economic and Technological Change: Present Status and Future Prospects* (London: Harwood, 1991). An example is the peacock's tail, which helps each peacock in the reproductive game and thus conveys a selective advantage despite the uselessness of the tail in survival-related functions. The same was true for the extinct Irish elk: its enormous antlers gave its bearers a putative advantage in mating, but they were apparently useless as a defensive tool, and furthered the demise of the species. One can easily think of products that survive because of their success in marketing and advertising despite demonstrable lower quality.

[25] Ernst Mayr, *One Long Argument: Charles Darwin and the Genesis of Modern Evolutionary Thought* (Cambridge, Mass.: Harvard University Press, 1991), pp. 160–1.

[26] For a detailed argument along these lines, see Stuart Kauffman, *At Home in the Universe: The Search for the Laws of Self-Organization and Complexity* (New York: Oxford University Press, 1995), p. 73.

projected to historical processes to cast light on the question why so much of historical change occurs in concentrated spurts of intense technological activity, such as the British Industrial Revolution.[27] Most recent research in modern evolutionary biology suggests that the dynamic of evolution, too, proceeded in intensive spurts separated by long periods of stasis rather than in linear progressions.[28]

The analogy with evolutionary biology underlines the rather unlikely nature of continuous technological progress. Stability in the systems of living beings is maintained by what biologists term *genetic cohesion*. Similarly, technology is subject to *technological cohesion*, basically meaning that on the whole technological systems will be stable and inert. It could be the case, of course, that the agents of change, whether they are mutations in DNA or new ideas occurring to people, are themselves highly nonlinear in their frequency. It is more plausible, however, to assume that changes in "mutagens" are relatively rare and that mutations occur at more or less uniform rates but are constrained by the inertia and resistance to change within the system. The likelihood of change taking place depends on the outcome of the struggle between novelty, thirsting for a chance to take place, and the old, fearful of any threat to the status quo. As Wesson has pointed out, "the most important competition is not among individuals and their lineages, but between new forms and old. The old must nearly always win, but the few newcomers that score an upset victory carry away the prize of the future." This paragraph, written as a comment on Darwinian evolution, mirrors the one written decades earlier by Schumpeter: "In capitalist reality, as distinguished from its textbook picture, it is not [price] competition which counts but the competition from the new commodity, the new technology . . . which strikes not at the margins of the profits of the existing firms but at their . . . very lives."[29] Schumpeter believed that pure competitive capitalism ensured that cases in which a superior technology would be rejected would be rare, but he also understood the fragility of capitalism in democratic society.

In the context of a struggle between the status quo and novelty, the nonlinear dynamic of historical evolution becomes more plausible. The technological status quo will create barriers that make it more difficult for new ideas to catch on, and at times may succeed in rigging the decision-making process so that novelty becomes almost impossible. Once these dams are broken, however, the torrent of innovation may become unstoppable, at least

[27] Joel Mokyr, "Punctuated Equilibria and Technological Progress," *American Economic Review*, 80(2) (May 1990): 350–4; Joel Mokyr, "Was There a British Industrial Evolution?" in J. Mokyr, ed., *The Vital One: Essays Presented to Jonathan R. T. Hughes* (Greenwich, Conn.: JAI Press, 1991), pp. 253–86.

[28] For an accessible summary, see Niles Eldredge, *Reinventing Darwin: The Great Evolutionary Debate* (London: Weidenfeld & Nicholson, 1995).

[29] Robert Wesson, *Beyond Natural Selection*. (Cambridge, Mass.: MIT Press, 1991), p. 149; Joseph A. Schumpeter, *Capitalism, Socialism and Democracy*, 3rd ed. (New York: Harper & Row, 1950), p. 84.

for a while. Precisely if the political arguments are not cast in terms of the perceived costs and benefits of the new technology itself, but rather in terms of the rules that are to be followed in making these decisions, such non-linearities become understandable.

The story becomes considerably more involved but also richer when we regard not only technology but also institutions as subject to evolutionary forces. Douglass C. North has stressed the idea that institutions evolve in that their dynamic can be described by stochastic shocks subject to selective filters, even if not all the implications of this approach were fully explored.[30] What we have, then, is two evolutionary systems, one epistemological (technology) and one political and social (formal institutions, customs, and other informal rules of behavior), that co-evolve over time.[31] An example is the emergence of American industrial capitalism after the Civil War, in which the technology of interchangeable parts and mass production assembly lines implied an enormous growth in the optimal scale of much of the manufacturing. This technology co-evolved with changes in the structure of business institutions, including the emergence of the modern hierarchical business corporation, labor unions, and the growth in efficiency and scope of capital and labor markets.[32] Such a continuous interactive co-evolution means that, if a foreign technology were transplanted into a society where the adapted institutions had not evolved jointly, serious incongruities and disruptions could be the result. The consequent resistance to technological change can, in this fashion, be re-interpreted in a wider context.

4 Markets or Politics?

Although the terminology here is different, the concept of heterogeneous aggregators is closest to the concepts enunciated by Olson in his *Logic of Collective Action* and *Rise and Decline of Nations*. Consider for simplicity an

---

[30] See Douglass C. North, *Institutions, Institutional Change and Economic Performance* (Cambridge: Cambridge University Press, 1990), p. 87.

[31] This idea was suggested to me by Dr John Kurien of the Center for Development Studies at Thiruvananthapuram. For a further discussion of co-evolution in a biological context, see Geerat Vermeij, "The Evolutionary Interaction among species," *Annual Reviews of Ecology and Systematics*, 1994. Whereas Vermeij's analysis deals primarily with interaction between two evolving species, there is no reason why his analysis cannot be extended to larger groups. Vermeij himself has repeatedly stressed the isomorphisms he sees between paleobiological and social history: Kauffman, *At Home in the Universe*, p. 217, suspects that "biological coevolution and technological coevolution . . . may be governed by the same or similar fundamental laws."

[32] Richard R. Nelson, "Recent Evolutionary Theorizing about Economic Change," *Journal of Economic Literature*, 33 (March 1995): 64.

economy that has to make a binary choice whether to adopt T_1 or not. While in a market economy such decisions are of course made by individuals, in most societies discontinuous and discrete changes in the main technique in use involve to some extent public decision-making. Patents have to be issued, environmental impact statements filed, and in many cases outright licences and support from some public authority are required.[33]

When, then, will opposition to the market as the arbiter of innovations emerge? To start with, assume for the sake of argument simply that all utility functions contain only income as an argument, and that the only effect that the transition from T_0 to T_1 has is to increase the real income of $\tilde{s}$ at individuals, to reduce the real income of s individuals such that $\Sigma_{s\sim} dY | T_1 > -\Sigma_s dY | T_1$. This means that the invention is socially preferable, but the potential for conflict is resolved only if the gainers use part of their augmented incomes to compensate the losers. Compensation would seem at first glance a reasonable way to resolve the problem, but in fact it rarely occurs directly because of the formidable problems of identifying the losers, measuring the dimensions of their loss, and overcoming the problems of moral hazard among losers as well as collective action among gainers. All the same, compensation does occur. The welfare and farm support systems in modern Western economies could be interpreted at least in part as mechanisms designed to compensate and placate groups that ended up at the short end of the stick in rapid industrialization and subsequent de-industrialization. If compensation does not occur, the losers will have an interest to band together to try to change the social decision rule from G_M to a rule that is more favorable to them. The way for them to do this is to circumvent the market, in our terms by reducing α, and then try to affect the aggregator G_D and/or G_V by political action. It is in this fashion that persuasion and rhetoric enter the story; in a "pure" market system, they need not enter the debate.

A major reason why people tend to remove the market as the sole arbiter of technological decisions and delegate part of the decision-making process to political bodies is that markets effectively truncate preferences over technology at zero. If one supports a new technique, one can vote "yes" by buying the new product or switching to the new technique. By not buying the product or refusing to switch, one can express indifference or dislike, but individuals have no control over what others do even if they feel it might affect them. In markets it is difficult to express a "no" vote. Another reason is that so much technology is part of the public sector: transport, public health, infrastructure, and the military require political approval of changes simply because these are sectors in which some form of prior market failure has been observed.

Above all, consumers seem to distrust the free market as an arbiter of new

[33] An example would be the adoption of railroads after the 1830s, which involved varying combinations of private and public decision-making in different countries. In Britain, the decision to adopt railways was largely a private decision made in the context of the free market; in other countries the government played a direct entrepreneurial role.

technology just because it is new. Whereas in a technologically static economy there may be no reason to distrust the invisible hand, the informational asymmetries and irreversibilities associated with the generation and adoption of new techniques seem to demand a cool and unbiased arbiter. It is feared that greedy entrepreneurs will sell asbestos-type products to the public and then abscond. Thalidomide-type disasters, however small compared with the benefits of advances in medical technology, produce a constant demand for government assurances that new products and techniques are safe. At the same time, it needs stressing that not all resistance to technological progress is necessarily conservative and in defense of some technological status quo. Many cases of social resistance to a new technique occur because there are two alternatives to T_0, T_1, and T_2. Left to the market, T_1 will be chosen; if some interest group wishes to use non-market mechanisms to bring about some alternative T_2, it is the *nature* of technological change they wish to influence, not its very existence.[34]

Self-interest, of course, counts too. Economists have used the term "rent-seeking" for the replacement of market decisions by government control or some other form of collective decision-making that benefits a small group or individual. Here we expand the standard definition of rent seeking to include "loss-avoidance." Historically, most of the resistance to new technological change had economic reasons: potential losers set up obstacles to obstruct innovation. The main question is why for some individuals technological change is income-reducing. Below I provide a typology of some of the more obvious sources of purely rational resistance to innovation.

4.1 *Unemployment*

One obvious reason for the resistance to innovation, widely believed since Ricardo's famous chapter on "Machinery," is that labor-saving technological change reduces the demand for undifferentiated labor, thus leading to unemployment and a possible decline in wages. As economists have long understood, this statement in and of itself cannot be accepted without working through the general equilibrium properties of an exogenous change in the production function. An invention that replaces workers by machines will have effects on *all* product and factor markets. An increase in the efficiency of production that reduces the price of one good will increase real income and thus will increase demand for other goods; the replaced workers may find employment in other industries, and their real wage may go up or down.

In an abstract general equilibrium world without adjustment costs, where all workers and productive assets can be costlessly converted from one usage to

---

[34] This is what sets aside the literature of "alternative" or "soft" technology advocated by Amory Lovins from the shrill and technophobe positions advocated by, say, Ivan Illich and Chellis Glendinning.

another, there is no a priori expectation that changes in production technology will necessarily reduce labor income and employment. In the real world, of course, temporary disequilibria can cause hardship to large subgroups of the population. Yet in some of the most widely studied instances, the feared patterns of technological unemployment did not materialize. Nineteenth-century Britain did not suffer from a secular increase in structural employment, feared by Ricardo and the Luddites alike. In a very different environment, it was widely feared that the mechanization of agriculture in Asia in the 1970s would lead to widespread rural unemployment; this did not occur.[35] Recent studies by labor economists find that the introduction of new technology is on balance associated with positive job *growth*. One such study flatly declares that "job growth and the introduction of new technology appear to be complements rather than substitutes. The Luddites were wrong."[36]

4.2 *Capital Losses*

A different problem occurs when physical capital is of a "putty–clay" variety: once shaped, it is difficult to convert to another use. This can be seen in a simple vintage model in which one product is produced by machines of differing efficiency. The lowest ranked machine earns a rent of zero; all other machines earn a rent that is proportional to the difference between the production cost of the least efficient machine in use and that of their own. The value of the asset can thus be determined by the present discounted value formula, in which the value of the asset is a function of this difference and *expected* future technological depreciation. A rise in the rate of technological change will reduce the market value of existing machines of older vintage, and so it might be expected that the owners will find a way to avert it if they can.

Yet in practice this happens rarely. The cases in which the owners of physical capital have fought against the introduction of new techniques are comparatively few. The reason must be that, while the physical qualities of machines can only rarely be altered, capital goods—including ownership in patents—can be bought and sold.[37] Thus, the owner of a set of machines that become

---

[35] M. J. Campbell, "Technology and Rural Development: the Social Impact," in M. J. Campbell, ed., *New Technology and Rural Development: The Social Impact* (London: Routledge, 1990), p. 26.

[36] David G. Blanchflower and Simon M. Burgess, "New Technology and Jobs: Comparative Evidence from a Two-Country Study," presented to the National Academy of Sciences Conference on Technology, Firm Performance and Employment, Washington DC, May 1995 (version cited dated Dec. 1995), p. 18.

[37] It is critical for this argument that patents do not categorically exclude some existing producers from licensing patents or having them assigned to them. When this happens, it is of course quite likely that existing producers will not be able to jump on the new bandwagon. For a survey of how common patent licensing and assignment already was in 19th-cent. America, see Naomi Lamoureaux and Kenneth Sokoloff, "Long-term Change in the Organization of Inventive Activity," presented at the National Academy of Sciences Colloquium on Science, Technology, and the Economy, Irvine, Calif. Oct. 20–22, 1995.

obsolete will take a loss on those machines, but he can always buy into the new technology by buying the new machines that yield the higher profits through lower costs. This explains, for instance, the relatively weak resistance to the introduction of steam engines despite the huge locational rents that were being secured by the owners of water mill sites. Industrialists using water power might have been losing when their mills fell into disuse, but they could make up for those losses by buying into steam technology themselves, which is precisely what happened in Lancashire during the British Industrial Revolution. In those cases in which capital markets favored some existing producers over others, however, this principle is violated, and in such cases resistance is to be expected.[38]

4.3 Non-pecuniary Losses

Another source of resistance to technological change is that it changes not just the *level* of average costs, but the overall *shape* of the cost function. While new technology thus reduces overall costs and increases efficiency, it may also change the minimum efficient size of the firm and the entry conditions to the industry. Thus, when the minimum efficient size of firms in the textile industry was hugely increased during the first Industrial Revolution, artisans and small domestic producers were effectively driven out of the industry. In a world without transactions and information costs and hence "perfect" capital markets, the costs of these changes would be mitigated by small producers combining into large firms and exploiting some of the economies of scale. This did occur at a larger scale than is usually appreciated.[39] The so-called "workshop system", in which workers hired space and a piece of equipment in a large building and worked on their own account without hierarchy and discipline, was prominent in many industries until well into the nineteenth century. All the same, during the Industrial Revolution, even before the famous Luddite and Captain Swing disturbances, there were some riots by artisans and self-employed producers threatened by factories.[40]

Workers, moreover, care about such non-pecuniary characteristics of the workplace, from safety and noise on the shopfloor to job satisfaction and

[38] A recent example is provided by Bruland. Norwegian fishermen in the 18th cent. resisted a new technique of multiple lines, which enhanced productivity but whose use was "confined to relatively well-off fishermen who could afford to invest in extra equipment and suitable boats." See Kristine Bruland, "Patterns of Resistance to New Technologies in Scandinavia: an Historical Perspective," in Bauer, *Resistance*, p. 131.

[39] Gregory Clark, "Factory Discipline," *Journal of Economic History*, 54(1) (March 1994): 132–5. In other societies, too, such workshops occurred early on in the industrialization process. In India, in industries such as cotton ginning, rice polishing, and flour milling, entrepreneurs often just provided the machines and their maintenance and charged a fee for processing from the workers. See Morris, "The Growth of Large-scale Industry," p. 675.

[40] Adrian Randall, *Before the Luddites* (Cambridge: Cambridge University Press, 1991).

decision-making authority. If new technology affects these characteristics negatively, workers will resist unless they can be bought off by employers through fully compensating wage increases, or can find new jobs similar to their old ones at zero cost to themselves. During the Industrial Revolution, a particular bone of contention was the attempt by employers to standardize products and reduce the leeway that artisans and domestic workers had in setting the parameters of the product. When the advantages of product standardization led to lower tolerance boundaries on the characteristics of output, from cotton cloth to musket balls, repeated attempts to enforce such standards ran into determined opposition.[41] Beyond that, technology change affects the regional distribution of production and employment, thus forcing workers to move from one region to another or from a rural to an urban area. New technology is often felt to destroy traditional communities. For some members of those communities that counts for little, whereas for others it counts for a great deal; thus, any kind of aggregator will lead almost inevitably to some subset of the population being dissatisfied.

4.4 *Human Capital*

The opportunities for conflict are much wider when we consider human capital.[42] Skills and experience are acquired over a lifetime, but the ability to learn new skills declines over the life cycle.[43] Workers beyond the student or apprentice stage can be expected to resist new techniques insofar as innovation makes their skills obsolete and thus irreversibly reduces their expected lifetime earnings. The new technology may be inaccessible to them for more reason than one; factories require a willingness to submit to discipline and hierarchy that the independent artisan was too proud to submit to. It is of no consolation to the older generation that their children may have no difficulty adjusting to

[41] Ken Alder, *Engineering the Revolution: Arms, Enlightenment, and the Making of Modern France* (Princeton: Princeton University Press, 1996), chs. 4–5.

[42] In a formal analysis of the emergence of resistance among skilled workers, Krusell and Ríos-Rull ingeniously capture an example of this kind of problem. They model an economy in which all capital is technology-specific human capital, and show that older workers who have invested in a skill that is specific to a technology threatened by obsolescence can be modeled as a "vested interest" for whom it is optimal to try to block the new technology: Per Krusell and Jose-Victor Ríos-Rull, "Vested Interests in a Positive Theory of Stagnation and Growth," *Review of Economic Studies*, 63 (1996): 301–29. For an analysis along similar lines and the important constraint on the effectiveness of such resistance by the openness of the economy, see Thomas J. Holmes and James A. Schmitz, "Resistance to New Technology and Trade between Areas," working paper, Federal Reserve Bank of Minneapolis, 1995.

[43] As *The Economist* put it recently, "What grown-up who spent years of childhood learning to tie shoes, to count to ten, to parse Greek or to find triple integrals does not now sigh at having to lipread the baffling instructions for a video recorder or for Windows 95? Almost every generation gets overtaken in some department of knowledge as new discoveries and unfamiliar technologies replace yesterday's learning": "Cranks and Proud Of It," *The Economist* (Jan. 20, 1996): 86–7.

the new regime, mastering the new technique and thus improving their material standard of living.

Again, the example of the British Industrial Revolution illustrates this point vividly. As the old domestic industries came increasingly under pressure from the more efficient factories, the older artisans by and large refrained from seeking employment in them; the reliance of factories on child and teenage labor was motivated by the ability of youths to learn the skills and adopt the docility required for the factory environment.[44] Some new technology was in fact deliberately designed to exclude males and to favor women and children, as was the case in the early factories of the Industrial Revolution.[45]

The protection of skills and specific human capital is often combined with other forms of rent-seeking through the creation of barriers to entry and the control of output. This is clearly a widespread interpretation of the European craft guild system which ruled urban artisans in many areas for many centuries. In pre-modern urban Europe, these guilds enforced and eventually froze the technological status quo.[46] Similar phenomena, mutatis mutandis, occurred in China.[47] It is important to stress that many of those guilds were originally set up to fulfill different functions, acting as clearing houses for information, organizational devices to set up training, mutual insurance support organizations, and sincere attempts to prevent opportunism and free riding on others' reputations. Yet over time many of them degenerated into technologically conservative bodies.[48]

In most of Europe, then, craft guilds eventually became responsible for a

---

[44] The classic text on this is still Sidney Pollard, *The Genesis of Modern Management* (Harmondsworth: Penguin Books, 1965), pp. 213–25. See also Arthur Redford, *Labour Migration in England, 1800–1850* (Manchester: Manchester University Press, 1926, reprint 1964); for a recent restatement see John S. Lyons, "Family Response to Economic Decline: Handloom Weavers in Early Nineteenth-Century Lancashire," *Research in Economic History*, 12 (1989): 45–91.

[45] Maxine Berg, *The Age of Manufactures, 1700–1820*, 2nd edn. (London: Routledge, 1994), pp. 144–55; Carolyn Tuttle, "Children Hard at Work during the Industrial Revolution," unpublished manuscript, Lake Forest College (1996), pp. 156–75.

[46] Kellenbenz, for example, states that "guilds defended the interests of their members against outsiders, and these included the inventors who, with their new equipment and techniques, threatened to disturb their members' economic status. They were just against progress": Herman Kellenbenz, "Technology in the Age of the Scientific Revolution, 1500–1700," in Carlo Cipolla, ed., *The Fontana Economic History of Europe*, (London: Fontana, 1974), Vol. 2 p. 243. Much earlier Pirenne pointed out that "the essential aim [of the craft guild] was to protect the artisan, not only from external competition, but also from the competition of his fellow-members." The consequence was "the destruction of all initiative. No one was permitted to harm others by methods which enabled him to produce more quickly and more cheaply than they. Technical progress took on the appearance of disloyalty": Henri Pirenne, *Economic and Social History of Medieval Europe* (New York: Harcourt Brace & World, 1936), pp. 185–6. For a similar description of the Italian guilds, see Carlo Cipolla, "The Economic Decline of Italy," in Brian Pullan, ed., *Crisis and Change in the Venetian Economy in the Sixteenth and Seventeenth Centuries* (London: Methuen, 1968).

[47] See Olson, *Rise and Decline*, p. 150, and Mokyr, *The Lever of Riches*, pp. 232–3.

[48] In a recent paper, S. R. Epstein has defended the technological role of craft guilds, pointing out that they fulfilled an important role in the dissemination and intergenerational transmission of technical information. There is no contradiction between such a role and the inherently conservative role played by craft guilds.

level of regulation that stifled competition and innovation. They did this by laying down meticulous rules about three elements of production that we might term "the three p's": prices, procedures, and participation. As guilds gained in political power, they tried as much as they could to weaken market forces as aggregators and tended increasingly to freeze technology in its tracks. The regulation of *prices* was inimical to technological progress because process innovation by definition reduces costs, and the way the inventor makes his profits is by underselling his competitors. Regulating prices may still have allowed some technological progress because innovators could have realized increased profits through lowering costs even if they could not undersell their competitors. To prevent this, *procedures* stipulated precisely how a product was supposed to be made and such technical codes, while originally designed to deal with legitimate concerns such as reputation for quality, eventually caused production methods to ossify altogether. Enforcing these procedures, however, was far more difficult than enforcing pre-set prices.

Finally, and in the long run perhaps the most effective brake on innovation, by limiting and controlling the number of entrants into crafts, and by forcing them to spend many years in apprenticeship and journeymanship, guild members infused entrants with the conventions of the technological status quo and essentially cut off the flow of fresh ideas and the cross-fertilization between branches of knowledge that so often is the taproot of technological change.[49] A particularly pernicious custom was the rigid division of labor between craft guilds so that each guild was confined to its designed occupation, a practice that occasionally required royal intervention to prevent egregious abuses.[50]

The exclusion of innovators by guilds did not end with the Middle Ages or even with the Industrial Revolution. In 1855, the Viennese guild of cabinet-makers filed a suit against Michael Thonet, who had invented a revolutionary

More controversial is his claim that guilds provided a cloak of secrecy which worked as a protection of the property rights for inventors. Even if such a system could be demonstrated to have existed, most authorities are in agreement that eventually much of the guild system was overtaken by technologically reactionary forces which, instead of protecting innovators, threatened them. See S. R. Epstein, "Craft Guilds, Apprenticeship, and Technological Change in Pre-modern Europe," mimeo, London School of Economics, 1995. An extreme example is the printers' guild, one of the most powerful and conservative guilds in Europe, which steadfastly resisted any innovation and as late as 1772 legally restrained one of its members from building an improved press: cf. Maurice Audin, "Printing," in *A History of Technology and Invention*, Vol. 3, *The Expansion of Mechanization, 1725–1860*, ed. Maurice Daumas (New York: Crown, 1979), p. 658.

[49] Particularly restrictive was the custom confining the intergenerational transmission of skills to kinship. In some industries, particularly in ironmaking, skills were the traditional realm of dynasties in which technological knowledge was kept as much as possible within the family. See Chris Evans and Göran Rydén, "Recruitment, Kinship, and the Distribution of Skill: Bar Iron Production in Britain and Sweden, 1500–1860," paper presented to a conference on "Technological Revolutions in Europe, 1760–1860," Oslo, May 31–June 2, 1996.

[50] Thus, in the 1560s, three Parisian coppersmiths invented improved *morions* (military helmets), but were prevented from producing them because the armorers held the exclusive rights to defensive weapons. In this case they were overruled by King Charles IX. Cf. Henry Heller, *Labour, Science, and Technology in France, 1500–1620*, (Cambridge: Cambridge University Press, 1996), pp. 95–6.

process for making bentwood furniture. The *Tischlermeister* claimed that the inventor was not a registered cabinetmaker. The suit was dismissed when the court made his workshop an "imperial privileged factory."[51]

The role of the guilds can go some way towards explaining the series of technological successes we usually refer to as the British Industrial Revolution, and why it occurred in Britain as opposed to the European Continent, although clearly it was only one of many variables at work.[52] Resistance was not confined to manufacturing; when large department stores were introduced into Germany following the French model in the later nineteenth century, small shopkeepers banded together and were able to persuade the major states in Germany to pass a special tax on large stores to protect the small merchants from the threat of modernization.[53]

Perhaps the arena in which the largest number of technological battles have been fought since the Industrial Revolution has been in free trade. Protection for domestic industries often was identical to protection for obsolete technology. While the battles against free trade and technological progress by no means coincide, their overlap is considerable, and free trade and an open economy are by far the best guarantees that an economy will use best-practice technology. This idea goes back at least as far as David Hume, who pointed out in 1742 that

nothing is more favorable to the rise of politeness and learning than a number of neighboring and independent states, connected together by commerce and policy. The emulation which naturally arises among those neighboring states is an obvious source of improvement. But what I would chiefly insist on is the stop [i.e. constraint] which such limited territories give both to power and authority.[54]

At the same time, free trade was hardly a *necessary* condition: Britain remained a protectionist country until the 1840s, and the United States followed highly protectionist policies in the last third of the nineteenth century, yet both were highly open to innovation.[55]

[51] Ekaterini Kyriazidou and Martin Pesendorfer, "Viennese Chairs," *Journal of Economic History*, 59(1) (March 1999): 143–66.

[52] In pre-revolutionary France the network of craft guilds and small producers, often supported by local authorities, was adamantly opposed to all technical innovation. See Pierre Deyon and Philippe Guignet, "The Royal Manufactures and Economic and Technological Progress in France before the Industrial Revolution," *Journal of European Economic History*, 9(3) (Winter 1980): 611–32. The Crown did its best to circumvent this conservative force by awarding privileges, pensions, and monopolies to successful innovators and inventors. Needless to say, resistance to innovation before the Industrial Revolution took many forms, not all of which depended on the guilds.

[53] E. Andrew Lohmeier, "Consumer Demand and Market Responses in the German Empire, 1879–1914," unpublished Ph.D. dissertation, Northwestern University, ch. 2.

[54] David Hume, "On the Rise and Progress of the Arts and Sciences" (1742), in David Hume, *Essays: Moral, Political and Literary*, ed. Eugene F. Miller (Indianapolis: Liberty Fund, 1985).

[55] The strong connection between openness and economic growth was recently demonstrated by Jeffrey Sachs and Andrew Warner, "Economic Reform and the Process of Global Integration," *Brookings Paper on*

In the past century, resistance to new production technology has come in part from labor unions. There is no compelling reason why labor unions must resist technological change: after all, as "encompassing organizations" they ought also to be aware of the undeniable benefits that new technology brings to their members *qua* consumers.[56] The growth of the labor movement's power in Britain is often held responsible for the declining technological dynamism of post-Victorian Britain. Resistance of organized labor slowed down technological progress in mining, shipbuilding, and cotton weaving.[57] Such resistance was not 100 percent effective, but Coleman and MacLeod may well be right when they judge that labor's resistance "reinforced the increasingly apathetic attitude of employers toward technological change."[58] In printing, London's notorious Fleet Street earned a reputation of stormy industrial relations, where management's major preoccupation was with avoiding disruptions to production, even at the expense of high unit labor costs and restrictions on technological innovation.[59] The crisis in the Bombay cotton industry in the 1920s and 1930s, when Bombay lost much of its market share to other areas, is attributed to the militancy with which Bombay trade unions fought against a technical and administrative rationalization of cotton mill practices.[60] In a recent paper, Susan Wolcott documents in detail how Indian workers were able to block successfully the implementation of larger spindles in the cotton spinning industry, not only in Bombay but also in Ahmedabad and Sholapur.[61]

In our own time, labor unions have been held responsible for impeding technological progress in many industries. In the European and American auto industry, for instance, they have resisted the closing of outdated plants and the introduction of the flexible work practices and reduced job classifications that have increased the efficiency of Japanese car manufacturers.[62] However, not *all* unions have taken a consistently conservative stance against new technology. In

Economic Activity, no. 1 (1995): 1–95. Oddly enough, the technological implications of the open economy are entirely neglected by Sachs and Warner in their list of links between openness and more rapid economic growth.

[56] See Alan Booth et al., "Institutions and Economic Growth," *Journal of Economic History*, 57(2) (June 1997): 416–44.

[57] For the cotton industry, see especially William Lazonick, *Competitive Advantage on the Shop Floor* (Cambridge, Mass.: Harvard University Press, 1990), pp. 78–114. In shipbuilding, for example, the boilermaker union limited the ability of employers to introduce pneumatic machinery after 1900. See Edward H. Lorenz, *Economic Decline in Britain: The Shipbuilding Industry* (Oxford: Clarendon Press, 1991), pp. 58–9.

[58] Donald Coleman and Christine MacLeod, "Attitudes to New Techniques: British Businessmen, 1800–1950," *Economic History Review*, 39 (1986): 588–611, on p. 606.

[59] Roderick Martin, "New Technology in Fleet Street, 1975–1980," in Bauer, *Resistance to Technology*, p. 194.

[60] Morris, "Growth of Large Scale Industry," pp. 622–3.

[61] Susan Wolcott, "The Perils of Lifetime Employment Systems: Productivity Advance in the Indian and Japanese Textile Industries, 1920–1938," *Journal of Economic History*, 54(2) (June 1994): 307–24.

[62] Holmes and Schmitz, "Resistance to New Technology" p. 29. See also Martin Kenney and Richard Florida, *Beyond Mass Production* (New York: Oxford University Press, 1993), p. 315.

post-1945 Sweden and Germany, for example, unions were induced to join coalitions aimed at increasing productivity. These unions were large and encompassing groups, and, as the Olsonian theory suggests, their membership benefited enough from technological progress for the benefits to outweigh the costs.

4.5 *Externalities*

The non-pecuniary aspects of new technology raise particular concerns when there are "external effects," that is, when new technology affects common resources. Much of the resistance by the environmental movement to superfast railroads, nuclear power, and advanced pesticides, for instance, deals precisely with the non-income effects of technological change. Again, such non-pecuniary effects are valued differently by different individuals, and thus the outcome that political aggregators determine will differ from the market outcome. In the standard case of externalities, common resources are not priced at their marginal social cost. In a static economy, arrangements will often emerge that minimize such discrepancies. New technology compounds the transactions costs with information problems. Thus, it is difficult enough to limit the use of *known* atmospheric pollutants, but it is far harder to enforce agreements when the damage is unknown or in dispute. Unknown effects on shared resources therefore aggravate disagreement and political resistance to technological progress.

  To conclude, there are good reasons for subgroups within an economy to try to dethrone the free market as the sole aggregator, that is to disallow the competitive price mechanism by itself to determine which technologies will be adopted and which will not. This effort has been undeniably successful; almost everywhere, some kind of non-marketing control and licensing system has been introduced that has some agency or group of experts approve new technology *before* it is brought to the market. The next issue then should be, why should the outcome of such a decision-making process differ substantially from the outcome of the market, and what are the sources of disagreement and debate between the different groups?

5 Political Action within an Aggregator

Given that society has determined the aggregator, that is, the "rules of the game" by which decisions are made, do social resistance and political action still make sense? Obviously, unless $\alpha = 1$, the non-market game is only beginning. Once the arena has been chosen, interest groups and ideologically committed activists will concentrate on getting the outcome they desire. The nature of the debate will differ, of course, depending on the arena and the motives of the opposition; in particular, there is a distinction between the adoption of known technologies by developing economies and that of new, wholly untried, technologies by economies on the technological frontier. We may distinguish the following forms of political action.

5.1 *Lobbying*

The pure case is that in which the "losers" discussed above lobby to get it rejected. Persuasion and political agitation do not make much sense if the distribution of gains over the population is continuous, since in that case every decision-maker already has made up his or her mind and nobody is strictly indifferent; in practice however there are likely to be discontinuities in the distribution, leaving a large number of "voters" indifferent to the implementation of T_1. These voters would be "rationally indifferent"; that is, because they have a negligible or zero stake in the outcome, it is hardly worth their while to master the often intricate details of new technologies. Lobbying then involves an attempt to persuade these "indifferent voters" to support or resist the new technology. In this context, Olson's notions of the *Logic of Collective Action* are central. When the losses are concentrated, as they often are, the losers are likely to be more easy to organize and to have more political clout even if the social gains outweigh the losses.

5.2 *Strategic Behavior and Logrolling*

It may be sensible in some cases to pretend to object to some technologies as part of a bargaining strategy. For instance, as already noted, workers may actually stand to benefit from a new technology, but may find it in their interest to resist it in order to eventually secure a larger part of the new technology or perhaps to secure increased rents elsewhere. There is historical evidence of the use of resistance to innovations as a bargaining chip even when the interests of both sides are unclear.[63] When a new and more efficient technology is

---

[63] As Martin points out in his analysis of the British newspaper debate, "it is rarely the case that a management totally united behind technological change is opposed by unions or employees totally opposed" (Martin, "New Technology in Fleet Street," p. 204). Within management and within workers there are often conflicting interests at work, and it is often as hard to predict which position each side is going to take as it is to predict the outcome.

introduced, there are rents to be dissipated; it makes sense for unions to resist the new technology unless they can be guaranteed an acceptable proportion of the rents generated.[64] Furthermore, if there is more than one negotiation going on at one time, groups may be trading off support or resistance for technologies that they actually do not care much about in order to secure support for their position on decisions that affect them directly.

5.3 Correlation Effects

Often new technology is viewed and depicted as "packaged" in a cultural—political deal that is undesirable even if the new technology in and of itself is. This kind of ambiguity flavors much of the political argument in non-Western nations and often is coupled with a cultural suspicion of foreigners. There is a sense that "the magical identity is development = modernization = Westernization." Especially when new technology takes the form of new products, it is often considered to be correlated with undesirable cultural and social side-effects. It is then rejected by some, not because of its inherent economic characteristics but because of these externalities.

The history of India illustrates this well. Headrick sums up the issue as follows:

The colonized [nations] were in an ambiguous position. Western technology had led to their defeat and captivity and threatened their culture and way of life. No one illustrates their ambivalent attitudes toward Western technology quite as well as Mohandas K. Ghandi, who wore handwoven garments made of homespun yarn but also used a watch, traveled by train, and kept in touch with his followers by telephone.[65]

In China and in the Islamic Middle East, too, the slow speed at which economic modernization occurred was in part the result of the association of more efficient production methods with an alien culture. Political action was aimed broadly at the culture with which the new technology was associated. Yet in recent times most cultures, suspicious as they may be of foreign influence,

---

[64] The most detailed work on the subject has been carried out by William Lazonick on the cotton industry. His conclusion is worth repeating: "Vested interests—in particular the stake that British workers had in job control and the historic underdevelopment of British management—stood in the way of . . . promoting the diffusion of advanced production methods." See William Lazonick, "Theory and History in Marxian Economics," in A.J. Field, ed., *The Future of Economic History* (Boston: Kluwer-Nijhoff, 1987), p. 303. Labor viewed the adoption of new machines with "acute suspicion." Rather than block the new machinery altogether, however, their resistance was often veiled in increased demands. To secure labor's acceptance, management had to make concessions that reduced the profitability of new machinery: Peter Payne, "Entrepreneurship and British Economic Decline," in B. Collins and K. Robbins, eds, *British Culture and Economic Decline* (New York: St Martin's Press, 1990), pp. 25–58.

[65] Daniel Headrick, *The Tentacles of Progress* (New York: Oxford University Press, 1988), p. 382.

have come to realize that they cannot afford to reject foreign technology lock stock and barrel.[66]

Such packaging of culture and technology can take other forms. It has been argued that some new technologies have especially negative effects on women, children, or members of other special social groups. When this occurs, resistance to the new technology may occur just because these groups are deemed by some to be vulnerable and thus worthy of protection even if they themselves stand to benefit from it. A prominent example of this type of argument is the work of Vandana Shiva, whose work combines feminism, environmentalism, and a fierce suspicion of Western technology.[67] In the West, too, technological progress was associated with powerful groups from which individuals felt alienated. Thus, technological resistance against, say, nuclear power might be viewed as "a blow to big business or big science." Sociological studies suggest, however, that such resistance is fairly rare.[68]

Some of the historical suspicion about new technology was related to its effects in promoting commercialization. Most technological change affects the proportion of total output that goes through the market. The Green Revolution, with its heavy reliance on purchased inputs (seeds, fertilizers, pesticides), raised serious objections on the basis of the alleged disruptions and violence that market penetration perpetrated on self-sufficient small communities, thereby causing the "depeasantization of the peasantry".[69] In principle, however, technological progress can be either market-enhancing or market-curtailing. Many of the household appliances developed during the twentieth century have led to the home production of cleaning and cooking services that had previously been carried out by hired household labor. Another correlation effect is the fear that new technology will lead to rationalization and secularization, undermining the power of religion and "traditional values."

5.4 *Irreversibilities and Path Dependence*

Another possibility occurs when a new technology is adopted initially and then subsequently some new information emerges or some change in preferences occurs that makes people change their minds. In that case the aggregator

---

[66] A notable example of this eclectic attitude is the economic nationalism preached by India's Bharatiya Janata Party, whose slogan is "Microchips, not potato chips" (*Business Week*, Oct. 23, 1995, p. 50).

[67] Shiva argues that modern technology destroys nature and is thus "associated with violence to women who depend on nature for drawing sustenance for themselves, their families, their societies." The Industrial Revolution created a "domination and mastery of men over nature [which was] also associated with new patterns of domination and mastery over women": Vandana Shiva, *Staying Alive: Women, Ecology, and Development* (London: Zed Books, 1988), pp. xvi–xvii.

[68] See Allan Mazur, "Opposition to Technological Innovation", *Minerva*, 13(1) (Spring 1975): 58–81, at 62.

[69] See Vandana Shiva, *The Violence of the Green Revolution* (London: Zed books, 1991), pp. 177, 190.

G itself remains but the outcome changes, so that $G(T_1|I) > G(T_0|I)$ but $G(T_1|I')$ $< G(T_0|I')$, where T_1 and T_0 are the two techniques and I and I' are two information sets. The very nature of new technological information is that it is irreversible; once learned, it is difficult if not impossible for society to "unlearn" a new technique, no matter how socially undesirable that technique may be. This kind of phenomenon might be called the *Pandora effect*. Even if society "regrets" its decision to move to T_1, it may not be able to return to T_0. If the possibility of this occurring is anticipated at time 0, society may decide not to adopt T_1, "so that we do not regret it later." This is especially the case with technology that can be used for both constructive and military purposes. The classic example of such a "regret" is the conversion of Lewis Mumford, one of the great minds of thinking about technology in the twentieth century, from technological enthusiast to technological skeptic because of the ravages wrought by World War II.[70] Certain inventions that misfired badly have also led to difficult controversies such as the current debates on pesticides, asbestos, and CFCs. Undoing the effects of this new knowledge is costly, and ending their use difficult to enforce.

Given the path-dependent nature of technological change, it may make sense for a subset of the population to resist a new technology even if it temporarily increases welfare, if there is an expectation that this technology will eventually lead to the development of further technologies that may be deemed undesirable.[71] In other words, technological change involves not just a choice between two techniques, but two different technological trajectories, such as nuclear vs. fossil fuel energy or direct vs. alternating current. This takes us back to the principle of correlation discussed above, but with an additional dynamic element. Political action is aimed at persuading the relevant decision-maker that a certain technological avenue is undesirable even if some initial features appear attractive. Thus, there is a sense, not entirely misplaced, that medical advances that made transplantations possible will eventually lead to markets in organs, or that the ability to identify the gender of fetuses through amniotic fluid tests may eventually lead to selective abortion to achieve gender selection. "Cyberphobia" is in part based on the futuristic fear that impersonal and inhuman machines will eventually govern society, and that the differences between people and machines will eventually become hazy. *In vitro* fertilization techniques have resulted in a fear of the mechanization of the human reproductive process, and the fluoridation of drinking water has raised concerns about socialized medicine and also about the (perhaps more realistic) power

[70] Thomas P. Hughes, *American Genesis: A Century of Invention and Technological Enthusiasm* (New York: Penguin Books, 1989), p. 448.

[71] An example would be the campaign conducted by the Foundation on Economic Trends, a Washington lobby dedicated to fighting the spread of biotechnology. As of now, there is no registered case of any damage caused by biotechnology. Yet the fear persists that, if these technologies took off, somehow others would emerge that would be extremely harmful.

of a state to affect unsuspecting individuals through the control of a network technology such as the water supply.[72] There is a fear that new technologies that initially work well will veer out of control and, like Frankenstein, eventually turn on their creators. Precisely because so many new technologies have ended up being used in totally different ways from those for which they were originally intended, there is a justified fear that, by producing new knowledge, we may be unleashing, like the Sorcerer's Apprentice, something we may not be able to control. The fundamental sense of concern is that some forms of technological change lead to a slippery slope toward some vaguely perceived but unacceptable future outcome, which—while never absolute— has affected much of the underlying thinking of technological conservatives.[73] A generalization of the Pandora effect would be that all might agree to prefer T_1 to T_0 but if T_1 leads in high probability to $T_2, \ldots, T_n$ and T_n is less desirable than T_0, T_1 will be resisted. It may well be the case that we would now be better off not knowing how to release nuclear energy, but this option no longer exists.

5.5 Diversity

Another concern is that new technology may lead to a decline in diversity and thus block future technological change. In agriculture this is literally true: settling on an optimal breed or variety may in fact be hazardous simply because the existence of parasites suggests that negative frequency dependence might be the optimal strategy. The Irish disaster of 1845–50 was caused by over-commitment to a seemingly superior crop.[74] In general, there is a conflict between the obvious advantages of standardization in network technologies and the need for diversity. While at times diversity is hopelessly inefficient (such as in the case of watch batteries), in other cases it keeps alive technologies that later on might be the base of important breakthroughs. New technology may thus be resisted because it reduces the array of future technological

[72] Fluoridation was first introduced in the USA in 1945. But in 1992 only 62% of Americans using public water enjoyed its benefits. In Western states, where the aggregator took the form of referenda rather than an imposition by elected representatives, adoption rates were generally lower (2% in Nevada, 16% in California). This reflects classical Luddite skepticism about "mass medication" but also correlation effects such as "mistrust of big government." There is no evidence of any negative side-effect of fluoridation except a minor discoloration of teeth when the quantities are higher than optimal. See *Scientific American*, 274 (2), (Feb. 1996): 20.

[73] Arnold Toynbee wrote in 1958 that, "if a vote could undo all the technological advances of the last three hundred years, many of us would cast that vote in order to safeguard the survival of the human race while we remain in our present state of social and moral backwardness", cited by Noel Perrin. *Giving Up the Gun: Japan's Reversion to the Sword, 1543–1879* (Boston: David R. Godine. 1979), pp. 80–1.

[74] This is strongly argued by Shiva in her criticism of the Green Revolution, where she maintains that high-yielding varieties in the long run will be more vulnerable to pests and diseases owing to lower genetic diversity (cf. Shiva, *Violence of the Green Revolution*, ch. 2).

choices. This seems to be the root of the suspicion with which American computer specialists regard Microsoft and Intel.

5.6 *Uncertainty and Heterogeneity*

Above all, however, there is inherent uncertainty in the adoption of genuinely new technologies, which makes any aggregator a matter of dispute. It is in the nature of new technology that its effects cannot be anticipated with accuracy.[75] Thus, *any* expected benefits and costs are to some extent unknowable, and the more radical the innovation, the deeper this ignorance. Suppose society agrees on the aggregator, but there is uncertainty as to the value of $G(T_1)$. This creates a double-barrelled problem. For one thing, individuals do not know what the value of $G(T)$ is and thus make decisions on the basis of a subjective probability distribution $F_i(T)$. Second, they weight the outcomes by a loss function $L_i(T)$. Disagreements occur both because of heterogeneity in F_i and heterogeneity in L_i. Even if individuals agree on the probability distribution of the outcomes, they could differ in their rate of risk aversion and in the shape of the loss function they associate with certain outcomes. Equally important, however, is heterogeneity in the expectations about the probability density function of $F(T_1)$. Resistance and political conflict will occur if the distribution is such that there are enough individuals who believe that $G(T_1) < G(T_0)$.

Let G_0 be the point at which the new and the old technologies "break even" and $f(G)$ be the number of people who believe the net benefits of the new technology to be G. Then, if

$$(1) \qquad \int_{-\infty}^{G_0} f(G)\mathrm{d}G < \int_{G_0}^{\infty} f(G)\mathrm{d}G,$$

the new technology will be "voted" in existence. Note how complicated the debate is: individuals might agree on the *mean* of the subjective probability density function (p.d.f.) and yet come to different conclusions if they disagree on the variance or even on the size of the left tail. If the probability assigned to a major disaster in a nuclear plant is estimated at 0.1 percent per year by some and 0.001 percent per year by others, their attitude towards the project may be radically different even if the rest of the p.d.f. looks remarkably similar. Precisely because of the unknown consequences of new technology, persuasion, pressure, and propaganda (that is, political action) will inevitably remain part of technological decisions.

In practice, it is difficult to disentangle heterogeneous expectations from

[75] Nathan Rosenberg, "Uncertainty and Technological Change," paper presented to the Federal Reserve Bank of Boston conference on Technology and Growth, Chatham, Mass., June 5–7 1996.

heterogeneous preferences. There are, however, obvious exceptions: the resistance to nuclear power in the West, especially, has been shown repeatedly to be strongly correlated with perceptions of danger.[76] With respect to nuclear power and genetic engineering, society is clearly divided into optimists and pessimists, whose subjective probability density functions over the outcomes of a new technology differ. Moreover, there is a tempting if invalid tendency to draw inferences from one technological outcome to another: the thalidomide affair has imposed restrictive brakes on the development of new drugs.[77] There is a serious spillover effect when one poorly executed project such as Chernobyl raises questions about the desirability of nuclear power altogether. Logical inferences from single events about the social costs and risks of entire new technologies are hard to make. James Jasper has noted that "the Three Mile Island accident in 1979 and the Chernobyl accident confirmed, interestingly, both the American antinuclear drift and the French pro-nuclear program. And neither accident did much to alleviate Swedish ambivalence about the future of its nuclear program."[78]

6 Systemic Resistance

A different reason why society might resist innovation that seems attractive on the surface has to do with cross-technique spillover effects. As we have seen, *all* evolutionary systems have some source of resistance to change, otherwise they might collapse into the indeterminacy Kauffman describes as his "supracritical region."[79] Yet the technological choices offer some sources of inertia that are not found in nature. Unlike biology, industry can mold its own selection environment by the development of rules of behavior that evolve spontaneously but the purpose of which is presumably to preserve the status quo and protect existing firms. Nelson points out that such action may be central in determining what design or system becomes dominant.[80]

Technology, too, occurs in "systems," meaning basically that components

---

[76] Mazur, "Opposition to Technological Innovation," p. 66. For more recent discussions, see especially Dorothy Nelkin and Michael Pollack, *The Atom Besieged* (Cambridge, Mass.: MIT Press, 1981), and James Jasper, "Three Nuclear Controversies" in Dorothy Nelkin (ed.), *Controversy: The Politics of Technical Decisions* (London: Sage Publications, 1992).

[77] Joachim Radkau, "Learning from Chernobyl for the Fight against Genetics?" in Bauer, *Resistance to New Technology*, pp. 335–55.

[78] James Jasper, "Three Nuclear Controversies", p. 108.

[79] Kauffman, *At Home in the Universe*, p. 294. Kauffman conjectures that "the enhanced diversity of goods and services can lead to a further explosion of the technological frontier . . . if the social planner deems them useful to the king."

[80] Nelson, "Recent Evolutionary Theorizing," p. 77.

that are changed will have effects on other parts with which they interact. This implies that a change in technique from T_0 to T_1 is likely to change costs subsequent to its adoption through unintended consequences to other components. Many of these occur through a variety of externalities or network effects: electrical equipment, trains, software, farming in open field agriculture —all share the problem of interrelatedness. In order to work, they require a uniformity we call standardization, and thus single members cannot change a component without adhering to the standards. Yet here, too, the analogy can be pressed too far: in technology—but not in nature—we can invent "gateway" technologies in which the incompatibilities are overcome, including for instance electrical convertors from 115 V to 220 V or railroad cars with adjustable axes that travel on different gauges. Positive feedback traps can occur in technological systems, but they tend to be rare in open economies because of competitive pressures from outside. Yet they do occur: American color TV has been "stuck" now for decades at a low-quality (low definition) screen. IBM-based computers struggled for years with the often paralyzing constraint of 640K RAM in "conventional memory," the nemesis of computer games and many multi-media applications. In both cases it has turned out to be costly and tricky, but not impossible, to devise a "gateway" solution.

The complementarities involved (broadcast reception in the case of TV; software–hardware in the case of computers) are characteristics of one of the most often occurring sources of technological inertia in history: frequency dependence.[81] A new technique cannot be successful until it is already adopted by a sufficiently large number of users. Similarly, in natural selection, new species cannot propagate unless they can mate with a sufficiently similar creature. This kind of model sounds almost discouraging, since in its strictest sense it means that only success succeeds, a blueprint for total stasis. Obviously, in *some* cases this hurdle can and has been overcome, but it should alert us that in normal situations new technological ideas that might on the face of it work well do not "catch on" and eventually vanish without a trace. IBM's OS/2 operating system, much superior to MS/DOS, was rejected because it was not sufficiently "compatible," as were DAT tape players and Beta-system VCRs.[82] A special case of frequency dependence is learning by doing, where average costs decline with cumulative output.

It is not always possible to know exactly how important these learning effects

---

[81] For a recent survey of this literature, see Brian Arthur, *Increasing Returns and Path Dependence in the Economy* (Ann Arbor: University of Michigan Press, 1994); see also Paul A. David, "Path Dependence in Economic Processes: Implications for Policy Analysis in Dynamical System Contexts," CEPR working paper, April 1992.

[82] The most famous but also controversial example is the DVORAK keyboard, thought to be superior to the standard QWERTY system. See Paul A. David, "Understanding the Economics of QWERTY: the Necessity of History," in W. N. Parker, ed., *Economic History and the Modern Economist*, (Oxford: Basil Blackwell, 1986), pp. 30–49; S. J. Liebowitz. and Stephen E. Margolis, "The Fable of the Keys," *Journal of Law and Economics*, 33 (1990), 1–25.

would have been in products that never made it to mass production. They are the outcome of an experiment never performed. Would airships have become safe and fast (in addition to being quiet and fuel-efficient) had the world of aviation not switched to fixed-wing aircraft in the interwar period? If Volkswagen and Toyota had tried to implement a steam engine in their mass-produced models, would steamcars have been perfected to the point where they could have put up as good a competition to the four-stroke internal combustion engine as the Diesel engine? Could the same be said for two-stroke engines, Wankel engines, and so on?

7 Concluding Remarks

One of the main rediscoveries of the new growth theory and recent thinking about economic development is the possibility of the poverty trap or multiple equilibria. Another way of thinking about the issues discussed in this paper is that it is possible for an economy to be "stuck" at a low level of income because the institutions it has are somehow inappropriate for technological progress. Usually the literature has thought of institutions as affecting the allocation of resources or the formation of capital. As technological progress, both home-made and imported, is one of the main engines of growth, the suitability of institutions for the successful adoption of new ideas is an important question. Simple economic models may be difficult to construct here, but by a combination of political economy and the lessons of economic history some insights into the causes and consequences of resistance and opposition to technological change can be drawn. The deeper question is whether sustained economic growth is the exception and stagnation the default, or whether, as argued especially by E. L. Jones in his *Growth Recurring*, economic growth is a natural condition for most economies, but more often than not political and cultural impediments drag an inherently dynamic economy into stagnation and poverty. This debate may seem to some a bit like an argument about whether a zebra is black with white stripes or the other way around. In either case, the political economy of technological progress must occupy its rightful place at center stage.

3 Economic Institutions and Development: A View from the Bottom

Oliver E. Williamson

1 Introduction

Applications of institutional economics to the study of economic development and reform has been growing, but its role is still modest.[1] That institutional economics has been invited to speak to these issues is because earlier approaches—dirigiste; get the prices right; get the property rights right—are perceived to be inadequate. That institutional economics has made only modest headway is partly because the New Institutional Economics is itself still in early stages of development (having taken shape only over the past thirty-five years, with a primary focus on developed economies[2]), and partly

---

[1] See Pranab Bardhan, "The New Institutional Economics and Development Theory," *World Development*, 17 (1989): 1389–96; Mustapha Nabli and Jeffrey Nugent, *The New Institutional Economics and Development* (New York: North-Holland, 1989); Elinor Ostrom, Larry Schroeder, and Susan Wyne, *Institutional Incentives and Practical Alternatives* (Boulder, Colo.: Westview Press, 1993); Mancur Olson, "Dictatorship, Democracy and Development," *American Political Science Review*, 87 (1993): 567–76; Barry Weingast, "Constitutions as Governance Structures," *Journal of Institutional and Theoretical Economics*, 149 (1993): 286–311; Barry Weingast, "The Political Foundations of Democracy and the Rule of Law," unpublished manuscript, 1995; Brian Levy and Pablo Spiller, "The Institutional Foundations of Regulatory Commitment," *Journal of Law, Economics, and Organization*, 9 (1994): 201–46; Douglass North, "Economic Performance through Time," *American Economic Review*, 84 (1994): 359–68; World Bank, *Annual Conference on Economic Development* (Washington, 1995); World Bank, *Bureaucrats in Business* (Washington, 1995).

[2] Eirik Furubotn and Rudolf Richter, "The New Institutional Economics: an Assessment," in E. Furubotn and R. Richter, eds., *The New Institutional Economics* (College Station: Texas A&M Press, 1991), pp. 1–32; Oliver E. Williamson and Scott Masten, *Transaction Cost Economics* (Aldershot: Edward Elgar Publishing, Ltd., 1995).

because applications to problems of economic development and reform are forbiddingly difficult.[3]

As Ronald Coase puts it,

The value of including . . . institutional factors in the corpus of mainstream economics is made clear by recent events in Eastern Europe. These ex-communist countries are advised to move to a market economy, and their leaders wish to do so, but without the appropriate institutions no market economy of any significance is possible. If we knew more about our own economy, we would be in a better position to advise them.[4]

Moreover, even if we are confident that "polities significantly shape economic performance because they define and enforce the economic rules," whereupon "an essential part of development policy is the creation of polities that will create and enforce efficient property rights," there is the further problem that "we know very little about how to create such polities."[5]

The New Institutional Economics operates at two levels. The macro level deals with the institutional environment or rules of the game. According to Douglass North, the institutional environment is "the humanly devised constraints that structure political, economic and social interactions. They consist of both informal constraints (sanctions, taboos, customs, traditions, and codes of conduct), and formal rules (constitutions, laws, property rights)."[6] The more micro level deals with the institutions of governance. These are market, quasi-market, and hierarchical modes of contracting (more generally, of managing transactions and seeing economic activity through to completion).

Inasmuch as economic development and reform deal with sectoral or economy-wide programs of a macro kind, the natural application of institutional economics to development is in a top-down way: how do economic development and reform vary with the condition of the institutional environment? Although that is an instructive way to proceed,[7] this paper adopts a bottom-up approach instead. The object is not to reconstruct the institutional environment from bottom-up building blocks, but rather to *interpret* the institutional environment through the lens of governance. This entails (1) examining the ramifications of the institutional environment (and changes therein) for governance, and (2) using core concepts that originate in the study of governance to interpret the polity. As illustrated by the recent World Bank study on *Bureaucrats in Business*, the microanalytics of investment and contracting are implicated. As developed therein, that study looked "at company experience in depth and creatively [applied] institutional analysis [of

---

[3] Ronald H. Coase, "The Institutional Structure of Production," *American Economic Review*, 82 (1992): 713–19; North, "Economic Performance."

[4] Coase, "Institutional Structure," p. 714.

[5] North, "Economic Performance," p. 366.

[6] Douglass North, "Institutions," *Journal of Economic Perspectives*, 5 (1991): 97–112, at p. 97.

[7] Weingast, "Political Foundations."

governance] to determine how contracts between management and government can serve as tools [of] reform."[8]

I begin with a sketch of the transaction cost economics approach to governance and explain how this helps to inform the study of the institutional environment. Three core governance concepts—credible commitment, bureaucracy/ bureaucratization, and remediableness—are then described in Section 3. The lessons of each for understanding the institutional environment (mainly the polity) and economic development and reform are then developed in Sections 4 and 5. Concluding remarks follow.

2 Governance

Transaction cost economics is concerned predominantly with the governance of contractual relations. Given that there are many alternative ways to organize a transaction (or a related set of transactions), which governance structures (modes of contracting) are used, when, and why? Vertical integration— whether to supplant market by hierarchy (whether to make rather than buy)— is the paradigm problem out of which transaction cost economics works. Whereas orthodox microtheory invokes monopoly purpose or efficient risk-bearing to interpret nonstandard and unfamiliar contracting and organizational practices (those that differ from simple and uniform price-mediated exchange[9]), transaction cost economics maintains that such practices more often have the purpose and effect of mitigating contractual hazards, thereby economizing on transaction costs.

2.1 *The Firm-as-Governance Structure*

Transaction cost economics is a much more microanalytic enterprise than is standard microeconomic theory.[10] Upon making the transaction the basic unit of analysis, the firm is no longer regarded principally as a technological entity (defined by economies of scale and scope) but as an organizational entity. Rather, therefore, than describe the firm as a production function (a technological construction), the firm is described as a governance structure (an

---

[8] World Bank, *Bureaucrats in Business*, p. xi.

[9] Kenneth J. Arrow, "Uncertainty and the Welfare Economics of Medical Care," *American Economic Review*, 53 (1963): 941–73.

[10] Kenneth J. Arrow, "Reflections in Essays," in George Feiwel, ed., *Arrow and the Foundations of Economic Policy* (New York: New York University Press, 1987), pp. 727–34.

organizational construction). David Kreps succinctly puts the issues as follows:[11] the firm is like individual agents in textbook economics, which finds its highest expression in general equilibrium theory.[12] The firm transacts with other firms and with individuals in the market. Agents have utility functions, firms have a profit motive; agents have consumption sets, firms have production possibility sets. But in transaction cost economics, firms are more like markets—both are arenas within which individuals can transact.

Upon describing firms and markets as *alternative* modes of organization, the decision to organize which transactions by which governance structures is predominantly explained by the differential transaction costs that attend each. The identification, explication, and mitigation of hazards is central to the exercise and, as discussed below, is vital to an understanding of the institutional environment. The rudimentary argument is this: (1) transactions differ in their attributes; (2) governance structures differ in their cost and competence (for adapting to disturbances and effecting hazard mitigation); and (3) efficiency purposes are served by aligning transactions with governance structures so as to effect a transaction-cost-economizing result. As John R. Commons perceptively recognized, "the ultimate unit of activity ... must contain in itself the three principles of conflict, mutuality, and order. This unit is a transaction."[13] Not only does transaction cost economics concur that the transaction is the basic unit of analysis, but it holds that governance is the means by which *order* is accomplished in a relation where potential conflict threatens to undo or upset opportunities to realize *mutual* gains.

The orthodox preoccupation with price and output thus gives way to the study of comparative economic organization. Transaction cost economics is nevertheless at one with orthodoxy in two crucial respects: an economizing orientation is maintained; and contracts, albeit incomplete, are examined in a farsighted way. Order is thus accomplished by looking ahead, perceiving potential hazards, and factoring these hazards back into the design of governance, thereby mitigating the hazards. Issues of credible commitment and remediableness (see Sections 3.1 and 3.3) are posed.

2.2 The Three-Level Schema

Although transaction cost economics is concerned mainly with the governance of contractual relations, governance does not operate in isolation. The comparative efficacy of alternative modes of governance varies with the

[11] David Kreps, "Corporate Culture and Economic Theory", in James E. Alt and Kenneth A. Shepsle, *Perspectives on Positive Political Economy* (Cambridge: Cambridge University Press, 1990), p. 96.

[12] See Gerrard Debreu, *Theory of Value: An Axiomatic Analysis of Economic Equilibrium* (New Haven, Yale University Press, 1959) and Arrow and Hahn, *General Competitive Analysis* (San Francisco: Holden-Day, 1971).

[13] John R. Commons, "The Problem of Contracting Law, Economics and Ethics," *Wisconsin Law Review*, 8 (1932): 3–26, at p. 4.

institutional environment on the one hand and the attributes of economic actors on the other. A three-level schema is therefore proposed, according to which the object of analysis (governance) is bracketed by more macro features (the institutional environment) and more micro features (the individual). Feedbacks aside (which are underdeveloped in the transaction cost economics setup), the institutional environment is treated as the locus of shift parameters, changes in which shift the comparative costs of governance. The individual is where the behavioral assumptions originate.

Although economic actors are commonly described in terms of what is analytically convenient (whence the appeal of hyper-rationality), transaction cost economics subscribes to Herbert Simon's view that "[n]othing is more fundamental in setting our research agenda and informing our research methods than our view of the nature of the human beings whose behavior we are studying."[14] The two behavioral assumptions out of which transaction cost economics works are (1) bounded rationality (on which account all complex contracts are unavoidably incomplete) and (2) opportunism (on which account mere promise unsupported by credible commitments poses contractual hazards). These behavioral assumptions apply symmetrically to *all* forms of organization, which is to say that economic actors in the private sector and public sector are described as being alike.[15]

Bounded rationality is defined as behavior that is "intendedly rational but only limitedly so."[16] Hyper-rationality is disallowed, but the economic agents to whom Simon refers are attempting effectively to cope. Neither nonrationality nor irrationality is therefore implied. Rather, the principal lesson of bounded rationality for economic organization is that all complex contracts are unavoidably incomplete.

Although many students of organization associate bounded rationality with myopia—in that economic actors are assumed to lack the wits to look ahead and take hazard-mitigating actions—that is more pertinent to the study of consumer behavior than it is in the commercial sector where more complex forms of hierarchical organization permit specialization. Transaction cost economics maintains that parties to commercial transactions not only look ahead, but perceive hazards and take hazard mitigation actions (in cost-effective degree).

It bears noting, however, that all contractual hazards would vanish were it not that bounded rationality is paired with opportunism. Given the absence of bounded rationality, comprehensive contingent claims contracting would obtain. Given the absence of opportunism, contract as promise would every-

---

[14] Herbert Simon, "Human Nature in Politics: The Dialogue of Pyschology with Political Science," *American Political Science Review*, 79 (1985): 293–304, at p. 303.

[15] Private sector: see Oliver E. Williamson, *The Mechanisms of Governance* (New York: Oxford University Press, 1996); public sector: see Olson, "Dictatorship."

[16] Herbert Simon, *Administrative Behavior*, 2nd edn. (New York: Macmillan, 1961 (1947), p. xxiv.

where be efficacious.[17] Confronted, however, with both bounded rationality and opportunism, there are posed contractual hazards to which alternative modes of governance are differentially responsive. This is the world with which transaction cost economics is concerned.

The nature and magnitude of these hazards varies both with the attributes of transactions and with the condition of the institutional environment. Recall that the institutional environment is defined jointly by the *rules of the game* (the formal constraints: constitutions, laws, property rights) and the *conditions of embeddedness* (the informal constraints: sanctions, taboos, customs, traditions, codes of conduct). Although transaction cost economics ordinarily takes the institutional environment as given and examines governance with reference to fixed background conditions, that is not the only way to proceed.

The first and most obvious way to relax this setup is to allow for *shifts* in the institutional environment: how do investment and the organization of economic activity change in response to shifts in the condition of the institutional environment? The second and more ambitious way to proceed is to *reshape* the institutional environment so as to effect a better microanalytic outcome: how does the bottom-up approach help to inform such an under-taking? The first of these is described here and the second is taken up in Section 5. As it turns out, actively reshaping the institutional environment is a rare event—to which the remediableness criterion is especially pertinent.

2.3 Shifts in the Institutional Environment

How do changes in property rights and contract laws influence investment and contracting? That is a straightforward query to which both the logic of organization and empirical analysis can be applied.[18] The effect of *changes* in the institutional environment *within* nation states and *differences* in the institutional environment *between* nation states can both be investigated in this way.

Unsurprisingly, more secure investment regimes will elicit more investment in durable, non-redeployable assets, ceteris paribus. Also, parameter shifts that change the relative costs of governance will induce transactions to be shifted into what have now become the (comparatively) lower cost modes. The overall composition of investment and contracting will reflect changes of both investment and organizational kinds.[19] Such considerations have begun to

---

[17] Oliver E. Williamson, *The Economic Institutions of Capitalism* (New York: Free Press, 1985), pp. 64–7.

[18] Logic of organization: see Oliver E. Williamson, "Comparative Economic Organization: the Analysis of Discrete Structural Alternatives," *Administrative Science Quarterly*, 36 (1991): 269–96; empirical analysis: see Edwin Mansfield, "Intellectual Property Protection, Direct Investment and Technology Transfer," Discussion Paper no. 27, International Finance Corporation, Washington, 1995.

[19] Michael Riordan and Oliver Williamson, "Asset Specificity and Economic Organization," *International Journal of Industrial Organization*, 3 (1985): 365–78; and Williamson, "Comparative Economic Organization."

make their way into the development literature, especially in relation to the differential efficacy of privatization as a function of the institutional environment.[20]

A noteworthy feature of this privatization literature is that nominal changes in contract and property laws do not necessarily imply effective changes. There is a need to go beyond the (nominal) laws on the books to consider the de facto laws, which brings in the mechanisms of enforcement. And there is a related need to ascertain the ease with which changes, once made, can be reversed, which brings in the polity. Issues of credible commitment are posed.

···

3 Three Core Concepts

The transaction cost approach to economic organization emphasizes (1) governance (as against technology), (2) the microanalytics of transactions and governance structures (as against price and output), (3) transaction cost economizing (as against monopoly purpose and/or efficient risk bearing[21]), (4) discrete structural (as against marginal) analysis, and (5) focuses on governance, as bracketed by the behavioral assumptions (bounded rationality; opportunism) from below and the institutional environment (rules of the game; condition of embeddedness) from above.

Three core concepts—credible commitment, bureaucracy/bureaucratization, and remediableness—also inform the way in which the study of governance proceeds. Although each of these concepts has its origins in the study of industrial organization, each has broad reach and applies also to the economics and politics of development and reform. Each concept is sketched here. Applications to the economics and politics of development and reform are taken up in Section 4 and 5.

---

[20] Levy and Spiller "Institutional Foundations"; World Bank, *Bureaucrats in Business*.

[21] Viewing the firm as a production function, the "legitimate" boundaries of the firm were defined by technology, whereupon extending the boundaries of the firm beyond those needed to realize economies of scale and scope was regarded as deeply problematic. There being little appreciation for the importance of organization, applied price theorists concluded that boundary extension had the purpose of facilitating price discrimination and/or creating barriers to entry. Ronald Coase captured the prevailing orientation to nonstandard and unfamiliar practices as follows: "if an economist finds something—a business practice of one sort or other—that he does not understand, he looks for a monopoly explanation. As in this field we are very ignorant, the number of ununderstandable practices tends to be rather large, and the reliance on a monopoly explanation frequent." Ronald Coase, "Industrial Organizations: A Proposal for Research," in V. R. Fuchs, ed., *Policy Issues and Research Opportunities in Industrial Organization* (New York: National Bureau of Economic Research, 1972), p. 67.

3.1 *Credible Commitments*

The concept of credibility, or the lack thereof, has played a significant role in the study of industrial organization, mainly in the context of credible threats. The credible threat issue is this: if A says to B that it will do X if B does Y, but should B do Y then A's best response is to do Z, then A's threat to do X is not credible. The study of strategic interfirm behavior has been vastly reshaped by sorting credible from noncredible threats. Analytical and public policy confusion—in both antitrust and regulation—prevailed before bluffs and credibility were distinguished.[22]

One of the benefits of credible threat thinking is that it induced students of industrial organization to work out of a farsighted (rather than myopic) setup. Indeed, the concept of credibility is equally—arguably, is even more—important in the context of credible commitments, where the issue is that of promise rather than threat. The farsighted contracting issue posed by promise is whether, if A promises B that it will take delivery under all state realizations save those in S_1, but A's best response is to take delivery only for state realizations in S_3, B will then project that A will cancel in both S_1 and S_2 unless added safeguards are introduced. The basic proposition here is that mere promise, without more, is not self-enforcing.

Given farsighted contracting, parties to a contract will not only be alert to possible future hazards, but they will have incentives to relieve those hazards—provided that this can be done in a cost-effective way. Contrary to Machiavelli, who worked out of a myopic logic and advised his prince to breach contracts with impunity, the farsighted prince will recognize that better terms can be had by devising ex ante safeguards that communicate confidence by deterring ex post opportunism. Contract is thus viewed as a triple (p, h, s)—where p is the price at which trade takes place, h is the hazard that accrues if no hazard mitigating action is taken, and s is the safeguard. It is elementary that, as between two identical buyers, only one of which offers a safeguard, the supplier will offer to supply on better terms (at a lower price) in the trade for which a safeguard has been provided.

The "obvious" way to provide a safeguard is to post a bond which is forfeited if the buyer should breach. However, pecuniary bonds pose problems of their own, of which contrived breach is an example. The study of economic organization becomes both much more complicated and much more interesting on that account. As it turns out, many nonstandard and unfamiliar forms of organization have the purpose and effect of providing credible commitments.[23]

[22] A. Dixit, "A Model of Duopoly Suggesting a Theory of Entry Barrier," *Bell Journal of Economics*, 10 (1979): 20–32; A. Dixit, "The Role of Investment in Entry Deterrence," *Economic Journal*, 90 (1980): 95–106.

[23] Oliver E. Williamson, "Credible Commitments: Using Hostages to Support Exchange," *American Economic Review*, 73 (1983): 519–40.

Because, however, contractual hazards and their mitigation have played such a negligible role in economics (the insurance literature and the preoccupation with risk aversion excepted), farsighted contracting and the ramifications for economic and political organization were long neglected—although that is now changing. Suffice it to observe here that (1) the identification, explication, and mitigation of contractual hazards is the central focus on transaction cost economics; (2) many of these hazards reside in the details of transactions and organization, on which account self-conscious attention to these details is needed; (3) a farsighted approach to contract in which credible commitments are featured has broad applications—including, as developed in Section 4, applications to political organization.

3.2 Bureaucracy/Bureaucratization

Bureaucracy is commonly regarded as "the problem," which indeed sometimes it is. But that obscures the fact that bureaucracy has a lot to recommend it and is also, frequently, "the solution." An accurate assessment of bureaucracy requires that we come to terms with both its strengths and its weaknesses. These need to be identified and explicated and the ramifications worked out.

3.2.1 Benefits

(a) *Bureaus as benevolent?*   It was once common to regard government as an omnipotent, omniscient, benevolent autocrat. Avinash Dixit summarizes recent theory and practice as follows: "Much of the [orthodox] theory, and almost all of the practice, of economic policy analysis views the making and implementation of the policy as a technical problem, even as a control engineering problem."[24] The earliest models assumed that policy was made by

an omnipotent, omniscient, and benevolent dictator. The work on the second-best removed the omnipotence. That on information removed the omniscience. However, the assumptions of benevolence and dictatorship have remained ... The normative approach continues to view policy-making as a purely *technical* problem. The implicit assumption is that once a policy that maximizes or improves social welfare has been found and recommended, it will be implemented as designed, and the desired effects will follow.[25]

Omnipotence permitted the government to fix any problem directly: if prices deviated from marginal cost, it reset them appropriately. If, moreover, some

[24] A. Dixit, *The Making of Economic Policy: A Transaction Cost Politics Perspective* (Cambridge, Mass.: MIT Press, 1996), p. 3.
[25] Ibid., p. 7.

prices were constrained but the government was nevertheless omniscient, then second-best adjustments could be prescribed. And even if omniscience could not be sustained, the government would still win in the comparison between the self-interested firm and the benign government agency, provided only that the two were identically informed.

Benevolence, like hyper-rationality, is plainly a convenient assumption. One of the lessons of transaction cost economics, however, is that all forms of economic organization are beset by opportunism. That has taken a long time to register. Thus, economists long resisted, but eventually conceded, that the separation of ownership from control mattered,[26] whereupon it was an extreme simplification to ascribe profit maximization (unfailing managerial stewardship) to the modern corporation. The same applies to the government: to ascribe social welfare maximization to politicians and bureaucrats is convenient but naive. Accordingly, just as "Economists studying business and industrial organization have ... developed richer paradigms and models [of the firm] based on the concepts of various kinds of transaction costs," so too will policy analysis benefit from "opening up the [public] black box and examining the actual workings of the mechanisms inside."[27] The upshot is that, rather than describe the firm/bureau/polity as a technical entity to which stewardship behavior is ascribed, the need instead is to describe the firm/bureau/polity as a governance structure to which agency problems accrue. Policy analysts have been slow to come to terms with that condition.

(b) *Hierarchy/coordination*   Coordination is the obvious answer to the question of what are the advantages of hierarchy in relation to the market. Internalizing externalities, thereby to coordinate the choice of decision variables, is one possibility.[28] Coordinated adaptations to disturbances—of a "conscious deliberate, purposeful" kind[29]—covers a more important class of circumstances. But if firms enjoy advantages in coordination respects, wherein do their disadvantages reside? That question needs to be both posed and answered.

3.2.2 *Costs*

One of the deep puzzles of economic organization is why a large firm cannot do everything that a collection of small firms can do (by replication) and occasionally do better (by selective intervention). If the large firm can replicate

---

[26] Adolph A. Berle and Gardner C. Means, Jr, *The Modern Corporation and Private Property* (New York: Macmillan, 1932).

[27] Dixit, "The Making of Economic Policy," p. 8.

[28] Otto A. Davis and Andrew Whinston, "Externalities, Welfare, and the Theory of Games," *Bell Journal of Economics*, 10 (1979): 20–32.

[29] Chester Barnard, *The Functions of the Executive* (Cambridge, Mass.: Harvard University Press, 1938 (15th printing 1962)), p. 4.

what the collection of small firms does in all circumstances in which autonomy works well and intervenes only when expected net gains can be projected, then bigger is always better. That leads to the counterfactual prediction that everything will be organized in one large firm. What needs to be explained then is where the combination of replication with selective intervention breaks down.

If nonstandard and unfamiliar forms of organization are to be understood in terms of the details, then that is where the costs of bureaucracy reside. As it turns out, issues of credible commitment are posed. Can a firm credibly commit to replicate—to respect autonomy among the operating parts—in all circumstances save those where expected net gains can be projected? Can an autonomous firm sell its assets to a common owner and credibly commit to manage those assets efficiently, reliably choosing efficient factor combinations and utilizing those assets with due care? Confronted with information asymmetries, where the advantage accrues sometimes to the owner and sometimes to the manager, and recognizing the propensity of each party to seek its own advantage, it becomes clear that the combination of replication and selective intervention cannot be reliably implemented. Instead, incentives are *unavoidably degraded* upon taking transactions out of the market and organizing them internally.[30]

Additionally, bureaucracies undergo changes over time as the membership acquires deeper knowledge and as coalitions and strategizing develop among the parts. Bureaucracy, like the law, has a life of its own.[31] It does not, therefore, suffice to choose hierarchy over market because immediate coordination benefits can be projected. Because incentives are degraded and future distortions are in prospect, these too need to be taken into account.[32]

3.3 Remediableness

One of the most common practices in public policy analysis is to compare an actual form of organization with a hypothetical ideal. Although this can be instructive, it is also fraught with hazards.

3.3.1 Asymmetrical standards

Appealing to a hypothetical ideal is unobjectionable as long as the limits of all feasible forms are recognized. A problem, however, arises if some forms are

---

[30] Williamson, *Economic Institutions*, ch. 6.

[31] Ibid.

[32] Actually, the intertemporal consequences of bureaucracy are mixed. Some take the form of benefits (more efficient codes and communication—see Kenneth J. Arrow, *The Limits of Organization* (New York: W. W. Norton, 1974)—while others take the form of cumulative distortions in the bureaucratic decision process—see Mancur Olson, *The Rise and Decline of Nations* (New Haven: Yale University Press, 1982). The latter increase relatively with time.

privileged. Ronald Coase remarked about this asymmetry as follows (emphasis added):

Contemplation of an optimal system may provide techniques of analysis that would otherwise have been missed and, in certain special cases, it may go far to providing a solution. But in general its influence has been pernicious. It has directed economists' attention away from the main question, which is *how alternative arrangements will actually work in practice*. It has led economists to derive conclusions for economic policy from a study of an abstract of a market situation. It is no accident that in the literature . . . we find a category "market failure" but no category "government failure." Until we realize that we are choosing between social arrangements which are all more or less failures, we are not likely to make much headway.[33]

Similar concerns were registered by Harold Demsetz in his examination of costly information and its ramifications for inefficiency.[34] The propensity to describe the government as an omnipotent, omniscient, or at least benevolent autocrat (as discussed by Dixit: see Section 2.2 above[35]) is in this same tradition. Such asymmetrical treatments of failure predispose public policy analysis in favor of particular outcomes. That is not a satisfactory state of affairs.

3.3.2 Inefficiency by design

Inefficiency by design sounds like a contradiction in terms—which it is, if the criterion is a hypothetical ideal. Given, however, that all feasible forms of organization are flawed, what appears to be inefficient may in fact be an effort to cope with property rights that are poorly defined and/or costly to enforce. Firms in these circumstances may decide to make rather than buy because outside procurement runs the risk that valued know-how will leak out.[36] Also, manu-facturers' agents sometimes incur added expenses, over and above those needed to develop the market, because these added expenses strengthen customer bonds in a cost-effective way, thereby helping to deter manufacturers from entering into the distribution stage and expropriating market development investments.[37] Similarly, franchisors will sometimes impose costly bonding on franchisees as a means by which to deter franchisees from violating quality norms.[38]

The common thread that runs through all of these examples is that insecure but legitimate property rights will be supported by added expenses in the

[33] Ronald H. Coase, "The Regulated Industries: Discussion," *American Economic Review*, 54 (1972): 194–7, at p. 195.

[34] Harold Demsetz, "Information and Efficiency: Another Viewpoint," *Journal of Law and Economics*, 12(1) (April 1969): 1–22.

[35] Dixit "Making of Economic Policy."

[36] David J. Teece, "Profiting from Technological Innovation," *Research Policy*, 15 (1986): 285–305.

[37] Jan Heide and George John, "The Role of Dependence Balancing in Safeguarding Transaction-Specific Assets in Conventional Channels," *Journal of Marketing*, 52 (1988): 20–35.

[38] Benjamin Klein and K. B. Leiffer, "The Role of Market Forces in Assuring Contractual Performance," *Journal of Political Economy*, 89 (1981): 615–41.

degree to which these are perceived to be the most cost-effective way to protect against the loss of value. Whether such added costs are inefficient cannot be established by reference to a hypothetical ideal.

To be sure, if it were always and everywhere the case that we could rely on "a [costless] legal system to define property rights and arbitrate disputes," then anyone "wishing to use a resource has to pay the owner to obtain it."[39] That would simplify matters considerably, and many economists have been drawn to the fiction of the Coase theorem. However, because it is expensive to define and enforce property rights through the courts, costly court-ordering needs to be evaluated in relation to alternative feasible private-ordering forms of organization. If the most cost-effective way to protect property rights is to incur private-ordering expenses of the kinds described above then—awaiting a superior measurement technology or other device by which property rights can be better protected—the resulting "inefficiency by design" is not inefficient in any remediable sense whatsoever.

3.3.3 Path dependency

Path dependency is another way of saying that history matters.[40] It is also believed to be a chronic source of inefficiency in economics and politics.[41] I am persuaded of the importance of path dependency but take exception with all inefficiency claims that are based entirely on comparisons with a hypothetical ideal (of which zero transaction costs is an example[42]).

Specifically, no inefficiency should be implied if one discovers, in the fulness of time, that it would have been better to have chosen Y over X at time zero if, at time zero, the best informed choice was X. To be sure, if a decision-maker could have looked ahead and did not, that is discreditable, perhaps even a blunder. Even such an error, however, does not necessarily imply inefficiency. From a systems point of view, it may be necessary to test the competence of managers to decide which of them get advanced and which do not. Unless that sorting process is not working, "mistakes" do not necessarily signal breakdowns.

A more common basis to claim path-dependent inefficiency is in the context of interdependencies among decision-makers. Thus, suppose that the average net benefits of adopting a technology increase with the number of adopters.[43]

---

[39] Ronald H. Coase, "The Federal Communications Commission," *Journal of Law and Economics*, 2 (1959): 1–40, at p. 14.

[40] Douglass North, *Institutions, Institutional Change, and Economic Performance* (New York: Cambridge University Press, 1990), p. 365.

[41] Brian Arthur, "Competing Technologies, Increasing Returns, and Lock-in by Historical Events," *Economic Journal*, 99 (1989): 116–31; North, *Institutions*.

[42] Ibid., p. 360.

[43] The example is similar to but different from the discussion of interdependency in Stanley Leiberman and Stephen Margolis, "Path Dependence, Lock-in, and History," *Journal of Law, Economics and Organization*, 1 (1995): 205–26.

Assume further that the choice of a technology has long-lasting consequences, in that the technology is both durable and non-redeployable. Suppose also that there are two technologies (A and B) and that the technology (say A) with the higher net benefit intercept has the lower slope. Assume further that there are N firms and that the average net benefit lines intersect at a value $\bar{N}$ that is less than but close to N.

All firms make their choice of technology simultaneously and independently. If all perceive that it is in their collective interests to choose B, then the efficient choice of B will be observed. But suppose that some fraction, say α, of the population is known to be confused and refers only to the intercept in making its choice. If that fraction is such that $(1-\alpha)N < \bar{N}$, and if it is not cost-effective to educate the confused fraction of the population—possibly because, even if agreement among the perceptive $(1-\alpha)N$ could easily be reached, education is prohibitively expensive, or because the cost of orchestrating collective action by the perceptive, thereby to provide education, is very great—then the choice of A (by both myopic and perceptive firms) will be observed.

Those who appeal to a hypothetical ideal will declare that the latter result is inefficient. Those who work out of the remediableness criterion will be more circumspect.

Lapses into ideal but operationally irrelevant reasoning will be avoided by (1) recognizing that it is impossible to do better than one's best, (2) insisting that all of the finalists in an organization-form competition meet the test of feasibility, (3) symmetrically exposing the weaknesses as well as the strengths of all proposed feasible forms, and (4) describing and costing out the mechanisms of any proposed reorganization. To this list, moreover, there is yet a further consideration: (5) making a place for and being respectful of politics. This last has been the most difficult for public policy analysts to concede.

Remediableness is a comparative institutional criterion, according to which the appropriate test of "failures" of all kinds—markets, hierarchies, and bureaus alike—is as follows. An extant mode of organization for which no feasible superior alternative can be described and implemented with expected net gains is presumed to be efficient. The burden of proof for rebutting this presumption is placed on those who take exception. Mere appeal to the fiction of zero transaction costs or to claims of path dependency do not alone discharge the burden.

4 Applications to Politics

Microanalytic reasoning, the idea of discriminating alignment, and the three core concepts set out in Section 3 are applied here to the puzzles of politics.

4.1 Credible Commitment

Credible commitment reasoning has its origins in the study of contract. Given the institutional environment (rules of the game and conditions of embeddedness), the focus turns to private ordering: what can the immediate parties to a transaction do to infuse contractual confidence? As heretofore described, transaction cost economics views governance as the means by which *order* is accomplished in a relation where potential *conflict* threatens to undo or upset opportunities to realize *mutual* gains.

Credible commitments infuse order by mitigating hazards, as a consequence of which parties make more specialized investments and engage in trade on better terms than they otherwise would—because they correctly infer that the hazards of investment and exchange have been reduced. Such reasoning not only applies at the level of governance, but carries over to the level of the institutional environment. As Barry Weingast has put it,

In important respects, the logic of political institutions parallels that of economic institutions. To borrow Williamson's phrase, the political institutions of society create a "governance structure" that at once allows the society to deal with on-going problems as they arise and yet provides a degree of durability to economic and political rights. Importantly, these help limit the ability of the state to act opportunistically.[44]

A farsighted state will thus recognize that organization matters and that it can take actions that increase confidence in both contracting and investment. But because politics is different, credible commitments may fail to materialize because of ignorance, front-loading, or looting.

The ignorance argument is that long-run efficiency reasoning does not come easily to politicians, who are more familiar and comfortable with power reasoning. The "invitation" by Mikhail Gorbachev, advising US companies to invest quickly in the Soviet Union rather than wait, is illustrative: "Those [companies] who are with us now have good prospects of participating in our great country . . . [whereas those who wait] will remain observers for years to come—we will see to it" (*International Herald Tribune*, June 5, 1990). That an experienced and sophisticated leader of a huge nation-state in the late twentieth century should choose carrot-and-stick reasoning rather than an offer of credible commitments to encourage investments suggests the counter-intuitiveness of credibility.

What Gorbachev evidently failed to understand is that the ready exercise of administrative discretion is the source of contractual hazard. Ready recourse to discretion not only places those who have already invested at greater hazard,

---

[44] Barry Weingast, "Constitutions as Governance Structures," *Journal of Institutional and Theoretical Economics*, 149, (1993): 288.

but also causes those who are contemplating investment to think again. The paradox is that fewer degrees of freedom (rules) can have advantages over more (discretion) if they make commitments more credible.[45] That is not an obvious result.

The institutional environment takes on special significance where the change in benefits takes the form not of redistribution but of expropriation. Have the requisite structural safeguards been created at the constitutional level, and are they respected in practice? If the requisite constitutional safeguards are weak or absent, are there other mechanisms that communicate confidence?[46] Do the customs in the community, for example, fill the gap? Or have de facto property rights been created, the effect of which is to deter governments from seizing or devaluing assets (even if this can be done without legal recourse), because adverse reputation effects will thereafter accrue?

The issues here are pertinent to the study of privatization[47] and, more generally, to the assessment of differential economic performance across juris-dictions that differ in de jure or de facto structural respects. How does the division of powers and parliamentary regimes differ in credibility respects? Is de facto practice more likely to differ from de jure rules in one of these regimes than another? How do background societal conditions (customs, mores) affect the calculus?

This is plainly a big order, and work of this kind is only now getting started.[48] The proposition, however, that credible commitment is a robust concept with application to both private-sector governance and the organization of politics seems secure. If, therefore, one wants to display the ramifications of one contracting mode in relation to another or one polity in relation to another, credible commitment reasoning turns out to be deeply informative.

4.2 Bureaucracy/Bureaucratization

Although Oskar Lange perceived that *"the real danger of socialism is that of a bureaucratization of economic life,* and not the impossibility of coping with

---

[45] Finn Kydland and Edward Prescott, "Rules Rather than Discretion: The Inconsistency of Optimal Plans," *Journal of Political Economy*, 85 (1977): 473–91.

[46] An example where they did not is Hungary, where Janos Kornai reports that "individuals or their parents [who] lived through the era of confiscations in the forties" discount "repeated official declarations" that they will not be expropriated again, which explains why "many of them are myopic profit maximizers, not much interested in building up lasting goodwill . . . or investing in long-lived fixed assets": Janos Kornai, "The Hungarian Reform Process," *Journal of Economic Literature*, 24 (1986): 1687–1737, at pp. 1705–6).

[47] See, especially, the work on telecommunications of Levy and Spiller, "Institutional Foundations."

[48] Douglass North and Barry Weingast, "Constitutions and Commitment: the Evolution of Institutions Governing Public Choice in 17th Century England," *Journal of Economic History*, 49 (1989): 803–32; David Soskice, Robert Bates, and David Epstein, "Ambition and Constraint: the Stabilizing Role of Institutions," *Journal of Law, Economics, and Organization*, 8 (1992): 547–60; Weingast, "Constitutions"; Weingast, "Political Foundations"; Gabriella Montignola, Yingyi Qian, and Barry Weingast, "Federalism, Chinese Style," unpublished paper, 1993.

the problem of allocation of resources"[49] (emphasis in original), he took the position that monopolistic capitalism was similarly beset by bureaucratization and that the study of bureaucracy "belongs" to sociology.[50] If, comparatively, capitalism and socialism are indistinguishable in bureaucratization respects, then attention needs to be focused on other features where the real differences reside. Even, moreover, if capitalism and socialism differed significantly in bureaucratic respects, Lange's fallback position was that the study of bureaucracy belonged to sociology. The proper study of economics, therefore, was resource allocation—even if this was a matter of only second-order importance.

Successive generations of students of comparative economic systems emulated that example. The study of control "plays no role in the socialist controversy"[51] and little thereafter. Instead, the study of comparative economic systems was preoccupied with technologies (firms-as-production functions) and techniques (marginal cost pricing; linear programming; activity analysis). Indeed, we are told that "Technology and human needs are universal. To start with just these elements has facilitated and intensified professional contacts and interactions between market and socialist countries."[52] Rather than introduce institutional differences that could disrupt the conversation between economists who lived under different social/political/economic systems, it is better to maintain harmony.

If, however, bureaucratic differences are where the real action resides, that was a fateful decision. To be sure, the theory of bureaucracy to which I refer in Section 3.2 above is in very primitive shape. Bureaucratic differences are nonetheless hugely responsible for the incentive and control differences that distinguish market and hierarchies; and I conjecture that similar considerations carry over to comparative economic systems.

Of special importance are the intertemporal distortions and transformations that predictably attend bureaucracy and are especially virulent in large public bureaucracies. Mancur Olson develops the argument with reference to the former Soviet Union as follows:

in the fullness of time, as more and more coteries of subordinates collude in their own interests, the system not only loses efficiency and output but also becomes a web of counter-theft and corruption that ultimately leaves the center impoverished. If the harshest punishments are imposed on even the faintest suspicion, then the bureaucratic competition that is indispensable to the system can be preserved somewhat longer, so

---

[49] Oskar Lange, "On the Theory of Economic Socialism," in Benjamin Lippincott, ed., *On the Economic Theory of Socialism* (Minneapolis: University of Minnesota Press, 1938), p. 109.

[50] Ibid., pp. 109–10.

[51] Benjamin N. Ward, *The Socialist Economy: A Study of Organizational Alternatives* (New York: Random House, 1967), p. 37.

[52] Tjalling Koopmans, "Concepts of Optimality and their Uses," *American Economic Review*, 67 (1997): 261–74, at pp. 264–5.

Stalinist purges can make the system work better. In the long run, nonetheless, the difficulties of covert collective action are bound to be overcome in more and more enterprises, industries, localities, and ethnic or linguistic groups. Thus it is a "law of motion" of Soviet-type societies that they must not only run down over time, but also become increasingly corrupt. Ultimately, it becomes, some say, "impossible to buy and easy to steal." More and more victims of the regime come to believe that he who "refrains from taking state property" is robbing his family.[53]

To be sure, other ex post rationalizations for the collapse of the former Soviet Union and Eastern Europe can be advanced. What is needed is to ascertain the refutable implications of each. Although the current state of bureaucracy/bureaucratization theory does not meet the test of being fully predictive, the proposition that bureaucracy is centrally implicated is at least plausible. Exploring that will require research attention to be concentrated on the study of bureaucracy—not in a contrived way, in which notions of benign governance are selectively invoked, but in a genuinely comparative institutional fashion, in which *common* behavioral assumptions are ascribed to economic actors in all governance structures whatsoever.[54] Implementing that, furthermore, requires the study of economics and organization theory to be joined.

4.3 Remediableness

Normative public policy analysis typically invokes benign government[55] and invariably holds that economics trumps politics. By contrast, positive public policy analysis recognizes that all feasible forms of organization are flawed and places economics in the (analytical) service of politics. Public policy analysts who work out of the remediableness criterion are understandably much more cautious in assessing politics. Rather than declaring that politics is inefficient whenever deadweight losses can be ascribed to political outcomes, which is common practice,[56] two questions are posed: "What's going on here?" and "Is it remediable?"

Many economists and public policy analysts are understandably discomfited by this role reversal. Much more satisfying to excoriate on politics—politicians know not what they do—than to ask how this vastly complicated process works and whether observed outcomes are remediable.

[53] Mancur Olson, "Russian Reforms: Established Interests and Practical Alternatives," unpublished paper, IRIS/University of Maryland, 1995, p. 26.

[54] James March and Herbert Simon, *Organizations* (New York: John Wiley and Sons, 1958); Oliver Williamson, *The Economics of Discretionary Behavior: Managerial Objectives in a Theory of the Firm* (Englewood Cliffs, NJ: Prentice-Hall, 1964); Ronald Coase, "The Regulated Industries: Discussion," *American Economic Review*, 54 (May 1964): 194–7: Harold Demsetz, "Information and Efficiency: Another Viewpoint," *Journal of Law and Economics*, 12(1) (April 1969): 1–22.

[55] Dixit, "Making of Economic Policy."

[56] George J. Stigler, "Law or Economics?" *Journal of Law and Economics*, 35 (1992): 455–68.

As discussed in Section 3.3, issues of inefficiency by design and history dependency are ones to which the criterion of remediableness relates in examining private-sector economic organization. Both concepts apply equally to politics.

Indeed, because political property rights are especially insecure, inefficiency by design is commonly observed in politics. Thus, if incumbent politicians perceive that the direct delivery of benefits to their constituencies can easily be reversed or redirected by a successor set of politicians with different preferences, then indirect programs that are more secure will be brought under consideration. If indirection is the only way to deliver legitimate political purposes with assurance,[57] then to declare that all convoluted programs are necessarily inefficient is unwarranted. In circumstances, moreover, where such protection is costly to devise, recourse to the heavy front-loading of benefits should come as no surprise.

More generally, to observe that a political program is "burdened" with large deadweight losses, as compared with a hypothetical ideal, is not dispositive. As in the private sector, so too in the political sector does the remediableness test apply. Such an inquiry takes the public policy analyst into the microanalytic details of transactions and public-sector governance in very much the same way as private-sector transactions and their governance have been studied by transaction cost economics.[58]

The issues here can be illustrated by examining the convoluted ways in which the polity sometimes accomplishes income redistribution. Consider the almost universal disdain with which the US sugar program is regarded, which program has been described by George Stigler as follows:

The United States wastes (in ordinary language) perhaps $3 billion per year producing sugar and sugar substitutes at a price two to three times the cost of importing the sugar. Yet that is the tested way in which the domestic sugar-beet, cane, and high-fructose corn producers can increase their incomes by perhaps a quarter of the $3 billion—the other three-quarters being deadweight loss. The deadweight loss is the margin by which the domestic costs of sugar production exceed import prices.[59]

The usual interpretation is that such deadweight losses represent inefficiency: "the Posnerian theory would say that the sugar program is grotesquely inefficient because it fails to maximize national income."[60] Such reasoning is widespread. Thus, North declares that "an efficient political

[57] Terry Moe, "Political Institutions: The Neglected Side of the Story," *Journal of Law, Economics, and Organization* (Special Issue), 6 (1990): 213–53; Terry Moe, "The Politics of Structural Choice: Toward a Theory of Public Bureaucracy," in Oliver E. Williamson (ed.), *Organization Theory* (New York: Oxford, 1997), pp. 116–53.
[58] Dixit, "Making of Economic Policy."
[59] Stigler, "Law or Economics?" p. 459.
[60] Ibid.

market would be one in which ... only legislation (or regulation) that maximized the income of the [population of] affected parties to the exchange would be enacted."[61]

Stigler objects to such a criterion because it fails to respect the political process: "Maximum national income ... is not the only goal of our nation as judged by policies adopted by our government—and government's goals as revealed by actual practice are more authoritative than those pronounced by professors of law or economics."[62] Indeed, he goes further: the "sugar program is efficient. This program is more than fifty years old—it has met the test of time."[63] By contrast with those who regard redistribution as problematic and even illegitimate, Stigler plainly interprets redistribution—even convoluted redistribution—as one of the legitimate purposes of government.

A somewhat backhanded way of ascribing legitimacy to redistribution is to view this as an unavoidable cost of democratic government. We may not like what we get, but it is part of the package. Thus, although less redistribution would be preferable to what we observe, we need to become reconciled with the political realities.

A more favorable construction is that redistribution is a central and foreseeable architectural feature of democratic politics. To be sure, that could be disputed: voters, after all, are poorly informed and many fail to participate. That, however, is scarcely dispositive if the key players are politicians and interest groups.[64] Both groups being well-informed and deeply strategic, we should expect to find that redistribution is the product of a strategic political calculus—which is consistent with much of the data.

But what, then, is to be made of redistribution that is accomplished in tortured ways as compared with less costly and feasible alternatives? Surely that is inefficient and ought to be reformed?

Maybe, but then again, maybe not. Two issues are posed. First, it is much easier to postulate more efficient alternatives—lump-sum transfers being an example—than it is to describe the enabling mechanisms. The latter is a much more demanding microanalytic exercise. Second, the apparent inefficiencies of politics sometimes serve intended purposes, which is to say that politics also exhibits inefficiencies by design. I have examined both of these issues elsewhere.[65] Suffice it to observe here that examining politics in a comparative institutional way with reference to a remediableness criterion can be a humbling experience for economists, compared with the usual practice of conducting normative public policy and political analysis with reference to a hypothetical ideal.

---

[61] North, *Institutions*, p. 360.

[62] Stigler, "Law or Economics?" p. 459.

[63] Ibid.

[64] Terry Moe, "Political Institutions: the Neglected Side of the Story," *Journal of Law, Economics, and Organization* (Special Issue), 6 (1990): 213–53, at p. 121.

[65] Williamson, *Mechanisms of Governance*, ch. 8.

5 Development and Reform

My purpose here is to sketch the lessons of bottom-up reasoning and the core concepts of credible commitment, bureaucracy/bureaucratization, and remediableness for the analysis of economic development and reform. Of these three concepts, remediableness is the most controversial, partly because it is also the most consequential. It nevertheless bears noting that any effort to craft reform needs to make express provision for credibility and allowance for both the differential costs of bureaucracy (as these vary with the polity) and the intertemporal transformations that accrue to bureaucratization.

The first stage of the remediableness test is *economic:* can a superior feasible form of organization be described?[66] Proposed alternatives that fail this test are properly regarded as hypothetical alternatives and can be dismissed as fanciful. Implicitly, if not explicitly, such alternatives violate one or both of the behavioral assumptions out of which transaction cost economics works. The second stage test is *political:* does the proposed alternative enjoy the requisite political support to be implemented? Both of these tests are controversial, especially the second.

The economic test disallows the standard gambit of ascribing benign intent to government regulation. Instead, government failures and market failures must both be admitted. If the government wins the organizational form competition on efficiency grounds, that will not be a contrived result but will be the outcome of a genuine side-by-side competition. Assuming that this is passed, the political test poses a further hurdle. Can the superior feasible economic alternative actually be implemented? If it cannot, then we need to get beyond feasability to make allowance for politics (and the political purposes served by what appear to be convoluted extant programs). This is where the need for economists to be more respectful of politics comes in. Modes of organization that are judged to be remediably inefficient in economic terms may qualify as efficient when politics is introduced. If economics does not trump politics but works in the service of politics, then we need to understand the latter.

This is not to say that all extant political outcomes qualify as efficient. Both general and particular objections can be registered. At the general level, a political system could be judged to be so lacking in merit as to be undeserving of respect. Even, moreover, within polities that, at a general level, are judged to be

---

[66] Another possibility is technological infeasibility: an alternative is described which violates the laws of physics—for example, a perpetual motion machine. But, whereas hypothetical ideals of a technological kind are instantly recognized as simplistic, hypothetical ideals of an organizational kind still get a hearing in many quarters.

above threshold, particular objections can be presented. As discussed else-where,[67] a presumption that a particular program is efficient can be rebutted by showing that (1) the program incurs vastly greater deadweight losses than had previously been disclosed; (2) the program has taken on a life of its own, of which capture is an especially troublesome possibility; (3) rival feasible alternatives are unfairly disadvantaged by second mover disadvantages or in other organizational respects; and/or (4) the extant program is otherwise the product of unacceptable initial conditions. As it turns out, overturning an efficiency presumption for a particular program in a polity that is judged to be above threshold at the general level is not easy—especially in an advanced economy.

Sometimes, however, bargains can be struck with developing economies that are not feasible in more advanced economies. That is because additional degrees of freedom accrue when economic aid is introduced into the calculus, which is the case when assessing developing (as against developed) economies where conditional economic aid can be used to strike bargains with an en-trenched polity. Reforms that would otherwise be unacceptable may become acceptable if the price is right.

It will be useful in this connection to appeal to the four-way classification of nation states shown in Figure 3.1, where the condition of the economy (developed or developing)[68] and the condition of the polity (above or below

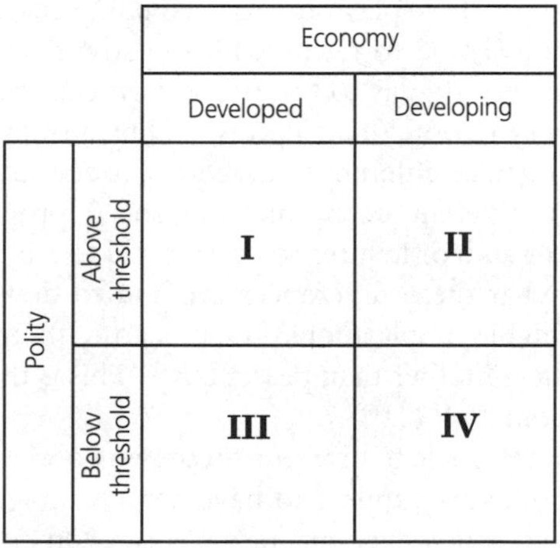

		Economy	
		Developed	Developing
Polity	Above threshold	**I**	**II**
	Below threshold	**III**	**IV**

Fig. 3.1

---

[67] Williamson, *Mechanisms of Governance*, ch. 8.

[68] The World Bank study, (*Bureaucrats in Business*, p. xvii) describes "developing economies" as those in which the 1992 per capita income is $8,355 or less and "industrial economies" as those in which the 1992 per capita income is $8,356 or more. For my purposes, developing economies probably have a lower per capita income, but I do not have a clean cut-off point.

threshold) are the key dimensions. Regarding the second of these, polities are judged to be below threshold if they lack the capacity reliably to deliver de facto democratic outcomes, where failures of democracy can take any of three forms: (1) the polity does not possess the requisite de jure democratic features; (2) the requisite de jure features are present but the conditions of embeddedness to support de facto democracy are lacking; and (3) the requisite de jure and embeddedness features are present but have been defeated by corruption (often with the support of the military). Both totalitarian and authoritarian states are implicated.[69]

5.1 *Cell I: Developed Economy, Above Threshold*

Nation states that are located in this cell are judged to be efficient. This is not to say that all have reached a degree of "perfection," or that differences between them are inconsequential. They are, however, irremediable, in that there is no realistic prospect for general reform. The economic and political institutions out of which such a nation state works are deemed to be acceptable.

Great Britain and France are examples of Cell I entries. It is elementary that the polities in these two countries differ and that these differences have consequential effects on social behavior and economic performance. Because both polities are above threshold, however, the need is to understand what the differences are and how these play out. As each polity is a syndrome of related attributes, we need to come to terms with the strengths and weaknesses of each—in a manner very similar to the transaction cost treatment of markets and hierarchies as a syndrome of attributes.[70] Thus, just as we expect markets and hierarchies to organize different transactions, so should we expect different polities to support different economic and social programs. Rather than regretting differences and/or failures to correspond to a hypothetical ideal, we need to ascertain what these differences are and to develop the systematic consequences (refutable implications) that accrue thereto. Understanding "What's going on here" rather than prescribing "This is the law here" is what the exercise is all about.

To be sure, were it possible to examine these two polities in the context of de novo choice, one polity may appear to have net advantages in relation to the other. De novo choices, however, are rarely posed. On-going polities that are above threshold and that enjoy the assent of the governed are ones for which there is no case for general reform. In that event, any case for reform must rest on policy particulars.

The sugar program discussed in Section 4.3 is an example of such a particular.

---

[69] Barry W. Poulson, *Economic Development* (Minneapolis–St Paul: West Publishing, 1994), p. 98.
[70] Williamson, "Comparative Economic Organization."

If it were the case that this program of redistribution had its origins in an early denial of the voting franchise to a subset of the population on which the current burdens are disproportionately concentrated, or if the deadweight losses of this program had not previously been disclosed and/or are judged to be unacceptably large, or if the program is the convoluted product of events that are deemed ex ante unimaginable and ex post unacceptable, then a judgment of efficiency would be withheld.[71] As it turns out, however, upsetting Stigler's rough-and-ready test-of-time criterion for ascribing efficiency is not easy—which is to say that it is difficult (but not impossible) to deny efficiency on one or more of these grounds.

5.2 Cell II: Developing Economy, Above Threshold

Similar considerations apply to a developing economy—with the added provision, however, that developing economies can sometimes be induced to make changes that developed economies cannot (at least if the economy in question is of only moderate size). Added latitude obtains if and as deals can be made between organizations that are administering economic aid and the polity in the developing country.

Absent an outside offer to supply aid as a condition of reform, the presumption is that the politicians in a country that is above threshold have already struck the deals that are perceived to be cost-effective and mutually beneficial. Subject to the same types of particular exception discussed above, such a state of affairs is deemed to be provisionally efficient. Absent an inducement from outside the system, the prevailing state of affairs is irremediable (and in that sense efficient).

As indicated, however, the conditional supply of aid by an outside agency will sometimes make it possible to strike deals that are perceived as an improvement both by incumbent politicians and by standard welfare economics criteria. What would otherwise be an irremediable condition thus becomes remediable—because a superior feasible alternative can be both described and implemented. The recent World Bank Policy Research Report on *Bureaucrats in Business* is pertinent. As Michael Bruno puts it in his foreword, the report

describes the formidable obstacles governments face when attempting to divest state-owned enterprises or otherwise improve their performance, [yet finds that] . . . some governments have indeed overcome the obstacles. Following a comprehensive reform strategy, they have divested when possible, and improved performance incentives for firms remaining in government hands. Trade and investment have usually followed,

---

[71] Williamson, *Mechanisms of Governance*, ch. 8.

bringing more rapid growth and enhanced opportunities for society at large. But why haven't more governments privatized or otherwise reformed state-owned enterprises? Reform entails political costs. Because politics is integral to reform, a study of reforms in public ownership cannot exclude political analysis. A key finding of the report is that *political obstacles are the main reason that state enterprise reform has made so little headway* in the last decade. The report makes an innovative attempt to objectively disentangle and measure the elements that constitute the political constraints on reform. While this is a significant contribution, we should also bear in mind that our analytical knowledge of political processes, though arguably older, is less complete than that of economic forces and motives. It is an area in which additional analytical work and more data will no doubt enhance our knowledge in the years to come.[72] (emphasis added)

As the authors of the report subsequently develop, the politics of reforming state-owned enterprises turns on three conditions: political desirability, political feasibility, and credibility.[73] On political desirability, transaction cost economics has little to say. The second and third conditions—feasibility and credibility— relate directly to remediableness and credible commitment considerations, both of which are core transaction cost economics concepts. Interestingly, more- over, the third core concept of transaction cost economics—the disabilities that accrue to government bureaucracy—is also pertinent. Thus, although Herbert Simon avers that "careful comparative studies have generally found it hard to identify systematic differences in productivity and efficiency between profit- making ... and publicly-controlled organizations,"[74] the World Bank study vigorously contests that position[75] and provides considerable evidence to the contrary. But for the differential burdens of government bureaucracy, the economic case for privatization would vanish.

The upshot is that transaction cost economics provides much of the requisite conceptual framework within which to deal with the politics and economics of development and reform. Because, however, the action resides in the details, this conceptual framework needs to be joined by deep local knowledge. That combination is precisely what the World Bank team brings.[76]

5.3   *Cell III: Developed Economy, Below Threshold*

Cell III describes authoritarian or totalitarian nation states for which there is little internal economic pressure for reform and for which a feasible economic

---

[72] World Bank, *Bureaucrats in Business*, pp. xi–xii.
[73] Ibid., pp. 10–14.
[74] Herbert Simon, "Organizations and Markets," *Journal of Economic Perspectives*, 5 (1991): 25–44, at p. 38.
[75] World Bank, *Bureaucrats in Business*, pp. 33–50.
[76] The World Bank study "looks at company experience in depth and creatively applies institutional analysis to determine how contracts between management and government can serve as tools to reform enterprises . . . It suggests policy courses to be pursued under different country and enterprise conditions": Ibid., p. xi.

deal to effect reform cannot be presented by outsiders. Such nation states can be condemned as oppressors of human and political rights, which can encourage political dissidents. Realistically, however, major reform is out of the question. At best, minor deals may sometimes be struck on particulars.

Mancur Olson appears to conclude similarly upon posing the question, "What special circumstances explain the cases where a more or less democratic or at least pluralistic government emerges out of an autocracy?"[77] If I understand his response to this query correctly, such reforms are less the product of conscious efforts than they are adventitious: "autocracy is prevented and democracy permitted by the *accidents of history* that leave a balance of power or stalemate—a dispersion of force and resources that makes it impossible for any one leader or group to overpower all of the others" (emphasis added).[78] Although those accidents of history can be identified after the fact, a predictive theory has yet to materialize.[79] If the instruments for a major reshaping of the institutional environment are rarely on the table— cataclysmic events like the Glorious Revolution, or the American Revolution, or the Russian Revolution being beyond the scope of "conscious, deliberate, purposeful" public policy analysis—then that condition needs to be admitted.

5.4 Cell IV: Developing Economy, Below Threshold

As there is greater economic pressure for reform in Cell IV, the possibility of striking a deal is improved. Hard-headed credibility considerations nevertheless apply.

Thus, de jure democratic reform could be for naught if the requisite societal embeddedness conditions are not satisfied.[80] The prospects are better if the informal embeddedness conditions—the sanctions, taboos, customs, traditions, and codes of conduct to which North refers[81]—are in place and the main obstacle is the military. In that event, a move from Cell IV to Cell II with the prospects of Cell I may be possible. But such a move is not easy to orchestrate.

Absent a realistic prospect for general reform, a lowering of sights is needed. Economic aid in the form of humanitarian relief (food, medical assistance) may be the extent of it. To expect a great deal more than this in nations where the relevant embeddedness conditions do not obtain is wishful thinking.

[77] Olson "Dictatorship," p. 573.

[78] Ibid.

[79] The principal example offered by Olson, as well as by North and Weingast, "Constitutions and Commitment," is the Glorious Revolution in England in the 17th cent.: see Olson "Dictatorship," p. 574.

[80] See Weingast, "Political Foundations," for a discussion of the importance of embeddedness.

[81] North, "Institutions," p. 97.

6 Concluding Remarks

My purpose has been to sketch the basic framework and key ideas out of which transaction cost economics works, and thereafter to apply these to the puzzles of economic organization, politics, and economic reform. As developed herein, some of the chronic puzzles in all three of these areas are better explained by going beyond orthodoxy and appealing to comparative contractual reasoning in which credible commitments, bureaucracy, and remediableness are featured.

Of these three concepts, remediableness has the most far-reaching ramifications for reshaping our understanding of economic development and reform. The recurring themes are these: (1) all feasible forms of organization are flawed in relation to a hypothetical ideal; (2) many practices that are regarded as reprehensible when viewed through the lens of price theory/ applied welfare economics actually serve efficiency purposes and/or are not remediable when examined through the lens of transaction cost economics; and (3) the readiness with which many economists and public policy analysts have condemned observed practice and prescribed public policy intervention should give way to more carefully delimited (selective) intervention; also, (4) the action resides in the details.

The key actors in the bottom-up approach to development and reform are the individuals, groups, and firms that are examining the current and prospective economic environment for allocating human and physical assets with reference to the perceived hazards and opportunities. The degree of credibility in the institutional environment turns out to be crucial for this purpose. Regimes that are perceived to be unreliable, unstable, or, even worse, predatory pose hazards. Not only will investments in human and physical capital vary systematically with the nature and magnitude of those hazards, but so likewise will organization.

4 Dictatorship, Democracy, and Development

Mancur Olson[1]

1 Introduction

In my student days, in reading Edward Banfield's account of the beliefs of the people in a poor village in southern Italy, I came upon a remarkable statement by a village monarchist. He said: "Monarchy is the best kind of government because the King is then owner of the country. Like the owner of a house, when the wiring is wrong, he fixes it."[2] The villager's argument jarred against my democratic convictions, although I could not deny that the owner of a country would have an incentive to make his property productive. Could the germ of truth in the monarchist's argument be reconciled with the case for democracy?

It is only in recent years that I have arrived at an answer to this question. It turns out that for a satisfactory answer one needs a new theory of dictatorship and democracy and of how each of these types of government affects economic development. Once this new theory is understood, one can begin to see how autocracies and democracies first emerge. I shall set out this conception in a brief and informal way and use it to explain some of the most conspicuous features of historical experience.

The starting point for the theory is that no society can work satisfactorily if it does not have a peaceful order and usually other public goods as well. Obviously, anarchic violence cannot be rational for a society: the victims of violence and theft lose not only what is taken from them but also the incentive

[1] This article was previously published under the same title in *American Political Science Review*, 87(3) (September 1993): 567–76. It is reprinted with permission of the American Political Science Assocation. I am grateful to the US Agency for International Development for support of my research on this subject through my Center for Institutional Reform and the Informal Sector (IRIS).

[2] Edward Banfield, *The Moral Basis of a Backwards Society* (Glencoe, Ill.: Free Press, 1958), p. 26.

to produce any goods that would be taken by others. There is accordingly little or no production in the absence of a peaceful order. Thus, there are colossal gains from providing domestic tranquility and other basic public goods. These gains can be shared in ways that leave everyone in a society better off. Can we conclude that, because everyone could gain from it, a peaceful order emerges by voluntary agreement?

From the logic of the matter, we should expect that in small groups a generally peaceful order will normally emerge by voluntary agreement but that in large populations it will not. The key to the matter is that each individual bears the full costs or risks of anything he or she does to help establish a peaceful order or to provide other public goods but receives only a share of the benefits. In a tiny group, such as a hunter–gatherer band, each person or family will obtain a significant share of the benefits of a peaceful order, and the net advantages of such an order are so great that even a single family's share of the gains can easily outweigh the sacrifices needed to obtain it. Moreover, when there are only a few, the welfare of each noticeably depends on whether each of the others acts in a group-oriented way. Thus, each family, by making clear that cooperation by another will bring forth its own cooperation but that noncooperation will not, can increase the likelihood that another will match its behavior, thereby increasing the incentive each has to act in the group interest. The theoretical prediction that sufficiently small groups can often organize for collective action is corroborated by countless observations.[3]

This prediction is also in accord with anthropological observations of the most primitive societies. The simplest food-gathering and hunting societies are normally made up of bands that have (including the children) only about 50–100 people. In other words, such a band will normally contain only a few families that need to cooperate. Anthropologists find that primitive tribes normally maintain peace and order by voluntary agreement, and that is to some extent what Tacitus, Caesar, and other classical writers observed among the less advanced Germanic tribes. The most primitive tribes tend to make all important collective decisions by consensus, and many of them do not even have chiefs. When a band becomes too large or disagreement is intense, it may split, but the new bands normally also make decisions by unanimous consent. If a tribe is in the hunting-and-gathering stage, there is also little or no incentive for it to subjugate another tribe or to keep slaves, since captives cannot generate enough surplus above subsistence to justify the costs of guarding them.[4] Thus,

[3] Mancur Olson, *The Logic of Collective Action* (Cambridge, Mass.: Harvard University Press, 1965).

[4] There is quantitative evidence from an exhaustive survey of ethnographic accounts showing that references to slaves are virtually absent in the accounts of the most primitive peoples but are rather common in more advanced agricultural societies. See L. T. Hobhouse, G. C. Wheeler, and M. Ginsberg, *The Material Culture and Social Institutions of Simpler Peoples* (London: Routledge & Kegan Paul, 1965). Slavery is unprofitable in hunting–gathering societies; see Mancur Olson, "Some Historic Variation in Property Institutions," mimeo, (Princeton University, 1967.

within the most primitive tribes of pre-agricultural history, the logical presumption that the great gains from a peaceful order can be achieved by voluntary agreement appears to hold true.

Once peoples learned how to raise crops effectively, production increased, population grew, and large populations needed governments. When there is a large population, the same logic that shows why small groups can act consensually in their common interest tells us that voluntary collective action *cannot* obtain the gains from a peaceful order or other public goods, even when the aggregate net gains from the provision of basic public goods are large.[5] The main reason is that the typical individual in a society with, say, a million people will get only about one-millionth of the gain from a collective good, but will bear the whole cost of whatever he or she does to help provide it, and therefore has little or no incentive to contribute to the provision of the collective good. There is by now a huge theoretical and empirical literature on this point, and the great preponderance of it agrees that, just as small groups can usually engage in spontaneous collectives, very large groups are not able to achieve collective goals through voluntary collective action.[6]

Thus, we should not be surprised that, while there have been much written about the desirability of "social contracts" to obtain the benefits of law and order, no one has ever found a large society that obtained a peaceful order or other public goods through an agreement among the individuals in the society.

··

2 The First Blessing of the Invisible Hand

Why, then, have most populous societies throughout history normally avoided anarchy? An answer came to me by chance when reading about a Chinese warlord.[7] In the 1920s China was in large part under the control of various warlords. These were men who led armed bands with which they conquered some territory and then appointed themselves lords of that territory; they taxed the population heavily and pocketed much of the proceeds. In addition, there

[5] Small tribes can sometimes form federations and thereby increase the number who can obtain collective goods through voluntary action; see Olson, *The Logic of Collective Action*, pp. 62–3. Some of the very earliest agricultural societies may have been of this character. But when the number of small groups itself becomes very large, the large-number problem is evident again and voluntary collective action is infeasible.

[6] For citations to much of the best literature extending and testing the argument in *The Logic of Collective Action*, as well as for valuable new analyses, see Russell Hardin, *Collective Action* (Baltimore: Johns Hopkins University Press, 1982), and Todd Sandler, *Collective Action: Theory and Applications* (Ann Arbor: University of Michigan Press, 1992).

[7] See James E. Sheridan, *Chinese Warlord: The Career of Feng Yu-hsiang* (Stanford: Stanford University Press, 1966).

were *roving bandits*, who plundered and moved on. The warlord Feng Yu-hsiang was noted for the exceptional extent to which he used his army to suppress such bandits and for his defeat of the relatively substantial army of the roving bandit White Wolf. Apparently most people in Feng's domain found him much preferable to the roving bandits.

At first, this seems puzzling: why should warlords, who were *stationary bandits*, continuously stealing from a given group of victims, be preferred, by those victims to roving bandits, who stole but soon departed? The warlords had no claim to legitimacy, and their thefts were distinguished from those of roving bandits only because they took the form of continuing taxation rather than occasional plunder.

The point is, if a bandit rationally settles down and takes his theft in the form of regular taxation, and at the same time maintains a monopoly on theft in his domain, then those from whom he exacts taxes will have an incentive to produce. The rational stationary bandit will take only a *part* of their income in taxes, because he will be able to exact a larger total amount of income from his subjects if he leaves them with an incentive to generate income that he can tax.

If the stationary bandit successfully monopolizes the theft in his domain, then his victims do not need to worry about theft by others. If he steals only through regular taxation, then his subjects know that they can keep whatever proportion of their output is left after they have paid their taxes. Since all of the settled bandit's victims are for him a source of tax payments, he also has an incentive to prohibit the murder or maiming of his subjects. With the rational monopolization of theft—in contrast to uncoordinated competitive theft—the victims of the theft can expect to retain whatever capital they accumulate out of after-tax income and therefore will also have an incentive to save and to invest, thereby increasing future income and tax receipts. The monopolization of theft and the protection of the tax-generating subjects thereby eliminates anarchy. Since the warlord takes a part of total production in the form of tax theft, it will also pay him to provide other public goods whenever the provision of these goods increases taxable income sufficiently.

In a world of roving banditry, there is little or no incentive for anyone to produce or accumulate anything that may be stolen and, thus, there is little for bandits to steal. Bandit rationality, accordingly, induces the bandit leader to seize a given domain, make himself the ruler of that domain, and provide a peaceful order and other public goods for its inhabitants, thereby enabling him to obtain more in tax theft than he could have obtained from migratory plunder.

Thus, we have "the first blessing of the invisible hand": the rational, self-interested leader of a band of roving bandits is led, as though by an invisible hand, to settle down, wear a crown, and replace anarchy with government. The gigantic increase in output that normally arises from the provision of a peaceful order and other public goods gives the stationary bandit a far larger take than he could obtain if he did not provide government.

Thus, government for groups larger than tribes normally arises not because of social contracts or voluntary transactions of any kind, but rather because of rational self-interest among those who can organize the greatest capacity for violence. These violent entrepreneurs naturally do not call themselves bandits but, on the contrary, give themselves and their descendants exalted titles. They sometimes even claim to rule by divine right. Since history is written by the winners, the origins of ruling dynasties are, of course, conventionally explained in terms of lofty motives rather than self-interest. Autocrats of all kinds usually claim that their subjects want them to rule and thereby nourish the unhistorical assumption that government arose out of some kind of voluntary choice. (These claims have an echo in some literature in the "transaction costs" tradition that attempts to explain the emergence of various kinds of governments partly or wholly through voluntary contracts and the costs of the transactions associated with them.[8])

Any individual who has autocratic control over a country will provide public goods to that country because he or she has an "encompassing interest" in it.[9] The extent of the encompassing interest of an office-holder, political party, interest group, monarch, or any other partial or total "owner" of a society varies with the size of the stake in the society. The larger or more encompassing the stake an organization or individual has in a society, the greater the incentive the organization or individual has to take action to provide public goods for the society. If an autocrat received one-third of any increase in the income of his domain in increased tax collections, he would then get one-third of the benefits of the public goods he provided. He would then have an incentive to provide public goods up to the point where the national income rose by the reciprocal of one-third, or three, from his last unit of public good expenditure. Though the society's income and welfare would obviously be greater from a larger expenditure on public goods, the gains to society from the public goods that a rational self-interested autocrat provides are nonetheless often colossal.

[8] See Yoram Barzel, Property Rights and the Evolution of the State, Manuscript (December 1993); Edgar Kiser and Yoram Barzel, "Origins of Democracy in England," *Journal of Rationality and Society*, 3 (1991): 396; Douglass North, *Growth and Structural Change* (New York: W. W. Norton, 1981); and Douglass North and Robert Thomas, *The Rise of the West* (Cambridge: Cambridge University Press, 1973). This literature is most constructive and interesting, but, to the extent to which it tries to explain government in terms of voluntary transactions, it is not convincing. North, while emphasizing transaction costs and contracts, also uses the notion of the "predatory state" and the logic of collective action in his account of the state, so his approach must be distinguished from Barzel's.

[9] For the definition of an encompassing interest and evidence of its importance, see Mancur Olson, *The Rise and Decline of Nations* (New Haven: Yale University Press, 1982). The logical structure of the theory that encompassing interests will be concerned with the outcome for society whereas narrow groups will not is identical with the logic that shows that small groups can engage in voluntary collective action but large groups cannot.

Consider, for example, the gains from replacing a violent anarchy with a minimal degree of public order.

From history, we know that the encompassing interest of the tax-collecting autocrat permits a considerable development of civilization. From not long after the first development of settled agriculture until, say, about the time of the French Revolution, the overwhelming majority of mankind was subject to autocracy and tax theft. History until relatively recent times has been mostly a story of the gradual progress of civilization under stationary bandits interrupted by occasional episodes of roving banditry. From about the time that Sargon's conquests created the empire of Akkad until, say, the time of Louis XVI and Voltaire, there was an impressive development of civilization that occurred in large part under stationary banditry.[10]

3 The Grasping Hand

We can now begin to reconcile the village monarchist's insight and the foregoing argument with the case for democracy. Though the village monarchist was right in saying that the absolute ruler has as much incentive to carry out repairs as the owner of a house, his analogy is nonetheless profoundly misleading. The autocrat is not in a position analogous to the owner of a single house or even to the owner of all housing, but rather to the owner of *all* wealth, both tangible and human, in a country. The autocrat does indeed have an incentive to maintain and increase the productivity of everything and everyone in his domain, and his subjects will gain from this. But he also has an incentive to charge a *monopoly* rent, and to levy this monopoly charge on everything, including human labor.

In other words, the autocratic ruler has an incentive to extract the maximum possible surplus from the whole society and to use it for his own purposes. Exactly the same rational self-interest that makes a roving bandit settle down and provide government for his subjects also makes him extract the maximum possible amount from the society for himself. He will use his monopoly of coercive power to obtain the maximum take in taxes and other exactions.

The consumption of an autocratic ruler is, moreover, not limited by his personal capacities to use food, shelter, or clothing. Though the pyramids, the

[10] Many of the more remarkable advances in civilization, even in historic times, took place in somewhat democratic or nondictatorial societies such as ancient Athens, the Roman Republic, the north Italian city-states, the Netherlands in the 17th cent., and (at least after 1689) Great Britain. The explanation for the disproportionate representation of nonautocratic jurisdictions in human progress is presented below.

palace of Versailles, the Taj Mahal, and even Imelda Marcos's 3,000 pairs of shoes were expensive, the social costs of autocratic leaders arise mostly out of their appetites for military power, international prestige, and larger domains. It took a large proportion of the total output of the Soviet Union, for example, to satisfy the preferences of its dictators.[11]

Some writers use the metaphor of the "predatory state," but this is misleading, even for autocracies. As we saw earlier, a stationary bandit has an encompassing interest in the territory he controls and accordingly provides domestic order and other public goods. Thus, he is not like the wolf that preys on the elk, but more like the rancher who makes sure that his cattle are protected and given water. The metaphor of predation obscures the great superiority of stationary banditry over anarchy and the advances of civilization that have resulted from it. No metaphor or model of even the autocratic state can therefore be correct unless it simultaneously takes account of the stationary bandit's incentive to provide public goods at the same time that he extracts the largest possible net surplus for himself.

Though the forms that stationary banditry has taken over the course of history are diverse, the essence of the matter can be seen by assuming that the autocrat gets all of his receipts in the form of explicit taxation. The rational autocrat will devote some of the resources he obtains through taxation to public goods, but will impose far higher tax rates than are needed to pay for the public goods since he also uses tax collections to maximize his net surplus. The higher the level of provision of public goods, given the tax rate, the higher the society's income and the yield from this tax rate. At the same time, the higher the tax rate, given the level of public good provision, the lower the income of society, since taxes distort incentives.

So what tax rate and what level of public good provision will the rational self-interested autocrat choose? Assume for the moment that the autocrat's level of public good expenditure is given. As Joseph Schumpeter lucidly pointed out, and Ibn Kalduhn sensed much earlier,[12] tax receipts will (if we start with low

---

[11] The theory offered here applies to communist autocracies as much as to other types, though it needs to be elaborated to take account of the "implicit tax-price discrimination" pioneered by Joseph Stalin. This innovation enabled Stalinist regimes to obtain a larger proportion of social output for their own purposes than any other regime had been able to do. This explains Stalin's success in making the Soviet Union a superpower and also the great military capacity of many communist regimes. Furthermore, it generated a unique dependence of the system on its management cadre, which ultimately proved fatal. For how the theory applies to communist autocracies and the societies in transition, see Christopher Clague and Gordon Rausser, eds., *The Emergence of Market Economies in Eastern Europe* (Cambridge, Mass.: Basil Blackwell, 1992), preface and ch. 4; Peter Murrell and Mancur Olson, "The Devolution of Centrally Planned Economies," *Journal of Comparative Economics*, 15 (1991): 239–65; and Mancur Olson, "From Communism to a Market Democracy," unpublished paper, Center for Institutional Reform and the Informal Sector, 1993.

[12] Joseph Schumpeter, "The Crisis of the Tax State," in *Joseph A. Schumpeter: The Economics and Sociology of Capitalism*, ed. Richard Swedberg (Princeton: Princeton University Press, 1991); and Ibn Kalduhn, *The Mugaddimah* trans. Franz Rosenthal (Princeton: Princeton University Press, 1967). Schumpeter's analysis was written in the highly taxed Austria–Hungarian Empire late in World War I.

taxation) increase as tax rates increase, but after the revenue-maximizing rate is reached, higher tax rates distort incentives and reduce income so much that tax collections fall. The rational self-interested autocrat chooses the revenue-maximizing tax rate.

Though the amount collected at any tax rate will vary with the level of public good provision, the revenue-maximizing tax *rate* for the autocrat should not. This optimal tax rate determines exactly how encompassing the interest of the autocrat in the society is; that is, it determines the share of any increase in the national income that he will receive. He will then spend money on public goods up to the point where his last dollar of expenditure on public goods generates a dollar's increase in his share of the national income. At this point, the gain to society will, as we know, be the reciprocal of his share.

Though the subjects of the autocrat are better off than they would be under anarchy, they must endure taxes or other impositions so high that, if they were increased further, income would fall by so much that even the autocrat, who absorbs only a portion of the fall in income in the form of lower tax collections, would be worse off.

There is no lack of historical examples in which autocrats for their own political and military purposes collected as much revenue as they possibly could. Consider the largest autocratic jurisdictions in Western history. The Bourbon kings of France (especially on the eve of the French Revolution) were collecting all they could in taxes. The Habsburg kings of Spain did the same. The Roman Empire ultimately pushed its tax rates at least to the revenue-maximizing level.

4 The Reach of Dictatorships and Democracies Compared

How would government by a rational self-interested autocrat compare with a democracy? Democracies vary so much that no one conclusion can cover all cases. Nonetheless, many practical insights can be obtained by thinking first about one of the simplest democratic situations. This is a situation in which there are two candidates for a presidency or two well-disciplined parties seeking to form the government. This simplifying assumption will be favorable to democratic performance, for it gives the democracy an "encompassing" interest rather like the one that motivates the stationary bandit to provide some public goods. I shall make the opposite assumption later. But throughout, I shall avoid giving democracy an unfair advantage by assuming better motivation. I shall impartially assume that the democratic political leaders are just as self-interested as the stationary bandit and will use any expedient to obtain majority support.

Observation of two party democracies tells us that incumbents like to run on a "you-never-had-it-so-good" record. An incumbent obviously would not leave himself with such a record if, like the self-interested autocrat, he took for himself the largest possible net surplus from the society. But we are too favorable to democracy if we assume that the incumbent party or president will maximize his chances of re-election simply by making the electorate as a whole as well-off as possible.

A candidate needs only a majority to win, and he might be able to "buy" a majority by transferring income from the population at large to a prospective majority. The taxes needed for this transfer would impair incentives and reduce society's output just as an autocrat's redistribution to himself does. Would this competition to buy votes generate as much distortion of incentives through taxation as a rational autocracy does? That is, would a vote-buying democratic leader, like the rational autocrat, have an incentive to push tax rates to the revenue-maximizing level?

No. Though both the majority and the autocrat have an encompassing interest in the society because they control tax collections, the majority in addition earns a significant share of the market income of the society, and this gives it a more encompassing interest in the productivity of the society. The majority's interest in its market earnings induces it to redistribute less to itself than an autocrat redistributes to himself. This is evident if we consider the option that a democratic majority would have if it were at the revenue-maximizing tax rate. At the revenue-maximizing tax rate, a minuscule change in the tax rates will not alter tax collections. A minuscule *increase* in the tax rate will reduce the national income by enough so that, even though a larger percentage of income is taken in taxes, the amount collected remains unchanged; and a tiny *reduction* in the tax rate will increase the national income so much that, even though a smaller percentage is taken in taxes, receipts are unchanged. This is the optimal tax rate for the autocrat because changes in the national income affect his income only by changing tax collections.

But a majority at the revenue-maximizing tax rate is bound to increase its income from a *reduction* in tax rates: when the national income goes up, it not only, like the autocrat, collects taxes on a larger national income, but it also earns more income in the market. So the optimal tax rate for it is bound to be lower than the autocrat's. The easiest arithmetic example comes from supposing that the revenue-maximizing tax rate is one-third and that the majority earns one-third of the national income in the marketplace. The rational autocrat will then find that the last dollar in taxes that he collects reduces the national income by three dollars. One-third of this loss is his loss, so he just breaks even on this last dollar of tax collection and is at his revenue-maximizing rate. But if a majority mistakenly chooses this same tax rate, it would be hurting itself, for it would lose two dollars (the same dollar lost by the autocrat plus one dollar of market income) from the last dollar it collected in taxes. Thus, a majority would maximize its total income with a lower tax rate and a smaller redistribution to itself than would be chosen by an autocrat.[13]

More generally, it pays a ruling interest (whether an autocrat, a majority, or any other) to stop redistributing income to itself when the national income falls by the reciprocal of the share of the national income it receives. If the revenue-maximizing tax rate were one-half, an autocrat would stop increasing taxes when the national income fell by two dollars from his last dollar of tax collection. A majority that, say, earned three-fifths of the national income in the market and found it optimal to transfer one-fifth of the national income to itself would necessarily be reducing the national income by five-fourths, or $1.25, from the last dollar that it redistributed to itself. Thus, the more encompassing an interest—the larger the share of the national income it receives taking all sources together—the less will be the social losses from its redistributions to itself. Conversely, the narrower the interest, the less it will take account of the social costs of redistributions to itself.

This last consideration makes it clear why the assumption that the democracy is governed by an encompassing interest can lead to much too optimistic predictions about many real-world democracies. The small parties that often emerge under proportional representation, for example, may encompass only a tiny percentage of a society and therefore may have little or no incentive to consider the social cost of the steps they take on behalf of their narrow constituencies. The special interest groups that are the main determinant of what government policies prevail in the particular areas of interest to those interest groups have almost no incentive to consider the social costs of the redistributions they obtain. A typical lobby in the United States, for example, represents less than one percent of the income-earning capacity of the country. It follows from the reciprocal rule that such a group has an incentive to stop arranging further redistributions to its clients only when the social costs of the redistribution become at least a hundred times as great as the amount they win in redistributional struggle.[14]

It would therefore be wrong to conclude that democracies will necessarily redistribute less than dictatorships. Their redistributions will, however, be shared, often quite unequally, by the citizenry. Democratic political competition, even when it works very badly, does not give the leader of the

[13] A mathematical and a geometrical proof of this conclusion and an analysis of many other technical questions raised by the present theory is available on request. [Most of these proofs as well as proofs of some other propositions are are now available in Martin C. McGuire and Mancur Olson, "The Economics of Autocracy and Majority Rule: The Invisible Hand and the Use of Force," *The Journal of Economic Literature*, 34 (March 1996): 72–96.

[14] Olson, *Rise and Decline*.

government the incentive that an autocrat has to extract the maximum attainable social surplus from the society to achieve his personal objectives.

....

6 "Long Live the King"

We know that an economy will generate its maximum income only if there is a high rate of investment, and that much of the return on long-term investments is received long after the investments are made. This means that an autocrat who is taking a long view will try to convince his subjects that their assets will be permanently protected not only from theft by others but also from expropriation by the autocrat himself. If his subjects fear expropriation, they will invest less, and in the long run his tax collections will be reduced. To reach the maximum income attainable at a given tax rate, a society will also need to enforce contracts, such as contracts for long-term loans, impartially; but the full gains are, again, reaped only in the long run. To obtain the full advantage from long-run contracts, a country also needs a stable currency. A stationary bandit will therefore reap the maximum harvest in taxes—and his subjects will get the largest gain from his encompassing interest in the productivity of his domain— only if he is taking an indefinitely long view, and only if his subjects have total confidence that their "rights" to private property and to impartial contract enforcement will be permanently respected and that the coin or currency will retain its full value.

Now suppose that an autocrat is concerned only about getting through the next year. He will then gain from expropriating any convenient capital asset whose tax yield over the year is less than its total value. He will also gain from forgetting about the enforcement of long-term contracts, from repudiating his debts, and from coining or printing new money that he can spend, even though this ultimately brings inflation. At the limit, when an autocrat has no reason to consider the future output of the society at all, his incentives will be those of a roving bandit, and that is what he will become.[15]

[15] When war erodes confidence about what the boundaries of an autocrat's domain will be, an autocrat's time horizon with respect to his possession of any given territory shortens—even if he believes he will remain in control of some territory somewhere. In the limit, complete uncertainty about what territory an autocrat will control results in roving banditry. The advantages of stationary banditry over roving banditry are obviously greatest when there are natural and militarily defensible frontiers. Interestingly, the earliest states in history emerged mainly in what one anthropologist call "environmentally circumscribed" areas, that is, areas of arable land surrounded by deserts, mountains, or coasts; see Robert L. Carneiro, "A Theory of the Origin of the State," *Science*, 169 (1970): 733–8. The environmental circumscription not only provides militarily viable frontiers but also limits the opportunity for defeated tribes to flee to other areas in which they could support themselves (as Carneiro points out). This in turn means that the consensual democracy characteristic of the earliest stages of social evolution is, in these geographical conditions, replaced by autocratic states earlier than in other conditions.

To be sure, the rational autocrat will have an incentive, because of his interest in increasing the investment and trade of his subjects, to promise that he will never confiscate wealth or repudiate assets. But the promise of an autocrat is not enforceable by an independent judiciary or any other independent source of power, because autocratic power by definition implies that there cannot be any judges or other sources of power in the society that the autocrat cannot overrule. Because of this and the obvious possibility that any dictator could, because of an insecure hold on power or the absence of an heir, take a short-term view, the promises of an autocrat are never completely credible. Thus, the model of the rational self-interested autocrat I have offered is, in fact, somewhat too sanguine about economic performance under such autocrats because it implicitly assumes that they have (and that their subjects believe that they have) an indefinitely long planning horizon.

Many autocrats have had short time horizons, at least at times: the examples of confiscations, repudiated loans, debased coinages, and inflated currencies perpetrated by monarchs and dictators over the course of history are almost beyond counting.

Perhaps the most interesting evidence about the importance of a monarch's time horizon comes from the historical concern about the longevity of monarchs and from the once-widespread belief in the social desirability of dynasties. There are many ways in which to wish a king well; but the king's subjects, as the foregoing argument shows, have more reason to be sincere when they say "long live the king." If the king anticipates and values dynastic succession, that further lengthens the planning horizon and is good for his subjects.

The historical prevalence of dynastic succession, in spite of the near-zero probability that the son of a king is the most talented person for the job, probably also owes something to another neglected feature of absolutisms. Any ruler with absolute power cannot, by definition, also have an independent source of power within the society that will select the next ruler and impose its choice upon the society. An independent capacity to install a new ruler would imply that this capacity can be used to remove or constrain the present autocrat. Thus, as is evident from modern dictatorships in Africa and Latin America, most dictatorships are by their nature especially susceptible to succession crises and uncertainty about the future. These uncertainties add to the problem of short time horizons that has just been described. In these circumstances, it may be advantageous to a society if a consensus emerges about who the next ruler will probably be, since this reduces the social losses arising from the absence in an autocracy of any independent power that could ensure a smooth succession. Given autocracy, then, dynastic succession can be socially desirable, both because it may reduce the likelihood of succession crises and because it may give monarchs more concern for the long run and the productivity of their societies.

7 Democracy, Individual Rights, and Economic Development

We have seen that, whenever a dictator has a sufficiently short time horizon, it is in his interest to confiscate the property of his subjects, to abrogate any contracts he has signed in borrowing money from them, and generally to ignore the long-run economic consequences of his choices. Even the ever-present possibility that an autocracy will come to be led by someone with a short time horizon always reduces confidence in investments and in the enforcement of long-run contracts.

What do the individuals in an economy need if they are to have the maximum confidence that any property they accumulate will be respected and that any contracts they sign will be impartially enforced? They need a secure government that respects individual rights. But individual rights are normally an artifact of a special set of governmental institutions. There is no private property without government! In a world of roving bandits, some individuals may have possessions, but no one has a claim to private property that is enforced by the society. There is typically no reliable contract enforcement unless there is an impartial court system that can call upon the coercive power of the state to require individuals to honor the contracts they have made.

But individuals need to have their property and their contract rights protected from violation not only by other individuals in the private sector, but also by the entity that has the greatest power in the society, namely, the government itself. An economy will be able to reap all potential gains from investment and from long-term transactions only if it has a government that is believed to be strong enough to last and inhibited from violating individual rights to property and to contract enforcement.

What does a society need in order to have a government that satisfies both of these conditions? Interestingly, the necessary conditions to ensure the individual rights required for maximum economic development are exactly the same conditions that are needed to have a *lasting* democracy. Obviously, a democracy is not viable if individuals, including the leading rivals of the administration in power, lack the rights to free speech and to security for their property and contracts, or if the rule of law is not followed even when it calls for the current administration to leave office. Thus, the same court system, independent judiciary, and respect for law and individual rights that are needed for a lasting democracy are also required for security of property and contract rights.

As the foregoing reasoning suggests, the only societies where individual rights to property and contract are confidently expected to last across generations are the securely democratic societies. In an autocracy, the autocrat will often have a short time horizon, and the absence of any independent power to assure an orderly legal succession means that there is always substantial uncertainty about what will happen when the current autocrat is gone. History provides not a single example of a long and uninterrupted sequence of absolute rulers who continuously respected the property and contract-enforcement rights of their subjects. Admittedly, the terms, tenures, and time horizons of democratic political leaders are perhaps even shorter than those of the typical autocrat, and democracies lose a good deal of efficiency because of this. But in the secure democracy, with predictable succession of power under the rule of law, the adjudication and enforcement of individual rights is not similarly short-sighted. Many individuals in the secure democracies confidently make even very-long-term contracts, establish trusts for great-grandchildren, and create foundations that they expect will last indefinitely, thereby revealing that they expect their legal rights to be secure for the indefinite future.

Not surprisingly, then, capital often flees from countries with continuing or episodic dictatorships (even when these countries have relatively little capital) to the stable democracies, even though the latter are already relatively well supplied with capital and thus offer only modest rates of return. Similarly, the gains from contract-intensive activities such as banking, insurance, and capital markets are also mainly reaped by stable democracies like the United States, the United Kingdom, and Switzerland. Though experience shows that relatively poor countries can grow extraordinarily rapidly when they have a strong dictator who happens to have unusually good economic policies, such growth lasts only for the ruling span of one or two such leaders. It is no accident that the countries that have reached the highest level of economic development and have enjoyed good economic performance across generations are all stable democracies. Democracies have also been about twice as likely to win wars as have dictatorships.[16]

....

8   The Improbable Transition

How do democracies emerge out of autocracies? It is relatively easy to see how autocratic government emerges and why it has been the predominant form of government since the development of settled agriculture: there is

---

[16] David A. Lake, "Powerful Pacifists: Democratic States and War," in *American Political Science Review*, 86 (1992): 24–37.

never a shortage of strong men who enjoy getting a fortune from tax receipts. It is much harder to see how democratic government can emerge out of autocracy.

It is a logical mistake to suppose that, because the subjects of an autocrat suffer from his exactions, they will overthrow him. The same logic of collective action that ensures the absence of social contracts in the historical record, whereby large groups agreed to obtain the advantages of government, also implies that the masses will not overthrow an autocrat simply because they would be better off if they did so. Historical evidence from at least the first pharaohs through Saddam Hussein indicates that resolute autocrats can survive even when they impose heinous amounts of suffering upon their peoples. When they are replaced, it is for other reasons (e.g. succession crises) and often by another stationary bandit.[17] What special circumstances explain the cases where a more or less democratic[18] or at least pluralistic government emerges out of an autocracy?

One obvious special circumstance is that, partly for the reasons just set out, the richest countries are democracies, and democracies have usually prevailed in the competitions with their major autocratic competitors, whether fascist or communist. The triumphant democracies have sometimes encouraged or subsidized transitions to democracy in other countries. In some cases, such as Germany, Japan, and Italy after World War II, the victorious democracies more or less demanded democratic institutions as a price for giving independence to the vanquished nations. The theoretical challenge is to explain not these transitions, but rather those that are entirely internal and spontaneous.

Easy as it would be to argue that the initially or spontaneously democratic countries were blessed with democratic cultures or selfless leaders, this would be an ad hoc evasion. The obligation here is to explain the spontaneous transitions to democracy from the same parsimonious theory that has been used in the rest of this essay.

The theory suggests that the key to an explanation of the spontaneous emergence of democracy is the *absence* of the commonplace conditions that generate autocracy. The task is to explain why a leader who organized the overthrow of an autocrat would not make himself the next dictator, or why any group of conspirators who overthrew an autocrat would not form a governing junta. We have seen that autocracy is a most profitable occupation and that the authors of most coups and upheavals have appointed themselves dictators. So

---

[17] For more examples of other types of reason, see Mancur Olson, "The Logic of Collective Action in Soviet-Type Societies," *Journal of Soviet Nationalities*, 1(2) (1990): 8–33.

[18] In the interest of brevity, democracy is here defined as competitive elections, social pluralism, and the absence of autocracy, rather than in terms of universal suffrage. Although how a narrower suffrage turns into a wider suffrage can be explained by straightforward extensions of the logic of the theory offered here, developing these extensions and testing them against the historical evidence would not be a small undertaking.

the theory here predicts that democracy would be most likely to emerge spontaneously when the individual or individuals or group leaders who orchestrated the overthrow of an autocracy could not establish another autocracy, much as they would gain from doing so. We can deduce from the theory offered here that autocracy is prevented and democracy permitted by the accidents of history that leave a balance of power or a stalemate—a dispersion of force and resources that makes it impossible for any one leader or group to overpower all of the others.

But this deduction does not give us any *original* conclusion: rather, it points directly toward one of the major inductive findings in some of the literature in history and in political science on the emergence of democracy. If the theory here is right, there must be a considerable element of truth in the famous "Whig interpretation" of British history and in the explanations of democracy offered by political scientists such as Robert Dahl and, especially, Tatu Vanhanen.[19] If the theory offered here is right, then the literature that argues that the emergence of democracy is due to historical conditions and dispersions of resources that make it impossible for any one leader or group to assume all power is right.

Yet it is also necessary to go back again to the theory for a crucial detail. Even when there is a balance of power that keeps any one leader or group from assuming total control of a large area or jurisdiction, the leader of each group may be able to establish himself as an autocrat of a small domain. A dispersion of power and resources over a large area can result in a set of small-scale autocracies but no democracy. If, however, the different contending groups are scrambled together over a wide and well delineated domain, then small autocracies are not feasible, either. They may not be feasible also if each of the leaders capable of forming a small-scale autocracy believes that a domain of that small scale would not be viable, whether because of aggression by other autocrats or for any reason.

If scrambled constituencies or any other reason rules out division of a domain into mini-autocracies, then the best attainable option for the leader of each group when there is a balance of power is power sharing. If no one leader can subdue the others or segregate his followers into a separate domain, then the only alternatives are either to engage in fruitless fighting or to work out a truce with mutual toleration. The provision of a peaceful order and other public goods will, in these circumstances, be advantageous for all of the groups; thus, the leaders of the different groups have an incentive to work out mutually satisfactory arrangements for the provision of such goods. Given peaceful conditions, there are great gains to leaders and other individuals in each

---

[19]   Robert Dahl, *Polyarchy: Participation and Opposition* (New Haven: Yale University Press, 1971) and Tatu Vanhanen, "The Level of Democratization Related to Socioeconomic Variables in 147 States in 1980–85," *Scandinavian Political Studies*, 12 (1989): 95–127.

group from being able to make mutually advantageous contracts with others, and therefore there is a common interest in establishing a disinterested and independent judiciary. With several groups, it is not certain in advance how elections will turn out, yet each group can, by allying with other groups, insure that no one other group will continually dominate elections. Thus, elections as well as consensual agreements among the leaders of the different groups can be consistent with the interest of the leaders and members of each group.

Though there are a fair number of democracies, there have not been many spontaneous and entirely autonomous transitions from autocracy to democracy. Most of the democracies in the English-speaking world owe a good deal to the pluralism and democracy that emerged in late seventeenth-century Britain, and thus do not tend to offer a completely independent test of the argument about the transition to democracy offered here.

Happily, the initial emergence of democracy with the Glorious Revolution of 1689 in England (and its very gradual transition from a democracy with a highly restricted franchise to universal suffrage) nicely fits the logic of the democratic transition predicted by the present theory. There were no lasting winners in the English civil wars. The different tendencies in British Protestantism and the economic and social forces with which they were linked were more or less evenly matched. There had been a lot of costly fighting, and, certainly after Cromwell, no one had the power to defeat all of the others. The restored Stuart kings might have been able to do this, but their many mistakes and the choices that ultimately united almost all of the normally conflicting Protestant and other political tendencies against them finally led to their total defeat.

None of the victorious leaders, groups, or tendencies was then strong enough to impose its will upon all of the others or to create a new autocracy. None had any incentive to give William and Mary the power to establish one, either. The best option available to each of the leaders and groups with power was to agree upon the ascendancy of a parliament that included them all and to take out some insurance against the power of the others through an independent judiciary and a Bill of Rights. (The spread of the franchise is too long a story to tell here. But it is not difficult to see how, once the society was definitely non-autocratic and safely pluralist, additional groups could parlay the profitable interactions that particular enfranchised interests had with them— and the costs of suppression that they could force the enfranchised to bear— into a wider suffrage.)

With a carefully constrained monarchy, an independent judiciary, and a Bill of Rights, people in England in due course came to have a relatively high degree of confidence that any contracts they entered into would be impartially enforced and that private property rights, even those of critics of the government, were relatively secure. Individual rights to property and contract enforcement were probably more secure in Britain after 1689 than anywhere else, and it was in Britain, not very long after the Glorious Revolution, that the Industrial Revolution began.[20]

Though the emergence of a democratic national government in the United States (and in some other areas of British settlement, such as Australia and Canada) was due partly to the example or influence of Great Britain, it also was due in part to the absence of any one group or colonial government that was capable of suppressing the others. The thirteen colonies were different from one another even on such important matters as slavery and religion, and none of them had the power to control the others. The separate colonies had, in general, experienced a considerable degree of internal democracy under British rule, and many of the colonies, because of the different religious and economic groups they contained, were also internally diverse. Many of the authors of the US Constitution were, of course, also profoundly aware of the importance of retaining a dispersion of power (checks and balances) that would prevent autocracy.

9 The Different Sources of Progress in Autocracies and Democracies

Since human nature is profoundly complex and individuals rarely act out of unmixed motives, the caricature assumption of rational self-interest that I have been using to develop this theory is obviously much too simple to do justice to reality. But it has not only simplified a forbiddingly complex reality but has also introduced an element of impartiality: the same motivation was assumed in all regimes. The results are probably robust enough to hold also under richer and more realistic behavioral assumptions.

The use of the same motivational assumption and the same theory to treat both autocracy and democracy also illuminates the main difference in the sources of economic growth and the obstacles to progress under autocracy and under democracy. In an autocracy, the source of order and the provision of other public goods, and likewise the source of the social progress that these public goods make possible, is the encompassing interest of the autocrat. The main obstacle to long-run progress in autocracies is that individual rights, even

---

[20] For striking evidence on how the growth of cities was much greater in medieval and early modern Europe in democratic or less autocratic regimes, see J. Bradford De Long and Andrei Shleifer, "Princes and Merchants: European City Growth before the Industrial Revolution," mimeo, Harvard University, 1992. In effect, the De Long–Shleifer paper is a test of the advantages of democracy that I put forward. [For a citation to the now-published paper and for a further development of the argument, see Ch. 5 below. *Eds.*]

to such relatively unpolitical or economic matters as property and contracts, can never be secure, at least over the long run.

Although democracies can also obtain great advantages from encompassing offices and political parties, this is by no means always understood;[21] nor are the awesome difficulties in keeping narrow special interests from dominating economic policy-making in the long-stable democracy. On the other hand, democracies have the great advantage of preventing a significant extraction of social surplus by their leaders. They also have the extraordinary virtue that the same emphasis on individual rights that is necessary to lasting democracy is also necessary both for securing rights to property and for enforcing contracts. The moral appeal of democracy is now almost universally appreciated, but its economic advantages are scarcely understood.

---

[21] Olson, *Rise and Decline*, and Mancur Olson, "A Theory of the Incentives Facing Political Organizations: Neo-corporatism and the Hegemonic State," *International Political Science Review*, 7 (1986): 165–89.

5 Overstrong Against Thyself: War, the State, and Growth in Europe on the Eve of the Industrial Revolution

J. Bradford De Long[1]

1 Introduction

1.1 The Problem

Begin with two observations. The first is from Mancur Olson:

[T]here is a strange dualism . . . In the absence of government, a powerful individual may physically possess something, but no one has any enforceable rights—there is no private property without government. Neither are there contracts, corporations, or patents . . .

[But] just as governments are essential for [economic development], so governments are also the greatest threat . . . [Only] governments . . . can expropriate property on a large scale . . . Thus, we arrive at the paradox . . . sustained economic development may require governments that are strong enough to last indefinitely, yet so limited and restrained that they do not use their overwhelming power to abrogate individual rights . . .[2]

[1] I would like to thank Greg Clark, Mancur Olson, Andrei Shleifer, and Jeffrey Weintraub for helpful discussions. The title is from John Milton, *Samson Agonistes*. Parts of the research underlying this paper have been supported by IRIS (the Institutional Reform and the Informal Sector center at the University of Maryland), by the National Science Foundation, and by the Alfred P. Sloan Foundation.

[2] Mancur Olson, "The Logic of Collective Action in Soviet-Type Societies," *Journal of Soviet Nationalities*, 1(2) (1990): 8–33.

The second is a comment made by a not-very-senior White House official after an inconclusive Clinton administration trade policy meeting:

What you economists don't see, is that you are pushing for the public interest. But there are other interests that can be more important.

I was outraged. What is the public interest but the appropriate utilitarian sum of private interests? What interest could possibly be more important?

But indeed, there *are* interests that are more important. Whether rulers feel themselves responsible to themselves alone, to God, or to the electorate; whether they sit in Washington's White House, in Agra's Red Fort, or in London's St James Palace, there are always other interests than the public interest in economic prosperity and development. "The President can't win reelection unless he carries Macomb County, and this is very important in Macomb County." "The protestant succession is not secure unless the king's dynastic interests in Germany are protected." "The smallholders and the unions are the political base of this government, and this policy is not in their interests." "No government in this country can survive large-scale urban discontent, so the price of imported foodstuffs in the capital must be kept low."

The brutal fact is that policies that generate sustained long-run economic growth *must* rank far down the list of concerns of those who meet in palace conference rooms to make policy. Maintaining the splendor and state appropriate for a prince; military survival; military conquest; redistribution of wealth *downward* in the income distribution to improve social welfare; redistribution of wealth *upward* to make the politically powerful happy—all these compete with policies that promise to increase the size of the pie but take a generation or more to do so.

Thus, a government—at least, a modern government able to enforce its writ throughout its territory—is "overstrong against thyself." The reference is to John Milton's *Samson Agonistes*, where Samson pulls down the temple of Dagon, killing the Philistines and himself. Since 1500 or so, governments have acquired enormous strength, not least from their ability to mobilize a larger share of their territories' resources to achieve their goals. And in many cases they have used their strength—their ability to tax and to mobilize—in a way that has brought their economies down in ruins, or at least into stagnation.

Some—like the anthropologist Ernest Gellner—believe that this trap that the growth of government sets for economic growth is the near-inevitable destiny of human societies. Growth and prosperity lead to powerful governments and priesthoods. Powerful governments and priesthoods can appropriate and mobilize resources from producers to achieve their goals. And their goals are not further economic growth and prosperity. As Gellner has written:

[Since the invention of agriculture] society as such is a trap, and moreover one from which it was almost impossible for mankind to escape. A stored surplus needs to be guarded and its distribution enforced. No principle of distribution is either self-validating or self-enforcing. Conflict is inevitable, and victors have every interest in permitting a return match . . . Few agrarian societies escape . . . Looking at those caught in the agrarian trap, we know that but for the Grace of God that would be our condition . . .[3]

We can see this trap in operation throughout history. Consider early modern Europe, where mercantile prosperity and imperial conquest gave great power to the Spanish king, which he used to try to reconquer northern Europe for the Catholic Church. Mercantile prosperity in Spain stagnated under the burden of this aggressive program of conquest and expansion. The other great powers of Europe also found sustaining economic growth inconsistent with the burden of achieving the politico-military goals of the rulers.

In early modern Europe, only one emerging European nation-state—Great Britain—managed to continue to grow its economy under the burden of maintaining the military effort required of an early modern European great power.

1.2 The Stakes

That the British economy did continue to grow under this burden—and triggered the Industrial Revolution—is of enormous importance to us. Without it we would not be here today. There is an alternative world, in which the British economy—like the economies of the continental European "great powers" of the early modern period—staggered under the burden of eighteenth-century war, and economic and mercantile activity regressed. Were we in that alternative world today, we might look at the burst of mercantile prosperity and growth in early modern Europe much as we look at the similar burst of prosperity in China under the Sung dynasty or in Greece after the Persian Wars—as a relatively happy era in human history, but one cut short and followed by stagnation owing to war and politics.

Instead, the human race today consists of perhaps a billion people to whom technology and enterprise give a standard of living that emperors of earlier centuries might envy. Look at the styles of life of the middle class in the developed world, or of educated elites in the developing world. Are their standards of living inferior to those of past emperors—like Tokugawa Ieyasu, Chandragupta Maurya, or Marcus Aurelius Antoninus? On an optimistic reading, perhaps three billion more people are on the "escalator to modernity"—living significantly better than their ancestors, and looking forward to a future in which their children will live better still. We may have

---

[3] Ernest Gellner, "Introduction," in Jean Baechler, John Halt, and Michael Mann, eds., *Europe and the Rise of Capitalism* (London: Blackwell, 1988).

escaped the trap in which most of humanity endured a low standard of living near subsistence, and where kings and priests skimmed off the surplus to accomplish their own projects unrelated to sustained economic growth.

Then again, we may not have permanently escaped the trap. There are today about one and a half billion people, several hundred million of them in India, who are *not* living better than their ancestors, and are *not* looking forward to significant improvement in material welfare over the next generation. There *is* a level of population at which our technological mastery would just keep the population fed, and Malthus's extremely unpleasant "positive checks" on population growth would come into operation once again. Regions in which more than 300 million people are living today may be under water by the end of the next century as a result of global warming. The world is not Utopia; only optimists think that it is rapidly moving toward Utopia. But the Industrial Revolution has at least opened the possibility that, if we manage our collective destiny properly, the human race will move toward Utopia in the future.

Our stake in the success of the Industrial Revolution is large: without it, we would probably be trapped in the traditional pattern of human civilization, with the bulk of the population made up of low-productivity near-subsistence artisans and farmers, and a brutal elite skimming off the surplus, instead of having at least the chance of attaining a permanently better destiny. We have a strong interest in understanding how, exactly, humanity achieved the Industrial Revolution.

There is an additional factor. Today's governments have goals and aims different from and more extensive than the conquest-and-splendor governments of earlier centuries: the redistribution of income in an egalitarian direction, and the redistribution of wealth in the direction of groups whose favor is politically essential for the ruling government. But the fundamental logic of rulership—and the temptation to sacrifice policies to achieve long-run growth to other goals—remains. Thus, the expanded role of the government has made taming government more urgent for us.

So how did first northwestern Europe, and then Great Britain, escape the trap of a government "overstrong against thyself"?

....

2 Princes and Merchants in Europe

2.1 The "Backwardness" of Europe

In the grandest sweep of world history, northwestern Europe is a backward region. Two thousand and fifty years ago the Roman politician Cicero could dismiss the island of Great Britain as a region not worth conquering because it was inhabited by barbarians too stupid even to make good slaves. It had no business being the most technologically advanced part of the world, and the home of transcontinental empires, in the second half of the millennium just coming to an end.

Looking down on earth from outer space a thousand, or two thousand, or three thousand years ago, northwestern Europe does not look like a region with high agricultural productivity, with a high middle-class standard of living, or a region that is likely to see an industrial revolution. High on the list must come the valleys of the Yellow, Yangtze, Ganges, Indus, Euphrates, and Nile Rivers, with perhaps other regions like Japan, Java, Al-Andalus, and the eastern Mediterranean basin. But northwestern Europe does not even make it onto the list of regions where an industrial revolution *might* be possible until about five centuries ago.

Between ten and five centuries ago a cessation of invasions, an improvement in climate, and the slow upward pressure of technological progress allowed Europe's populations to recover (see Figure 5.1). Population had recovered from the lows it had reached in the "Dark Ages." Although population growth was slow and interrupted by plague and famine, improvements in the basic agricultural technology needed to farm the heavy, forest soils of Europe meant that by 1600 or 1700 Europe could support a population of 80 million or so—perhaps twice its level under the Roman Empire (see Figure 5.2).

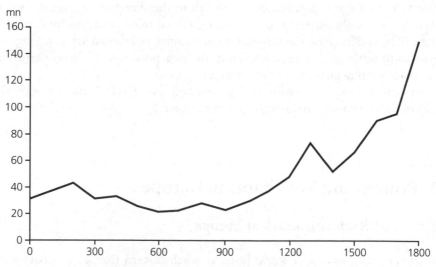

Fig. 5.1 European Population up to 1800

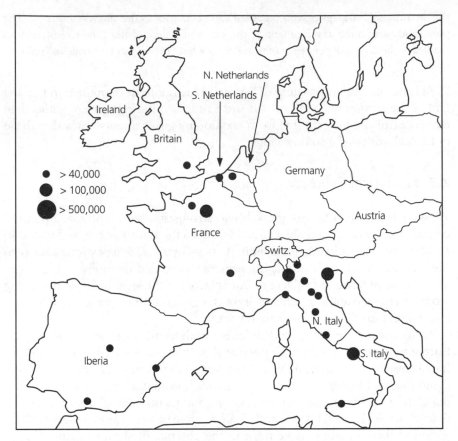

Fig. 5.2 Population of European Cities, *c.* 1500

2.2 *Princes and Merchants*

As the historian Charles Wilson noted, there is an interesting pattern to the growth of European cities:

The two areas which in 1500 represented the richest and most advanced concentrations of trade, industry, and wealth were the quadrilateral formed by the Italian cities Milan, Venice, Florence, and Genoa; and the strip of the [southern] Netherlands that ran from Ypres north-east past Ghent and Bruges up to Antwerp. It was not merely coincidence that these were the areas where the tradesmen of the cities had been most successful in emancipating themselves from feudal interference, and in keeping at bay the newer threat of more centralized political control offered by the new monarchies. In the fleeting intervals between the storms of politics and war, men here glimpsed the material advance that was possible when tradesmen were left in peace unflattered by the attentions of strategists who regarded their activities as the sinews of war . . . The precocious economic development of the cities of Italy and the Low Countries was cradled in the civic independence of those cities where merchants had achieved political power . . .[4]

At least one important cause of European *mercantile* development in the first half of the second millennium was the existence of self-governing cities, free from control and by large free from taxation by governments—whether those of feudal lords or of absolutist kings.

2.3 *Statistical Evidence*

Wilson's eye noted that city growth was strongest where centralized political control was weak. Andrei Shleifer and I noticed the same pattern, and wrote an article in 1993 quantifying this insight.[5] City growth had a very strong allergy to the presence of strong, centralizing princes who called themselves "absolute" in the sense of being not subject to but creators of the legal order, and a strong attraction to mercantile republics: city-states governed by representative or not-so-representative oligarchies of merchants.

According to De Long and Shleifer, each century in which a western European region (one of nine that we analyzed: Iberia, southern Italy, northern Italy, Austria, Germany, France, southern Low Countries, northern Low Countries, and Britain) was ruled by a strong "absolutist" prince saw its urban population fall by roughly 180,000 people, and its number of cities with more than 30,000 fall by roughly one and a half, relative to what the experience of *that* region in *that* era would have been in the absence of absolutist rule. If each region in Europe had experienced an additional century and a half of absolutist rule before 1650, the urban population living in cities of 30,000 or more in 1650 would have been reduced from 4.7 to 2.6 million. Instead of 40 or so cities of more than 30,000, with 10 cities of 100,000 population or more, Europe in 1650 might have had some 22 cities of more than 30,000, with 6 cities of 100,000 population or more—approximately the degree of urbanization that Europe had possessed in 1200, and probably insufficient to support the mercantile prosperity and web of exchange that was a necessary precondition for the Industrial Revolution[6] (see Table 5.1).

[4] Charles W. Wilson, "Trade, Society, and the State," in *The Cambridge Economic History of Europe*, vol. IV, *The Economy of Expanding Europe in the Sixteenth and Seventeenth Centuries* (Cambridge: Cambridge University Press, 1967).

[5] J. Bradford De Long and Andrei Shleifer, "Princes and Merchants: European City Growth Before the Industrial Revolution," *Journal of Law and Economics*, 30(2) (October 1993): 671–702.

[6] Applying the quantitative estimates to the Continent as a whole may overestimate the impact of political régimes on economic growth: perhaps absolutist rule by strong princes displaced city growth beyond their borders to some degree, rather than crippling urban growth in absolute terms. But there is no doubt that freedom from rule by a strong prince was a prerequisite of urban growth in pre-industrial Europe.

Table 5.1 Basic Regression Results: People, Cities, or Proportion of Cities per Century

Dependent variable	Effect of strong princely rule	Variance explained	Standard error	Region controls?	Era controls?
Growth in population of cities over 30,000	−178.47 (48.53)	0.70	156.70	Yes	Yes
Growth in population of cities over 30,000	−79.65 (40.40)	0.48	185.13	No	Yes
Growth in number of cities over 30,000	−2.28 (0.82)	0.54	2.63	Yes	Yes
Growth in number of cities over 30,000	−1.52 (0.60)	0.36	2.75	No	Yes
Proportional growth in population of cities over 30,000	−0.30 (0.24)	0.49	0.76	Yes	Yes
Proportional growth in population of cities over 30,000	−0.15 (0.16)	0.37	0.76	No	Yes

2.4 *Directions of Causation*

Could high urban populations be a cause rather than a consequence of freedom from rule by strong princes? Perhaps city-states with ample populations were good at hiring soldiers to fight off attempts to incorporate them into nascent empires.

Of course. But this does not lead us to doubt *our* interpretation of the importance of freedom from a strong state. The underlying variation on which the estimates of De Long and Shleifer are based is the result of the political and military accidents of European history. For example, Friedrich I von Hohenstaufen, "Red Beard," loses his wars to bring northern Italy under his control, and its city-states remain independent; Robert I d'Hauteville, "the Crafty," and his brothers win their wars to bring southern Italy under their control, and its city-states become part of the "prototype absolutism" that was the Kingdom of Sicily in the first few centuries of this millennium. In the year 1000, southern Italy outstripped northern Italy in agricultural productivity, population, and urbanization; by 1500, after five centuries of absolutist rule in the south, southern Italy was a backwater compared with the productive and urban north.

For another example, the Spanish King Felipe II Habsburg, "the Prudent," sends his lieutenant the Duke of Alba to impose royal power on and suppress heresy in the Low Countries. Alba's government, the "Council of Blood," triggers wide-scale revolt. This was brought under control in the southern half, but in the northern half water barriers and the navy of the embryonic Republic of the Netherlands provide an edge that allows the Dutch Revolt of Willem I Nassau, "the Silent," to succeed. Thereafter the northern provinces that were to become the modern-day Netherlands flourish, while the southern provinces that were to become modern-day Belgium stagnate for centuries.

All these wars could have ended otherwise, and nearly did.

2.5 Incentives of the Rulers

Why should the success of an urban region at maintaining effective political independence be so important a determinant of growth and prosperity?

In pre-industrial Europe, a city-state was typically ruled by an oligarchy of merchant-burghers. Larger units—dutchies, kingdoms, and empires—were ruled by quasi-hereditary princes whose professions were those of warriors. The origins of the medieval European city as a center of commerce with a dominant class made up of merchants (rather than, for example, a dwelling place of landlords, or a center of religion) are obscure and complex.[7]

Nevertheless, the fact that European city-states were ruled by merchants who had a direct interest in economic prosperity—while larger units were ruled by princes whose only similar direct interest was in military power—had important consequences. Consider a ruler who "taxes" an economy, where taxes are interpreted, very broadly, to include *all* transfers to the state or its functionaries, from the cost imposed on citizens forced to quarter soldiers in their homes to sums of money paid to royal justiciars to get them to hear one's legal case. Denote by t this "tax" rate imposed on an economy, with total productive output $X(t)$, and assume that, as the tax rate goes up, the productivity of the private economy declines:

$$(1) \qquad \frac{dX(t)}{dt} < 0.$$

At what rate did such a ruler choose to tax? A prince sought to maximize "revenue"—either for opulent display, to fight off invasions from neighboring princes, or for offensive war. In most cases a strong prince found the pressure to spend every possible shilling, florin, and guilder on war irresistible: as much as 90 percent of revenue was spent on war. Thus, a prince found himself driven to pushing the "tax" rate up until:

$$(2) \qquad t = \frac{X(t)}{-(dX(t)/dt)}.$$

This is the "Laffer" tax rate, as in Brennan and Buchanan[8] (see Figure 5.3).

A far-sighted prince interested in fighting off next year's invasion as well as

[7] Max Weber, *Economy and Society* (Berkeley: University of California, 1968).
[8] Geoffrey Brennan and James M. Buchanan, *The Power to Tax: Analytical Foundations of a Fiscal Constitution* (Cambridge: Cambridge University Press, 1980).

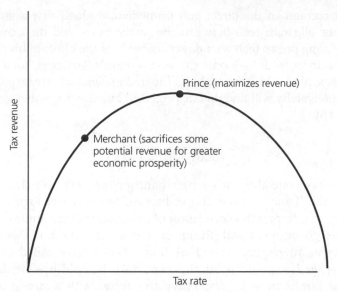

Fig. 5.3 Choice of "Taxation" for Princely and Merchant-Dominated Governments

this year's, or one with confidence in the stability of the dynasty,[9] may perform the revenue maximization calculation implicit in (2) over a long time horizon. A beneficent prince may shade the tax rate downward; a prince who values cruelty and the brutal display of power for its own sake may shade it upward above the level that satisfies equation (2); but the logic of the situation forces the prince toward a revenue-maximizing tax rate.

Consider, by contrast, government by merchant oligarchs, or more generally a government in which landlords or burghers with substantial private wealth have an important role in powerful representative assemblies. Their well-being depends to a considerable extent on their private incomes. And their private incomes depend on economic prosperity. And an increase in state revenue will seem to them no bargain if it leaves their businesses and rents impoverished.

For example, Lorenzo di Medici, "the magnificent," guided the government of Florence for half of the fifteenth century. Yet his prestige and comfort depended not so much on the revenues in the city's treasury as on the prosperity of the Medici Bank. Self-interested merchants and landlords, then, have objectives more appropriately modeled by some function,

(3) $$tX(t) + U[X(t)],$$

[9] But no one should believe that dynasties are stable. Consider, for example, the kings of England between 1066 and 1715. As De Long and Shleifer document in "Princes and Merchants", something went seriously awry in 18 of the 31 royal successions in this period. There was only a 13% chance that the legitimate heir who was grandson, granddaughter, grandnephew, or other relative of an English monarch would inherit the throne without disturbance in the line of succession.

that takes account of the direct and immediate tradeoff that a government of merchant oligarchs feels between the public purse and their own private purses. A ruling prince feels an indirect tradeoff, as the effect of his policies on economic activity feeds back onto the government's resources; but a merchant oligarch must place a higher weight on the maintenance of private prosperity.

Such an oligarchy will find that its preferred tax rate is not that given by (2) but instead by

$$t = \frac{X(t)}{-(dX(t)/dt)} - \frac{dU[X(t)]}{dX(t)}.$$

Thus, the "tax" rate that such a merchant government will choose will be lower than the "Laffer" tax rate chosen by a ruling prince (see Figure 5.4).

One way to interpret this correlation of independent mercantile domination of city-state government with European economic growth is that economic growth seems to require what Karl Marx would have called the *political hegemony of the bourgeoisie*: political power must be held by—or the holders of political power must be responsive to—those with a strong interest in economic development. Lacking this political configuration, economic growth will slow and stagnate, for the state's potential demands are unlimited. Thus, Marx's emphasis on the need for political revolution before capitalism—and economic growth—can flourish: the "feudal" or the "absolutist" government forms a superstructure incompatible with the requirements of the mode of

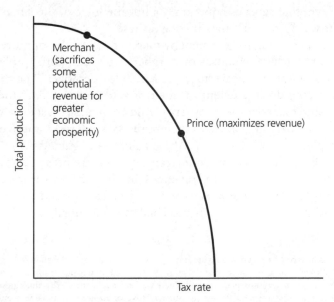

Fig. 5.4 Total Economic Activity for Princely and Merchant-Dominated Governments

production, and must be replaced if there is to be progress rather than the "mutual ruin of the contending parties."

At least one road to successful development requires the establishing of identity between political rulers and economic entrepreneurs interested in growth, or at least the establishing of a community of interest between those two groups.

2.6 The Weakness of Europe's Military Aristocracies

Many loose ends remain. How did Europe's city-states evolve their peculiar political structure? What was it about the culture that allowed economic growth to take advantage of the political opening created? But there is one loose end that is overriding. How can merchants—specialists in production and exchange—maintain political control, even in limited regions, against princes—specialists in violence and coercion? This is a serious problem—so serious that nowhere else in this millennium do we see anything like the regions of substantively independent self-governing city-states seen in Europe.

In the civilizations of Islam, for example, the great historian-statesman Ibn Khaldun describes an urban, mercantile world always subject to invasion and conquest by nomadic warrior societies. The standard way of ensuring civil order is to allow and encourage one of the warrior clans to become rulers and protectors. But, as Ibn Khaldun[10] saw the cycle—in which he participated—the cultural consequences for a warrior aristocracy of being the ruling class of an urban, mercantile civilization undermine its ability to provide an effective defense. And a century later, the urban, mercantile civilization finds itself once again without effective defense against the next wave of invasion and conquest.

It is difficult to escape the conclusion that the military successes of self-governing city-states in Europe owe a great deal to the relative incompetence and ineptness of Europe's warrior aristocracies in the first half of this millennium.

Certainly European military technology does not seem to have been up to the standards of Asia and North Africa. Those parts of Europe, including Hungary and Silesia, subjected to a Mongol reconnaissance-in-force in the early thirteenth century were unable to offer any effective resistance.

2.7 The End of the City-State Era

European kings and princes, however, did not remain relatively weak forever. In the middle of the twelfth century the German emperor Friedrich I von Hohenstaufen, "Red Beard," and at the beginning of the fourteenth century the

[10] Ibn Kahldun, *The Mugadimmah* (Princeton: Princeton University Press, 1967).

French king Philippe IV Capet, "the Handsome," would send their armies south and north, respectively, to attempt to establish their authority and rule over the city-states of Flanders and of Lombardy. Both met with disaster. The militia of the Weaver's Guild of Flanders unhorsed so many French knights at the Battle of Courtrai that it is also called the "Battle of the Golden Spurs"—after the golden spurs the knights wore that were taken as booty by the weavers. The pikemen of the Lombard League inflicted a decisive defeat on Friedrich's army at Legnano, which led to the Peace of Konstanz—at which Friedrich I abandoned all claims to jurisdiction over or revenues from the city-states of northern Italy.

However, a whole complex of technological, organizational, and political changes—usually called the "military revolution"—greatly amplified the ability of European princes to mobilize and sustain large armies, and brought the era of city-state autonomy to an end in the sixteenth century. In the mid-sixteenth century the king of Spain, Felipe II Habsburg "the Prudent," sent an army north to the Low Countries under the command of his favorite, Fernando Alvarez de Toledo, the Duke of Alba. His government, called either the "Council of Troubles" or the "Council of Blood," had no trouble suppressing resistance in defense of the region's traditional "liberties"—until the failure of the over-committed Spanish government to pay the army triggered a mutiny. The only obstacle the armies of the father of Felipe II, Charles V of Ghent, had faced in their conquest of northern Italy were the armies of the French king Francois I Valois—the forces of the Italian city-states themselves were simply not an obstacle.

3 The Military Revolution

3.1 Technology and Organization

Thus, between 1500 and 1600, the military—political dynamic of Europe changed drastically. In the late fifteenth century, when the kings of France began to launch military expeditions into northern Italy, the total sizes of armies mobilized was quite small—perhaps 20,000 soldiers in the expeditionary force, and perhaps 50,000 *at most* on all frontiers and garrisons. But by the middle of the sixteenth century, Charles V Habsburg "of Ghent"—King of Aragon and Castile, Count of Burgundy, Emperor of the Holy Roman Empire, Archduke of Austria, King of Hungary, Bohemia, etc.—would mobilize on the order of 150,000 soldiers for the last stage of his lifelong wars with France (see Figure 5.5).

The sources of this "military revolution" were many. First came changes in

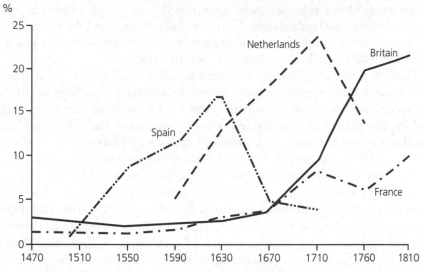

Fig. 5.5 Approximate Armies as a Share of Adult Male Manpower, 1470–1810

military technology: gunpowder and the pike. But more important was the increase in administrative capacity: for the first time, European monarchs had the clerks to count their soldiers, and the systems of accounting and revenue collection to allow them to levy taxes rather than call for feudal contributions and levies.

Projecting the size of the government, and of its budget, is an extremely hazardous enterprise for pre-modern Europe. But we can count soldiers more or less, and compare them to what we guess about the adult male population of the country. And such counts indicate that by the middle of the sixteenth century Spain was paying for armies that amounted to perhaps 8 percent of its adult male population; by 1590 Spain's armies and navies amounted to perhaps 12 percent of its adult population; and at the peak of military effort in the Thirty Years War, around 1630, armies amounted to perhaps 17 percent of the adult male population of Spain. And we can guess that state military expenditure then amounted to 15–20 percent of national product, and to a much higher share of *marketed* economic product.

In the late fifteenth century, England had been the most effective proto-state in Europe: Henry V of Lancaster's armies amounted to perhaps 3 percent of England's adult male manpower. This success in military mobilization can be traced back to the Norman conquest of England in the eleventh century, which created a degree of centralization, of royal power vis-a-vis aristocrats, and of bureaucratic infrastructure not reached in other European countries until the sixteenth century.

But by 1550 the sole European great power was Spain. Other European states—Britain, the Netherlands, Austria, Prussia, Russia, and the peculiar case of France—were to follow it, reaching similar and sometimes higher peaks of relative military mobilization. But Spain was the first.

There is a considerable literature on the "decline of Spain."[11] But from a demographic and expenditure population, the extraordinary thing is not that Spain declined (and in 1670 could not mount the kind of military effort that it had for the preceding century and a half), but that it had stood head-and-shoulders above the other monarchs and countries of Europe in terms of its ability to mobilize society in the pursuit of war for so long. American treasure helped—but its quantitative impact on Spanish finances was less than the conquest of a new European province like Lombardy or Flanders. The major cause of Spanish predominance in military affairs was that it was the first regime to acquire the administrative expertise necessary to run through the array of financial expedients that became standard for absolutist monarchies. Thus, it is worth looking into the relationship between state power, the political—military goals of the ruling prince, and Spain's economic relative decline in more detail.

3.2 The Decline of Spain

The military effort made by the Spanish monarchy rose steadily from the beginning of the sixteenth into the early seventeenth century. The centralization of authority in the hands of the successors of Ferdinand and Isabella, the prestige gained by the completion of the Christian reconquest of Spain, the willingness of monarchs to assume the power to raise taxes through a broad variety of expedients, and the availability of American treasure to finance war had transformed Spain from a middle-rank European power into the greatest European power (at least insofar as its ability to project military force is concerned) for nearly two hundred years. Its ability—unique for its age—to mobilize resources allowed it to project power all over western and central Europe in an attempt to reconquer lands that had adopted Protestant heresies for the Catholic Church, and to secure the position of the ruling Habsburg dynasty as the leading dynastic house in Europe.

Paul Kennedy has convincingly—though non-quantitatively—argued that Spain was the first power to suffer from "imperial overstretch." The wars of the

---

[11] See e.g. J. H. Elliott, "The Decline of Spain," in Carlo Cipolla, ed., *The Economic Decline of Empires* (London: Methuen, 1970); J. H. Elliott, *Richelieu and Olivares* (Cambridge: Cambridge University Press, 1983); and J. H. Elliott, *The Count–Duke of Olivares: The Statesman in an Age of Decline* (New Haven: Yale University Press, 1986).

Counter-Reformation entailed a degree of military mobilization in Spain larger than any previously attempted in Europe. Supporting this mobilization required money on a scale previously unseen in Europe.

And the extra efforts needed to gain the final extra quantum of gold or silver to support Spain's armies was obtained in ways that were potentially disastrous for the economy. For example, consider the first two financial decisions taken by the Spanish King Felipe IV upon his accession at the beginning of the Thirty Years' War: to renew the coinage of copper so that silver could be exported to pay for armies abroad (with disastrous consequences for Spanish merchants' ability to purchase imports); and to confiscate the Seville merchants' share of the silver from the American treasure fleet of 1620, giving them copper in exchange (and guaranteeing that throughout the reign of Felipe IV merchants would demand a healthy risk premium for any precious-metal transactions that might come under the power of the Spanish monarchy.

J. H. Elliott[12] summarizes the "series of well-known images" that mark the relative economic decline of Spain: "vagabondage, the contempt for manual labor, monetary chaos and excessive taxation." The heart of Spanish absolutism was the highly taxed province of Castile, which possessed a tax and forced-contribution system that "left the villager of Castile and Andalusia very little inducement to remain on the land." And contemporary observers blamed large-scale government debt for the decay of Castilian commerce—those with a taste for risk found the expected returns higher from lending to the government.

Under Felipe IV, for example, the servants of the crown displayed what Elliott calls "both zeal and ingenuity" in raising revenue:

the introduction of a [new] tax on the first year's income from [bureaucratic] offices . . . a salt tax, which provoked a rising in Vizcaya . . . [A]ppropriated a year's income from the Archbishopric of Toledo . . . [C]ollection of a voluntary *donativo* to help save Flanders and Italy . . . [Confiscation of] half the yield of all *juros* [an important form of government bond] held by natives, and the entire yield of those belonging to foreigners—a device . . . employ[ed] in succeeding years . . . [A] new tax in the form of stamped paper . . . obligatory for all legal and official documents . . . [Seizure of] 487,000 ducats in American silver, [and] "compensation" in the form of [the] unwanted *juros* [whose yield had been confiscated six lines above] . . .

These expedients cannot have had a healthy impact on Spain's economy.

In Adam Smith's time, the tax system of Spain was held up as an example of how *not* to sustain economic growth. Smith believed that a misunderstanding of the true incidence of taxation—"the notion that duties upon consumable goods were taxes on the profits of merchants"—was partially responsible for

---

[12] Elliot "Decline of Spain."

the extraordinary damage done to the Spanish economy by its system of public finance. *The Wealth of Nations* contains a discussion of

the famous Alcavala of Spain . . . at first a tax of ten per cent . . ., afterwards of fourteen per cent . . . upon the sale of every sort of property . . . repeated every time the property is sold. The levying of this tax requires a multitude of revenue officers sufficient to guard the transportation of goods, not only from one province to another, but from one shop to another . . . Through the greater part of a country in which a tax of this kind is established, nothing can be produced for distant sale. The produce of every part of the country must be proportioned to the consumption of the neighborhood. It is to the Alcavala, accordingly, that Ustaritz imputes the ruin of the manufactures of Spain. He might have imputed to it likewise the declension of agriculture, it being imposed not only upon manufactures, but upon the rude produce of the land.[13]

A tax policy more destructive to the division of labor, and more hostile to mercantile commerce, can hardly be imagined.

The collapse when it came was remarkably sudden. By the second half of the seventeenth century, Spain was no longer a great power. There had been a decline in the flow of American treasure; a decline in urban population and prosperity as a result of high taxes; a decline in urban prosperity as a result of the expulsion of Jews, Muslims, suspected Jews, suspected Muslims, people with Jewish ancestors, and people with Muslim ancestors—expulsions that may have forced out a fifth of the population of the Crown of Aragon; a decline because of too many state bankruptcies and repudiations of its debt; and revolts in nearly all the outlying provinces of Spain itself. By 1670 Spain could no longer mobilize the armies and navies it had mobilized in the days of Charles V Habsburg "of Ghent," his son Felipe II Habsburg "the Prudent," or his grandson Felipe IV Habsburg.

Thus, the century and a half of Spanish political dominance was also a century of relative economic decline. Lisbon and Madrid—two "parasite city" capitals, in the sense of Bairoch,[14] that were dependent on the state—grew. But there is little counterpart in Spain to the growth of Lyons as a textile center, or of Bordeaux as an export center. Even counting Madrid, the urban population of Spain stagnated in the years 1550–1650, in sharp contrast to the rapid rise in urban population in contemporary England, France, or the Netherlands (see Figure 5.6).

3.3 The Stagnation of the Dutch Republic

The bureaucratic and administrative tools that Spain had pioneered were soon copied. They were partially copied in France, which slowly increased the size of

---

[13] Adam Smith, *An Inquiry into the Nature and Causes of the Wealth of Nations* (London, 1776).

[14] Paul Bairoch, *De Jericho a Mexico: Villes et Economie dans l'Histoire* (Paris: Gallimard, 1985).

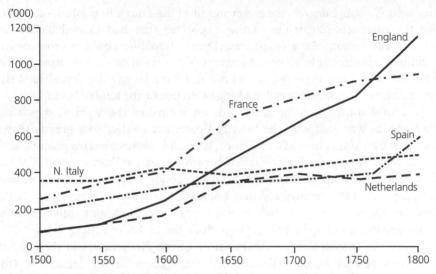

Fig. 5.6 Population of the Five Largest Cities in each Region, 1500–1800

its armies and navies from perhaps 1 percent of the adult male population in the late fifteenth century to perhaps 8 percent in the wars of Louis XIV Bourbon, "the Sun King," at the end of the seventeenth century and in the wars of Napoleon at the end of the eighteenth. They were also copied further to the east, as rulers of Austria, Prussia, and Russia followed in Spain's footsteps by imposing excises, selling offices to nobles to raise cash, borrowing and repudiating, and eventually drafting soldiers to such an extent that Prussia, at least, was called "not a state with an army, but an army with a state." These rulers pushed military effort to the breaking point of their regimes as well, ruling through ideologies that proclaimed the legal order to be their instrument subject to change at their will, and constrained in their exactions only by fear of rebellion.

But the most interesting factor is that the 'absolutist" regimes of princes in the seventeenth and eighteenth centuries were *not* the leaders in terms of proportional military mobilization. As Figure 5.5 shows, the peak in terms of relative military effort was probably reached in the Netherlands, where in 1710, during the wars begun by Louis XIV's attempt to conquer and annex the Netherlands, the country was paying for an army and a navy that together amounted to perhaps 24 percent of its adult male population.

One source of the northern Netherlands' extraordinary military mobilization was the complete absence of a prince from its political structure. The leader of the government was sometimes, but not always, a member of the dynastic house of Orange, but as the elected executive of a republic rather than as a monarch. To some degree, the government of the Dutch Republic looked a lot like the merchant-oligarchies of the city-states that had existed before the military revolution. As a result, the Dutch Republic could borrow nearly unlimited amounts at low rates of interest of 3 percent or so: merchant-princes were known to pay their debts, and did not have to pay the default and risk premiums that lenders charged the king of France or the king of Spain.

A second source was the life-and-death nature of the wars in which the Netherlands was engaged. The heavily Protestant Netherlands greatly feared conquest by a king, Louis XIV of France, who had just revoked his grandfather's "Edict of Nantes" providing toleration for Protestants in France. Louis XIV had thus inflicted significant damage on his own economy by driving his Protestant minority out of the country and into England, Germany, and the Netherlands. And he seemed likely to follow the same re-catholicizing policies if he succeeded in extending his borders to include the Low Countries.

Hence the extraordinary military effort of the Netherlands in their defensive wars against Louis XIV—and the willingness of the legislature (the Estates-General) of the seven provinces that made up the Dutch Republic to finance war through a tax system that was widely reputed to be the heaviest in Europe.

Thus, the Netherlands in the late seventeenth and eighteenth centuries does *not* fit the model of a relatively low-tax jurisdiction because of the powerful voice that the mercantile community had in the government: instead, it was a relatively high-tax jurisdiction. Merchants, and those with a direct material interest in economic growth, continued to have a large influence on the government. Nevertheless, taxes were high because of the fear on the part of the mercantile—Protestant community of the consequences of losing a major war.

And it looks as though the overtaxed Netherlands, in the eighteenth century, fell victim to Paul Kennedy's "imperial overstretch." Thirty years of constant warfare against France must have left the Dutch Republic in the early eighteenth century with a national debt equal to three or four times the national product, suggesting a debt service burden of 12–20 percent of national product and 18–30 percent of *marketed* economic activity.

It is no surprise that contemporary observers saw the eighteenth-century Dutch Republic as the most heavily taxed jurisdiction in Europe. And no surprise that observers like Boxer[15] write of an eighteenth-century decline in agriculture, and blame "the oppressive incidence of provincial taxation and the burden of the excise network" as "two reasons why a considerable number of farmers in North Holland left the land . . ."

This was also the diagnosis of informed and sophisticated contemporary

---

[15] C. R. Boxer, *The Dutch Seaborne Empire* (New York: Alfred A. Knopf, 1965).

observers. Adam Smith, for example, noted that "in Holland the money price of the bread consumed in towns is supposed to be doubled by means of . . . taxes . . ." He went on to report that such "heavy taxes upon the necessaries of life have ruined, it is said, [Holland's] principal manufactures, and are likely to discourage gradually even their fisheries and their trade in ship-building . . ." With public revenues slightly more than half of British levels, but with a quarter of Great Britain's population, the "inhabitants [of the Netherlands] must . . . be much more heavily taxed" than the inhabitants of Britain.

In spite of his judgment of their ruinous effect on the Dutch economy, Smith went on to argue that the levying of such high taxes "upon the necessaries of life [is] . . . no impeachment of the wisdom of that [Dutch] republick, which, in order to acquire and maintain its independency, has, in spite of its great frugality, been involved in such expensive wars as have obliged it to contract great debts . . ."[16]

Population and per-worker productivity in the Dutch Republic appear to have been no higher at the end of the eighteenth century than at the end of the seventeenth. The Dutch Republic at the end of the eighteenth century was still the richest and most prosperous area in Europe, but its lead over much of the rest had been substantially eroded.

Elsewhere the pattern appears much the same. Absolutist monarchies had powerful abilities to tax selected portions of their economies: they had little ability to tax the wealth of landlords and nobles, and they had little ability to tax consumption that did not flow through the market. But merchants and farmers who produced for sale were fair game. And almost everywhere, the mercantile economy was squeezed to the point of stagnation to support the politico-military interests of absolutist monarchs, or—in the case of the Dutch Republic—to defend the country against attack.

The cities of northern Italy—the richest region in Europe at the end of the Middle Ages, and the home of the Renaissance—never significantly participated in early modern economic growth. As Figure 5.6 shows, the population of the five largest cities of northern Italy did not grow significantly for three centuries. France and the Netherlands saw significant city growth at the end of the sixteenth and in the first half of the seventeenth centuries, but the populations of their largest cities then leveled off as well, coincident in time with the wars of attempted conquest launched by Louis XIV against the Netherlands. Only England saw rapid city growth continue into the second half of the seventeenth and the eighteenth centuries.

---

[16] Smith, *Wealth of Nations*.

4 The Anomaly of Britain

4.1 *Origins of the British Military State*

The mass mobilization of Britain's economy for war follows the same pattern as that of the Dutch, albeit a century or so later. The Dutch Republic had been militarized under pressure of the campaign by the Spanish to defeat its revolt and reconquer it for the Spanish monarchy, and was then further militarized in the context of the defensive struggle against Louis XIV of France. The British aristocracy deposed a king, James II, for religious reasons in 1688. James II fled into exile at the court of Louis XIV of France. The restoration of the Catholic James II to the throne of largely Protestant Great Britain thereupon became a war aim of Louis XIV, and Britain was thus drawn into the series of wars that began in 1689.[17]

With the religious order of the country at stake, taxes that would have been unthinkable in any previous age were gladly voted by Parliament to fight the French. An intrusive infrastructure of tax collectors and customs agents was established. And Britain's military mobilization began. By 1760, Britain's armies and fleets amounted to perhaps one in five of Britain's adult males. Certainly more than 15 percent of national product, perhaps more than 20 percent, was spent on Britain's military in the peak military effort years of the Seven Year's War (see Figure 5.7). The British state in the mid-eighteenth century was strong enough to defeat France at sea, subsidize France's land-based enemies when they took up arms, conquer the Caribbean islands and North America, and begin the conquest of India.

Just as the "decline of Spain" has generated a large literature, a good deal of which appears oddly misfocused in light of the demographics and finance of military mobilization, so the victory of Britain over France in the series of wars that began in 1689 and ended only in 1815 has generated a large literature, much of which focuses on England's strategic advantages.

But from a demographic–financial standpoint, Britain's victory is not surprising: its parliamentary regime was simply much better at taxing (and at borrowing as well–parliamentary rule meant a greatly lessened risk of default) than was the French.

Moreover, the British state sustained its military effort for an extraordinarily long time. Between 1756 and 1815, a span of 59 years, there were only twenty-two years of "peace." Figure 5.7 details the military effort—and the debt repayment effort necessary because of the military effort—mounted by

---

[17] For a superb and masterful overview of the rise of the British military state, see John Brewer, *The Sinews of Power: War, Money, and the English State, 1688–1763* (New York: Alfred A. Knopf, 1989).

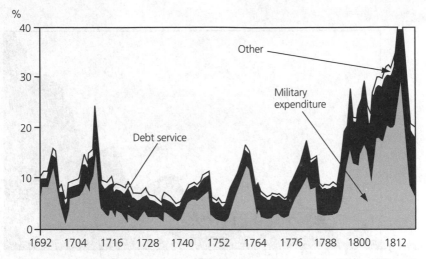

Fig. 5.7 Components of Government Expenditure as a Share of Trend National Product, 1692–1812

the British crown during the long eighteenth century. The consequences of Britain's massive military mobilization for its national debt, and for the amount of national product the British government extracted in taxes, were as you would expect. The high taxes levied were not high enough to cover wartime peaks in expenditure; hence the debt mounted as a share of trend national product throughout the eighteenth century. It peaked during the American Revolution at around 130 percent of a year's national product; and peaked at the end of the Napoleonic Wars at something like three times trend national product (Figure 5.8).

All other European states—absolutist like Spain or non-absolutist like the Netherlands—appear to have been unable to maintain both economic growth and the degree of military effort that being a European great power in the sixteenth, seventeenth, and eighteenth centuries required. Why don't we tell the same story about eighteenth-century Britain—a prosperous economy that staggered and eventually collapsed under the burden of the war expenditures required by a parasitic, aggressive, expansionistic, and imperialist government? How did Great Britain achieve its unique success?

4.2 *Adam Smith*

First, it was far from clear to contemporaries watching the British state in the eighteenth century that it *would* succeed. Observers like Adam Smith would

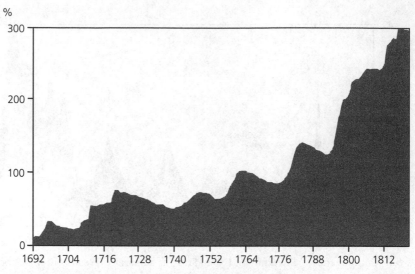

Fig. 5.8 British Debt as a Proportion of Trend National Product, 1692–1820

repeatedly praise the British tax system's efficiency. For example, he wrote that "the people of France . . . it is generally acknowledged, are much more oppressed by taxes than the people of Great Britain"; and yet,

in 1775 and 1766, the whole revenue paid into the treasury of France, according to the best, though, I acknowledge, very imperfect accounts which I could get . . . [was] not the half of what might have been expected, had the people contributed in the same proportion . . . as . . . Great Britain.[18]

But Smith did not believe that the relative efficiency of the British tax system would protect Great Britain from the adverse economic consequences of the cost of fighting its eighteenth-century wars. He wrote of the uniform "progress of the enormous debts which at present oppress, and will in the long-run probably ruin, all the great nations of Europe . . ." He took readers of *The Wealth of Nations* on a tour of the public finances of all the major European powers:

The practice of [running up large debts during wartime and then consolidating the post-war indebtedness into long-term bonds] has gradually enfeebled every state which has adopted it. The Italian republicks seem to have begun it . . . Spain seems to have learned the practice from the Italian republicks, and (its taxes being probably less judicious than theirs) it has, in proportion to its natural strength, been still more enfeebled . . . France . . . languishes under an oppressive load . . . The republic of the United Provinces [of the Netherlands] is as much enfeebled by its debts as either Genoa or Venice.

[18] Smith, *Wealth of Nations*.

And he finished by asking the rhetorical question: "Is it likely that in Great Britain alone a practice, which has brought either weakness or desolation into every other country, should prove altogether innocent?"[19]

Supporters of Britain's fiscal—military establishment in the mid-eighteenth century advanced two arguments that its policies were sustainable. First, British peacetime revenues did exceed peacetime expenditures plus interest, and there was a "sinking fund" to buy back the outstanding principal of the debt. Second, Britain's tax system was fairer and put less of a burden on the economy.

But Smith did not believe that the "sinking fund" provided any economic security. Governments would raid the sinking fund: even "during the most profound peace, various events occur which require an extraordinary expence, and government finds it always more convenient to defray this expence by misapplying the sinking fund . . ." Raising taxes was difficult, for "every new tax is immediately felt . . . [But] a momentary suspension of the [re]payment of the debt is not immediately felt by the people, and occasions neither murmur nor complaint . . . Hence the usual misapplication of the sinking fund." Smith saw correctly the steady rise in debt as a share of national product that took place throughout the eighteenth century.

Smith also was not reassured by the relative efficiency and fairness of the British tax system in the eighteenth century:

The system of taxation established in those [other] countries, it may be said, is inferior to that of England. I believe it is so. But it ought to be remembered, that when the wisest government has exhausted all the proper subjects of taxation, it must, in cases of urgent necessity, have recourse to improper ones. The wise republick of Holland has upon some occasions been obliged to have recourse to taxes as inconvenient as the greater part of those of Spain. Another war begun before any considerable liberation of the publick revenue had been brought about . . . may . . . render the British system of taxation as oppressive as that of Holland, or even as that of Spain . . . Let us not . . . rashly conclude that [the British economy] is capable of supporting any burden; nor even be too confident that she could support without great distress a burden a little greater . . .[20]

Thus, it was not obvious to contemporaries that a prosperous eighteenth-century Britain was consistent with the imperial policy and military expenditures necessary for Britain to play the role of an eighteenth-century European great power. From their perspective, at least, the same forces that made a strong state inconsistent with advancing mercantile prosperity in Holland, France, and Spain were at work in Britain as well. The concluding pages of *The Wealth of Nations* are a plea for the reformation of British policy—either

[19] Smith, *Wealth of Nations*.
[20] Ibid.

distribute the burden of financing Britain's wars more widely, so as to eliminate the risk that "imperial overstretch" would push the British economy into the condition of Holland's or Spain's, or abandon empire and fight the wars of continental Europe.

4.3 *Wrong Answers*

Some of the standard answers for Britain's continued economic success throughout the eighteenth century found in the history books are clearly wrong. As we have seen, it is *not* the case that Britain's status as an island exempted it from the military effort characteristic of continental European powers. It maintained a navy second-to-none *and* it spent enough on a land army to, at times, be a significant factor in the military balance on the northern European plain. It is *not* the case that the early growth of representative government in Europe placed a check on the expansion of public spending. Rather the reverse: parliamentary power made it possible for Britain to mobilize a *greater* share of national product for war than could its continental adversaries.

4.4 *Possible Right Answers*

Instead, the reasons for Britain's escape from the trap that history set for Enlightenment-era economies appear to be four in number. These are considered below in rough order of increasing probable importance.

4.4.1 *Ideological preconditions for mobilization*

When Britain's military mobilization began, it began all at once, as a near-unanimous decision by the political nation in response to the succession crisis of 1688. Thus, Britain's tax system was widely seen as fairer and less destructive than the exemption-ridden systems that continental absolutist monarchs had to construct to maintain political support for their military adventures.

As noted above, when Britain entered the European power struggle, the religious order of the country was immediately placed at risk. In most early modern wars kings fought for prestige and provinces, nobles fought for honor and plunder, and soldiers fought for pay. From the moment Britain became a participant in the wars of early modern Europe, its kings were fighting not just for prestige and provinces, but for their very right to wear the crown; its nobles were fighting not just for honor and plunder, but to preserve their property against the overturn that might well follow the reversal of the Protestant religious settlement; and all were fighting for their souls.

Thus, taxes that would have been unthinkable in any previous age, or in any other emerging nation-state, were gladly voted by Parliament to fight the French. An intrusive infrastructure of tax collectors and customs agents was established. Elsewhere in Europe, aristocrats fought tooth and nail—with substantial success—for exemption from the taxes levied by seventeenth and eighteenth-century states. In Britain the aristocrats loaded taxes on themselves for fear of the consequences of military defeat and the return of the Roman Catholic Stuart dynasty that they had deposed in favor of the house of Orange and then of Hanover.

Had British absolutism grown up gradually, it would almost surely have a had a less fair and less efficient tax system, resting on a smaller tax base, in a pattern similar to that of continental absolutisms: the king would have acquired the power to tax the economy as a whole by offering selective exemption to the nobles who staffed the *estates* and the *parlements* that had retained the feudal right to be consulted before royal action became law. The consequences for the mercantile economy of a given level of expenditures would have been significantly more damaging had Britain's military state emerged otherwise than in response to the threat to the Protestant succession posed by the potential return of the exiled James II.

4.4.2 Victory and empire

Second, Britain won its eighteenth-century wars. While British victory over Indian princes, American tribes, and the Dutch, French, and Spanish navies in the struggle for trade and empire was not *the* cause of British economic growth, it did plausibly add an extra 5 or 10 percent to the national product. In a context in which the key to avoiding economic stagnation is broadening the tax base on which the burden of fighting the next war is placed, the economic benefits of empire may well have been important.

It is here, if anywhere, that the benefits of the "representative" character of British government are to be found. Supplies for war had to be voted by Parliament, an assembly of landlords with financiers and merchants mixed in. The government had to maintain the confidence of the monarch in order to retain power, but it also had to retain the confidence of Parliament. Throughout the eighteenth century, kings were eager to project British military power onto the European continent proper—the dynastic interests of William III as Stadholder of the United Provinces, and of Georges I, II, and III as Electors of Hanover.

Mercantile interests in Parliament were more willing to vote for war if the government would adopt a "navy first" strategy; thus, the requirement of maintaining parliamentary confidence led the government to adopt a military strategy oriented more toward the mercantilist and imperial maritime power that Britian became. Representation—constraints on the monarch—did not diminish the size of the war effort appreciably, but in all probability did shift its direction somewhat.

4.4.3 The late arrival of the modern state

Third, the early modern state—capable of mobilizing 10–20 percent of national product for war—came to Britain relatively late, in 1690 rather than in 1550. Thus, the British economy had an extra century and a half to grow without having to bear the burden of a large military establishment. It is hard to see the late arrival of the modern state in Britain as due to anything other than luck: the shakiness of the Tudor dynasty and the foreignness of the Stuart dynasty prevented the kind of consolidation of authority that was ongoing in Spain, France, and Prussia in the sixteenth and seventeenth centuries.

Thus, Britain's national debt was an insignificant fraction of national product as late as 1688. By that time Spanish absolutism, and its consequent wars, had burdened the Spanish economy for nearly two hundred years; and French absolutism, begun by Henry IV and Cardinal Richelieu, was three-quarters of a century old. A late start gave the burden of early modern wars less time to press down on the British economy.

4.4.4 Demography

Fourth and probably most important, however, British peak military effort coincided with an extraordinary demographic upswing which provided a larger resource base, on which the debt left over from the last generation's wars placed a smaller burden.

Thus, in the last analysis, a large part of the answer must be demographic. Britain's population in 1800 was two and a half times its population in 1600; in contrast, France's population in 1800 was only one-half more than in 1600; Holland's only one-third more, and Spain's, only one-quarter more. If Britain's population had been stagnant in the eighteenth century (and if Britain had maintained its historical military effort), by the end of the American Revolution in 1783 Britain's national debt would have been not 1.3 times a year's national product but 2.1 times—and its national debt in 1820 would have been not three times a year's national product but seven times. Such a debt would have imposed an unsustainable burden on the economy: perhaps 28 percent of national product would have been levied in taxes to pay debt service in 1820, a burden that a growing economy could not have stood.

Many histories of Europe dwell on the fortunate coincidence of an "agricultural revolution" in Britain coming just on the eve of the Industrial Revolution, making it possible. Such histories usually see the agricultural revolution as allowing the release of labor from subsistence farming to industrial production. But here we see another, possibly more important, implication—of an "agricultural revolution," and of changes in Europe's climate that made the north somewhat more hospitable.

Without rapid population growth in eighteenth-century Britain, it is possible that we would not be here today: the burden of eighteenth-century wars might well have strangled economic growth. Indeed, Jeffrey Williamson[21] has convincingly argued that the burden of fighting Britain's wars did slow growth significantly. Remove Britain's demographic upswing, and Williamson's calculations of "crowding out" imply a British economy shrinking in terms of output per capita from 1780 to 1820.

It is important to stress that Britain's escape from the above scenario was the result of a fortunate combination of causes: a nation united for war, the late arrival of the modern state, the plunder from overseas empires, and (most important) the demographic upswing—all had nothing to do with each other. It is easy to imagine a world in which one, two, three, or all four of these factors were missing.

Had one of these four factors been missing, it is likely that Britain would still have been the site of the first Industrial Revolution. Remove two or more of the factors, and it is likely that we would now have to write the history of eighteenth-century Britain as we do the history of sixteenth-century Spain or seventeenth-century Holland: as an era of mercantile brilliance and political power that ended in long-run economic stagnation and decline.

5 Conclusion

In the first half of this millennium, European economic growth was enabled in part by the relative ineptness of Europe's military aristocracy: only in Europe were self-governing city-states able to maintain their independence against centralizing princes; only in Europe did merchants have a chance to rule, and to shape policies that saw economic growth as an end in itself, rather than as a means to courtly splendor or to military power.

In the third quarter of this millennium, the traditional centers of the European economy—the Mediterranean coast of Aragon, northern Italy, the southern half of the Low Countries around Antwerp, Brussels, Ghent, Bruges,

---

[21] Jeffrey Williamson, "Why Was British Growth So Slow During the Industrial Revolution?" *Journal of Economic History*, 44(3) (1984): 687–712.

and Lille —went into decline, in large part because of the burden of financing the military effort made possible by the new bureaucracies of "absolutist" monarchs.

Britain—and only Britain—was able to be a European great power, to finance its wars at whatever level of spending seemed necessary, and still to see sufficient economic growth in the eighteenth century to trigger an Industrial Revolution. This is an extraordinary event, and not one fore-ordained. Contemporary observers like Adam Smith, in his *Wealth of Nations*, wrote of the likely ruin of European economies—not exempting Britain's—under the burden of national debt created by the enormous war expenditures made possible by the military mobilizations undertaken by early modern states.

5.1 *Lessons Learned*

What lessons can we draw for economic development today from this excursion into the minutiae of early modern history? What advice should governments take, and those of us who are concerned about institutional and constitutional frameworks to constrain and empower governments? The lessons appear to be four:

The first and most important lesson is: *be lucky*. Of the perhaps six European proto-nation-states that in the sixteenth through eighteenth centuries acquired the potential to tax and mobilize 10 or more percent of national product, all but one used this power in a way that severely retarded economic growth. And that country's escape is due in large part to a fortunate coincidence of many different factors—or, in other words, in large part to good luck.

The second lesson is: *do not expect too much*. Rates of per capita output growth in the developing world since 1945—even including Africa, and even excluding the East Asians—appear to be roughly twice what European countries accomplished in the nineteenth century, when they had similar shares of their populations in agriculture. Given the extra roles played by modern governments, and given the difficulties faced by even the most technologically advanced pre-industrial economies in continuing growth under the burden of their more limited governments, I believe that we should be grateful for the development progress that has been made rather than disappointed that progress has not been faster.

The third lesson is: *unite the nation*. Britain's military effort was based on a system of finance established in the context of an emergency, near-universal consensus of the political nation that a stronger state was necessary. Absolutism in France, or Spain, or even the Netherlands was the result of bargaining between the central authority and other politically powerful groups: we will back your authority to tax the economy if we are granted significant exemptions and special privileges. Comparing British and French public finances on the eve of the French Revolution, it seems clear that British public finance caused much less discontent—and probably much less distortion and damage to the economy.

The last lesson is: *do what can be done to raise economic growth higher on the list of policy-makers' priorities*. This is difficult, because, at least from the high seats of rulers and politicians, other considerations rank higher than policies to enhance long-run economic growth *for what seem to politicians and princes to be good reasons*. Woodward writes of how it was "ridiculous to talk to politicians about the distant future. To mention [benefits achieved at] 'infinity' [in the future] was patently absurd . . . More vividly . . . he was presenting [President] Clinton with costs that would be paid in his presidency and benefits that would come several presidencies into the future."[22] Yet politicians pursue not only *material* but also what Max Weber termed *ideal* interests—the approval of one's peers, confidence in one's religious salvation, glory, and honor are very real, and are powerful motivations of human action.

And here economists can perhaps have some impact: to some degree, we can play with the minds of politicians and princes. We can, by our collective approval and disapproval, help assure them that adopting policies with long-term development benefits will give them a favorable place in the history books—"William the Good" as opposed to "Ronald the Badly Advised"— and an old age in which they are honored and respected advisers and elders, rather than reviled as the standard-bearers for failed policies. The work is difficult. The effects are marginal at best.

Yet still the work is worth doing.

I was lucky enough to work for Lloyd Bentsen when he was Treasury Secretary. He told me a story that President Kennedy had told him. He spoke of an aged and retired French commander, Marshall Lyautey, giving instructions to the head gardener of his country estate: ". . . and I want to plant two rows of oak trees," the Marshall said, "one on each side of that drive. Start planting them tomorrow."

"But my Marshall," the gardener replied, "those trees will take fifty years to grow!"

"Oh," said the Marshall. "In that case, there is no time to lose. Start planting them this afternoon."

---

[22] Robert Woodward, *The Agenda* (New York: Simon & Schuster, 1994).

6 The Swedish Model: A Comment on Mancur Olson's Analysis

Erik Moberg

1 The Rise and Decline of the Swedish Model

For a long time in this century many Swedes were proud of their country. From a relatively poor and backward position, it developed into one of the three or four most productive economies in the world. At the same time, the Swedish welfare state gradually took form. The public systems of education, medical care, and other social services grew. Poverty was almost entirely eradicated and people's standard of living, while growing, became more and more equalized. At the end of the 1960s, the public expenses constituted about 45 percent of the GDP, and there were no deficit problems. Internationally, *the Swedish model* became a concept loaded with positive values.

The 1960s were the heyday of that model. Then, gradually, things started to deteriorate. Sweden's growth rate became slower and in some years, the latest of which are 1991, 1992, and 1993, even turned negative. The production per capita is now below that of at least fifteen other industrialized countries. Unemployment has risen dramatically.[1] The retarded growth has been accompanied by continuously increasing public expenses. In 1990 they constituted a good 60 percent of GDP. The state's debt has risen to roughly 80 percent of the country's GDP. Almost half of this is owed to creditors abroad. The crisis is now deep and severe. For many people the Swedish model has become a warning rather than an ideal.

---

[1] The official figure is around 12% (Nov. 1997), but other methods of measurement give considerably higher levels; e.g., Ståhl and Wickman have calculated that only about 80% of those who would be employed in an ideal labor market are, in fact, employed. Their unemployment figure is thus about 20%. See I. Ståhl and K. Wickman, *En miljon utan jobb: Suedosclerosis III* (in Swedish) (Stockholm: Timbro, 1995).

It is hardly surprising that some scholars found this pattern remarkable. First, Sweden's achievements during the period of advance could certainly not have been taken for granted. From a conventional economic point of view, one would rather have predicted that Sweden's extremely large welfare state, with its unusually high taxes and exceptionally generous social insurance, by severely disturbing incentives would badly hamper economic performance. But that did not happen. Economic growth and the welfare state seemed quite compatible, and it was therefore important to ask exactly how and why? What was the Swedish secret? Then, when such questions seemed to have been answered, Sweden's economic performance gradually began to worsen. This, of course, was also bound to astonish. How could a country that once performed so remarkably well, now be worse off than most other comparable countries?

One scholar who has discussed these problems is Mancur Olson, and he has done so in two works in particular. The one is the booklet 'How Bright are the Northern Lights? Some Questions about Sweden,[2] which deals mainly with the long, successful pre-crisis period. The other work, the article "The Devolution of the Nordic and Teutonic Economies,"[3] deals with the crisis after the happy years.

2 Olson on Sweden's Success

Olson starts his discussion about the successful period by putting two nicely related questions:[4]

1. Why isn't the Swedish economy performing better than it is?
2. Why isn't the Swedish economy performing worse than it is?

Olson's answer to the first question relies on mainstream economics and draws attention to the compressed wage differentials, the high level of transfers, and the high taxation in Sweden. This answer, I think, is obviously correct and there is not much to discuss about it. The really interesting question is the second one: how is it that Sweden, in spite of its seemingly big obstacles to growth, performed so remarkably well, and in fact better than most other nations?

[2] The book is based on the Crafoord Memorial Lecture given by Mancur Olson at the University of Lund, Sweden, in 1986: Mancur Olson, How Bright are the Northern Lights? Some Questions about Sweden (Lund University Press, 1990).

[3] Mancur Olson, "The Devolution of the Nordic and Teutonic Economies," American Economic Review, Papers and Proceedings, May (1995).

[4] Olson, Northern Lights.

But even if the second question is the crucial one, I think that Olson's interpretation of the question is worth a comment. The obstacles that Olson has in mind are the large public sector and the fully developed welfare state. In essence, therefore, he asks why Sweden's extreme welfare politics did not hamper economic growth more than it did. This question is certainly worth asking, but it is nonetheless remarkable. Keeping Olson's own well known theory of national development in mind, a slightly different interpretation of the question would be more natural.[5]

What I am thinking about is Olson's contention that stable societies become increasingly sclerotic with age. The basis for this is two propositions that are derived from Olson's logic of collective action and are presented, among other places, in *The Rise and Decline of Nations*.[6] The first one says that "[s]table societies with unchanged boundaries tend to accumulate more collusions and organizations for collective action over time," and the second one that "[o]n balance, special interest organizations and collusions reduce efficiency and aggregate income in the societies in which they operate and make political life more divisive." According to this, therefore, one would expect Sweden to be quite sclerotic since it is old and stable; and it would be natural to think about the second question as about why Sweden, being such an old and stable society, was not performing worse than it was.

Now, my reason for thinking that Olson's interpretation of the question should be avoided is that, in a sense, it takes the emergence of the Swedish welfare state for granted. The welfare state is brought into the discussion as a reason for putting a question, for which Olson's theory already has an excellent reason, and therefore the existence of the welfare state does not appear as something that needs an explanation of its own—which, indeed, I think it does.

After this we can now turn to Olson's answer to his second question. First, and contrary to many persons' beliefs, he says that a large public sector does not necessarily impede economic growth very much. He presents statistics supporting his assertion and also provides an explanation. Advanced welfare politics, as we know, is always associated with substantial redistributions, but such redistributions can be of different kinds.

Olson makes a distinction between explicit and implicit redistributions. An *explicit redistribution* is a cash transfer from taxpayers to particular beneficiaries, which are commonly deemed to deserve or need the money. An *implicit redistribution*, on the other hand, usually refers to the favoring of some selected people or firms by a new law of some kind; examples are tariffs or quotas favoring some particular industry. By their advocates, such laws are often said to be good for the society at large, and their redistributional character is

---

[5] Mancur Olson, *The Rise and Decline of Nations: Economic Growth, Stagflation, and Social Rigidities* (New Haven: Yale University Press, 1982).

[6] Ibid. p. 74.

thus concealed. An explicit redistribution will increase the public sector; an implicit one usually does not. Olson also argues that implicit redistributions, for several reasons, may disturb people's incentives much more than explicit ones, and thus may be more harmful to economic growth. "Inconspicuous redistributions," he writes, "are often also more costly to society than conspicuous ones: the costs that are not noticed are less likely to be minimized."[7] The deadweight losses resulting from an implicit redistribution may easily become many times bigger than the favors enjoyed by the beneficiaries.

Now, Olson submits that the Swedish welfare state to a large extent uses explicit rather than implicit redistributions, and that is the first part of his explanation of Sweden's surprisingly good performance. In a second part he goes on to draw attention to the importance, especially for a small country, of the policies for international trade. He asserts, again perhaps contrary to many persons' beliefs, that free trade is very important for economic growth; and again he presents statistics showing that protective measures, such as quotas and tariffs, almost universally impede growth drastically. This, of course, exemplifies the harmful effects of implicit redistributions; the basic mechanism is that the protected firms, when not exposed to competition from countless foreign firms, can easily form cartels which will harm the national economy at large. Sweden, however, has never had a significant protective wall for manufactured goods, and that is the second part of Olson's explanation of Sweden's good performance.

Olson's explanation seems plausible but also leads to new questions about the causes behind the explicit redistributions and the non-existent protective wall. In his answers to these secondary questions, Olson emphasizes that Sweden's lobbying organizations, to a large extent, have been quite encompassing, and thereby inclined to abstain from destructive policies. An encompassing organization, in Olson's terminology, is an organization whose members represent a large share of the country's income-earning capacity. Since such organizations and their members to a large extent are affected by their own activities, they have strong incentives to be, from a general point of view, prudent. In Olson's words, "Encompassing organizations have some incentive to make the society in which they operate more prosperous, and an incentive to redistribute income to their members with as little excess burden as possible, and to cease such redistribution unless the amount redistributed is substantial in relation to the social cost of the redistribution."[8] The opposite to encompassing organizations is narrow organizations, which, from a general point of view, are likely to behave irresponsibly.

The power in Olson's explanation of Sweden's surprisingly good performance thus comes from his assertion that Sweden's lobbying organizations to

---

[7] Olson, *Northern Lights*, p. 60.
[8] Olson, *Rise and Decline*, p. 74.

such a large extent are encompassing rather than narrow. True, he also dis-cusses some ad hoc factors, exogenous to his own theory, such as the quality of Swedish economists and some historical experiences of the Swedish exporting industries; but these elements are marginal and may be disregarded here. The obvious next question therefore is: how is it that the Swedish organizations are so encompassing?

This question Olson answers only tentatively. In some places he indicates that Sweden's smallness and homogeneity may be an explanation, and certainly there may be some truth in this.[9] First, smallness and homogeneity often go together. When, for example, a large piece of something, say a big rock, is divided into parts, those parts, individually, are likely to be more homogeneous than the original piece. Second, both smallness and homogeneity may favor encompassing organizations. If, for example, the costs for creating an organiz-ation depend only on the organization's absolute size, and not at all on its size in relation to the society at large, then, automatically, organizations will become more encompassing the smaller the country is. Also, it is reasonable to assume that the costs of an organization are higher the more heterogeneous a country is, which makes encompassing organizations in homogeneous countries more likely than in other countries. Thus, it is not unreasonable to think about smallness and homogeneity as causes of encompassedness. But neither is it, I think, very convincing; the arguments are too vague.

We may thus conclude that Olson's answer to his second question, about the surprising success of Sweden, in terms of encompassing organizations is basically sound, even if the mechanisms behind the encompassing organiz-ations, and the emergence of the welfare state, remain obscure. Furthermore, Olson devotes hardly any space to the mechanisms by which lobbying organizations influence government. This is important, since the prudence or non-prudence of the organizations would not matter if they had no influence.

3 Olson on Sweden's Crisis

We may now turn to Olson's account of the Swedish crisis in later years.[10] The basic question, of course, is why Sweden, which earlier performed so well, has become so overwhelmed by troubles. Olson's answers are short and tentative and, it should be said, do not claim to be anything else.

He suggests for example that the prior successful development may have

---

[9] See e.g. Olson, "Devolution," p. 24.
[10] Ibid.

led to overconfidence in the Swedish model, and thereby to "overshooting."[11] "The country," he writes, "came to believe that it could redistribute even more without excessive social costs." This argument is of course sensible, but also very vague; furthermore, it is unrelated to Olson's basic ideas about organizations, and in that sense is ad hoc.

This last criticism does not apply to another line in Olson's reasoning, in which he argues that the organizations that were earlier quite encompassing may have become less so, and therefore, according to his theory, also less responsible. In this argument Sweden's economic performance is considered as a reflection of the degree of encompassedness of its organizations. Olson here applies an idea that he has presented in several publications,[12] namely that encompassing organizations are inherently unstable and are likely to disintegrate into a number of narrow organizations. This disintegration, according to Olson, is caused by the same mechanisms as the emergence of narrow organizations within a society without any organizations. Basically, a minority within a large encompassing organization will find itself in the same situation as a minority in a society without lobbying or cartelistic organizations. These minorities will find the encompassing organization and the state, respectively, quite similar. Neither of them articulates the particular interests of the minorities, and these will therefore try to organize. In the one case it is the society without organizations that is changed, and in the other the society with encompassing organizations. In both cases the end result is a society with a lot of narrow organizations.

This idea about the encompassing organizations' instability raises some questions. How, for example, if they are inherently unstable, could encompassing organizations ever come into existence? To put the question somewhat differently, is there an equilibrium level of encompassedness or narrowness? If so, at which particular level is an organization narrow enough not to be threatened by further disintegration? What, in fact, hinders equilibrium to occur when every "organization" has one member only, or in other words when there are no organizations at all? And, if so, how is it that organizations ever appear? These questions, obviously, are only new variations of the basic question already put, concerning the determinants of an organization's degree of encompassedness or narrowness.

The idea about disintegrating encompassing organizations, even if generally true, is also, I think, of limited relevance for Sweden. First, the moderate disintegration that has occurred has consisted of deviations from the traditional centralized wage bargaining and is thus a labor market phenomenon not necessarily related to lobbying. Second, since a plausible main effect of the

---

[11] Olson, "Devolution," p. 24.

[12] E.g. Mancur Olson, "An Appreciation of the Tests and Criticisms," *Scandinavian Political Studies*, March (1986); Olson, *Northern Lights*; Olson, "Devolution."

decentralization is wider wage differentials, it is not clear that the results are harmful.[13] Third, since the first deviations from centralization occurred about ten years after the first signs of the economic crisis, in the beginning of the 1970s, the causal order, if any, should not be from disintegration to crisis, but from crisis to disintegration—when the trough is empty, the horses bite. This, again, brings us back to the question about the basic mechanisms determining the extent to which an organization is encompassing.

Olson's dealing with the crisis period is, in my opinion, less convincing than his handling of the period of success. Some of his ideas are vague and un-related to his own mainstream thinking. Another idea—that of disintegrating encompassing organizations—certainly belongs to his own theoretical frame-work, but fails to convince anyway. Olson is thus not only unsuccessful in bringing the two phases of the Swedish development under a common theoretical hat, but he also falls short of giving a plausible explanation for the crisis per se.

---

4 The Constitutional Factor

Some of the questions left unanswered by Olson require, I believe, some constitutional facts to be taken into account. Sweden has a parliamentary constitution with proportional representation. This determines the character of the political parties and therefore, as we shall see, is also relevant for the problems discussed here.

Parliamentarism is a method for appointing the executive, according to which the people first elect the legislature, which in turn appoints the executive. The legislature and the executive are thus, in a sense, appointed in the same popular elections. In a pure parliamentary system, the executive can further-more remain in office only as long as it enjoys the confidence of a majority in the legislature, and this requirement is therefore often referred to as the *parliamentary principle*. The other main system is the presidential one, which uses separate popular elections for appointing a president and thereby also the rest of the executive.

A parliamentary system depends, for its functioning, on the existence of stable, centralized, and disciplined political parties in a way that a presidential system does not. The reason is that the parliament's confidence in the

---

[13] P. A. Edin and R. Topel, *Wage Policy and Restructuring: The Swedish Labor Market sine 1960,* in R. Freeman, B. Swedenborg, and R. Topel, eds., *Reforming the Welfare State: The Swedish Model in Transition* (Chicago: National Bureau of Economic Research/Chicago University Press, 1997).

executive, in order to be reliable and lasting, cannot be ad hoc, accidental, or anonymous. The confidence expressed by a transient majority of individual members of the legislature cannot, it is easy to realize, have much value. The confidence has to be expressed by one or a few stable and identifiable actors, which, in effect, means consolidated political parties. A parliamentary system however is not dependent only on such parties; conversely, I submit, it also gives strong *incentives* for the formation of that kind of parties; and sometimes also for forming big parties.[14] The reason is that centralized leadership, stability, and discipline enhance a negotiating party's credibility and reliability and thereby its chances of becoming a member of the executive, a membership that often is quite attractive, or even lucrative.[15]

The proportional electoral system with multi-member constituencies can be compared with a plurality system with single-member constituencies (first past the post). The choice here affects the parties in two ways. First, the plurality system has a strong tendency to reduce the number of parties, in the extreme to two parties, whereas there are no such reductive forces operating in the proportional system.[16] Second, in contrast to the plurality system, the proportional system puts strong *means* for enhancing discipline, and thus for the creation of stable and cohesive parties, in the hands of the party leaderships. The main factor here is that the candidates for the legislature are largely dependent on the party leadership, both for nomination and for campaigning.

Now, I submit, these mechanisms can be used for explaining the character of the Swedish party system. There are seven parties, which on the whole are disciplined, stable, and cohesive. There are no strong forces reducing the number of parties. The Social Democratic party is quite big. The incentives to discipline come from the parliamentarism, and the means from the proportionalism. As a contrast, we may think about the United States with presidentialism and plurality. There, as we should expect, we find two main parties with low discipline.

These matters affect the distribution of power. In the Swedish system the

[14] A big party often has the advantage of being the component from which a coalition-building process starts. Even small parties, however, may have advantages by fitting well into minimum winning coalitions in Riker's sense. See W. H. Riker, *The Theory of Political Coalitions* (New Haven: Yale University Press, 1962). The incentives related to size are thus quite complicated.

[15] The idea that parliamentarism is dependent on stable, cohesive parties is generally accepted in political science. The converse idea—that parliamentarism enhances those party properties—is to my knowledge not discussed in a systematic way at all; and when the topic occasionally arises for some reason the idea is sometimes supported, sometimes discarded. An example of the latter is given by Sartori when he writes that "– party solidification and discipline [in parliamentary voting] has never been a feedback of parliamentary government": G. Sartori, *Comparative Constitutional Engineering: An Inquiry into Structures, Incentives and Outcomes* (London: Macmillan, 1994), p. 95.

[16] Maurice Duverger claimed that the tendency of a plurality system to enhance a two party system came close to being "a true sociological law." M. Duverger, *Political Parties: Their Organization and Activity in the Modern State* (New York: John Wiley, 1964), p. 217. This relationship, often referred to as "Duverger's law," is not however generally accepted in political science.

consolidated and disciplined parties can, as an approximation, be considered as unitary actors. The power is concentrated to the hierarchical summits of the parties. This does not mean, of course, that individuals are not important. It does however mean that the individuals almost exclusively play their roles within the parties. The individuals have a say in determining the party positions, and more so the higher up they are in the party hierarchy. When it comes to dealings with actors outside the party, for example with other parties, or with the electorate in campaigns, or with lobbying organizations, it is however usually the party as such, or the party leadership, that acts. Furthermore, during the current election period, the governmental power is held by the very few parties belonging to the executive or to the parliamentary majority supporting the executive. The US pattern is quite different. There, the party restrictions on the behavior of the president, and on the members of the Congress, are very weak indeed. All these individuals—several hundred—can therefore be considered as fairly independent actors. The power is spread out not only between the president and the Congress, but also among all the members of the Congress.

These different patterns should be of great importance. It thus seems likely that the *transaction costs* of political processes depend critically on the number of independent actors taking part.[17] The number of independent actors is likely to affect the possibilities of building decisive majorities or blocking minorities, the character of the lobbying processes, and the expediency of various strategies in the political competition.

One particular aspect likely to be affected by the patterns described is the relation between voters (the principals) and the political main actors (the agents), whether these are parties or individuals. Two types of such relation are particularly interesting: the one may be called delegation, the other instruction.

Delegation is, in a way, the simpler of the two and many people are familiar with it from experiences in ordinary clubs and the like. When people in such associations elect presidents, secretaries, and so on, they usually do not require more than that they have confidence in the persons elected. They just want to be able to rely on them to act in accordance with common sense in the interests of the club. Feeling such confidence, they are happy to delegate the decision-making to the people elected. For the most part such a system works well, but if, for some reason, a delegate starts to act in ways of which the members disapprove, there are usually provisions in the club's charter for displacing the

[17] The transaction cost concept was, as we know, introduced by Ronald H. Coase in economics, and by James M. Buchanan and Gordon Tullock in constitutional analysis. See J. M. Buchanan and G. Tullock, *The Calculus of Consent: Logical Foundations of Constitutional Theory* (Ann Arbor: University of Michigan Press, 1962); R. H. Coase, "The Nature of the Firm," *Economica*, 4 (1937). In economics low transaction costs are generally considered desirable, but in politics, where the majority rule usually reigns, it is not necessarily so. Low transaction costs may, for example, facilitate the formation of majorities exploiting the outsiders.

functionary. This rather simple kind of relation occurs not only in clubs, but also in politics.

Instruction, on the other hand, prevails when the voters do not limit themselves to picking representatives in which they have confidence, but also require that they shall execute a certain program, which may be worked out in a rather detailed way. Therefore, at the same time as people are elected, a program that those elected are obliged to implement is, in fact, adopted. The program may very well be, and often is, formulated by the candidates who want to get elected. Different candidates for political positions thus offer to carry through different programs if they are elected. This, however, is fully consistent with the view that, once a candidate is elected, the program can be considered as an instruction *from* the voters *to* the elected.

It is easy to see that in reality, *mixtures* of delegation and instruction often occur. This, however, does not preclude the fact that sometimes the element of delegation dominates and sometimes the element of instruction. My hypothesis is that the Swedish system has a tendency towards instruction, whereas the US system has a tendency towards delegation.

The reason is simple. In a parliamentary system a campaigner, which in that case is a party, will be able to fulfill its promises if its electoral success is big enough. If, for example, a party alone gets more than 50 percent of the seats in the legislature, it can, by itself, form an executive and implement all its promises immediately. A presidential system is, in this respect, different. Imagine a person running for the presidency, or for a seat in the Congress. In both cases everybody knows that the person, after the election, and however great the electoral success, will not, without further cumbersome and yet uncertain negotiations, be in a position to deliver on his or her campaign proposals. Exactly for that reason, it would not be particularly clever, and perhaps even a bit ridiculous, to let detailed proposals, or instructions, dominate the campaign. It seems more expedient for the candidate to emphasize his or her own personal qualities, thereby indicating a capacity for prudent action in various future situations which, at the moment of the election, are impossible to foresee. That, on the whole, is what such candidates seem to do, and their resulting relation to the voters, therefore, is primarily one of delegation.

5 Lobbying

Olson's lack of detailed ideas about how lobbying organizations influence government is, as I see it, a salient deficiency in his argument. In order to highlight this lacuna, we can consider a society with no lobbying organizations at all. From one point of view, such a society may be thought of as an extremely flexible and effective market economy, suffering from no sclerosis whatsoever. It is, however, also possible to think about all the individuals in the society as an equal number of organizations, which, then, are as narrow, and thereby as irresponsible, as they could possibly be. From this point of view, the society would be sclerotic in the extreme. This latter position is, of course, absurd, for the very simple reason that the individuals, considered as organizations, could not hope to influence the politicians. In spite of this, there is hardly anything in Olson's works that excludes this last position, since they do not contain, or refer to, any theory of influence. If, however, we take the constitutional setting into account, the outlines of such a theory become visible. I am thinking about two points in particular.

First, the obvious targets for the lobbyists are the centers of political power, which, in a parliamentary system, means the party leaderships. The lobbying will thus be concentrated at the summits of the political hierarchies. In a presidential system, on the contrary, the lobbyists will approach individual members of the legislature, or perhaps small occasional groups of such members. Thus, in a parliamentary system the lobbyists' counterparts are few and powerful, whereas in a presidential system they are numerous and, individually, much less powerful.

Second, the lobbyists are likely to ask for what they can get. In the parliamentary setting, with its inclination towards instruction, the lobbyists are therefore, to a large extent, likely to ask for various new reforms. Such demands are, without any value attached to the words, constructive or creative. In the presidential situation, with its tendency towards delegation, the demands will have a different tendency. Since the mechanism of instruction works badly, the lobbyists are more likely to play a negative, or a blocking, role. They will probably find it difficult to induce the politicians to bring in specified new reforms, but will find it easy to tell the politicians what not to do, and the politicians are likely to find that information valuable.

These ideas may be related to the widespread opinion that lobbying is a characteristic trait of the political life in the United States, and that lobbying there is more developed, and more influential, than in other democracies. This, I think, is wrong. Rather, I think that lobbying in the United States, where the targets are so many and so dispersed, cannot be restricted to a few closed rooms as in a parliamentary system, but unavoidably becomes open and visible to everybody. It is also, for the same reasons, less effective, and requires more resources, than lobbying in parliamentary countries. This view is compatible not only with the well known, and well published, lobbying activities on Capitol Hill, but also with the relatively slow development of the public expenditures in the USA, and the country's good long-term economic growth.

6 The Emergence of Encompassing Organizations

We can now return to the mechanisms behind the encompassing Swedish lobbying organizations, and the rise of the welfare state. In doing so I will at first emphasize that these things, obviously, cannot be given an exclusively constitutional explanation: other factors, such as people's ideas, certainly matter as well. But even if the constitution is not a sufficient condition for the encompassing organizations, and for the welfare state, it may nonetheless be a necessary one. I find it difficult to imagine Swedish society in another constitutional setting.

As for the issue of encompassedness, it may first be noted that some of the Swedish organizations are closely linked with political parties. In particular, the blue-collar workers' national confederation of trade unions, Swedish Landsorganisationen or just "LO," is closely related to the Social Democratic Party, not only ideologically, but also in a technical and organizational sense. In fact, it is common to talk about the unions and the party as the two branches of the labor movement. Similar, though not equally close, relations exist between the farmers' national organization and the Center Party, which is strong in the countryside. These close relationships presuppose that both parties are reasonably consolidated, and that they have lasting and clear identities. It is difficult to imagine similar relations between a consolidated organization such as the Swedish LO and loose conglomerates such as the Democratic and Republican Parties in the United States. Thus, there is a constitutional background here.

The unions engage in two important activities: bargaining for wages and other conditions of employment, and lobbying the governmental power (which often means the Social Democratic Party) on a wide range of societal issues, including legislation for the labor market. It seems likely that the unions, in their roles as bargainers, have a wish to control the labor markets and the supply of labor, and that these goals are more easily satisfied the more encompassing, and the more centralized, the union movement is. Consequently the unions are also likely to lobby for laws facilitating the fulfillment of these ambitions.[18] The Social Democratic Party, in turn, is likely to welcome encompassing unions able to provide campaign funds and mobilize voters. In Sweden, with its prevailing political ideas and its constitution tuned for "instruction," the emergence of encompassing organizations should therefore

---

[18] One example of an implemented legal rule of this kind is the explicit exclusion of the labor market from the area of application of the general law safeguarding market competition. Another example is the law about collective bargaining, including the very liberal rules regulating the organizations' use of blockade, boycott, and similar measures for enforcing outsiders into the framework of collective bargaining.

not come as a surprise. This tendency toward encompassedness, however, is also likely to have been stimulated by the Labor Movement's socialism. Certainly a socialist movement, with its inclination toward centralism and planning, will build encompassing organizations rather than narrow ones when able to do so.

7 The Rise of the Welfare State

These intimate relationships between the unions and the Social Democratic Party have furthermore been a fertile ground for the Swedish welfare state. The resulting consolidated, long-lasting organizational structures are able to develop and to harbor successively more and more elaborated, detailed, and comprehensive ideas about the construction of the society, and to implement them. Certainly, as Olson holds, these ideas are prudent in the sense that they are about the well-being of the society as a whole, and the contrast with careless policies of narrow organizations is thus sharp. Still, the prudence has a leftist touch.

Sweden has long had a large number of successful and technically innovative private enterprises. A deeply rooted commercial and entrepreneurial mentality is an obvious feature in the nation's culture. The tendency towards nationalization of the means of production has mostly been weak. Rather, production has mainly been considered the role of the private enterprises, while the creation of a comprehensive social security system has been considered an important public task.[19] The social security system is here taken in a wide sense to include, for instance, the laws regulating the labor market. Those laws are, in fact, constructed in such a way that the labor organizations, within wide limits, are virtually able to determine the wage level. Thus, it is hardly the employers and their organizations, which are quite weak, that restrain the wages, but rather the threat of unemployment.[20] That threat, however, is considerably alleviated by the generous, almost completely publicly financed, transfers for the unemployed.[21] Turning from the labor market to the general social security

[19] The social security system, it may be added, has been valued by its supporters not only because it alleviates human problems, but also because it functions as a built-in stabilizer over the business cycle. See E. Lundberg, "The Rise and Fall of the Swedish Model," *Journal of Economic Literature*, March (1985), p. 14.

[20] This weakness is, to a large extent, a consequence of the nature of the weapons of strike and lockout. Laws of the kind mentioned in n. 18 above are also important in this context.

[21] Apart from being welcomed by the unemployed, these generous public transfers are also important for the organizations themselves. Without such transfers, unemployed (and therefore unsatisfied and disloyal) members could easily threaten an organization with disintegration. These generous transfers thus illustrate how the political power helps organizations in their ambition to become, and remain, encompassing. This point is made by I. Ståhl and K. Wickman in *Suedosclerosis II* (in Swedish) (Stockholm: Timbro, 1994) pp. 27 f.

system, it is enough for our purposes to state its far-reaching, and generally generous, character. In spite of the extensive use of explicit rather than implicit redistributions, this entails two important risks.

First, people may engage in rent-seeking behavior, which means that they will try to become members of groups entitled to transfers of various kinds. Second, the state may become committed to very large, and almost unpredictable, future expenses. If, for example, for some reason the number of unemployed suddenly expands rapidly, unemployment transfers will increase drastically.

8 From Success to Crisis

Sweden's smallness, and its direct contacts with foreign markets, are important for understanding its predicament. Mancur Olson has emphasized that a liberal trade policy is of crucial importance for the effectiveness of the economy, but that is not the only aspect. A small and open country must also be extremely flexible and able to adapt rapidly to all kinds of price changes in the international environment. With increasing advantages of scale and specialization, and thereby increasing dependence on foreign trade, this need for flexibility is continuously growing. Important parts of the Swedish society, and in particular the labor markets, have however become increasingly *less* flexible, which has increased the vulnerability to price shocks. The crude price hikes in the 1970s and, more important, the sharply increased real interest rates in the beginning of the 1990s, were therefore ill-fated.[22]

This should go a long way toward explaining the crisis. When a price shock hits an inflexible country such as Sweden, the needed adaptation comes only very slowly. In the meantime, the formidable social security system starts working. Most important, wages do not adapt when necessary but instead stiffly escalate their yearly percentages, as required by tradition, "justice," and the public philosophy. Unemployment therefore increases drastically, and so do the public expenses; and the crisis is upon us.

---

[22] A detailed account of "the real interest shock" is given in Ståhl and Wickman, *Suedosclerosis II*.

7 Affirmative Action and Reservations in the American and Indian Labor Markets: Are They Really That Bad?

Edward Montgomery[1]

1 Introduction

The subject of quotas for minorities in employment, education, or the political process is a controversial one in many countries of the world. In the United States, the debate over the costs and benefits of affirmative action programs rages at both national and local levels.[2] In India, Malaysia, Sweden, Fiji, Malaysia, South Africa, Canada, Great Britain, Romania, and many parts of the former Soviet Union, the issue of minority group quotas is a contentious one.[3] Proponents of these programs argue for them on equity grounds as a way to achieve social justice and to rectify the damage from historical discrimination in a society. Opponents also raise counter-equity arguments to the effect that these programs involve reverse discrimination and codify the very racial or ethnic stereotypes and focus in a society that they are designed to remove.

[1] I wish to thank Mancur Olson, David Montgomery, Arijit Sen, Anand Sway, Rachel Kranton, Debashish Bhattacharjee, Alok Ray, and seminar participants at the Madras Institute for Development Studies and the Indian Institute of Management for helpful comments and discussions. All errors and opinions are strictly my own.

[2] Witness the recent cancellation of affirmative action plans in university admissions and government contracting in the states of California, Texas, Louisiana, and others. Legislation has also been introduced at the national level to end minority affirmative action plans.

[3] It should be noted that in some cases quotas or affirmative action programs are geared toward a numerical majority group. In some cases this is because the protected or targeted groups have expanded to include a majority of the population (typically through the inclusion of women), while in others the targeted groups were always the numerically dominant part of the population (e.g. ethnic Malays or Fijians).

While much of the debate focuses on these equity considerations, efficiency arguments have also been raised on both sides. Proponents argue that these programs encourage minority skill acquisition and help overcome information-based discrimination, while opponents cite the economic costs of filling positions on grounds other than "merit" and the potential disincentives for minorities to achieve because they will be guaranteed "token" positions. Despite the heat of the debate, little light has been cast about what effects these programs really have on any of these dimensions.

In this paper I propose to discuss the theoretical and empirical evidence of the economic effects of affirmative action or quota type programs. The focus will be on the effects on wages and employment in the labor market as well as on the acquisition of skills. I also consider how the dynamics of collective action may turn these programs, which were designed to be temporary and limited in scope, into larger, more permanent ones.

This topic is important to those concerned with political and social equity. It is also important for those interested in economic growth or development. As India (and the United States) continues with the process of market liberalization, the performance of the labor market is, and will be, of vital importance to the success or failure of these efforts. The question of whether, and by how much, quotas (reservations) or affirmative action plans enhance or retard labor market performance and economic efficiency is important. Recent work by Robert Lucas, among others, suggests that human capital externalities are an important source of economic growth.[4] Even without subscribing to the role of human capital embodied in some of these models, it should not take much to convince economists and policy-makers of the importance of skill acquisition. To the degree that imperfections or institutional barriers in the labor market affect the returns to skill acquisition adversely, resources may be allocated inefficiently and society may under-invest in human capital and grow more slowly.

As stated above, the defense of these programs (or attack on them) has been based, in part, on considerations other than economic efficiency. I do not consider these here, nor do I consider affirmative action or quotas as they apply to attempts to insure minority representation in the political process. This is not to imply that these are not important issues, but simply that they are beyond the rubric of this paper, which, while designed to see what lessons or implications can be drawn from the experience with these programs in the United States, does not purport to capture all of the institutional, historical, religious, and sociological factors affecting caste or group outcomes in the Indian economy.

The format of the paper is as follows. In Section 2 I briefly review some of

---

[4] Robert Lucas, "On the Mechanics of Economic Development," *Journal of Monetary Economics*, 22 (July 1988): 3–42.

the institutional and historical details concerning reservations and affirmative action plans in the United States and India. Understanding the context in which these programs arose and their scope is vital to modeling or empirically understanding their impact. In Section 3 I discuss theoretical models of the effects of these programs. Emphasis is placed on highlighting the role of initial assumptions in predicting the impact of these programs. The goal is to develop insight as to when and under what circumstance one might expect these programs to have beneficial or harmful effects on economic performance. Given the fact that reservations in India apply primarily to government employment, I develop a two-sector model of the labor market. The purpose of this model is to examine the impact of affirmative action programs in just one part of the economy where individuals have higher skills than in the non-covered sector. Finally, I consider the dynamic effects of quotas on skill acquisition and productivity.

Section 4 reviews empirical studies of the effects of affirmative action in the United States. The paucity of micro-level data prevents me from systematically analyzing the effects of reservations in India. Thus, the empirical evidence can only be viewed as suggestive of the potential impact of expansions in the reservation system in India. Section 5 draws conclusions about the efficacy of these programs. Since part of the controversy over reservations in India (and affirmative action in the United States) revolves around the expansion in the coverage of these programs to include the Other Backward Castes and non-minorities, I also consider how in a dynamic context the scope of these programs might change over time to include more groups.

2   Sketch of Some Institutional Details and Background

2.1 *India*

Cox describes the caste system in India as having both a religious and an economic dimension.[5] Each caste had a traditional occupation which was regarded as both a duty and a reserved niche. The *jajamai* system dictated that by birth heritage each person was to be assigned a narrow range of jobs to which he could supply labor. Economic necessity or growth has led to some

---

[5] Oliver Cromwell Cox, *Caste, Race and Class: A Study in Social Dynamics*, (New York: Monthly Review Press, 1959).

Table 7.1 Shares of Scheduled Castes and Tribes in Indian Population, by State, 1981

States	Castes			Tribes		
	Total	Male	Rural	Total	Male	Rural
Andaman	0.000	0.000	0.000	0.118	0.108	0.159
Andhrapradesh	0.149	0.149	0.164	0.059	0.060	0.073
Arunpradesh	0.005	0.005	0.003	0.698	0.648	0.730
Assam	n/d	n/d	n/d	n/d	n/d	n/d
Bihar	0.145	0.144	0.152	0.083	0.081	0.089
Chandigarh	0.141	0.141	0.237	0.000	0.000	0.000
Dadr and Nagar	0.020	0.018	0.019	0.788	0.771	0.816
Delhi	0.180	0.180	0.230	0.000	0.000	0.000
Goa	0.022	0.021	0.019	0.010	0.010	0.011
Gujarat	0.072	0.072	0.070	0.142	0.140	0.191
Haryana	0.191	0.191	0.207	0.000	0.000	0.000
Himpradesh	0.246	0.248	0.252	0.046	0.046	0.049
Jammu-Kashmir	0.083	0.082	0.093	0.000	0.000	0.000
Karnataka	0.151	0.150	0.165	0.049	0.049	0.060
Kerala	0.100	0.101	0.108	0.010	0.010	0.012
Lakshadweep	0.000	0.000	0.000	0.938	0.926	0.966
Madhya Pra	0.141	0.142	0.145	0.230	0.223	0.278
Maharastra	0.071	0.071	0.075	0.002	0.090	0.127
Manipur	0.012	0.013	0.014	0.273	0.272	0.328
Meghalaya	0.004	0.004	0.003	0.806	0.786	0.861
Nagaland	0.000	0.000	0.000	0.840	0.801	0.897
Orissa	0.147	0.146	0.151	0.224	0.221	0.243
Pondicherry	0.160	0.162	0.217	0.000	0.000	0.000
Punjab	0.269	0.270	0.302	0.000	0.000	0.000
Rajasthan	0.170	0.171	0.177	0.122	0.120	0.149
Sikkim	0.058	0.055	0.054	0.233	0.222	0.236
Tamil Nadu	0.183	0.183	0.218	0.011	0.011	0.014
Tripura	0.151	0.151	0.159	0.284	0.282	0.315
Uttarpradesh	0.212	0.211	0.231	0.002	0.002	0.002
West Bengal	0.220	0.218	0.262	0.056	0.055	0.074
Mizoram	0.000	0.000	0.000	0.935	0.899	0.950

regional variation in these caste occupational norms within India. Nonetheless, mobility across occupations tends to occur only for the caste as a whole, rarely for an individual. The lowest castes (the Dalits or untouchables) occupied the lowest jobs, i.e. agricultural laborer and sweeper, which when combined with religiously justified social ostracism served to relegate them to the bottom of the economic and social heap.

As seen in Tables 7.1 and 7.2, 1980 Census data indicate that there is substantial variation in the representation of members of Scheduled Castes (Dalits) and Scheduled Tribes across states in India. In some states Scheduled Castes make up almost 30 percent of the population (Pondicherry), while in others they account for less than 1 percent (Arunpradesh). Scheduled Tribes range

Table 7.2 Representation of Scheduled Castes and Tribes by Occupation and State, 1981

States	Farm workers			Marginal workers			Main workers		
	Total	SC	ST	Total	SC	ST	Total	SC	ST
Andaman	0.067	0.000	0.000	0.037	0.000	0.135	0.332	0.000	0.263
Andhrapradesh	0.294	0.431	0.429	0.035	0.039	0.046	0.423	0.503	0.494
Arunpradesh	0.366	0.066	0.464	0.030	0.030	0.031	0.496	0.427	0.504
Assam	n/d	n/d	n/d	n/d	n/d	n/d	n/d	n/d	n/d
Bihar	0.235	0.315	0.320	0.027	0.030	0.088	0.297	0.364	0.371
Chandigarh	0.007	0.006	0.000	0.002	0.004	0.000	0.347	0.338	0.000
Dadr and Nagar	0.296	0.095	0.360	0.081	0.155	0.092	0.408	0.263	0.419
Delhi	0.008	0.007	0.000	0.003	0.003	0.000	0.319	0.302	0.000
Goa	0.087	0.050	0.168	0.046	0.052	0.086	0.306	0.348	0.389
Gujarat	0.194	0.180	0.349	0.050	0.046	0.096	0.322	0.314	0.406
Haryana	0.172	0.182	0.000	0.033	0.036	0.000	0.284	0.289	0.000
Himpradesh	0.243	0.273	0.324	0.080	0.080	0.106	0.344	0.357	0.408
Jammu-Kashmir	0.183	0.206	0.000	0.139	0.168	0.000	0.304	0.282	0.000
Karnataka	0.239	0.302	0.351	0.035	0.038	0.042	0.368	0.411	0.430
Kerala	0.110	0.219	0.316	0.039	0.058	0.047	0.267	0.363	0.405
Lakshadweep	0.000	0.000	0.000	0.046	0.000	0.049	0.197	0.000	0.179
Madhya Pra	0.293	0.307	0.427	0.045	0.045	0.071	0.384	0.405	0.463
Maharastra	0.239	0.251	0.406	0.038	0.042	0.053	0.387	0.402	0.479
Manipur	0.277	0.307	0.424	0.028	0.065	0.011	0.403	0.390	0.479
Meghalaya	0.315	0.042	0.357	0.025	0.014	0.026	0.434	0.334	0.450
Nagaland	0.347	0.000	0.396	0.007	0.000	0.007	0.475	0.000	0.470
Orissa	0.245	0.278	0.352	0.053	0.057	0.096	0.327	0.364	0.398
Pondicherry	0.116	0.304	0.000	0.018	0.041	0.000	0.287	0.387	0.000
Pubjab	0.170	0.194	0.000	0.021	0.034	0.000	0.294	0.290	0.000
Rajasthan	0.210	0.222	0.283	0.061	0.060	0.118	0.305	0.320	0.322
Sikkim	0.296	0.254	0.304	0.017	0.015	0.026	0.466	0.424	0.445
Tamil Nadu	0.240	0.372	0.392	0.024	0.032	0.031	0.393	0.459	0.482
Tripura	0.199	0.183	0.335	0.026	0.019	0.051	0.296	0.279	0.361
Uttarpradesh	0.218	0.262	0.317	0.015	0.020	0.027	0.292	0.317	0.369
West Bengal	0.155	0.215	0.331	0.019	0.021	0.053	0.283	0.296	0.415
Mizoram	0.305	0.037	0.322	0.037	0.000	0.039	0.417	0.822	0.397

from over 90 percent of the population in Lakshadweep to less than 1 percent in Tamil Nadu. Both groups tend to make up a higher percentage of the rural population than they do of the urban population. This is reflected in their high concentration among farm workers. The fact that Scheduled Castes and Tribes have not achieved overall economic parity is indicated by their over-representation among the lowest paid marginal workers. Further, as seen in Table 7.3, literacy rates for both groups still lag substantially behind the rest of the population. While there is substantial across-state variation in literacy for both groups, their attainment is generally about 60 percent of the overall literacy rate. Since literacy is a minimal requirement for higher paying jobs, this educational deficiency continues to hamper economic progress for the Scheduled Castes and Tribes.

Table 7.3 Literacy Rates, by State and Caste, 1981

States	Districts	Total Population		Scheduled Caste		Scheduled Tribe	
		Mean	Std	Mean	Std	Mean	Std
Andaman	1.00	0.52	1.00	–	–	0.31	1.00
Andhrapradesh	23.00	0.29	0.09	0.18	0.08	0.10	0.06
Arunpradesh	1.00	0.21	1.00	0.37	1.00	0.14	1.00
Bihar	31.00	0.26	0.06	0.11	0.04	0.22	0.18
Chandigarh	1.00	0.65	1.00	0.37	1.00	–	–
Dadr and Nagar	1.00	0.27	1.00	0.51	1.00	0.17	1.00
Delhi	1.00	0.62	1.00	0.39	1.00	0.00	–
Goa	1.00	0.57	1.00	0.38	1.00	0.26	1.00
Gujarat	19.00	0.42	0.08	0.41	0.14	0.22	0.10
Haryana	12.00	0.36	0.06	0.21	0.07	–	–
Himpradesh	12.00	0.40	0.08	0.32	0.10	0.38	0.15
Jammu-Kashmir	14.00	0.24	0.07	0.52	0.29	–	–
Karnataka	19.00	0.38	0.09	0.21	0.06	0.20	0.07
Kerala	12.00	0.70	0.08	0.56	0.09	0.39	0.19
Lakshadweep	1.00	0.55	1.00	–	–	0.53	1.00
Madhya Pra	45.00	0.27	0.08	0.19	0.08	0.10	0.06
Maharastra	26.00	0.44	0.09	0.36	0.09	0.25	0.10
Manipur	1.00	0.41	1.00	0.34	1.00	0.40	1.00
Meghalaya	1.00	0.34	1.00	0.26	1.00	0.32	1.00
Nagaland	1.00	0.43	1.00	–	–	0.40	1.00
Orissa	13.00	0.32	0.09	0.22	0.05	0.15	0.05
Pondicherry	1.00	0.56	1.00	0.32	1.00	–	–
Pubjab	12.00	0.41	0.08	0.24	0.11	–	–
Rajasthan	26.00	0.23	0.06	0.13	0.04	0.12	0.07
Sikkim	1.00	0.34	1.00	0.28	1.00	0.33	1.00
Tamil Nadu	16.00	0.47	0.10	0.32	0.11	0.28	0.14
Tripura	1.00	0.42	1.00	0.34	1.00	0.23	1.00
Uttarpradesh	56.00	0.28	0.08	0.16	0.06	0.36	0.31
West Bengal	16.00	0.38	0.12	0.24	0.08	0.15	0.10
Mizoram	1.00	0.60	1.00	0.84	1.00	0.60	1.00

The Indian Constitution attempted to eliminate the caste system and caste discrimination. Article 17 abolished untouchability and its practice in any form, while Article 15 outlawed discrimination based on religion, caste, race, sex, or place of birth. The Constitution included special provisions to protect the Dalits from "social injustice and all forms of exploitation."[6] In addition, India adopted what some Americans would refer to as "Affirmative Action" and others would call "quotas," for the Scheduled Castes in public-sector employment and education in 1943 and for the Scheduled Tribes in 1950. Not only has the federal

[6] Articles 335 and 29(2) deal with discrimination in employment and the reservation of positions in public employment. Article 46 adds the protection against injustice. See Biswajit Banerjee and J. B. Knight, "Caste Discrimination in the Indian Urban Labour Market," *Journal of Development Economics*, 17 (1985): 277–307, for a discussion of caste discrimination in the labor market.

government adopted a reservation system, but almost every state government has reservations for members of the Scheduled Castes and Tribes and some cover Other Backward Castes as well.[7] It should be noted, however, that the extension of anti-discrimination laws to private-sector employers did not occur until the Untouchability (Offenses) Act was amended in 1976.[8]

Since 1947, the level of reservations for competitive vacancies in public service at the federal level has risen from 12.5 to 15 percent for Scheduled Castes and from 5 to 7 percent for Scheduled Tribes (to match their percentage of the population). Banerjee and Knight note that these set-asides increased to almost 17 percent for direct recruitment jobs, and that the system has been expanded to cover not only entry-level government jobs but also those filled on the basis of promotion within certain classes (Classes II, III, and IV).[9] Galanter noted that Indian state governments have also adopted reservations on employment that range from 5 to 25 percent of jobs for members of the Scheduled Castes and between 3 and 80 percent for Scheduled Tribes.[10]

The federal reservation system in India extends beyond restricting competition for certain vacancies. It attempts to increase the supply of potential applicants from the protected groups by raising maximum age limits, lowering minimum examination qualifying scores, waiving fees, giving training, and providing travel allowances for travel to interviews. The Indian government also reduces or exempts the Scheduled Castes from the payment of tuition and fees in government and aided schools, provides books and meal subsidies, and offers scholarships to them for post-secondary education. About 20 percent of the positions at technical schools are reserved for members of the Dalits.

Many Indian states also have enacted reservations in education for members of the Other Backward Castes. The pool of potential applicants for these positions was further enlarged by raising the maximum age limit by three years and reducing the minimum qualifying marks by 5 percent. As these groups are larger (and better off economically) than the Dalits, this has been a source of tension over the reservations in India.

While the Other Backward Castes generally have no problem filling all of their reserved slots in higher education, members of the Scheduled Castes and Tribes do not fill all the slots reserved for them at medical, engineering, and

---

[7] See Marc Galanter, *Competing Equalities*, (Berkeley: University of California Press. 1984), ch. 4. Galanter notes that reservations for Other Backward Castes appear in at least 13 states and are most common in the south of India. In other states Other Backward Castes share the same reservation as the Scheduled Castes and Tribes.

[8] Ibid. ch. 4.

[9] Banerjee and Knight, "Caste Discrimination." Classes II, III, and IV correspond to attendant (peon), clerical, and other administrative jobs respectively. Class I refer to senior administrative positions.

[10] Galanter, *Competing Equalities*.

agricultural colleges.[11] Further, despite these reservation policies, it remains true that the Scheduled Castes are less likely to enter secondary and post-secondary education than non-scheduled castes and that they have a substantially lower completion rates at all levels of schooling. These discrepancies are not as severe at the lowest educational level (literacy), but they rise with the level of education. This is reflected in the fact that the Scheduled Castes accounted for 16.7 percent of illiterates in 1971 (compared with 14.6 percent of the population) but only 7 percent of the primary and middle school finishers and 3.2 percent of the matriculate or college graduates.

Despite the constitutional prohibitions against discrimination, evidence suggests that in many rural villages the practices of untouchability remain. Cox, Beteille, Berreman, and Lakshmanasamy and Madheswaran, in their various studies of the caste system, conclude that social discrimination against the Scheduled Castes is less virulent in urban settings, but remains a fact of Indian life.[12] Further, some evidence suggests that even within the government sector discrimination persists with regard to promotions and hiring for those jobs where personal interviews are allowed.[13]

2.2 United States

As in India, the US Constitution (the 14th Amendment) outlaws discrimination on the part of government. It was not until the 1960s that major anti-discrimination legislation with regard to private actions was passed.[14] The Civil Rights Act of 1964 and the Equal Pay Act of 1965 represented milestones in the anti-discrimination legislative process which ultimately led to legislation to outlaw discrimination on the basis of race, religion, sex, age, disability status, veterans status, and ethnic origin.[15]

Smith and Welch and Donohue and Heckman conclude that the evidence is unclear as to what role to ascribe to civil rights legislation for black economic

[11] Ibid. p. 63.

[12] Cox, *Caste, Race and Class*; Andre Beteille, *The Backward Classes in Contemporary India* (Delhi: Oxford University Press, 1992); Gerald D. Berreman, *Caste and other Inequities* (Delhi: Folklore Institute, 1979); T. Lakshmanasamy and S. Madheswaran, "Discrimination by Community: Evidence from Indian Scientific and Technical Labour Market," *Indian Journal of Social Science*, 8 (1995): 59–77.

[13] Galanter, *Competing Equalities*, p. 99.

[14] The 14th Amendment to the Constitution prohibits states (or the government) from passing laws that discriminate. This prohibition of state-sponsored discrimination was initially interpreted in the Plessey v. Ferguson case to allow "Jim Crow", or separate-but-equal, laws to stand. Not until 1954, in Brown v. the Board of Education, did the Supreme Court of the USA strike down this type of statute and prohibit the government from engaging in segregationist policies.

[15] Some state and local governments have also extended protection on the basis of sexual orientation and household composition.

progress in the 1960s and 1970s.[16] In the South, where discrimination was legally institutionalized, the evidence suggests a stronger role than in the North, where black economic gains have been more modest.[17] The declining relative position of blacks in the 1980s has been ascribed more to declining school quality and skills than to a rise in discrimination.[18] Nonetheless, despite improvements, recent audit studies by the Urban Institute and others suggest that discrimination continues to affect the lives of minorities in the United States.

The requirement that employers take active measures to remove discrimination was initiated in Executive Orders 11246 and 11375, which covered the behavior of federal contractors. Starting in 1968, these contractors were required by the Office of Federal Contract Compliance Programs (OFCCP) to present written "affirmative action" plans, complete with goals and timetables, to rectify "imbalances" in their employment practices with regards to race and gender. The penalties for failing to do so range from disbarment from government contracts to fines.[19] The OFCCP and the Equal Employment Opportunity Commission (EEOC), the two agencies charged with enforcing anti-discrimination laws, expanded the size of their staffs and the number of cases brought fairly continuously until the early 1980s, with their attention increasingly focused on sex discrimination cases.[20]

Part of the controversy over affirmative action plans in the United States revolves around the degree to which the goals and timetables required in the statutes have become quotas. Despite the fact that the 1964 Civil Rights Act (and all subsequent amendments) explicitly proscribe the use of quotas, opponents argue that employers' fear of governmental or individual legal action has effectively established a de facto quota system in the United States. Proponents counter that the lax enforcement of both equal pay and affirmative

[16] See James P. Smith and Finis Welch, "Affirmative Action and Labor Markets," *Journal of Labor Economics*, 2 (April 1984): 269–301; and John Donohue and James Heckman, "Continuous versus Episodic Change: the Impact of Civil Rights Policy on the Economic Status of Blacks," *Journal of Economic Literature*, 39 (December 1991): 1603–43.

[17] I know of no studies that have examined in detail the importance of civil rights legislation in the recent economic progress of women. This may alter previous conclusions on the effects of these laws as serious attention to sex discrimination by the EEOC is a relatively recent phenomena (1980s). The fact that the gender composition of many occupations has changed substantially over the last 20 years, while the wages of women have risen relative to men in the 1980s, suggests a possible benefit of these laws.

[18] See Chinhui Juhn, Kevin Murphy, and Brooks Pierce, "Accounting for the Slowdown in Black–White Wage Convergence," in *Workers and their Wages: Changing Patterns in the United States*, ed. Marvin Kosters (Washington: American Enterprise Institute Press, 1991). It should be pointed out that Leonard and others find evidence that the decline in EEOC enforcement efforts over the past decade has had an adverse effect on the relative position of blacks.

[19] Disbarment is rarely used as a penalty. The first example of such a penalty did not occur until 1974 and the penalty had been imposed just 26 times (as of the early 1980s). See Jonathon Leonard, "Anti-Discrimination or Reverse Discrimination: the Impact of Changing Demographics, Title VII, and Affirmative Action on Productivity," *Journal of Human Resources*, 19 (Spring 1984): 145–72, and "The Impact of Affirmative Action on Employment," *Journal of Labor Economics*, 2 (October 1984): 439–63.

[20] See Smith and Welch, "Affirmative Action."

action requirements means that these timetables are simply paper goals and not quotas. To the degree that this is true, the effects (either positive or negative) of affirmative action plans in the United States will provide a lower-bound estimate of the effects of similar programs in India or other countries where the reservations are explicit quotas.

3 Theoretical Considerations

In this section I consider theoretical models of the cost and benefits of affirmative action or quota programs. I examine the degree to which predictions of the economic consequences of these programs rely on the continued existence of discrimination and the form that it takes. There is a wide range of models that yield somewhat different conclusions about the efficacy of these programs. Becker's seminal work on the economics of discrimination analyzed the effect on employment and earnings of employer, worker, or customer "taste" or prejudice in a competitive economy. These models predict that discriminators "pay" for their tastes via lower profits or higher prices[21]. As seen in Table 7.4,

Table 7.4 Summary of Implication of the Impact of Quotas in Alternate Models of Discrimination

Employer	
Case 1	If no discrimination exists, policy leads to: (*a*) increased minority employment in covered sector; (*b*) no changes in minority wages or productivity.
Case 2	If all employers are prejudiced, then (*a*) relative minority earnings are higher in the covered than in the non-covered sector; (*b*) minority "wait" unemployment exists; (*c*) employment in covered sector falls relative to that in the non-covered sector.
Co-worker	
Case 1	If segregation existed prior to government action, then there is an increase in relative minority employment in the covered sector.
Case 2	If all minorities work in covered sector, then covered-sector wages exceed non-covered-sector wages.
Case 3	If minorities are employed in both sectors, then all minority workers will be in non-covered sectors; wages will be the same within and across sectors.
Customer	If quotas apply to sector with discrimination customers, then (*a*) majority productivity is higher in covered than in non-covered sector, while the reverse holds for minorities; (*b*) relative minority employment in the covered sector increases; (*c*) minority relative wages are higher or unchanged.

Source: Lawrence Kahn, "Customer Discrimination and Affirmative Action," *Economic Inquiry*, 26 (July 1991): 555–71

[21] See Gary Becker, *Economics of Discrimination*, 2nd edition (Chicago: Chicago University Press, 1971).

even within Becker-type models, the source of the discrimination (customers, co-workers, employers) is found to affect the direction and impact of quotas or affirmative action requirements. Further, differences in a country's technology, institutions, population distribution, discrimination patterns, and other factors also alter the conclusions about the efficacy of these programs. Thus, in this section I will illustrate that, contrary to the certitude with which both proponents and opponents make their claims, there is not a simple answer as to whether the benefits of quotas are positive or negative.

A challenge for any theory of discrimination is to explain what appears to be its persistence. In Becker-type taste models, competitive economic forces will tend to erode or eliminate these differences.[22] That is, employers, customers, or employees with below-equilibrium tastes for discrimination have an incentive to "cheat" on the prevailing social norms. Thus, for discrimination to persist, the taste for discrimination, or the inclination to discriminate, needs to be extreme enough to dominate the economic incentive to cheat, or there must be other market imperfections (or government action) that allow discrimination to persist.[23]

Statistical discrimination models have the potential advantage of not requiring a large degree of animus in order to generate long-run discriminatory equilibrium. However, since they rely on the presence of imperfect information, they are likely to provide a good explanation of the persistence of discrimination only where latent productivity is very costly to observe. Further, the types of trait that are hard to observe must be sensitive to wage incentives.

Akerlof develops a model of caste or ethnic discrimination that is consistent with the persistence of discrimination or the absence of "cheating" on the dominant or discriminating groups's tastes.[24] The key enforcement mechanism is that transactions that break the caste taboo change the subsequent behavior of other agents in the economy. Caste (or group) serves not only to identify how one will be treated by another individual in a transaction, but also how all other members of that group will treat you in subsequent transactions. Thus, someone who violates caste taboos changes all subsequent behavior of uninvolved parties with respect to the violator of caste norms.

The key assumption necessary to maintain a discriminatory equilibrium is that members of the lowest caste are not free to set up their own economy, independent of the others' castes, and be as well off as they are under the caste

---

[22] If discrimination takes the form of nepotism for the favored group, then employer discrimination will not be eliminated. There are no market forces to bid away favored workers who are receiving more than their marginal products if firms are willing to accept lower profits. Unlike the standard employer discrimination model, this formulation gives majority or favored workers an incentive to preserve the discriminatory equilibrium as they are getting above (rather than equal to) their reservation marginal products.

[23] It is also possible that persistence can result in an employer discrimination model if the firm's cost function is upward sloping. This effectively limits expansion and prevents non-discriminators from driving out discriminating firms.

[24] See George Akerlof, "The Economics of Caste and of the Rat Race and other Woeful Tales," *Quarterly Journal of Economics*, 90 (November 1976): 599–618.

system. Given the highly interdependent nature of rural production, this condition seems likely to hold, although in urban settings it may be less binding. In any case, this condition serves to not only to put a floor on the level of resources that the lowest caste can receive, but also to explain why this group might not seek to actively change the system.

The caste system imposes penalties for workers, employers, and customers for violating caste employment rules, and results in workers being segregated into their caste-specific occupations or jobs. In equilibrium, no customer has an incentive to buy from a cheating firm and no employer has an incentive to hire outcast workers. Since the marginal product of the worker depends on his job assignment, the result will be an income distribution skewed along caste lines. This caste equilibrium is stable but not Pareto-optimal, since in a Pareto-optimal equilibrium all workers would be employed in the higher-wage occupations or jobs and would receive the same wage.

Reservations in this world allow employers to hire members of the lower castes for skilled jobs. This would be mutually beneficial if, as part of compliance with the law, social or caste sanctions could be avoided. Donohue and Heckman have argued that this is an apt characterization of the behavior of southern textile firms in the United States. Prior to the 1964 Civil Rights Act, black employment was negligible.[25] It grew dramatically after the law's passage as employers could now engage in welfare (profit)-enhancing employment decision and avoid the social sanctions previously evoked from hiring blacks.

The welfare-enhancing benefits of quotas in this world occur in part because worker productivity is *job*, and not individual, specific. Thus, reassigning individual workers to different occupations generates no output loss. With the economy operating in the caste or discriminatory equilibrium, pre-quotas, reservations, or equal opportunity laws must be welfare-enhancing since they reduce existing distortions at no cost. In general, this model suggests then that in economies or industries where discrimination exists, and where most heterogeneity is job and not individually related, affirmative action plans or reservations will be nondistortionary and will lead to an increase in social welfare and output.

Welch develops a neoclassical model that is useful for illustrating the conditions under which quotas will tend to have *distortionary* effects on wages, employment, and output.[26] A key difference from the Akerlof framework is that here heterogeneity is individual rather than job-related. The one-sector version of this model assumes that output is given by

(1) $$q = f(a, b),$$

[25] Donohue and Heckman, "Continuous versus Episodic Change."
[26] See Finis Welch, "Employment Quotas for Minorities," *Journal of Political Economy*, 84 (August 1976): S105–39.

where a and b are the number of skilled and unskilled workers respectively. Quotas take the form of a requirement that employers hire r skilled minority workers for every majority worker. If these quotas are to bind, or to lead to more than a reshuffling of workers between firms, then $r > \pi_a$, where π_a is the percentage of skilled minorities in the population.

In this Becker-type model, discrimination takes the form of a subjective devaluation of the minorities' marginal product. The perceived productivities of minority skilled and unskilled workers are thus $\alpha_a f_a$ and $\alpha_b f_b$ respectively, where $\alpha_i \leq 1$ indicates the amount of discrimination. With $\alpha_i < 1$, discrimination exists, and wages, employment (for minorities), and output will be lower than if discrimination did not exist ($\alpha_i = 1$).

If equal pay laws are imposed without quotas (or without prohibitions on discrimination in hiring), minority employment and output in the economy will be further reduced.[27] Thus, as noted in Kahn, equal pay laws without anti-employment discrimination protection simply transfer the discrimination from the wage to the employment side of the labor market.[28]

If equal pay laws are combined with quotas, then the wage paid to skilled minority and majority workers will be a weighted average of their marginal products, or $f_a (1 + \alpha_a r)/(1 + r)$, since there are r minority workers for every skilled majority worker. This results in a transfer of income between minority and majority skilled workers. Note that if discrimination is absent, or if equal pay is not required or enforced, this transfer will not occur. Further, if the economy was at full employment prior to the quota, then the fact that $r > \pi_a$ means that there will be a surplus of skilled majority workers post-quota. Quotas are harmful in this context, as aggregate employment and output are reduced. It can be shown that the fall in output depends on the degree to which $r > \pi_a$ and on the skilled workers' share of output in the economy.

In thinking about the effects of reservations in government employment in India, or of affirmative action among federal contractors in the United States, a more appropriate framework allows for the presence of two sectors (covered/ uncovered), since much of employment in both countries is *not* under any requirement to practice affirmative action or reservations. The uncovered sector in India is the private sector, while the covered sector is public employment. In the United States the covered sector includes public-sector employers and federal contractors, while the uncovered sector includes nonfederal contractors.

In this context, the imposition of reservations (much like the presence of unions) is equivalent to a tax on the supply of skilled majority labor in the covered sector. This "tax" induces a shift in skilled workers to the uncovered

---

[27] Again, this assumes that discrimination exists, or $\alpha_i < 1$.
[28] Lawrence Kahn, "Customer Discrimination and Affirmative Action," *Economic Inquiry*, 26 (July 1991): 555–71.

sectors, raising the wages of both skilled minority and majority workers who remain in the covered sector.[29] Employment and output in the covered sector will fall, but that in the uncovered sector will increase. The movement of skilled workers to the uncovered sector will initially lead to a reduction in wages of skilled workers in the uncovered sector, and to an increase in wages for unskilled workers in that sector. What happens to unskilled wages in the covered sector depends on the relative skill intensity of the two sectors and on whether unskilled workers are gross substitutes or complements for skilled workers. In the United States it seems plausible that the covered sector is more skill-intensive than the uncovered sector. Whether this is true in India can be debated, but it seems plausible, as the mean level of educational attainment in the public sector is higher than in the private sector as a whole (including agriculture). Given a higher skill intensity in the covered sector, then if unskilled workers are complements, their wages fall in the covered sector. This in turn induces a migration of unskilled workers to the uncovered sector. If they are substitutes, wages will tend to rise for unskilled workers in the covered sector (as they did in the uncovered sector).

Overall, we expect that income for minorities (both skilled and unskilled) will unambiguously be higher, and that majority unskilled workers in both sectors and majority skilled workers in the covered sector are also likely to gain from quotas. The losers are the skilled majority workers now found in the uncovered sector.[30] This is consistent with the observation that in India and the United States quotas are viewed with the most hostility by skilled workers who claim to have been displaced, and that skilled members of minority groups are their biggest advocates.

The social costs of quotas in this context involve the inefficient allocation of labor and output between these sectors. An additional concern with quotas in developing countries is that the movement of skilled workers to the "uncovered" sector may take the form of international migration or a "brain drain." This would add to the welfare loss associated with quotas as it involves a reduction in the stock of a nation's human capital (and the loss of any social investment in skills via public education), which is a cause for concern. It should

---

[29] It is theoretically possible that wages of skilled workers in the covered sector might fall. If the elasticity of substitution in the covered sector is less than the elasticity of product demand, $\sigma_c + \eta < 0$, then it is possible that enough outmigration of unskilled workers from the covered sector could leave the skilled–unskilled worker ratio in the covered sector actually higher than before the quota. This would result in lower wages for skilled majority workers in the covered sector. This outcome, while possible, seems implausible.

[30] The models outlined above apply only to quotas on skilled workers. Given the plausible assumption that $\pi > r$ for unskilled workers, reservations for them will only generate a reallocation of unskilled minority workers from the uncovered to the covered sector. This assumption must hold unless quotas are set above the respective population ratios, given the assumption that quotas bind for skilled workers. These quotas will benefit unskilled minorities at the expense of unskilled majority workers if wages are higher in the covered sector. Since this is inconsistent with equilibrium in the demand for unskilled workers, there should be no net effect on income or wages from this type of reservation.

be noted, however, that reservation will increase emigration only to the extent that skilled worker wages are depressed enough to cover the psychic and monetary costs of international migration. Only in countries or occupations where the level of reservations is high relative to the supply of skilled minority workers (so that substantial displacement of majority workers occurs), is this likely to be a major concern.[31]

It should be noted that, to the degree that covered-sector firms are prevented by quota constraints from hiring skilled majority workers, wages for skilled workers in the two sectors will diverge. If equal pay laws are in effect, this wage differential generates the incentive for firms to engage in skill bumping, whereby unskilled minorities are classified as skilled workers by firms.[32] Since the alternative wage for skilled majority workers is $w_{2a} \leq w_{1a}$, the incentive to bump will exist as long as the loss from paying an unskilled minority the same wage as a skilled worker $(w_{1a} - w_{2b})$ is recouped by being able to hire a skilled majority worker at the uncovered-sector wage $(f_{1a} - w_{2a})$.[33] In equilibrium, bumping will occur until an equality exists between these conditions, generating a transfer of income between majority and minority workers. Output in this economy will be *higher* than without bumping. Covered-sector employment rises, and the extra cost of the reclassified minority workers is paid for by the majority skilled workers who gained access to covered-sector jobs. Interestingly, simulations suggest that, if the reclassified minority worker's marginal product is not below that of other unskilled workers, the social costs of quotas are negligible.

While quotas or reservations might result in some "skill bumping" or relabelling of unskilled minority workers, it is also possible that they may have a more dramatic affect on the decision to invest in becoming skilled in the first place. Lundberg and Startz, Milgrom and Oster, and Coate and Loury develop statistical or information-based discrimination models in which skill acquisition is endogenous.[34] In particular, they consider how employers' use of group

---

[31]   The size of a country's or a sector's elasticity of labor demand and supply will also determine if this effect is large. Wages will fall more, inducing more emigration, if these elasticities are low.

[32]   If the equal pay constraint was not binding, skilled majority workers might try and bribe skilled minority workers to work with them so that they may gain access to covered sector jobs. Thus, skilled minority workers would receive higher wages or rents equal to this wage differential. This would alleviate the excess demand for covered-sector employment and would convert these programs into pure income redistribution programs with little attenuate social costs.

[33]   This loss is less than that indicated in Welch, "Employment Quotas," as he assumes that a misclassified skilled worker has a marginal product *less* than he would in an unskilled job. Although misclassification leads to a loss in output relative to having a skilled worker in the job, it is not clear why the marginal product of an unskilled worker in a skilled job should be even lower than it would be if that individual were in the right job. See Smith and Welch, "Affirmative Action."

[34]   Shelly Lundberg and Robert Startz, "Private Discrimination and Social Intervention in Competitive Labor Markets," *American Economic Review*, 73 (June 1983): 340–7; Paul Milgrom and Sharon Oster, "Job Discrimination, Market Forces, and the Invisibility Hypothesis," *Quarterly Journal of Economics*, 102 (August 1987): 453–76; and Stephen Coate and Glenn Loury, "Will Affirmative Action Policies Eliminate Negative Stereotypes?" *American Economic Review*, 83 (December 1993): 1220–40.

identifiers in making inferences about individual productivity will affect decisions to invest in human capital.[35] If employers are less able to evaluate investments in human capital for minorities, then one would expect them to receive a lower return, invest less, and receive lower average wages as a result of lower average productivity. Thus, with endogenous worker productivity, employer beliefs of lower average productivity for minorities can become self-fulfilling, even if the innate ability distributions are the same.

Milgrom and Oster and Coate and Loury consider the question of what impact affirmative action or equal opportunity laws would have in a world with statistical discrimination and endogenous skill determination. Interestingly, both of these papers generate scenarios in which affirmative action or quotas are welfare-enhancing.[36] In Milgrom and Oster, firms discriminate in job assignments in order to hide workers from outsiders. Firms have private information on worker ability which is revealed to the outside world only through promotions or new job assignments. If the extent of private information (*invisibility*) is higher for minorities, then employers will have both the incentive and the ability to hide them in lower paying jobs. Minorities will find that their returns to investment in skills that cannot be readily determined by the market are less, so they will acquire fewer skills and be on average less productive. Affirmative action will have ambiguous effects because, while it reduces the number of qualified minorities who were assigned to low-level jobs and improves job matching, it also results in promotions for some unqualified workers.[37] In the long run, inefficiency in job assignment and skill acquisition is lower, output is higher, and average earnings and promotion probability differences between majority and minority workers decline.

Coate and Loury develop a matching model in which employers hold negative stereotypes of the minority productivity.[38] In this model, when the returns to acquiring signals of ability is low, or if signals are relatively uninformative, temporary versions of affirmative action programs will be optimal in eliminating stereotypes. Conversely, if the representation of skilled minorities is low relative to the quota, and the payoff to skill bumping is high, then the return to investing in skills (and hence the level of investment) might actually fall. Intuitively, which effect dominates depends on whether minorities react to the affirmative action job guarantees by relying on skill bumping or

---

[35] Welch, "Employment Quotas," also analyzes the effects on the return to education or skill in taste models of discrimination with quotas. Absent skill bumping, minority skilled wages rise relative to majority workers, generating convergence in underlying skill distributions. With skill bumping, the predictions are ambiguous and depend on the underlying cause of the initial inequality.

[36] Milgrom and Oster, "Job Discrimination"; Coate and Loury, "Affirmative Action Policies."

[37] These policies need to be combined with wage scales in order to have these properties. Affirmative action by itself would not eliminate the kind of discrimination they discuss.

[38] As with most statistical discrimination models, individual employers or workers have no incentive to correct misinformation. Since investment decisions are based on group beliefs or behavior, individuals cannot change their own payoffs and hence will not try.

increase their investments in skills now that their probability of being able to utilize them successfully has risen. A necessary condition for investment to fall is that minorities are a relatively small share of total employment. If quotas include women or other large population groups, the cost to employers of engaging in sufficient skill bumping will be high and quotas will be unlikely to lead to a decline in minority group skill investments.

We have considered the effects of quotas when worker productivity is determined by the job and by the individual and where discrimination is taste or information-based. I would like now to consider a somewhat different institutional context, in which worker rewards (pay) are tied not to the absolute level of their marginal product but to their relative productivity. Lazear and Rosen and others have provided a theoretical rationale for why firm internal labor markets or other hierarchical institutions might find this type of reward structure optimal.[39] These rank-order arrangements have been used to explain the large payoffs to CEOs of corporations, sales commissions based on relative performance, sporting tournament structures, and political campaigns. In addition, university admissions and some rationed government jobs are based on an applicant's relative ranking and not the absolute level of the individual's scores.

Schotter and Weigelt provide an interesting look at the impact of dis-crimination, equal opportunity, and affirmative action laws within the context of rank-order tournaments.[40] Discrimination (unfair tournaments) reduces the level of effort expended by both majority and minority workers.[41] Discrimin-ation increases (decreases) the likelihood that a majority (minority) worker will win at every effort level, leading to a decrease in investment from *both* groups. Thus, equal opportunity laws have the potential to increase both minority and majority worker effort, raising aggregate output.[42]

Even in the absence of discrimination, tournaments may be uneven because access to credit markets or other factors make the cost of effort (or investment) greater for minorities than for majority workers. These uneven tournaments yield lower effort than fair tournaments. The imposition of affirmative action in an uneven environment leads to lower effort (and output) from both groups. Schotter and Weigelt suggest, for plausible parameter values, that the fall in effort from minorities will not be enough to offset the advantage given them by an affirmative action program so the probability of labor market success will

[39] Edward Lazear and Sherwin Rosen, "Rank-Order Tournaments as Optimum Labor Contracts," *Journal of Political Economy*, 89 (October 1981): 841–64.

[40] Andrew Schotter and Keith Weigelt, "Asymmetric Tournaments, Equal Opportunity Laws, and Affirmative Action: Some Experimental Results," *Quarterly Journal of Economics*, 107 (May 1992): 511–40.

[41] When discrimination takes the additive form, or does not vary with the level of effort, the marginal payoff to effort is unaffected.

[42] This is not necessarily welfare-enhancing, as both groups would prefer to exert less effort. As in Akerlof, "Economics of Caste," the rat race properties of these tournaments increase output but may lower welfare.

rise. Thus, while output rises when discrimination is present and quotas are imposed, it tends to fall under these institutional arrangements if discrimination no longer exists.

These predictions rely on the assumption that workers know the nature of their payoff structure or the link between effort and potential rewards. In the real world, as Schotter and Weigelt note, this may not hold. Consequently, individuals may mistake luck (random success or failure) for differences in underlying ability, prejudice, or costs of investment. This creates the possibility that agents will drop out or give up if they feel that they are at a substantial disadvantage. Experimental evidence by Schotter and Weigelt suggests that this is indeed an important consideration. Even without discrimination, affirmative action programs in this circumstance can lead to *more* output, as disadvantaged groups react to the increased chance of winning by playing rather than withdrawing.

This spillover, or unintended benefit, of affirmative action programs comes from the fact that agents whose probability of success is small may move to the zero effort corner solution. Anecdotal evidence from the United States and India is supportive of this notion that reservations are perceived as important even though employment in the covered sectors is a remote possibility for the majority of the minority population.[43] Surveys suggest that reservations are instrumental in creating the impression that it is possible for a member of the minority group to succeed at the highest levels. Thus, even though the likelihood that the average inner-city black in the United States, or rural Dalit in India, gets one of the reserved slots is low, when the payoff is sufficiently positive they may be induced to expend effort or acquire skills. The result may be that they are better able to compete for a series of lower-level prizes (e.g. becoming literate, completing primary or secondary school). Thus, affirmative action in one sector of the economy may have collateral benefits in inducing individuals not to drop out, raising output in the uncovered sector and the economy.

4 Empirical Evidence

Given the lack of strong theoretical predictions about the likely efficacy of affirmative action type policies, it is useful to see what the empirical evidence accumulated to date suggests. Unfortunately the absence of good micro-level data precludes an effective empirical test of many of the propositions discussed

---

[43] See Galanter, *Competing Equalities*, ch. 4.

in this paper. Further, I do not know of any systematic attempts to measure the effects of reservations in India. Consequently, I limit this section primarily to a review of existing empirical work on the effects of affirmative action programs in the United States. Some evidence on the extent and success of reservations in Indian states will also be presented. Nonetheless, the empirical evidence will only suggest what might be the likely consequences of these reservations.

First, since the effect of quotas depends to a large degree on whether discrimination still exists, it is useful to review recent work on the extent or existence of labor market discrimination. The fact that discrimination has persisted long after the passage of anti-discrimination laws in the United States and India might seem self-evident. Proving discrimination or the disparate treatment of comparably skilled individuals, however, is problematic given the fact that the econometrician is unable to observe all the factors determining an individual's productivity. Nonetheless, there exist a plethora of empirical studies examining race and gender wage differentials in the United States.[44] Most seem to conclude that there are persistent unexplained wage differentials along racial and gender lines. Some recent ones have attributed this residual gap to school quality differences, and to gender socialization and family responsibility differences.[45]

Given the econometric difficulties in controlling for these unobservable factors, audit studies have been employed to test for the existence of discrimination in hiring, housing rental, and automobile purchase.[46] These audit studies, while not completely randomizing racial assignment, come closer to controlled tests of the effects of discrimination. Moreover, they seem to find persistent evidence of racial differences in treatment. Interestingly, there is also some evidence to support the conclusion that anti-discrimination laws lead to increased non-employment for minorities. Their employment-to-population ratios and unemployment rates have risen relative to those for majority workers over this period. This is consistent with the two-sector models' prediction of a gap between wages in the covered and uncovered sectors, and with

---

[44] See Richard Freeman, "Black Economic Progress after 1964: Who Has Gained and Why? in *Studies in Labor Markets*, ed. Sherwin Rosen (Chicago: University of Chicago Press, 1981); and Francine Blau, *The Economics of Men, Women and Work* (Englewood Cliffs, NJ: Prentice-Hall, 1992).

[45] See Derek Neal and William Johnson, "The Role of Pre-market Factors in Black–White Wage Differentials," NBER Working Paper no. 5124, May 1995.

[46] For hiring, see Jerry Newman, "Discrimination in Recruitment: an Empirical Analysis," *Industrial and Labor Relations Review*, 32 (1978): 15–23.; Margery Turner, Michael Fix, and Raymond Struyk, *Opportunities Denied, Opportunities Diminished: Discrimination in Hiring* (Washington: Urban Institute Press, 1991); and David Neumark, "Sex Discrimination in Hiring in the Restaurant Industry: an Audit Analysis," NBER Working Paper no. 5024, 1995. For housing rental, see John Yinger, "Measuring Racial Discrimination with Fair Housing Audits: Caught in the Act," *American Economic Review*, 76 (December 1986): 881–98. For studies on discrimination in automobile purchase, see Ian Ayres and Peter Siegelman, "Race and Gender Discrimination in Bargaining for a New Car," *American Economic Review*, 85 (June 1995): 304–21.

the effect of more effective enforcement of equal pay than equal employment laws in a world with continuing discrimination.

A second issue to examine is whether the beneficiaries of affirmative action or quotas are those that our theoretical model predicts. The empirical evidence on the effectiveness of affirmative action programs is summarized in Kahn.[47] The results are generally in line with our theoretical predictions. Every study to date has found that employers in the covered sector respond to the presence of affirmative action requirements by increasing their utilization of minorities.[48] The effects seem to be larger for blacks than for women, although this may be due to the relatively recent attention paid to affirmative action for women. Minorities also seem to experience wage gains in the covered sector relative to the uncovered sector. This positive effect on wages seems to be larger for more educated (skilled) blacks than for the less educated (skilled).

Contrary to what one might expect if affirmative action were really quotas, the evidence suggests that the employment gains for minorities came in growing firms and not through the displacement of majority workers. Further, although firms that promised to increase their utilization more did so, they consistently failed to reach their stated objectives. Finally, the productivity of minority workers, and of the covered sector as a whole, is no lower than that of white male employees, or the uncovered sector. Thus, skill bumping or mislabelling unqualified minorities seems to be of limited significance. Recent work by Holzer and Neumark again finds little evidence that skill bumping is a major concern, as minority new hires or promotions at firms that practice affirmative action do not appear to be significantly less qualified than majority workers.[49] Thus, the evidence for adverse output or welfare effects associated with affirmative action seems to be missing.

There is also little direct evidence of beneficial effects of affirmative action on output. Ayres and Cramton found some positive effects of affirmative action when they examined the recent FCC auction of licenses to slices of the radio spectrum.[50] Minority bidders were given preferred terms as part of an affirmative action plan. The net result was more minority bids and greater representation of minority firms. Although this result is not surprising, the fact that the government succeeded in generating *more* bid revenue from these auctions is. Their evidence suggests that the bid price of majority contractors also rose, generating an increase in net revenues for the government. As in the

---

[47] Lawrence Kahn, "Customer Discrimination and Affirmative Action," *Economic Inquiry*, 26 (July 1991): 555–71.

[48] See Leonard, "Anti-Discrimination" and "Impact of Affirmative Action"; Smith and Welch, "Affirmative Action"; and Donahue and Heckman, "Continuous versus Episodic change."

[49] Harry Holzer and David Neumark, "Are Affirmative Action Hires Less Qualified? Evidence from Employer–Employee Data on New Hires," mimeo, 1996.

[50] Ian Ayres and Peter Cramton, "Pursuing Deficit Reduction through Diversity: How Affirmative Action at the FCC Increased Auction Competition," *Stanford Law Review*, forthcoming.

Schotter—Weigelt experiment, subsidizing competition from one group where markets are thin had the effect of increasing effort from all groups and thereby increasing output.

Ayres and Cramtom also find evidence that the same result can be found with regard to government contractors. Here again, a key feature is that a limited number of firms typically bid for the work. Enacting affirmative action programs to subsidize one class of bidders results in substantially lower contract prices, with the reduction being sufficient to more than offset the subsidy costs of the affirmative action program. It would be of interest to investigate whether the same positive effect of affirmative action holds in thin labor markets or where the incumbent workers have some degree of monopoly power (perhaps at the senior management or professional occupations).

Data on the extent or effect of reservations in India seem to be limited. Systematic analysis requires micro-level data to capture the level of worker skills and to control for factors other than reservations that may have impact on hiring and promotion decisions for members of the protected castes. Nonetheless, reservations may have played a role in the significant growth in the representation of the lower castes and tribes in government employment that has occurred over the past forty years. In 1951 the Scheduled Caste share of federal government employment ranged from 9.4 percent in the lowest jobs (Class IV) to 0.6 percent in the highest jobs (Class I). By 1979 the Dalit had increased their representation to 19.3 percent of the lowest jobs and 4.8 percent of the highest. Although they remain under-represented relative to their share of the population (14.6 percent) in all but the lowest jobs, they significantly improved their employment in all public-sector jobs over this period.

The impression that reservations played a role in this expansion is reinforced by comparing Scheduled Caste and Scheduled Tribe employment in public undertakings (contractors) before and after reservations were extended to them in the mid-1960s. In 1965, fourteen years after the passage of anti-discrimination laws and the imposition of reservations at the federal level, Scheduled Castes members still accounted for only 0.20 percent of Class I jobs, 1.07 percent of Class II, and 0.92 percent of Class III jobs at public undertakings in 1965. However, 10 years after reservations were imposed on public undertakings, the percentage of employment in each of these job classes accounted for by members of the Scheduled Castes had increased by at least *150 percent*, rising to 1.4 percent of Class I, 3.0 of Class II, and 13.7 of Class III jobs in 1975.[51] While some of this growth may be due to general improvement in the skills and other factors affecting employment of these castes, the changes are again suggestive of the role played by reservations in enhancing the employment of the lower castes in India.

[51] See Galanter, *Competing Equalities*, for evidence of similar progress for the Scheduled Tribes.

A potentially fruitful area to examine is the effect of cross-state variation in the level of reservations on attainment. Given the fact that many Indian states differ in the level and timing of changes in their reservations, this could serve as a potential "natural experiment" to test the effects of these programs. Further, some states have extended coverage under reservations to Other Backward Castes, generating variation in the share of the population covered by the program. In 1980 Tamil Nadu increased its reservation for Other Backward Castes (OBCs) to 50 percent of Class III and IV jobs, while 18 percent were reserved for the Scheduled Castes and Scheduled Tribes. Conversely, Himachal Pradesh reserved only 5 percent of these jobs for the OBCs.

While the existence of cross-state variation in the level of these reservations suggests little about their likely impact, it is informative to see to what degree states succeeded in meeting their goals. Data from 1980 show that, while in some states these reservations were met, in other states the reservations, especially for higher level jobs, were not. For instance, in Karnataka 15 percent of jobs were reserved for members of the Scheduled Castes and their employment ranges from 8.8 percent of Class II jobs to 21 percent of Class IV jobs.[52] On the other hand, in Madhya Pradesh reservations were set at 15 percent for Scheduled Castes and 18 percent for Scheduled tribes, while employment for these groups never exceeded 12 percent of any job class.[53] In general, reservation levels were more likely to be met at lower job classes, while for Class I jobs they seem to seldom be met.

It also would be of interest to examine whether these different reservation levels are correlated with state-level education attainment, output growth, occupational attainment, and other measures of economic performance. Further, the extent to which state reservation goals are met, and the causes of shortfalls, merits examination. Unfortunately, this task will have to await further investigation.

5 Conclusions

The results of this paper suggest that conclusions about the likely effect of quotas or affirmative action programs are ambiguous. The theoretical discussion suggests that the impact on both the targeted minority group and the majority population depends upon assumptions about the source and existence of discrimination, underlying technology, the representations of the various

---

[52] All data are from "Reservations for Other Backward Castes," Report of the Mandal Commission, 1980.
[53] It reached 12% in Class IV jobs for the Scheduled Castes.

groups, and the presence of other distortions in the labor market. While these models, and the empirical evidence, suggest that minorities benefit from these programs, the size of this effect is uncertain. Whether these programs have the long-run effect of increasing minority incentives to invest in skill acquisition is also unclear. Evidence for the United States and India is suggestive of improved educational attainment for these groups, but the causal link to reservations or affirmative action is unproven. It is also true that there is an absence of evidence to support the conclusion that these programs have had a major distortionary impact on the workings of the labor market. Despite the heat generated by the debate over these programs, the evidence to date fails to suggest that they have had a major impact on the lives of minority populations. Whether this means that the market prevents these government programs from having a major impact, or that efforts to expand and apply these laws has been lax, cannot be determined from evidence to date.

Despite the lack of hard evidence, one way or the other these programs have generated substantial political debate. The theoretical discussion above suggests that this is not surprising since, if effective, the programs embody a transfer of income from majority to minority workers and perhaps the loss of rents generated by past discrimination (nepotism). That income or rents are transfered when these programs are in place is consistent with the pressures observed in many countries to expand the list of potential claimants for protection or by moves to eliminate the programs altogether.

While these programs are often initiated to protect or rectify wrongs against a small targeted population, they have expanded dramatically. In the United States, and in some Indian states, the protected groups cover a majority of the population. This is not to say that these groups are any less deserving, or that an expanded sense of social justice is inappropriate. The point is that, where the government can serve to extract rents, or be used to redistribute resources, individuals and groups have an incentive to insure that it does so in their direction. A concern for the future might well be that, while as presently constituted these programs costs may be small (or negative), their impact could be quite different as the pool of covered workers grows.

Finally, in both India and the United States, affirmative action and reservations were seen initially as a temporary necessity, not a permanent program. Much like the "infant industry" argument in international trade, temporary quotas were thought to give the protected groups an opportunity to overcome deficiencies in their stock of capital (human) or to establish "reputations" to overcome information-based barriers to employment. Once these investments are undertaken (under the assumption that no discrimination remains), quotas will no longer be necessary to insure that the minority population can compete with the majority population. The knowledge that the quotas are temporary insures that the requisite investments are made while the targeted groups have a competitive advantage. Matsuyama and others have shown that temporary quotas can be optimal from a social welfare prospective.[54]

A problem that arises is that, for these quotas to induce the correct investment behavior, the government must be able to credibly commit to the removal of these protections at some date in the future. Unfortunately, Matsuyama shows that, in the context of oligopolistic industries, the problem of dynamic inconsistency will prevent the government from making such a commitment, effectively rendering these programs permanent features.

An example of just this phenomena may perhaps be seen in the system of reservations in the Indian political process. These were originally to have expired after a predetermined interval, but they have been extended three times since then. Thus, rather than being part of a temporary program lasting ten years, they have become something that looks more permanent and have lasted an additional *thirty years*.[55]

Dynamic inconsistency is more likely to result if the beneficiaries of the quotas are a small group of, say, oligopolistic firms or a few politicians who can easily solve the collective action problem. In the case of labor market quotas, each member of the protected minority group has a smaller stake in their preservation, and hence it becomes harder to solve the coordination problem necessary to get the government to maintain these programs.

Interestingly, as Coate and Loury already suggested, quotas have been shown to delay rather than accelerate investments in skills or reputation.[56] While this need not always be the case, it is of interest to note that even opponents of quotas in the trade literature find that price (wage) subsidies (tariffs) or subsidies for investing (schooling and training) do not appear to produce these adverse affects.[57] These types of program, even if permanent, have been shown to be optimal from a social welfare prospective. Such programs, when combined with effective anti-discrimination laws in pay and employment, may be the most effective long-run mechanism to insure that the original goals of affirmative action in the United States and reservations in India are met.

---

[54] Kiminori Matsuyama, "Perfect Equilibria in a Trade Liberalization Game," *American Economic Review*, 80 (June 1990): 480–492.

[55] Galanter, *Competing Equalities*, p. 46.

[56] Coate and Loury, "Affirmative Action Policies."

[57] See Gene M. Grossman and Hendrik Horn," Infant Industry Protection Reconsidered: the Case of Informational Barriers to Entry," *Quarterly Journal of Economics*, 103 (November 1988): 767–87; and Kaz Miyagiwa, and Yuka Ohno, "Closing the Technology Gap under Protection," *American Economic Review*, 85 (September 1995): 755–70, for further discussion of tariffs and quotas and the infant industry problem in trade.

8

Communities and Development: Autarkic Social Groups and the Economy

Russell Hardin

1 Group Autarky

While not alone in their diversity, India and the United States are unusual in the degree to which they face problems of including different groups in their polities and economies. Political and economic inclusion are not logically connected. For example, some social groups, such as the Jews of Europe in earlier times and the Chinese outside China, have managed to be economically well connected while remaining politically and socially isolated. But it is typically true in many societies today that political and social separation is associated with a high and even comparable degree of economic separation. In general, economic separation of a group from the larger economy, which can verge on autarky for some groups within a larger national economy, entails lower productivity and poorer prospects of growth from specialization than would be expected for a group that is economically integrated into the larger economy.

China is distinctively different from India and the United States in that it has no substantial subgroups. There are ethnic differences and even some religious differences, although these are relatively insignificant and there is little or no political organization around these differences. There are also linguistic differences which might be called merely differences of dialect although the so-called dialects are commonly as different as the differences within the European Romance, Slavic, or Teutonic language families. But even these differences are relatively unimportant and unlikely to be the basis of demands for political preference. In part this is because there is a national language, or dialect—Mandarin Chinese—that is relatively accessible to all and is the native language of few.

Hence, China and India are developing nations with quite different social structures. India's *social structure* of competing and often conflicting groups is much more nearly like that of the United States, while China's relatively open and permeable *economy* is more nearly like that of the United States. China has the advantage, in comparison with the United States and especially with India, of an economy that is not broken into socially determined autarkic groups.

In general, autarky will depress productivity and income. In a world of competing states, free migration would drain those with potentially high earnings from a society that, by government fiat, enforced more nearly egalitarian distributions. Hence, a policy of egalitarianism might require substantial autarky, as in socialism in one country. But such autarky inherently hinders economic productivity. Similarly, group autarky within a society will hinder productivity, and especially productivity growth, if the autarky is economic as well as social. The scale of the American economy is smaller because the Old Order Amish, Indians on tribal reservations, and inner-city blacks are virtually out of the American market. But the Amish, reservation Indian, and inner-city black economies are radically smaller than they would be if they were more fully integrated with the national market. Segregation of communal groups that entails both social and economic segregation is evidently a much more widespread and perhaps intransigent problem in India than in the United States.

Many advocates of group difference insist that something would be lost if all groups were assimilated socially and economically. I wish to address the problems that such groups, especially communal groups, pose for economic productivity and development. I will also consider the normative claims for maintaining group differences through governmental preferences of various kinds. It is commonly asserted that government should support such groups by protecting them against the ravages of full integration in the larger society, perhaps in analogy with traditional views that government should protect individuals in various ways against the depredations of other individuals.

Allowing groups their own autarkic existence often seems normatively unproblematic. But it raises two practical questions with normative implications. First, how do we deal with the costs inflicted on children of their parents' desire for autarky? Second, how should we allocate the costs of such autarky, if there are any, between the autarkic group and the rest of society? There is a huge literature in political philosophy on the first of these questions, and I will address it only briefly below. The most common view on this question in western philosophy and politics is roughly that of John Stuart Mill. While adults should be allowed the autonomy to go their own way if they wish, children may justifiably be protected by government until they reach such age as to be capable of autonomy. There is very little literature of any kind on the second of these questions, and it is this question I wish to address here. In particular, I will be concerned with the economic costs of social group autarky.

2 Social Interest

To weigh the problem of socially autarkic groups, we must draw a distinction that is often not necessary for explanation of behavior, but is often taken to be relevant for the moral judgment of groups and their lives. This is a distinction that is commonly drawn by defenders of communal group norms: a distinction between economic and social interests. Economic interests seem relatively easily translatable into income. Social interests might also be translated into economic interests, although many advocates of various social interests insist on distinguishing them. Rather than argue this point, I wish to give as much ground to the advocates of communal social interests as plausible in order to address the implications of social group autarky.

Some advocates of social interests also insist that they take precedence over economic interests in any moral assessment of them when the two kinds of interest come into conflict. The distinction becomes important politically in debates over policies on economic growth. Growth in mere GDP, it is supposed, should not override concern for various groups' social interests, such as their interest in maintaining their community, their religion, their language, or their values, especially as expressed in their group-specific norms.

There is a vague tradition of thought that makes claims for the moral superiority of social over economic interests. In common discourse, social interests are simply held to be less crass than economic interests or, less articulately, are simply held to be right and inviolable. In western political philosophy the claim of moral superiority may result from a distorted appreciation of the protection of religious liberty in the tradition of liberalism that follows from John Locke. But the actual concern of early liberals is that of the illiberal Thomas Hobbes. It is to protect politics and economic life from the intrusions of religiously motivated violence and coercion. The American constitutional protections of religious liberty are similarly designed to keep religious differences and conflict out of politics.

In general, one should be wary of claims for moral superiority of group demands for political preference, especially when such preference comes at great cost to others. Most of the claims of social groups in our time do seem to entail costs to others. Even if these latter costs are "merely economic," however, as in the higher food costs that protection of the way of life of farmers entails for consumers, they should not obviously be trumped by the supposedly more moral social benefits. For utilitarians, of course, neither kind of good trumps the other in principle: rather, they must be weighed against each other. Even for non-utilitarians, however, neither kind of good can trump the other in principle. If it did, then we would have to conclude that even massive economic costs are justified by trivial social benefits. While many western moral philosophers write as though this conclusion were sensible, it cannot be entertained as a plausible political principle. Indeed, it was against such views that Hobbes, Locke, and early liberals saw the need to block absolutist religious claims on the polity.

From the logic of collective action,[1] it follows that social groups would not be able spontaneously to act on their own behalf unless their members individually saw the moral or social interests of the group as trumping their own individual economic interests enough to get them to donate time and money to the group cause. Apart from such moral commitments, they might act politically through voting, if they vote. And they might be mobilized by a political entrepreneur, who benefits from leadership. An odd implication of such entrepreneurship is that it can actually heighten the sense people might have of their group identity. The entrepreneur creates the group in order to be able to lead it. Creating or heightening identification with such a group may then lead to or deepen conflict between that group and the rest of its society. This is the story of Slobodan Milosevic and Franjo Tudjman, two of the most cynically destructive and bloody so-called leaders of our time.

In a further perverse twist in enabling collective action despite the logic against it, groups can develop strong norms of exclusion that are enforced against outsiders and aberrant insiders by the spontaneous actions of individual group members. These norms can be self-enforcing at the level of the group because enforcement of them can be in the interest of individual group members. As with political entrepreneurship, the development of such norms then heightens identification with the group. Such norms under-gird the autarky of social groups of many kinds. And they can stimulate interest in entrepreneurial leadership of such groups. Elsewhere, I have argued that, because these effects are essentially grounded in interest, the moral claims for groups that seem articulate in their self-proclamation may in fact be misplaced.[2] Indeed, groups with essentially universalist values cannot reinforce their members' commitments with norms of exclusion and the sanctions that these entail. It is only groups with narrowly defined, group-specific interests that can do so.

---

[1] Mancur Olson, *The Logic of Collective Action* (Cambridge, Mass.: Harvard University Press, 1965).

[2] Russell Hardin, *One for All: The Logic of Group Conflict* (Princeton: Princeton University Press, 1995), ch. 7.

3 Some American Examples

To clarify the distinction between social and economic interests, consider two groups. The first group is the Lubavitch community of Brooklyn, whose interest seems clearly to be a social interest in protecting their way of life. The second group is farmers, whose interest is ostensibly the economic interest of protecting their income when harvests are so large as to drive prices down to levels that would reduce them to poverty.

Members of the Lubavitch community have a way of life that they want to maintain. This way of life is richly communal and religious, and in the firm beliefs of many, it entails isolation from the corrupting larger society. Substantial isolation would require economic autarky, which would entail poverty and, very likely, destruction of the community. The Lubavitchers compromise on a remarkable version of partial autarky by employing themselves in their own community in communal industry. They survive economically through the grace of other Jews in the larger society who support them through donations and by buying the religious artifacts that the Lubavitchers manufacture.

Suppose the supportive buying and the donations ended. Then the Lubavitcher way of life would cease to be economically viable. They might then seek support from government, but this seems fairly clearly a case of non-economic, social interest that government might not support any more than it would underwrite the efforts of commercially failed rock singers whose preferred way of life is full-time rock singing.

Compare the situation of the Lubavitchers with that of American farmers over the past two centuries when the need for farmers has declined as agricultural productivity has risen dramatically. The protection of farmers is commonly demanded as a group benefit. In a largely agrarian nation under democracy, the group of small farmers can be a very large political interest. Such protection is commonly discussed, both in political discourse and in political–economic analyses, as a matter of economic interest. The supports that farmers seek are universalistic in the sense that anyone who goes into farming in relevant ways is entitled to them. It is not the community of farmers as such, but the individual farmers who are supported. And the supports are essentially straight cash.

Yet, much of the rhetoric of support for farmers is couched in quite different terms. In the United States the issue, ostensibly, is to support the family farm, a particular way of life. Genuinely to protect the way of life of farmers might eventually require the production of vastly too much food that then, in order to keep incomes of farmers high enough to keep them on the farm, would have to be destroyed rather than consumed. This has marginally been the effect of

American farm supports, but it would have to be carried to much greater extreme if most farmers and their children did not leave the farm, thereby giving up their way of life. Alternatively, government could simply pay farmers to stay on the farm without producing food, as American government does in part. But if carried to extremes, this policy would finally destroy the supposed way of life of farmers even while keeping them on the farm.

Hence the interest of farmers, a very important group in most societies, is ambiguously defined even though the form of the support is straightforwardly economic. Farm interests seem economic and are commonly treated as economic in the group-theory literature in the West. But they can in many ways better be seen as a social interest, perhaps especially in nations in which peasants or farmers are a very large fraction of the workforce. Their concern is not economic productivity so much as their way of life. They wish to protect that way of life despite the forces of efficiency that undercut it. Indeed, in many nations, what many farm workers have wanted is to achieve the way of life of independent farmers, and they have demanded land reform that would allow them to have that life. It seems unlikely that they would readily have accepted merely a steady income in lieu of land. It was the land and its way of life that they wanted.

Many industrial leaders are similar to farmers in that they want economic subventions or protections that go against the forces of efficiency. One might therefore say they too wish merely to protect a way of life. But this seems much less compelling as a characterization of their desires or demands. They might, unlike the peasants who sought land reform, readily trade in one company or one occupation for another that paid better. In this era of freer international trade, the concern of many workers begins to seem like a concern to protect a way of life.[3] But they, too, are more nearly concerned with level of income. In principle, they could sometimes continue their work lives at lower wages in order to compete with lower-cost imports, but they would not settle for this, and many of them would surely happily change jobs for higher pay in some other capacity.

---

4 Individuals and Groups

Spontaneous economic actors are of two kinds. There are individuals who largely seek their own benefits, and there are groups that seek benefits for distribution to individuals within the group and, arguably, group-level goods

---

[3] This is a commonly stated concern. For example, when Bethlehem Steel recently shut down the last blast furnace at its home plant in Bethlehem, Pennsylvania, laying off 1,800 workers, the plaint of the workers and their union leaders was that they were losing their way of life (*New York Times*, 19 November 1995: 1.27).

that are not distributable to the members. Because there is generally a need for government to oversee many economic provisions such as the maintenance of order and the enforcement of legal agreements, we generally have relatively strong governments that are, incidentally, capable of distributing benefits while maintaining legal and political order. Hence economic actors can both *seek* benefits through entrepreneurial success in the market and *demand* benefits from government. With rare exceptions, individuals cannot do the latter unless they do so under entitlement or other benefit programs established for defined groups. Individuals therefore generally attempt to be productive on their own or to gain government benefits as group members.

Spontaneously mobilized or defined groups typically are also of two kinds: those organized around a specific economic *interest*, such as production or consumption of some economic value, and those organized around a specifically defined non-economic *group*, such as an ethnic group. Groups organized around a specific interest can have constantly changing membership depending on who does or does not share the interest. Groups organized as such for the sake of the actual group typically have relatively stable memberships and often exclude others from the benefits they seek or enjoy. One can imagine a third kind of group, mobilized around very general economic interests such as the maintenance of generally useful infrastructures or the introduction of laws that would increase efficiency of interactions. This kind of group would generally oppose the demands of the other two kinds; but, because its interest is relatively universal, we can generally expect such a group to be relatively weak politically except when its votes are counted.

Economic growth depends centrally on the easy possibility of individual economic failure. This means that in actual experience economic growth will be coupled with frequent individual economic failure. A corollary of this is that, in a period of economic growth in a nation as diverse as India or the United States, *many social groups will fail as groups*. This will be true particularly for groups whose vaunted way of life is not economically viable in a dynamic economy, as thoroughgoing communal autarky is not economically viable. Efforts to protect such groups are effectively efforts to dampen growth and economic efficiency, just as efforts to protect individuals from failure by guaranteeing their success would dampen growth.

It is relatively easy to design universal welfare floors to protect individuals who fail economically. It is not easy to define analogous "floors" to protect groups as such when they fail. Individual members of groups can be protected under the general welfare floor for all individuals. But there is not a set of interests that groups per se have in common that can be made the elements of a universal floor for groups. If such groups are to be protected, any particular failed group will commonly have to be protected by an ad hoc program designed specifically for it.

Against many government policies that tend to destroy them, however, groups as such can often be protected without great cost to others. For example, some groups are given protection against universalizing educational programs by allowing them to have their own schools. When the government policy is one that generally benefits individuals, the group that rejects the benefit can typically be accommodated easily enough. But social groups cannot easily be protected against economic forces that undercut them without great effect on economic growth.

5 Special Status for Social Groups

Suppose we nevertheless conclude that social or moral status should be protected in some cases. What could be the form of relatively general principles for deciding when there is a proper case? One fairly simple principle is to perhaps include any group that is, at least with respect to the value being protected, autarkic. For example, a religious group might worship as it pleases because it does not interfere with anyone else when it does so; but it could not impose its religious principles on non-adherents against their objection. This is Locke's and Mill's position on religious liberty and it is arguably the position of the US Constitution on religious freedom.

This principle of autarky could be applied to any value or norm that a group wants protected and not merely to religious values or practices. It is a rough analog of Mill's harm principle, which he proposed for determining the range of individual liberty. Under the harm principle, I should be allowed to do anything I wish so long as I cause no harm to anyone else. So long as I meet this specification, I can be an atheist and reject religious requirements for salvation, I can put myself at risk for any reason that motivates me, I can even do harm to myself.

Ways of life generally "need" protection only when they are not economically viable. But that raises the question of why others in a society should subsidize a group's way of life. The claim of the moral rightness of the group's difference might suffice for defending against deliberate efforts to break down the group; it does not suffice for imposing a duty on others to care for it. Groups that are not viable may simply perish without anyone being actively to blame for their perishing.[4] In an era of dynamic economic change, we can

---

[4] There is a debate in ethics over whether there is a great moral difference between killing and letting die. While I think the moral difference is not great when "letting" has a relevant, clear causal sense, I think there is a substantial difference between metaphorically killing a community and metaphorically letting one die. In this case, the difference is between (a) supporting the tastes or preferences of the community in question by imposing a burden on others and (b) letting the community fail as a community while its members go on to live with changed preferences or reduced expectations. The latter difference is analogous to the difference between supporting someone in an economically failed venture rather than letting them fail economically. In these latter cases, the members of the failed community and the individual who fails in some economic enterprise typically have other options available to them.

expect groups to perish from within as the blandishments of the more dynamic economy of the larger society draw individuals out of the social group that cannot autarkically keep up with that larger society. This is not unlike the failure of egalitarian national experiments in our era in the face of blandishments from inegalitarian alternatives to which the most capable could migrate.[5] Moral defense of egalitarianism is inadequate to make it viable. Similarly, the moral defense of community is inadequate to make it viable.

Even defining an interest as collective often poses an obstacle to individual achievement. For example, if my group seeks some benefit, such as price supports for its products, its success might prevent me from producing as freely as if I were in a competitive market. Similarly, a profession can gain recognition that then gives it power to block individual professionals from various actions. In this case, the group gains power over its own membership, which is then defined not by some standard objective criterion but by its deliberate choice. Indeed, even if my group merely spontaneously organizes and adopts some norm for membership, it might exclude me if I behave in otherwise normal ways.[6] If it then seeks some benefit from government, it might work to exclude me from that benefit. In these and many other ways, collective achievement can be the enemy of individual autonomy and achievement. Groups come to compel individuals and to decide their fates.

One odd exception to this tendency of collective action to block individual effort is that defining an interest as collective often seems to justify leadership of the relevant group. Leaders then can, and typically do, become individual entrepreneurs whose status and careers turn on their success in managing the groups they lead. In effect, they extract resources from the group while acting as agents of the group to extract resources from the larger society to benefit the group. While their end might be the group and the life within it, their actual actions are largely in the world in which the group must live. Yet, without entrepreneurial leadership, many groups would have no prospect of politicking for their interest.

The possibility of special status for a group on the grounds of its social or moral interest raises an inherent ambiguity. Policies to protect such status commonly imply economic benefits at a cost to others. But this means that many groups might contrive claims of special status. And, in fact, it is common for groups that seek some benefit to assert that they have some special social or moral status that justifies their preferential treatment by government, as happened historically in the effort to create the powerful professional associations discussed below.

---

[5] Russell Hardin, "Efficiency vs. Equality and the Demise of Socialism," *Canadian Journal of Philosophy*, 22 (June 1992): 149–61.

[6] Hardin, *One for All*, ch. 4.

6 Conflict between Special-Status Social Groups

Giving social groups special status raises two big issues: conflicts between groups, and conflicts of interest within a group. The first can sometimes be minor if a group can pursue its values with relative autarky; the second is chiefly a matter of intergenerational differences in interests, which can be enormous. In this section I wish to address the first of these issues. Then, in Section 7, I will discuss briefly the issue of conflicts of interest internal to a social group.

Some ways of life are exclusionary, as is the Lubavitcher way of life. Lubavitchers do not wish to find new recruits in the larger society and would not welcome intruders in their community, although they would likely welcome the "return" of descendants of the Lubavitch community who have left the community; Serbs do not want Bosnian Muslims; Hutus do not want Tutsis; and Sikhs do not want Hindus in their own communities. They want separation, and they commonly follow norms of exclusion.[7]

It would be hard to object to such exclusion if the groups were autarkically unrelated, as the Lubavitchers in the United States are relatively unrelated to the rest of the polity. But typically, such groups interact heavily through the larger economy and society of which they are part. And they often practice their norms of exclusion *in that larger economy* as well as "within" the narrower confines of their own community. Perhaps the most important action that government takes against specific groups in many societies is to break their exclusion of others in the larger economy. The American system of affirmative action and the Indian preferences for members of Scheduled Castes are measures in favor of excluded groups. They have their effect, if any, through their impact on the power of relevant exclusionary groups, specifically by overriding those groups' norms of exclusion.

A social group whose program is exclusionary poses a particularly severe problem if it actually gains power. Once in power, it or its leaders may choose to seek group benefits principally by extracting resources from others or by restricting job and other opportunities to their own group members.

Consider several kinds of groups that have asked for or been granted special status on social or moral grounds There have been many of great importance, such as children, women, and the elderly. But let us focus on professional groups, religious groups, status groups, ethnic groups, especially minority ethnic groups, and linguistic groups. Religious, status, ethnic, and linguistic groups are commonly accorded special status in many nations today. Status groups are of special significance in India. Professional groups might seem an

[7] Ibid.

odd fit in this list, and indeed they are a peculiar variant on the claim of special status. The way in which they overtly fail the test of the principle of autarky is, however, instructive for considering other groups.

The various kinds of social group canvassed below differ in one very important respect: the degree to which they are exclusive and how the exclusion works. Professional groups require exclusion to gain their privileges; that exclusion is legally enforced when they gain legal control over licensing. Status groups are fundamentally grounded in an exclusion that is enforced spontaneously by members of the groups through norms of exclusion. Religious, ethnic, and linguistic groups are not grounded in exclusion, although religious and ethnic groups might practice exclusion and ethnic groups very often do so. Linguistic groups very often might even prefer inclusion. For example, the French seem actively to want *others* to speak French.

6.1 *Professional Groups*

Professional groups in the United States originally gained political recognition on the claim that they had moral commitments to public service and that their status had to be protected from crass market forces. Those professions today are extraordinarily powerful and exclusive. But almost no one, other than perhaps a few elderly lawyers and doctors, seriously contends today that their sometimes spectacular earnings are justified by their special moral status. That argument worked to gain power for the groups, and power worked to gain them massive benefits. They are now relatively free to dispense with the original argument of their moral superiority, and should indeed be embarrassed to invoke it to their clientele. Instead of the original argument of special moral status, many professionals today claim rather that they command their great incomes because they have expertise with high market value.[8] This claim might be more readily tested if their services were offered in a market less under the control of their professional organizations, but it is at least more nearly credible than was the earlier claim of special moral commitment.

The professionals' historical claim was peculiar. They claimed not that they had a moral status that was per se one that should trump economic interests: rather, they claimed that they were themselves especially moral on behalf of their clientele. They claimed that such moral commitment was necessary for service when the clientele could not judge the quality of the service rendered, so that the clientele could not judge between good and bad service that was merely offered on an open market.

There is little reason to suppose that professional groups merit any special

---

[8] Steven Brint, *In an Age of Experts: The Changing Role of Professionals in Politics and Public Life* (Princeton: Princeton University Press, 1994).

consideration as distinct social groups with moral or social interests. There may be compelling arguments that there are problems of market failure that justify the licensing and regulation of professionals in the interest of their clients. But social autarky and norms of exclusion are misplaced for such groups.

6.2 *Religious Groups*

Social autarky for religious groups need not have economic consequences, but, if coupled with norms of exclusion, it can. Laws and wider social norms that prohibited Jews from owning real property in medieval and later Europe did have economic consequences. Indeed, those laws, coupled with rival Catholic and Jewish interpretations on Biblical injunctions on lending at interest, virtually created the Jewish hegemony over lending, banking, and some aspects of merchandising. But in recent times Catholics, Jews, and Protestants have become interchangeable in Western economies, even when some of them have maintained strong religious communal ties.

There are some religious groups in the United States—notably the Luba-vitchers of Brooklyn and the Old Order Amish—that are so thoroughly autarkic that their way of life does have economic consequences, although the economic losses are borne mostly by the members of these groups rather than by the larger society. And some groups still practice enough exclusion, even in their business relations, that there are distinctively Catholic, Jewish, Mormon, and other firms grounded in norms of religious exclusion, just as there are distinctively Irish, Anglo-Saxon, German, southern, and so forth firms grounded in norms of ethnic exclusion. Similarly, in India ethnic and religious affiliations commonly determine the leadership of economic enterprises, so that there are Hindu, Muslim, and Sikh firms.

The Old Order Amish pose an extreme example of autarky that is relatively complete. It ranges from social to economic. The Old Order Amish insist on withdrawing their children from schooling altogether after about age 14 in order to protect them against the blandishments of the larger world by, essentially, keeping them ignorant of such blandishments. Moreover, they have won special dispensation from the Supreme Court to follow their policy despite its violation of state laws on the education of minors.[9]

While many people in the larger society object to this special dispensation for the Amish, they do not do so on the ground that it costs others: the Amish are almost fully autarkic within the larger society of the United States. Rather, they object to it as an unreasonable trammeling of Amish children, whose lack of education constrains their further lives and makes them far less autonomous than they would otherwise be. Hence, once they are adult, although they might

---

[9]   *Wisconsin v. Yoder et al.*, 406 US, pp. 205–49.

be free in principle to lead different lives, in practice they are relatively disqualified from doing so: they are best qualified to stay at work in the narrow community of the Old Order Amish.

In India in recent years, Hindu nationalism has been a disruptive, sometimes violent, force. By law, political discourse in India must be secular. Nevertheless, Hindu nationalists have become militant, organized, and articulate. Their goal is to make India a sectarian Hindu nation despite its very large minority religious groups. In this, they wish to reverse the message of Gandhi, who said, "We must cease to be exclusive Hindus or Muslims or Sikhs, Parsees, Christians or Jews. Whilst we may staunchly adhere to our religious faiths, we must be Indians first and Indians last."[10] Edward Desmond supposes that the Hindu nationalist movement suffers from ideological weakness because most Indians are far more likely to identify with their linguistic group, their region, and their caste than with "the Hindu nation."[11]

The Hindu nationalists do not seek protection by government of their way of life. They seek to take over government and to suppress other religious groups, especially Muslims. If religious and other values were really to be protected by government, contrary to the vision of early liberals, government might follow the model of early professional regulation and regulate (and sanction) clerics to protect the interests of their clientele. Presumably none of the advocates of government intervention on behalf of religious values would want anything of the sort. The Hindu nationalists in India and the Christian fundamentalists in the United States want government to be subject to their beliefs.

6.3 *Status Groups*

Status groups are defined entirely by social creation of categories that depend on norms of exclusion to keep some people out of high-ranking groups, thereby de facto putting them into lower-ranking groups. There can be many layers of exclusion from a topmost to a nearly bottom-most group, each excluding all those below. Status groups have been fundamentally important in social order throughout history. In many classical societies, there was some group that could be called aristocratic and other groups with inferior social ranks. In cities in the most developed parts of the world, there are typically local aristocracies who exclude the rest of the city dwellers as well as all or most outsiders from their parties and other social activities, sometimes even from their business and economic relations as much as possible.

Because status groups are grounded in exclusion that is enforced spon-

[10] Edward W. Desmond, "Storm over India," *New York Review of Books* (14 May 1992): 37–40, at p. 37.
[11] Ibid., p. 40.

taneously by norms of exclusion, they are inherently communal. Their norms therefore cannot survive outside the relevant community. Economic development that brings geographic mobility undercuts them. The local aristocracies of such regional cities as New Orleans, Toulouse, and Heidelberg have no cachet outside those cities.

The most impressively articulated system of status groups is that of India's caste system. The Indian caste groups are analogous to local aristocracies in traditional communities that are not very permeable. They may also be reinforced by associated religious values and beliefs and they have sometimes been reinforced by legal and political power. But they are largely spontaneously enforced when members of higher castes actively invoke norms of exclusion against all members of lower castes and aberrant members of their own caste, although at the village level there is often de facto political power behind the norms. For example, in June 1994, in the state of Bihar, a lower-caste girl eloped with an untouchable boy. With the approval of the village council, the boy's head was smashed and the girl was whipped and branded.[12] The brutality of communal justice in such cases is comparable to that of the salish in Bangladesh and the lynching that was common in the United States through the earlier part of the twentieth century. The village councils historically made no distinction between morals and law and, despite the rise of essentially universalistic law and justice, they continue to govern according to rules that differ by caste and gender.[13]

The Hindu caste system is in many ways almost an ideal example of the autarkic separation of various groups from each other. Each caste has its own proper moral and social code and there is no presumption that there is a correct, universal code for all—other than the universal principle of adherence to the norms of one's caste. Members of one caste would not judge the different code of another caste but would, rather, think it merely the right code for that caste even while it would be wrong for their own caste.

Autarky for status groups is likely to have deleterious effects on the larger society, especially if groups of higher status have special claims on available resources in some realm. The aristocrats of Europe controlled most European land and some castes in India have access to some employments that are denied to other castes. While legal constraints on caste employment have disappeared and there are even legal preferences for some castes, the ingrained social norms have not fully passed. Therefore, the possibilities for greater productivity from better use of talent are undercut, to the special detriment of those who are excluded, but also to the general detriment of the larger economy. Outsiders often decry the Indian caste system and its shackles, but a

---

[12] *Economist* (8 October 1994): 17.

[13] Christoph von Fürer-Haimendorf, *Morals and Merit: A Study of Values and Social Controls in South Asian Societies* (Chicago: University of Chicago Press, 1967), pp. 163–4.

residue of social class distinctions still shackles Western societies, perhaps especially England, and racism, which can be seen as a compounding of status and ethnic discrimination, is endemic in many Western societies and is especially destructive in the United States.

After the Chinese revolution, China broke the hold of certain status groups by frontally attacking and destroying individuals of high status in local communities. India has attempted to break the hold of status groups through affirmative policies to support those of low status rather than by attacking those with high status. The Chinese device has probably been more immediately effective, not least because it was more brutal. The status of the landed aristocracy of Europe was broken very slowly by a massive economic transition from production based on the land to production based in cities. The massive economic transition underway in India is likely to have a similar effect on the power of status groups over the economy.

Together, the lower castes, untouchables, and tribespeople constitute about 70 percent of the Indian population. Hence, under democracy one might expect lower castes to gain power if politics is fought on caste lines. That is what has been happening in many regions of India in recent years. In Uttar Pradesh, for the first time, an openly caste-based coalition of parties has gained power. Even leaders of national parties, such as Janata and Congress, must bow to the pressures of majorities who want job and other preferences for lower castes.[14] Oddly, caste, which is a Hindu creation with religious sanction, may stand in the way of Hindu nationalism because it so severely divides Hindus.

6.4 *Linguistic Groups*

Successful social autarky for linguistic groups is inherently harder than for ethnic and religious groups. Linguistic minority groups have poorer access to a nation's economy than do the linguistic majority or the speakers of the national language. For example, those in China who master Mandarin Chinese and those in Canada who master English have broader opportunities than those who do not. Those who begin with the national or majority language as their own language have a decided advantage over those who do not. Maintaining a group's identity when it speaks a minority language is therefore much more costly than merely maintaining the religious identity of a group that is free to compete in the economy on relatively equal terms with those of other religions. When members of a language community learn another language for

---

[14] Desmond, "Storm Over India," p. 34.

economic reasons, they have simultaneously learned it for other possible ends, such as to develop ties with other communities.[15]

Members of a language community are almost naturally excluded from other language communities. No deliberate exclusion, no norm of exclusion, is necessary. Merely the costs of dealing with people who do not speak one's language are sufficient to cause de facto exclusion. Yet, within a language community, there may be a norm of exclusion enforced against those who abandon the language or, especially, against the children of those who have abandoned it and have raised their children in a different language.[16] Such an intra-group norm of exclusion raises the costs to a member of the group of adopting another language. Hence, linguistic groups may strive to be more broadly autarkic than many other kinds of social group. They have to be, merely in order to sustain their communities. But the costs of such autarky, when the autarky includes economic separation as well as linguistic and social separation, can be massive.

If we adopt the principle of autarky to judge the extent to which a group should be allowed to practice its own norms, linguistic groups pose a major problem: how to equalize opportunities for political participation. We might agree that the costs of political participation to some substantial degree should be borne by the whole citizenry. If some group faces unequal costs, it is then up to the larger society to redress the difference. There are two parts to this issue. First, there are the costs of participation to ordinary citizens in electoral politics. Second, there are the costs of giving groups voice, the costs of political leadership or representation of groups. For the first of these, it should not cost one person much more to vote than it costs another. Clearly, there cannot be full equality of costs of participation unless the polling places go to the voters rather than the other way around. But within the realm of practicality, such mechanical costs can be substantially equalized.

In multi-lingual nations such as India, Belgium, Canada, and the United States, equalization of costs further requires making various voting materials available in all the relevant languages. Unfortunately, this does not resolve the difficulties of minority language groups. The real costs of voting for most people are the costs of becoming adequately informed to be able to vote intelligently in their own interest. This requires education for literacy and beyond. If minority

[15] In New York City, Puerto Rican English has become gendered for economic reasons. Puerto Rican women speak a different dialect from that spoken by Puerto Rican men: women speak white English; men speak black English. Why? Because women get jobs in offices as clerks and secretaries; men get jobs as blue-collar laborers. In New York, these two job markets are white and black respectively. The socio-linguist William Labov says this is the only instance he knows of gendered English (talk at New York University, winter 1995).

[16] Amy Wu, an ABC, or American-born Chinese, speaks English but not Cantonese. When she visits Chinese restaurants in New York's Chinatown without her Cantonese speaking relatives, she is scorned with treatment worse than that accorded non-Chinese. She quotes a friend who says, "You're either in or out" (*New York Times*, 10 December 1995: 13.25).

language groups are educated in the predominant language of the nation, their groups are severely undercut. If they are educated in the languages of their groups, the extra costs of informing them for intelligent voting may be substantial. Even then, they may not have access to adequate news coverage to give them understanding and information comparable to what is available in the predominant language. In Belgium and Canada, education and communication in two different languages are handled well enough to overcome disparities in costs to voters. In the United States and India the problems are far more severe, and the disparities are great for some language groups.

The second problem, that of the costs of giving groups voice, is far more difficult to overcome. Nativists commonly claim that minority language speakers can expect to be equal in a society only if they switch, at least for their children and further generations, to the predominant language. The claim is almost certainly true in fact, both economically and politically. Representation of a permanent minority group on the grounds of its social characteristics alone undercuts the possibility of representation of other issues within the group. The majority population can politic on various issues for differential benefit. Consider a very simplistic model in which each citizen spends the same total amount of time and resources in politicking for various causes. Those who use part of their time and resources politicking for their social group have less time for other matters. They will therefore tend to be less well represented on other matters.

Achieving political equality may genuinely require switching to the predominant language. But this is tantamount to giving up one's group. A liberal response to that complaint is that it is individuals, not groups, who matter. However, even if one accepts this response, one can still object that the adult members of a minority language group are not merely group members, but are also individuals. And the movement of their children and grandchildren out of their language brings enormous losses to many of these people. They virtually die before their time—or, rather, their community dies out, leaving them increasingly isolated. They might wish to claim that switching languages also brings losses to their children and grandchildren. The liberals could respond that the tradeoff for those losses is greater gains. The committed member of the minority group might answer that the gains are not greater except economically; the losses are moral and social and they are ignored in the liberal's vision.

In the end, the liberal can say little more than "Take it or leave it." Generally, the children and grandchildren will take the majority language if doing so makes a big difference to their economic opportunities, just as peoples around the world commonly learn second languages according to utility. The older generation of a minority language group will simply lose out unless it is able politically to insure the protection of its group by requiring the education of its children in the minority language. This political victory might ensure the economic disadvantage of future generations of the group while securing the life of the group. In this respect, it is analogous to the choice of the Old Order Amish to hobble their children by blocking their education and thereby their opportunities outside the Amish community. The striking feature of this resolution is that such a group may be relatively autarkic in its society, at least if it is geographically concentrated so that schooling is not radically more expensive for its children than for others. Indeed, if the group shares the values of the American Old Order Amish, it might require much less investment in education than the larger society would offer to other children.

Autarky for linguistic groups within a society is likely to have substantial economic consequences, surely for the autarkic groups themselves but also plausibly for the larger society if its market would benefit from being at a larger scale. In late nineteenth-century France, the large number of distinct groups and languages within French borders were seen as an obstacle to national unity and to nationalist aspirations. These groups were converted into French-speakers within a generation or two.[17] This conversion seems likely to have eased the way for economic productivity. For example, it made it easy for a youth leaving the farm to go to any city in France that might offer the greatest opportunity for employment, rather than only to the few places where the local language would be spoken. It simultaneously made it easier for communities to assimilate and disappear, to the dismay of older generations in those communities. (It may also have eased the way for French nationalism in World War I. The latter result was perhaps the chief concern of those who pushed for a single national language.)

India and China have adopted variants of the French solution to their polyglot languages. India has used English as one of its national languages. This is not an ideal solution, for the obvious reason that English is not trivially easy to learn for speakers of the various families of languages in India. China under the mandarin system ruled its empire of varied peoples through mandarins educated in the official language of the empire. That language survives today as the natural choice as national language. Its use is much easier than the use of English in India because of the peculiarities of the Chinese written language, which allows common meanings with quite different sounds to be uniformly represented. Hence, anyone who is literate in a Chinese dialect can read Mandarin. By good fortune, therefore, China escapes the problem of possibly autarkic linguistic groups. By misfortune, India faces a severe problem. Indeed, the lack of a national language may well weigh against the development of literacy, not least because literacy in varied languages would lead to even stronger identification with the relevant linguistic groups, and hence to harsher conflicts between such groups.

[17] Eugen Weber, *Peasants into Frenchmen: The Modernization of Rural France, 1870–1914* (Stanford, Calif.: Stanford University Press, 1976).

6.5 *Ethnic Groups*

Ethnic groups are often simultaneously religious and linguistic groups, which means that they are often both exclusive and excluded. This complexity has been a recipe for uncounted disasters throughout the twentieth century. Majority ethnic groups often want autarky that is relatively complete, excluding others from the majority economy, polity, and society.

As a rule, and as is also true for religious groups, the practice of exclusion by the enterprises of particular ethnic groups need not be substantially important to economic prospects of their society in general if there are competitive firms of other groups or even merely competitive firms with open, non-exclusionary recruitment. Where there is adequate competition, the chief losers from such exclusion are likely to be the firms that practice it, because they will not make choices on strict productivity grounds. This sanguine conclusion does not follow, however, in a context in which there is a prevalent, strong norm of social exclusion or prejudice. For example, where anti-black racial prejudice ruled social and economic relations in the United States, blacks were the clear losers, so much so that it would seem implausible to suppose that the prejudicial businesses suffered more than blacks did.

7 Conflict within a Special-Status Group

It is intellectually hard for a group to proclaim universalistic commitment to the idea of group autonomy, because the ground on which the group claims autonomy for itself may be that there is something inherently right about its values. And it is intellectually hard for a liberal who is committed to individual autonomy, whether from Millian or Kantian principles, to accept claims of group autonomy. Group autonomy de facto seems to involve control over the making of the next generation and perhaps also control over the behavior of even the current generation. Group autonomy at its extreme means that the Salman Rushdies of the world may be killed on behalf of the groups whose values they offend and that claim them as members.

We might be able to protect individuals against such depredations as the fatwa against Salman Rushdie, but we still face the intergenerational problems that lie at the heart of the debate over the normative appeal of community. Defenders of communitarian ideals insist that the liberal vision is one of a vacuous individual because individuals are of necessity created by communities. There is no over-arching principle according to which we can say creating people in the image of one community or one set of ideals is better than creating people in the image of another. Liberals might almost agree, adding chiefly that the people we create should be reasonably autonomous and not just the puppets of some community. Debate on this issue has so far shown little progress beyond a statement of the problem.

Successful economic growth requires some cynicism on the part of government toward the claims for the special nature of social groups and the demand that they be given special protection. Indeed, government effort might often rather be directed at protecting individuals from domination by their groups. One might wish to ground the claim for cynicism in the supposition that what groups claiming a moral or social interest really want is merely economic support. But I think that would be false. They often genuinely do want protection of their particular way of life, the practice of their norms, and so forth. The larger society might lose nothing from such protections except for the economic costs, as when farmers are protected against economic forces that would allow the importation of much cheaper food. In many cases, the chief losers are apt to be the future generations of the group whose current generation of leaders wants to be or is being protected.

In a defense of the prevalence of politics over values, one might assert that the benefits of the many in the larger society outweigh the exclusive benefits of the few in some group. But one need not make a strongly moral claim that this is true against those who assert the categorical difference between social and economic interests. One can settle for a simple Hobbesian claim about the objective facts of the matter. It is generally likely to be true that the many will prevail politically in a conflict over some group's exclusionary values insofar as the political decisions are relatively democratic. This is a generally sufficient claim in many contexts. It fails in contexts in which it is essentially the many who want a special protection against the few or even the exploitation of the few. In many nations with ethnic or religious divisions, there is a majority ethnic or religious group which, given democratic power, would happily suppress or exploit minority groups.

8 Concluding Remarks

Social groups need pose no problem for the larger society and economy unless they practice norms of exclusion that affect the economy. Oddly, the most harmful instances of the practice of such norms may typically be by majority or dominant groups rather than by minority groups of whatever kind. However, even the practice of norms of exclusion need not greatly affect the economy, but can be restricted to social matters of marriage and residence. Hence there is no substantial reason for opposition to social autarky for groups whose separation from the larger society has no negative effect on the larger economy or on the economic prospects of other groups.

At the same time, there is no universalist ground for government protection of the social interests of groups that wish to maintain social autarky. Indeed, for anyone who objects to the group control over children to try to keep them bound to the group, there is reason for government protection of young group members against their groups.

Policies directed at the group as a whole are tantamount to policies directed at each and every member of the group. Universalistic protections of everyone independently of membership in any subgroup in the society do not suppose any special status. For example, protections of rights, as in constitutional bills of rights, are universalistic. And programs of affirmative action, even though they might name groups, can be universalistic in the sense that they are directed at making the economic and political status of all more nearly equal. Such protections might provoke severe political conflict just because they break the power of special status.

Dealing with separatist groups, as in Kashmir, may raise far more complex issues which I have not addressed here. Such groups often can achieve separation only at great cost to others in their society. Indeed, this may be nearly always true, because few groups are geographically separated to such an extent as to make political separation into geographically distinct nations possible. The separation of Bangladesh from Pakistan was one of the closest examples of such separation in modern times and even that probably had destructive effects on many individuals who were living in the wrong part of the former Pakistani nation.

Another issue not discussed here is the problem of intolerant groups that are willing to use violence to achieve their goals of control or separation. Sporadic and spontaneous outbursts of violence, such as the periodic and occasional urban riots in the United States and the anti-Sikh riots in Indian cities following the assassination of Indira Ghandi in 1984, are common in many societies without seeming to pose a general threat to social stability. But the organized use of violence by groups, as in the recent rise of Hindu militancy, could become a devastating problem. The destruction of the mosque in Ayodhya and the anti-Muslim riots in Bombay in December 1992 and January 1993 were evidently driven by extremist leaders, such as Bal Thackeray of Shiv Sena, a reputedly well armed and organized militant group.[18] Violent militia groups have assisted the rise to power of fascist parties in many nations, and they have

---

[18] *New York Times* (17 April 1994): 1.3.

been willing to wreak extraordinary damage in India, throughout the Middle East, the United States, and many other nations in recent years. Their control is a task that no liberal, democratic government has mastered.

Apart from separatist and violent groups in some societies, the most difficult type of group difference to deal with is likely to be that of linguistic groups. For such groups, simple social autarky is not feasible if they are to be part of the larger economy. To be a more nearly equal part of that economy, their members must necessarily adopt the dominant language for at least part of their lives. And when they do, they are apt to weaken the bonds of their linguistic community over them. But there is hardly any practical alternative to their adopting the dominant language unless they are willing to suffer substantial economic disadvantages in comparison with others in their own society. Indeed, for the vast majority of languages currently spoken in the world, there is little alternative to quitting those languages if the children of their speakers are to enter the broader world in which they could prosper.

Status groups inherently also affect economic relations, but it is hard to conceive a defense of their rightness that could plausibly trump concern to block their harms to the economic prospects of either the society or excluded individuals. Religious and ethnic groups could be socially autarkic without affecting larger economic relations. They generally do not need protection from the state against anyone except possibly their own members, but there is no compelling argument for why the state should "paternalistically" suppress individuals' actions on behalf of the groups of which they are ostensibly members. Hence, *even granting the claim that moral or social interests trump economic interests is insufficient to justify state protection of ethnic, religious, or status groups*. The only plausible survivor of that claim is linguistic groups, for whom social autarky cannot be achieved without substantial economic effects and effects on political equality.

9 Law from Order: Economic Development and the Jurisprudence of Social Norms

Robert D. Cooter

1 Precursors

This paper has various intellectual precursors. Proponents of decentralization have long admired social norms because they arise spontaneously, outside the state.[1] The informality of social norms, however, caused scholars to underestimate their importance relative to formal law, until empirical research proved that social norms often control behavior in spite of the law. To illustrate, American businesses frequently remain rationally ignorant of the legal consequences of the contracts that they sign;[2] borrowing by small business in Taiwan often occurs outside of formal law;[3] and many Peruvian businesses systematically break the law to circumvent excessive regulations.[4]

The formal analysis of social norms developed through the application of game theory.[5] The economic analysis of social norms draws upon a funda-

---

[1] F. A. Hayek, "Planning and the Rule of Law," in his *The Road to Serfdom* (Chicago: University of Chicago Press, 1976); and Bruno Leoni, *Freedom and Law* (Indianapolis: Liberty Fund, 1991).

[2] Stewart Macaulay, "Non-contractual Relations in Business: a Preliminary Study," *American Sociology Review*, 28 (1963): 55.

[3] Jane Kaufman Winn, "Informal Financial Practices of Small Businesses in Taiwan," *Law and Society Review*, 28(2) (1994): 193–241.

[4] Hernando de Soto, *The Other Path: The Invisible Revolution in the Third World*, translated by June Abbott (London: Tauris, 1989).

[5] Edna Ullmann-Margalit, *The Emergence of Nors* (Oxford: Clarendon Press, 1977); Jack Hirshleifer, "Evolutionary Models in Economics and Law: Cooperation versus Conflict Strategies," in his *Economic Behaviour in Adversity* (Chicago: University of Chicago Press, 1987), Ch. 9; Robert Sugden, "Reciprocity: The Supply of Public Goods Through Voluntary Contributions," *Economic Journal*, 94 (1984): 772–987; and Michael Taylor, *The Possibility of Cooperation* (Cambridge: Cambridge University Press, 1987).

mental result in game theory: one-shot games with inefficient solutions, such as the prisoner's dilemma, often have efficient solutions when repeated between the same players.[6] This generalization grounds the "utilitarianism of small groups," by which I mean the tendency of small groups to develop efficient rules for cooperation among members.

The utilitarianism of small groups has been demonstrated for cattle ranchers, Chinese traders, medieval merchants, and contemporary diamond merchants.[7] Research on property rights has revealed variety and detail in the political arrangements by which small groups manage their assets.[8] Note that utilitarianism applies to social groups in which people have repeated transactions with each other, but not to social categories that classify together people who seldom interact with each other.[9] Furthermore, one group may develop norms that benefit its members by subordinating people from other groups.[10]

The analysis of social norms developed independently from the public finance literature on market failures, which began with Pigou's account of external costs.[11] Samuelson's distinction between public and private goods increased the level of mathematical precision.[12] This tradition has a clear

---

[6] Drew Fudenberg and Eric Maskin, "The Folk Theorem in Repeated Games with Discounting or with Complete Information," *Econometrica*, 54 (1986): 533–54; and R. Axelrod, *The Evolution of Cooperation* (New York: Basic Books, 1984).

[7] Cattle ranchers, see Robert C. Ellickson, *Order without Law: How Neighbors Settle Disputes* (Cambridge, Mass.: Harvard University Press, 1991); Chinese traders, see Janet Landa, "A Theory of the Ethnically Homogeneous Middleman Group: an Institutional Alternative to Contract Law," *Journal of Legal Studies*, 10 (1981): 349–62; and Janet Landa, "The Political Economy of the Ethnically Homogeneous Chinese Middleman Group in Southeast Asia: Ethnicity and Entrepreneurship in a Plural Society," in *The Chinese in Southeast Asia: Ethnicity and Economic Activities*, ed. L. A. P. Gosling and L. Y. C. Lim (Singapore: Maruzen Asia Publishing, 1983); medieval merchants, see P. Milgrom, D. North, and B. Weingast, "The Rule of Institutions in the Revival of Trade: the Law Merchant, Private Judges, and the Champagne Fairs," *Economics and Politics*, 2 (1990): 1–23; and Avner Grief, "Contract Enforceability and Economic Institutions in Early Trade: the Maghribi Traders' Coalition," *American Economic Review*, 83 (1993): 525–48; contemporary diamond merchants, see Lisa Bernstein, "Opting Out of the Legal System: Extralegal Contractual Relations in the Diamond Industry," *Journal of Legal Studies*, 21 (1992): 115–57.

[8] Thrainn Eggertsson, "Analyzing Institutional Successes and Failures: a Millennium of Common Mountain Pastures in Iceland," *International Review of Law and Economics*, 12 (1992): 423–37, 1992; D. N. McCloskey, "The Economics of Enclosure," and "The Persistence of English Common Fields," both in *European Peasants and their Markets*, ed. W. N. Parker and E. L. Jones (Princeton: Princeton University Press, 1975); Elinor Ostrom, *Governing the Commons: Evolution of Institutions for Collective Action* (Cambridge: Cambridge University Press, 1990); and Robert Ellickson, "Property in Land," *Yale Law Journal*, (1993).

[9] Eric Posner, "The Regulations of Groups: The Influence of Legal and Nonlegal Sanctions on Collective Action," *University of Chicago Law Review*, 63 (1996): 133; Eric Posner, "Law, Economics and Inefficient Norms, *University of Pennsylvania Law Review*, 144 (1996): 1697.

[10] George A. Akerlof, "A Theory of Social Custom, of which Unemployment may be One Consequence," *Quarterly Journal of Economics*, 94 (1980): 719–75; George A. Akerlof, "Discriminatory, Status-based Wages among Tradition-oriented, Stochastically Trading Coconut Producers," *Journal Political Economy*, 93 (1985): 265–76; and Richard H. McAdams, "Cooperation and Conflict: the Economics of Group Status Production and Race Discrimination," *Harvard Law Review*, 96 (1995): 338–433.

[11] A. C. Pigou, *The Economics of Welfare*, 4th edn. (London: Macmillan, 1950).

[12] Paul Samuelson, "The Pure Theory of Public Expenditure," *Review of Economics and Statistics*, 36 (1954): 387–9; Paul Samuelson, "Diagrammatic Exposition of a Theory of Public Expenditures," *Review of Economics and Statistics*, 32 (1954): 350–6; and William Baumol, "On Taxation and the Control of Externalities," *American Economic Review*, 62 (1972): 307.

prescription: markets for private goods, government for public goods, taxes for externalities. Coase challenged this tradition by arguing that externalities can be cured in the market, provided that transaction costs do not obstruct private bargains.[13] My paper retains Coase's view that markets cure many externalities and rejects his view that bargaining provides the mechanism. Instead, I propose a mechanism with better empirical support: social norms.

2 Agency Game

Production and exchange require people to cooperate with each other, such as stockholders and managers in a corporation, or managers and workers in a factory. The "agency game" is the paradigm developed in game theory for cooperation in business. In the agency game the first player to move, the "principal," decides whether or not to make an investment of 1. If no investment is made, the game ends and the players receive nothing. If an investment is made, the second player, the "agent," decides whether to cooperate or appropriate. Appropriation is merely redistributive: the agent appropriates the principal's investment of 1. Consequently, the sum of the payoffs in the northeast quadrant of Figure 9.1 is 0. Cooperation by both players is productive: the investment of 1 grows to 2. When the agent cooperates, the principal recovers his investment and the players split the product (each player receives 0.5). Consequently, the sum of the payoffs in the northwest quadrant of the figure equals 1. The most efficient cell in the table contains the highest sum of the payoffs, so investment and cooperation is the most efficient outcome.

If the agency game is played only once, the agent's best move is to appropriate. Knowing this, the principal concludes that his best move is not to invest. The one-shot game has a unique, unproductive solution.

An enforceable contract, in which the agent promises to cooperate, solves the problem of cooperation. To illustrate, the costless recovery of expectation

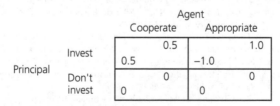

Fig. 9.1 Agency Game

[13] Ronald Coase, "The Problem of Social Cost," *Journal of Law and Economics*, 3 (1960): 1–44.

damages gives the principal an incentive to invest, regardless of the probability of the agent's breach of contract, and costless collection of expectation damages gives the agent a strong incentive to perform. Enforcement of contracts, however, typically requires coercion by a third party such as the state. Another solution can be found that does not require the state: the commitment of principal and agent to an enduring relationship. Commitment solves the problem of cooperation through repetition of the game. (The exceptions to this generalization need not concern us here.[14])

3 Tentative Agency Relationships

The fabric of modern business transactions, however, is not law or commitment. Instead, I will analyze the agency game with tentative relationships, which solve the problem by social norms. To model tentative relationships, repeat the agency game indefinitely often, but change the assumption about the number of players. Instead of assuming that there are only two players, assume that there are indefinitely many players, who form into pairs to play each round of the game.

After each round, some of these partnerships continue and others end. Partnerships end when the principal dissolves the relationship after the agent appropriates. Consequently, appropriators play only once with any particular principal. Cooperators repeat the game with the same partner. However, cooperative partnerships can end amiably after an unpredictable change in business conditions makes the relationship unproductive. Assuming stable business conditions, cooperators form relatively stable partnerships, whereas appropriators form relatively brief partnerships.[15]

The equilibrium concept for this game draws on evolutionary theory.[16] Think of players as hosts for competing behaviors and ask which of these behaviors will survive in competition with the others. Selection favors the behavior with a higher payoff. Assume that the proportion of players using a

[14] Glenn W. Harrison and Jack Hirshleifer, "An Experimental Evaluation of Weakest Link/Best Shot Models of Public Goods," *Journal of Political Economy*, 97 (1989): 201–25; and Jack Hirshleifer and Juan Carlos Martinez Coll, "What Strategies Can Support the Evolutionary Emergence of Cooperation?" *Journal of Conflict Resolution*, 32 (1988): 367–98.

[15] Rudolf Schussler, "Anonymous Exchange Cooperation," paper read at 4th International Conference on Social Justice Research, Trier Germany, 1993; and Robyn Dawes and John Orbell, "Social Welfare, Cooperators' Advantages, and the Option of Not Playing the Game," paper read at 4th International Conference on Social Justice Research, at Trier, Germany, 1993.

[16] Abhijit Banerjee and Jorgen W. Weibull, "Evolution and Rationality: Some Recent Game-Theoretic Results" in B. Allen (ed.), *Economics in a Changing World* (New York: St Martins Press, 1996).

particular strategy increases as long as that strategy produces above-average payoffs. Conversely, the proportion of players using a strategy decreases as long as that strategy produces below-average payoffs. Competition tends to eliminate all below-average strategies, so that every strategy surviving in equilibrium earns the same rate of return. In an internal equilibrium, some players cooperate and others appropriate, and both strategies earn the same expected payoff, as required to survive.

It is easy to see why both strategies might earn the same expected payoff. When a partnership dissolves, the players must search for new partners, which uses resources and time. Appropriating agents form unstable relationships and repeatedly search for partners, so appropriators expect a high payoff occasionally. In contrast, cooperating agents form stable relationships and seldom search for partners, so cooperators expect a modest payoff often.

In commodity markets, a stable, internal equilibrium usually exists when an increase in the quantity of production causes the cost of production to increase. Similarly, in the agency game, a stable, internal equilibrium usually exists when an increase in the proportion of appropriators causes the expected payoff from appropriation to decrease. (The necessary conditions are straightforward to explain.[17])

A stable equilibrium is depicted in Figure 9.2. The vertical axis shows expected payoffs and the horizontal axis shows the proportion of agents who appropriate. As the proportion of appropriators increases, the payoff to co-operation falls a little, because cooperating agents who do not have a partner must search longer to find one. This effect, however, is much larger upon appropriators, who continually search for new partners, so the payoff to appropriation falls quickly as the number of appropriators increases. The intersection of the curves in Figure 9.2 indicates that appropriators and cooperators expect the same payoff, as required for equilibrium, which occurs when approximately 20% of agents appropriate.

If enforcement were costless, the most efficient outcome would occur when none of the agents appropriates. Given costly enforcement, the gain from more cooperation must be balanced against the cost of deterring more appropriators, so the efficient outcome occurs when a positive proportion of agents appropriate.

---

[17] As the proportion of appropriating agents increases, more partnerships dissolve more often. Some of the principals released from these relationships look for new partners. Consequently, the *release* of principals from existing partnerships tends to *lower* the expected cost of a successful search by an agent for a partner. Another force, however, works in the opposite direction. As the number of appropriators increases, investment becomes less profitable and some principals withdraw from the industry. *Withdrawal* of principals from the industry *increases* the expected cost of a successful search by an agent for a partner. On balance, more appropriators cause search costs to increase when the withdrawal effect dominates the release effect. Thus, a stable equilibrium usually exists when the "withdrawal effect" dominates the "release effect." For a similar, formal model, see Schussler "Anonymous Exchange Cooperation."

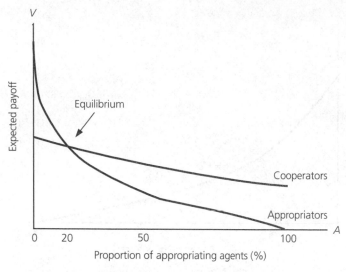

Fig. 9.2 Equilibrium Strategies of Agents

Now I turn from strategies to signals. In a community, people talk a lot about what everyone ought to do. What people say about morality may be used to signal their behavior.[18] In the agency game, some people will say that agents ought to cooperate and an agent who disagrees may signal that he is likely to appropriate, in which case principals will not form a partnership with him. Every agent benefits by signaling "cooperation," regardless of whether his real strategy is cooperation or appropriation, so the signaling equilibrium is uniform.

In the agency game, a uniform signaling equilibrium represents a consensus about the strategy that agents *ought* to follow. People who believe that agents ought to cooperate may be willing to punish agents who appropriate. The informal punishments that people use to enforce norms include gossip, rebukes, and shunning. For example, people who break the norms of a profession may suffer loss of reputation, censure, or expulsion from professional organizations. Punishing appropriators may cost something in time, effort, discomfort, money, or the risk of retaliation. I will say that people who are willing to pay such a price have internalized the norm.

Figure 9.3 depicts the fact that some people are willing to pay more than others to enforce a norm. The vertical axis represents costs of enforcement, *c*, and the horizontal axis represents the proportion of players, *E*, who enforce the

---

[18] Natural expressions for emotion make character translucent, which conveys an evolutionary advantage on people by facilitating forms of commitment: see Robert Frank, *Passions within Reason: The Strategic Role of Emotions* (New York: Norton, 1988).

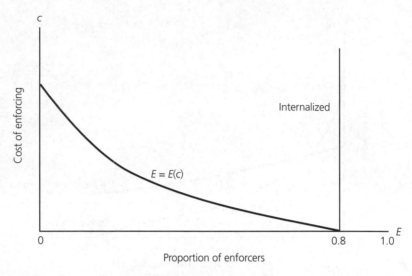

Fig. 9.3 Willingness to Punish

norm. As the cost of enforcing the norm increases, fewer players are willing to pay the higher cost. Thus, the function $E = E(c)$ slopes down to indicate that the expected cost of enforcing c must decline in order for enforcers E to increase.[19] According to the figure, 80 percent of the players will pay something to enforce the norm, which implies that they have internalized it, whereas 20 percent will pay nothing to enforce it.

Now I relate the three elements of the analysis of social norms: strategy, signal, and punishment. For any level of enforcement E in Figure 9.3, there exists a curve indicating the expected rate of return to appropriators in Figure 9.2. To depict this connection between punishment and strategy, Figure 9.4 combines Figures 9.2 and 9.3. Assume that punishing appropriators costs c_1, as shown in the right side of Figure 9.4, which results in enforcement $|E_1$. In the left side of the figure, the curve labeled "Appropriators $|E_1$" corresponds to enforcement level E_1. Given this expected payoff curve, the equilibrium proportion of appropriators equals A_1 and the expected payoff to agents equals V_1.

Now consider the effects of a fall in the cost of punishment. If the cost of punishing appropriators falls to c_2, as depicted in Figure 9.4, enforcement rises to E_2, which results in the "Appropriators E_2" curve. The fall in the expected payoff for appropriators causes the equilibrium proportion of appropriators to fall to A_2, and the expected payoff for agents rises to V_2. Thus, an increase in the willingness of players to punish appropriators in the agency game causes

[19] Here is a strict definition of terms, using the density function $f(s)$ over willingness to pay to enforce the social norm: $E = 1 - \int_0^c f(s)$.

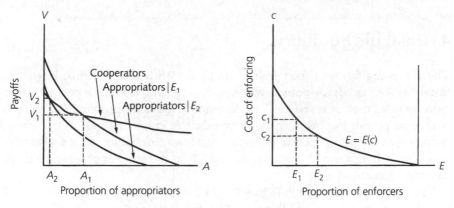

Fig. 9.4 Appropriation and Punishment

more cooperation and production, which benefits everyone. The benefits even extend to appropriating agents, whose expected payoff inevitably rises to the same equilibrium level as cooperating agents.

The agency game achieves the highest level of production when everyone cooperates and no one appropriates. I have shown that the level of cooperation and production in the agency game depends upon the willingness of players to punish appropriators. Self-interested principals may punish appropriators in order to discourage future partners from appropriating. Self-interested players, however, do not consider the general deterrence value of punishing appropriators, which benefits everyone. Self-interest favors free-riding on the enforcement efforts of others, which results in an inefficient equilibrium with too much appropriation.

Models of social norms, however, must consider behavior that is not narrowly self-interested. Internalization of a norm may cause players to punish appropriators as a matter of principle, not self-interest. So the internalization of social norms is crucial to their effectiveness. (While noting the importance of internalization, I leave its analysis to psychologists, who have studied it for generations.[20])

---

[20] See e.g. Sigmund Freud, *The Ego and the Id*, trans. Joan Riviere (New York: W. W. Norton, 1962); Jean Piaget, *The Moral Judgement of the Child*, trans. Marlorie Gabain (Glencoe, Ill.: Free Press, 1948); Lawrence Kohlberg, "Stage and Sequence: the Cognitive-Development Approach to Socialization," in *Handbook of Socialization Theory and Research*, ed. D. A. Goslin (Chicago: Rand McNally, 1969); Robert B. Chaldini, Carl A. Kallgren, and Raymond R. Reno, "A Focus Theory of Normative Conduct: a Theoretical Refinement and Reevaluation of the Role of Norms in Human Behavior," in *Advances in Experimental Psychology*, ed. M. P. Zanna (New York: Academic Press, 1991); and M. Sherif, *The Psychology of Social Norms* (New York: Harper, 1936).

4 Unstable Equilibria

The preceding figures depict stable equilibria. With social norms, however, instability can occur. A person who spontaneously punishes someone often risks confrontation or revenge. This risk tends to fall as the proportion of people willing to punish increases. In other words, the enforcer's cost of punishing decreases as the proportion of enforcers increases. Instability occurs when the cost of punishing wrongdoers decreases rapidly as the number of players willing to punish increases.

These facts are depicted in Figure 9.5. Whereas Figure 9.4 treats the cost of punishment as exogenous, Figure 9.5 treats it as endogenous. The curve denoted $c = c(E)$ in the right side of the figure depicts the relationship between the expected cost of punishing someone who breaks a social norm, denoted c, and the proportion of people willing to pay that cost, denoted E. As the proportion of enforcers E rises, the expected cost of enforcement c falls.

Bear in mind the difference between the functions $E=E(c)$ and $c=c(E)$. The function $E=E(c)$ describes the number of enforcers E who are willing to pay the cost c of enforcement. In other words, $E(c)$ is the willingness to pay for enforcement (the demand curve); $c=c(E)$, however, describes how many enforcers are required to sustain a given cost of enforcement. In other words, $c(E)$ is the cost of enforcement (the supply curve).

If the actual number of enforcers equals the number required to sustain the current cost of enforcement, the cost of enforcement remains constant. In other words, an intersection of the curves $E(c)$ and $c(E)$ indicates an equilibrium in the number of enforcers and the cost of enforcement.[21] If the actual number of

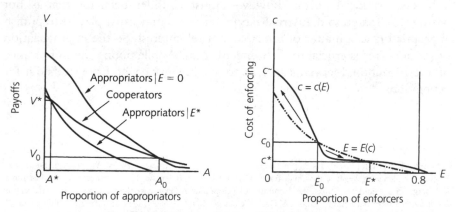

Fig. 9.5 Decreasing Cost of Punishment

[21] To be precise, an equilibrium is a pair of values $(E^\star, c^\star)$ such that $E^\star=E(c^\star)$ and $c^\star=c(E^\star)$.

enforcers falls short of the number required to sustain the current cost of enforcement, the cost of enforcement will rise. Conversely, if the actual number of enforcers exceeds the number required to sustain the current cost of enforcement, the cost of enforcement will fall.

The directional arrows in Figure 9.5 indicate the dynamics of the system. The actual number of enforcers falls short of the number required to sustain the current cost of enforcement at points to the left of (E_0,c_0). So any disturbance that causes c and E to deviate to the left of the equilibrium (E_0,c_0) will cause the system to move to the corner equilibrium at $(0,c\sim)$, where $E=0$. When $E=0$, the absence of enforcement causes the appropriator's expected payoff to correspond to the curve labeled "Appropriators$|E=0$" in Figure 9.5, which results in the equilibrium (A_0,V_0). Low enforcement thus results in a high proportion of appropriating agents and a low expected payoff to everyone.

The actual number of enforcers exceeds the number required to sustain the current cost of enforcement at points just to the right of (E_0,c_0) in Figure 9.5, so the cost of enforcement will fall. Any disturbance that causes c and E to deviate to the right of the equilibrium (E_0,c_0) will cause the system to move to the stable equilibrium at $(E^\star,c^\star)$. The point $(E^\star,c^\star)$ is a stable equilibrium because any small deviation from it causes the system to return to this point. The stability conditions can be summarized as follow:

- If $E(c)$ cuts $c(E)$ from below, the enforcement equilibrium is stable.
- If $E(c)$ cuts $c(E)$ from above, the enforcement equilibrium is unstable.

I have shown that (E_0,c_0) is an unstable equilibrium. Instability is more likely under two conditions. First, a small increase in the number of enforcers causes a large decrease in the cost of enforcement, which makes $c(E)$ steeply sloped; for example, $c(E)$ slopes steeply when large numbers of enforcers enjoy much security, whereas isolated enforcers bear much risk. Second, a small decrease in the price of enforcement causes a large increase in the number of enforcers, which makes $E(c)$ flat; for example, $E(c)$ is flat when many people who internalize the norm will pay a small amount to enforce it, but no one will enforce it at substantial personal cost.

When $E=E^\star$ in the figure, the high level of enforcement causes the payoff to appropriation to correspond to the curve labeled "appropriators$|E^\star$," which results in the equilibrium $(A^\star,V^\star)$. High enforcement thus results in a low proportion of appropriating agents and a high expected payoff to everyone.

In this figure, either many people enforce the norm or no one enforces it,[22] with the tipping point at (E_0,c_0). If the system begins at a level of enforcement above the tipping point, it "tips in" to a high level of enforcement of the norm. A high level of enforcement causes almost all agents to cooperate, thus

---

[22] This possibility is discussed by Taylor, *Possibility of Cooperation*, p. 145; and Mark Casson, *The Economics of Business Culture: Game Theory, Transaction Costs, and Economic Performance* (Oxford: Clarendon Press, 1991): p. 83.

approaching the most efficient situation in which no agents appropriate. Conversely, if the system begins at a level of enforcement below the tipping point, it "tips out" and low levels of enforcement result in low levels of cooperation. Later I discuss how law can cause such a system to tip into a high level of enforcement.

5 Distribution and Critical Morality: Agency Bargaining Game

As explained, every agent in the game above has an incentive to signal "cooperation." I want to modify the bargaining game to illustrate a situation with mixed signaling, not uniform signaling. As depicted in Figure 9.1, cooperation produces one unit of output which the principal and agent split. Instead, modify the game by assuming that the parties bargain over how to split the production from cooperation. Before forming a partnership, the parties must bargain to an agreement that the agent receives α% of the product and the principal receives $(1-\alpha)$%, as depicted in Figure 9.6.

The best bargaining strategies depend upon details of the model that I leave unspecified, such as the cost of searching for a new partner when bargaining fails. Under reasonable assumptions, however, bargaining will settle into an internal equilibrium, with some players signaling that they bargain hard and other players signaling that they bargain soft. Hard bargainers spend more time searching for partners and receive a large share of the cooperative surplus less often, whereas soft bargainers spend less time searching for partners and receive a smaller share of the cooperative surplus more often.

The incentives for signaling by agents differ between cooperating and bargaining. As explained, all agents have an incentive to signal cooperation, regardless of whether their real strategy is cooperation or appropriation. This

		Agent	
		Cooperate	Appropriate
Principal	Invest	α / $1-\alpha$	1.0 / -1.0
	Don't invest	0 / 0	0 / 0

Fig. 9.6 Agency Bargaining Game

fact explains why societies generate a consensus of opinion condemning deception and fraud in business. In contrast, all agents do not have an incentive to signal that they will adopt the same bargaining strategy. This explains why societies do not generate a consensus over how to distribute the gains from cooperation.

Soft bargaining promotes cooperation and avoids bargaining breakdowns, so a social norm requiring parties to bargain softly would increase production. Such a social norm, however, is unlikely to evolve. I defined a social norm as a consensus obligation. A consensus favoring soft bargaining is unlikely to arise because the signaling equilibrium is mixed. In the absence of a consensus, few people will internalize the obligation and enforcement will be low. Instead of consensus obligations, people will disagree about how they ought to bargain. Soft bargainers will appeal to a critical morality that imposes a higher standard on people than the one acknowledged by hard bargainers.

....

6 Third-Party Effects

In the game described above, the activities of a partnership affect its members and no one else. In reality, many business transactions affect third parties. I modify the agency game in Figure 9.7 to allow for external effects. To keep the numbers simple, I assume that investment by the principle has external effects in 10 percent of cases (e.g. injury, discharge of pollution, congestion of resource) and no external effects in 90 percent of the cases. When externalities occur, their value equals -2.

Figure 9.7 summarizes the resulting payoffs. The numbers in the lower left corner of each cell indicate the payoff to the principal and agent, respectively. The numbers in the upper right corner of each cell indicate the external cost to the third party. Its probability is shown in the column heading. If the principal

		Payoff to 3rd party and its probability	
		No externality probability = 0.9	Externality probability = 0.1
Total payoff to principal and agent	Invest and cooperate	0 1	−2 1
	Don't invest	0 0	0 0

Fig. 9.7 Principal-Agent and Third Party

and agent fail to form a partnership and no investment occurs, then the partners receive 0 and the third party receives 0. If a partnership forms, the principal invests, and the agent cooperates, then the principal and agent each receive 0.5 and the third party loses 2 with probability 0.1. If a partnership forms and the principal invests, the third party loses 1 with probability 0.1.

Assume that the partners can foresee whether or not their activities fall into the 10 percent of cases with external effects. Given foresight, efficiency requires the partners to forgo their activities in the 10 percent of cases with external effects, and efficiency requires the partners to invest and cooperate in the 90 percent of cases without external effects. We assume that partners and third parties cannot bargain to produce the efficient result. The question is whether or not an efficient social norm will evolve.

The answer depends upon the incentives to signal and punish. Assuming the players of the game form a human community, they will discuss and debate the question of whether or not a partnership should proceed under circumstances where its activities yield 1 for partners and cost 2 for third parties. For the sake of efficiency, players ought not to proceed in these circumstances. The evolution of such a social norm depends upon the level of coherence in the community.

The members of a coherent community will make convincing moral arguments for utilitarian obligations. To illustrate, people will say that everyone in the community should give the same weight to the harms they cause to others as to the benefits that they receive for themselves. Community coherence will cause its members to internalize the norm and punish violators. A high level of enforcement will provide an incentive for partners to conform to the norm. Conversely, community incoherence will lead to the externalization of the norm and deficient punishment of violators, in which case actors have little incentive to conform to the norm.

Figure 9.8 illustrates these facts. The right side of the figure, like the right side of Figure 9.5, depicts the cost of enforcing social norms. In a coherent community, people are willing to pay for enforcement, as indicated by the function labeled "$E=E(c)|$coherent," which results in the high equilibrium level of enforcement E^*. The left side of the figure depicts the immediate payoff to an actor from producing and the expected cost of punishment imposed on an actor who violates the social norm by creating an externality. The high level of enforcement E^* deters actors from violating the norm, as indicated in the left side of the figure by the fact that enforcement E^* causes the expected punishment to exceed the immediate payoff from the acting.

In contrast, people in an incoherent community are less willing to pay for enforcement, so the curve on the right side of Figure 9.8 shifts down to "$E=E(c)|$incoherent," which results in the low equilibrium level of enforcement $E=0$. The low level of enforcement $E=0$ does not deter actors from violating the norm, as indicated in the left side of the figure by the fact that the

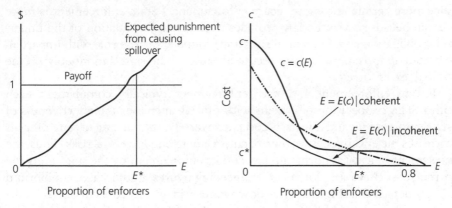

Fig. 9.8 Equilibrium with Spillovers

immediate payoff from the partnership exceeds the expected punishment caused by enforcement $E=0$.

In the simple agency game, self-interest of the parties creates a uniform signaling equilibrium, which provides the consensus about obligations as needed for the evolution of a social norm. In the agency game with externalities, however, self-interest does not necessarily produce uniform signaling. Instead, a consensus requires individuals to recognize their common interest in the group's efficiency and fairness. I use the phrase "coherent community" to mean a society whose members recognize this common interest and act upon it.

One cause of coherence is symmetry among the members of the community. By "symmetry," I mean that everyone has the same probability of being the injurer, and the same probability of being the victim, of external costs in the future. For example, everyone in a certain group might have the same probability of being the injurer or victim of an automobile accident, or the polluter or pollutee from exhaust fumes. Symmetry enhances agreement among people about the best rule for governing future harms.[23]

7 Jurisprudence of Social Norms

The preceding figures depict the informal enforcement of social norms by private persons, not state enforcement. According to Locke, the state can pro-

[23] Such a rule is "ex ante Pareto efficient." For a discussion, see Robert D. Cooter and Tom Ulen, "An Economic Case for Comparative Negligence," *New York University Law Review*, 61 (1987): 1067.

242 Robert D. Cooter

vide more certain and more secure enforcement.[24] State enforcement is more certain because a written law provides a canonical formulation of the underlying obligation and, in an ideal situation, courts apply the rule with impartiality. State enforcement is more secure because of the state's monopoly on the official use of force.

Private enforcement and state enforcement typically complement each other. The cooperation of citizens with officials increases the effectiveness of state enforcement and lowers its costs. Conversely, the backing of state officials increases the effectiveness of private enforcement and lowers its risks. Thus, the enactment of a social norm into law and its enforcement by the state shifts the private cost curve $c(E)$ down in the preceding figures. In the stable equilibrium $(E^\star,c^\star)$ depicted in Figure 9.5, a downward shift in the cost curve $c(E)$ shifts the equilibrium to a higher level of private enforcement above $A^\star$. In other words, public enforcement "pulls in" more private enforcement, rather than "crowding out" private enforcement.

State enforcement has another potentially powerful effect. If most citizens in Figure 9.5 believe that most citizens will enforce the social norm, then the system will move to the stable, internal equilibrium $(E^\star,c^\star)$ with a high level of enforcement $A^\star$. Conversely, if most citizens believe that few citizens will enforce the social norm, then the system will move to the unstable, corner equilibrium with a low level of enforcement. Thus, Figure 9.5 depicts a self-fulfilling prophecy. In such a social system, state enactment can sometimes tip society into conformity with the law merely by causing citizens to *believe* that most of them will enforce it.

For example, the city of Berkeley, California, recently enacted an ordinance requiring owners to clean up after their dogs (the "pooper-scooper" law). Enactment of the law clarified vague social norms concerning courtesy. After the law's passage, people became more aggressive toward discourteous owners of dogs. Apparently it is easier to say "Obey the law" than to say "Don't be so rude." Most owners now clean up after their dogs, so the sidewalks are much cleaner.

In another example, many local jurisdictions in America have recently enacted ordinances prohibiting smoking in public buildings such as airports. Before these ordinances were enacted, people smoked at will and nonsmokers seldom complained to smokers. After the ordinances were enacted, officials posted signs prohibiting smoking in public buildings. Although officials almost never enforce the prohibitions, the signs seem to have made nonsmokers believe, correctly, that other nonsmokers would support complaints against smokers. Enacting the ordinance has apparently tipped the balance in favor of private enforcement of the social norm.

---

[24] John Locke, *The Second Treatise of Civil Government*, ed. Thomas I. Cook (New York: Hafner, 1961 (1690)).

I have shown how state enforcement of social norms can reduce violations of the underlying obligation. Now consider what happens when the state imposes laws that undermine social norms. To undermine a social norm, the state creates obstacles to its private enforcement. For example, morality may require the fulfillment of promises to perform acts forbidden by the state, such as paying interest on a loan that exceeds the ceiling set by usury laws. Obstacles to private enforcement raise its costs, as indicated by an upward shift in the cost curve $c(E)$ in the preceding figures. In the stable equilibrium depicted in Figure 9.5, an upward shift in the cost curve $c(E)$ shifts the equilibrium to a lower level of private enforcement. It also increases the probability that random shocks will cause the system to reach the corner solution characterized by a low level of enforcement.

Using Figure 9.6, I extended the agency game to encompass bargaining strategies. The signalling equilibrium is apparently not uniform for bargaining strategies, which creates an obstacle to community consensus about what people ought to do. When consensus obligations are missing or incomplete, there is no social norm for the state to enforce. Instead, the state must choose among competing versions of morality, a situation that runs the risk of fostering a low level of informal enforcement and private cooperation with public officials.

External costs, as depicted in Figure 9.8, pose another problem. When external costs exceed internal benefits of a particular action, a coherent community will tend to reach agreement that people ought not to engage in the activity. The recognition of this social norm may raise the level of informal punishment for violators sufficiently to deter them. If the private costs of punishing violators is too high, or if a group of people lack the moral resources of a coherent community, then state enforcement may be required to prevent external harm.

....

8   Conclusion: Economic Development

This theory has some practical implications for economic development. In a developing economy with relatively free trade, business will tend to develop efficient norms to regulate private interactions. In these circumstances, the role of state law can be limited to correcting failures in the market for norms. Failures tend to occur because private, informal punishment insufficiently deters wrongdoing. In these circumstances, state enforcement of social norms can increase private cooperation and production. However, successful state enforcement typically requires a close alignment of law with morality, so state officials enjoy informal support from private persons.

Business law and morality get out of alignment in states suffering from legal centrism, such as over-regulation or central planning. In these circumstances, the realignment of business law with morality is needed to reduce corruption and create the private basis for effective public laws. To realign business law with morality, business law should be remade to reflect the best business practices.

The problem of aligning law with morality is especially acute when business activities create external costs. In these circumstances, mixed signaling incentives prevent the emergence of social norms restraining externalities. The emergence of social norms requires sufficient coherence in the community to develop a critical morality. Class, ethnic, or factional strife creates incoherence and fragmentation of social norms. An analysis of critical morality and the internalization of norms transcends economic traditions, but without such an analysis economics cannot fully comprehend the decentralization of law.

10 The Nature of Institutional Impediments to Economic Development

Pranab Bardhan[1]

1 Introduction

With the decline of the pervasive influence of Walrasian models in economics in recent years, it is now generally recognized that "institutions matter" and that the associated incentive structures substantially influence economic performance. But beyond this general agreement, there are still many differences among reasonable people on which institutions affect the process of development and how. In particular, different institutional economists emphasize different institutional impediments to development. The purpose of this paper is to bring these contrasting positions into the open and to express some of the concerns of the "old" institutional economists (emphasizing distributive conflicts) in a somewhat newer format, while drawing examples from the process of Indian economic development. For our present purposes we define "institutions" very generally (and vaguely) as social rules, conventions, and other elements of the structural framework of social interaction.

The New Institutional Economics literature points to some very important features of institutional failures that cause or prolong underdevelopment, particularly the legal and contractual structures and rules of third-party enforcement which are necessary for most arms'-length market transactions.

[1] I received valuable comments on an earlier draft from Avinash Dixit, Avner Greif, Margaret Levi, Dilip Mookherjee, Douglass North, Jeffrey Nugent, and James Robinson. Remaining errors are no doubt due to my laxity in following up on all of their suggestions.

Let us follow a by now well known account, as in North.[2] In a small, closed, face-to-face peasant community, transaction costs are low but production costs are high, because specialization and division of labor are severely limited by the extent of market defined by the personalized exchange process of the small community. In a large-scale complex economy, as the network of inter-dependence widens the impersonal exchange process gives considerable scope for all kinds of opportunistic behavior, and the costs of transacting can be high. In Western societies, over time, complex institutional structures have been devised to constrain the participants, to reduce the uncertainty of social interaction, and in general to prevent the transactions from being too costly and thus to allow the productivity gains of larger-scale and improved technol-ogy to be realized. These institutions include elaborately defined and effectively enforced property rights, formal contracts and guarantees, trademarks, limited liability, bankruptcy laws, and large corporate organizations with governance structures to limit problems of agency and, as Williamson has emphasized, of incomplete contracting and ex post opportunism.[3]

Some of these institutional structures are non-existent or weak or poorly devised and implemented in less developed countries. In these countries the state is either too weak to act as a guarantor of such rights and institutions and/or much too predatory in its own demands, posing a threat to such rights and institutions. The state is also sometimes captured by special-interest groups and lobbies that do not have, to use Olson's phrase, an "encompassing interest" in the productivity of the society and thus may prolong socially inefficient property rights.[4]

The preceding two paragraphs provide a capsule summary of some of the major insights generated by the New Institutional Economics literature in our understanding of underdevelopment as an institutional failure. I happen to agree with much of this diagnosis, but in this paper I shall focus, to a large extent, on my differing emphasis on (a) institutional impediments as outcomes of distributive conflicts, (b) the collective action problems these impediments exacerbate, and (c), in view of the critical need for coordination, on a more complex and nuanced role of the state, which many (but not all) states fail to adopt. Recent Indian economic history will provide the context of the discussion.

---

[2] D. C. North, *Structure and Change in Economic History* (New York: W. W. Norton, 1981); D. C. North, *Institutions, Institutional Change and Economic Performance* (New York: Cambridge University Press, 1990).

[3] O. Williamson, *The Economic Institutions of Capitalism* (New York: Free Press, 1985).

[4] M. Olson, *The Rise and Decline of Nations: Economic Growth, Stagflation, and Social Rigidities* (New Haven: Yale University Press, 1982).

2 Collective Mechanisms for Contract in Pre-modern Times

Beyond the face-to-face village community, the institutions that a society develops (or fails to develop) for long-distance trade, credit, and other inter-temporal and interspatial markets where the transactions are not self-enforcing provide an important indicator of that society's capacity for development. In this context the analyses of North, of Greif *et al.*, and of Greif have pointed to the importance of institutions like the merchants' guilds (for example those in Italian city-states, or the inter-city guilds like the German Hansa), the law merchant system (of private judges recording institutionalized public memory at the Champagne fairs, which provided an important nexus of trade between northern and southern Europe), the Maghribi traders' coalition, and the community responsibility system in the Mediterranean and European trade during the late Medieval commercial revolution between the eleventh and the fourteenth centuries.[5] These institutions facilitated economic growth by reducing opportunism in transactions among people largely unknown to one another and providing a multilateral reputation mechanism supported by frameworks of credible commitment, enforcement, and coordination.

In the informal enforcement of mercantile contracts, those dependent on bilateral reputation mechanisms (i.e. where the cheater is punished only by the party that is cheated) are usually more costly than multilateral reputation mechanisms (where punishment is inflicted by a whole community to which the party that is cheated belongs) or a community responsibility system (in which a whole community is jointly liable if one of its members cheats). In the case of bilateral reputation mechanisms, simple efficiency-wage considerations suggest that, in order to keep a long-distance trading agent honest, the agent has to be paid by the merchant (the principal) a wage higher than the agent's reservation income, whereas in more "collectivist" forms of enforcement this wage need not be as high, since the penalty for cheating is higher or else peer monitoring makes cheating more difficult. But in a world with information asymmetry, slow communication, and plausibly different interpretations of facts in a dispute, an uncoordinated multilateral reputation mechanism may not always work, and may need to be supplemented by a more formal organization to coordinate the expectations and responses of different members of the collectivity and to enforce the penalty. In medieval Europe

---

[5] North, *Institutions*; A. Greif, P. Milgrom, and B. Weingast, "Coordination, Commitment, and Enforcement: the Case of the Merchant Guild," *Journal of Political Economy*, (August 1994), A. Greif, "Trading Institutions and the Commercial Revolution in Medieval Europe," in A. Aganbegyan, O. Bogomolov, and M. Kaser, eds., *Economics in a Changing World*, vol. 1 (London: Macmillan, 1994).

the merchants' guilds provided such an organization. In governing relations between merchants and their various towns and the foreign towns with which they traded, they had the ability to coordinate the merchants' responses to abuses against any merchant and to force them to participate in trade embargoes. This credible threat of collective action from the guilds enabled the medieval rulers to commit to respecting the property rights of alien merchants, and thus facilitated exchange and market integration.[6] Of course, the strategic considerations involved in such coordination and commitment give rise to multiple equilibria in theoretical frameworks and to the historical context specificity of such institutional arrangements and the path dependence of their evolution.

In pre-colonial India, while more in-depth research on these lines is greatly needed, there is plenty of evidence that, contrary to the description popularized by colonial sociology of an inert, caste-ossified, "Asiatic" society under an oriental despotic state, there was a vigorous and far-flung mercantile economy operating with some indigenous institutions of trust and commitment in long-distance trade and credit. These institutions included negotiable credit instruments like the *hundi* (or bills of exchange), caste-based mercantile family firms and their branch agencies (*kothis*), mercantile *panchayats* (local courts), multi-caste assemblies of "respectable merchants" which adjudicated business disputes and imposed penalties for breaches of trust (firms kept lists of creditable merchants whose credit notes—*sahajog hundis*—could expect a rapid discount in the bazaar), multi-caste trading corporations of merchants and bankers, townsmen and religious specialists, associations of wholesale commission agents (*arethias*) and insurers (*bimawallas*), and so on.

Just as the merchants' guilds in medieval Europe had a positive role beyond their narrow cartelizing operations, the Indian castes served economic functions much beyond the restrictive practices of the rent-seeking distributive coalitions with which they are sometimes associated, for example in Olson.[7] Caste-based mercantile associations and courts provided credible mechanisms of commitment, enforcement, and coordination which facilitated the process of impersonal commercial exchange. One should also note that many sociologists, following the writings of Marx and Weber on India, have assumed that the caste system has paralyzed the development of wider solidarities in Indian economic life. Recent historical research has questioned this narrow view. For

[6] As Greif *et al.* point out in "Coordination," the usual interpretation of merchant guilds as mere cartels presents a puzzle: "If the purpose of the guilds was to create monopoly power for the merchants and to increase their bargaining power with the rulers, why did *powerful* rulers during the late medieval period cooperate with alien merchants to establish guilds in the first place? What offsetting advantages did the rulers enjoy? The puzzle is resolved if the guild's power enabled trade to expand to the benefit of the merchants and rulers alike."

[7] Olson, *Rise and Decline.* Mokyr also ascribes India's technological backwardness largely to the caste system; see J. Mokyr, *The Lever of Riches* (New York: Oxford University Press, 1990).

example, describing the mercantile culture around Benares in North India in the eighteenth century, Bayly writes:

While the mercantile population possessed a consciousness of caste and caste institutions which were more or less effective in matters of ritual, this did not preclude the formation of wider merchant organizations and bonds of trust which stretched across the boundaries of caste . . . Most trades were multi-caste ventures, and in their dealings with each other or with the authorities, merchants needed common institutions . . . Conceptions of status and mercantile honor also overrode caste for it is evident that trade and credit relations over long distances could not have survived without them. "Credit-worthiness," having one's *hundis* accepted in the bazaar, keeping regular commercial books, being frugal rather than "expensive": these were the measures of respectability which are mentioned regularly in commercial cases and they are witness to a consistent mercantile "public opinion." At the pinnacle of merchant society stood the members of the Naupatti Sabha (Society of Nine Sharers) themselves who functioned as a final panel of arbitration among merchants on matters such as debt, the division of assets in family partitions, bankruptcy, and the status of mercantile custom on legal instruments . . . To all intents and purposes then, an *ad hoc* "law merchant" existed. Excommunication remained the usual sanction for caste assemblies, but what were the sanctions available to this wider mercantile opinion? . . . The failure of one's credit in the bazaar was a sentence of commercial and sometimes of physical death. But the sanctions of Hindu religion were also available. Oaths were made in Ganges water and in the name of tutelary deities, or with the witness of a Gosain (belonging to an ascetic order) who was technically above caste and kin . . . The ultimate sanction was to have Brahmins mutilate themselves before the door of a debtor in order to heap spiritual demerit on him (*dharna*); this was only the most dramatic instance of the role of popular religion in reinforcing mercantile trust.[8]

Examples of the use of religious morality in sanctioning business conduct in other parts of the world include the Confucian code of ethics among Chinese businessmen in Southeast Asia and the Islamic moral code among the "trading diasporas" in West Africa.[9]

---

[8] C. A. Bayly, *Rulers, Townsmen and Bazaar: North Indian Society in the Age of British Expansion 1770–1870* (Cambridge: Cambridge University Press, 1983).

[9] In their detailed study of a Moroccan market in the 1950s, Geertz, Geertz, and Rosen report that religious authorities and business leaders play an important role in defining norms of acceptable commercial conduct and in sanctioning deviations. See C. Geertz, H. Geertz, and L. Rosen, *Meaning and Order in Moroccan Society* (Cambridge: Cambridge University Press, 1979).

3 Alternative Institutional Mechanisms for Development

In spite of all the indigenous institutions of a thriving mercantile economy that existed in pre-colonial India, the development of sequentially more complex organizations suited for industrial investment and innovations, as occurred in the West, was aborted, and India remains one of the poorest countries in the world. I shall desist from blaming it all on the policies of the colonial administration, not because I think they are unimportant (in some ways, particularly in terms of their "sins" of omission rather than commission, I believe they are crucial in explaining the performance of the Indian economy over the last century and a half), but because I want to keep away from the familiar litany of nationalist historiography and to confine myself to a discussion of indigenous institutional impediments to development, linking up with my critical assessment of the literature on the New Institutional Economics in its own terrain.

Greif, in his comparative study of the distinct trajectories of economic organization of two pre-modern societies—the Maghribi traders of the eleventh century and the Genoese traders of the twelfth—concludes by pointing our attention to the fact that the Maghribis' "collectivist" organization (based on multilateral reputation mechanisms and informal codes of conduct and enforcement) resembles that of contemporary developing countries, whereas the Genoese "individualistic" organization (based on bilateral punishment with more formal methods of communication and enforcement) resembles that of the developed West.[10] The latter system is presumably more likely to induce formal, i.e. legal and political, institutions of enforcement which facilitate industrial capital formation and innovations. The pre-colonial Indian mercantile organizations were clearly of the former type, based on multilateral reputation and communal enforcement. The legal and contractual structures were more formalized in the colonial period (the joint-stock companies with limited liability came only after the middle of the nineteenth century, around the same time they came in to vogue in Britain), but many of the modern Indian business houses were an outgrowth of the earlier mercantile family firms.

The dramatic success story of rapid industrial progress in Southeast Asia in recent decades, often under the leadership of Chinese business families who are organized under similar "collectivist" principles, makes one wonder how much of an institutional impediment this form of economic organization really is. As the Loury–Coleman–Putnam emphasis on the importance of "social capital" as

[10] A. Greif, "Cultural Beliefs and the Organization of Society: a Historical and Theoretical Reflection on Collectivist and Individualist Societies," *Journal of Political Economy* (October 1994).

a major determinant of economic performance gains more recognition in the social sciences, one hopes there will be more work on the mechanisms through which this form of capital works in Chinese-led entrepreneurial organizations.[11] In a study of seventy-two Chinese entrepreneurs in Hong Kong, Taiwan, Singapore, and Indonesia, Redding shows how, through specific social networks of direct relationship or clan or regional connection, they build a system dependent on patrimonial control by key individuals, personal obligation bonds, relational contracting, and interlocking directorships.[12]

As Ouchi had noted some years back, when ambiguity of performance evaluation is high and goal incongruence is low, the clan-based organization may have advantages over market relations or bureaucratic organizations.[13] In clan-based organizations, goal congruence (and thus low opportunism) is achieved through various processes of socialization; performance evaluation takes place through the kind of subtle reading of signals, observable by other clan members but not verifiable by a third-party authority.

In general, institutional evolution in poor countries is usually judged in terms of deviations from the "right" path of institutional development that brought about "the Rise of the West"; in view of the rise of the East in the last half century, the time may have come to rethink the canonical model of institutional development from the point of view of economic growth, and to consider how the "collectivist" organization may be reshaped in particular social–historical contexts to facilitate industrial progress and whether clan-based or other particularistic networks can sometimes provide a viable alternative to contract law and impersonal ownership. In East Asia in general (including Japan) corporate transactions have often been relation-based rather than rule-based, and the state, as we note later, has played a much more active role, particularly in the financial market, compared with the Western countries. The problems of relation-based systems, much commented upon in the wake of the recent financial crises in East Asia, should not blind us to the positive role they played in the early stages of industrial transformation.

[11] G. Loury, "A Dynamic Theory of Racial Income Differences," in P. A. Wallace and A. Le Mund, eds., *Women, Minority, and Employment Discrimination* (New York: Lexington Books, 1977); J. S. Coleman, *Foundations of Social Theory* (Cambridge, Mass.: Harvard University Press, 1990); and R. D. Putnam, *Making Democracy Work: Civic Traditions in Modern Italy* (Princeton: Princeton University Press, 1993).

[12] As Redding points out, "Many transactions which in other countries would require contracts, lawyers, guarantees, investigators, wide opinion-seeking, and delays are among the overseas Chinese dealt with reliably and quickly by telephone, by a handshake, over a cup of tea. Some of the most massive property deals in Hong Kong are concluded with a small note locked in the top drawer of a chief executive's desk, after a two-man meeting." (One hears similar stories about the Hasidic diamond traders of New York and about firms in industrial districts in Northern Italy.) Of course, as may be expected, such arrangements in the Chinese business families are somewhat constrained by too much reliance on centralized decision-taking and control, internal finance, relatively small-scale operations, and in the case of large organizations, a tendency to subdivide into more or less separate units, each with its own products and markets. See S. G. Redding, *The Spirit of Chinese Capitalism* (New York: Walter de Gruyter, 1990).

[13] W. G. Ouchi, "Markets, Bureaucracies, and Clans," *Administrative Science Quarterly* (March 1980).

North points out that some of the traditional institutions of exchange (he gives as examples caravan trade, or the North African *Suq*) did not evolve into more complex organizations as in early modern Europe because they lacked the inherent dynamic linkage with other institutions that would insure against the moral hazards, adverse selection and enforcement problems of the expanding exchange process: "there is no incentive to alter the system."[14] But as North would probably agree, such explanations are ultimately inadequate and somewhat circular. We cannot explain underdevelopment in terms of such institutional atrophy, because it is quite possible that the traditional institutions of exchange did not evolve in North Africa *because* low growth in the volume of trade and the low rate of return for the traditional bazaars did not provide an incentive to devise new institutions to reduce enforcement costs. In empirical work in institutional history, there is this perpetual identification problem.

4   A More Nuanced Theory of the State

A major institutional deficiency that blocked the progress of the mercantile into the industrial economy in India as in other poor countries relates to the financial markets. Even when mercantile family firms thrived in their network of multilateral reputation and enforcement mechanisms, the latter were not adequate for supporting the larger risks of longer-horizon industrial investment. These firms, by and large, had a limited capacity to pool risks and mobilize the capital of society at large in high-risk, high-return industrial ventures. The usual imperfections of the credit and equity markets emphasized in the literature on imperfect information are severe in the early stages of industrial development. The investment in learning by doing is not easily collateralizable and therefore is particularly subject to the high costs of information imperfections. The role of the government can become very important here, as Gerschenkron had emphasized for the late industrializers of Europe. There are, of course, cases, even in India, where coordination and mutual support among merchant families aided their transition to the industrial economy without much help (actually, with some hindrances) from the colonial government; for example, as Bayly notes:

In Ahmedabad, the one case of a "traditional" merchant city which industrialized from inside, it was several of the leading families who controlled resources and status within

[14] North, *Institutions*.

the trade guilds who went into the cotton mill ventures. No small man could go it alone. But if the leaders of the community who could themselves call on a wide range of security and information made the initial move, then others would follow.[15]

More often, however, such coordination in investment and risk-taking on the part of the merchant families was missing. Here clearly is a case of "strategic complementarities" and positive feedback effects resulting in multiple equilibria.[16] This is particularly important when externalities of information, and the need for a network of proximate suppliers of components, services, and infrastructural facilities with economies of scale, make investment decisions highly interdependent and raising capital from the market for the whole complex of activities particularly difficult.[17] Historically, in some countries the state has played an important role in resolving this kind of "coordination failure" by facilitating and complementing private-sector coordination. The colonial Indian state obviously did not.[18]

In much of the literature on the New Institutional Economics the importance of the state is recognized, but only in the narrow context of how to use its "monopoly of violence" in the enforcement of contracts and property rights on the one hand, and of how to establish its credibility in not making confiscatory demands on the private owners of those rights on the other.[19] This dilemma is implicit in the standard recommendation in this literature for a "strong but limited" government. It is, however, possible to argue that in the successful cases of East Asian development (including that of Japan) the state has played a much more active role, intervening in the capital market sometimes in subtle but decisive ways, using regulated credit allocation (sometimes threatening withdrawal of credit in not-so-subtle ways) in promoting and channeling industrial investment, underwriting risks and guaranteeing loans, establishing public development banks[20] and other financial institutions, en-

[15]   Bayly, *Rulers*.

[16]   This has a long history in the postwar development literature, from P. Rosenstein-Rodan, "Problems of Industrialization of Eastern and Southeastern Europe," *Economic Journal* (June–September 1943), to K. Murphy, A. Shleifer, and R. Vishny, "Industrialization and the Big Push," *Journal of Political Economy* (October 1989). For more recent theoretical contributions to this literature, see the special issue on "Increasing Returns, Monopolistic Competition, and Economic Development" in the *Journal of Development Economics* (April 1996).

[17]   For an account of the great financial difficulties faced by enterprising groups like the Tatas at Jamshedpur or by Walchand at Visakhapatnam in pre-Independence India, see R. K. Ray, *Industrialization in India: Growth and Conflict in the Private Corporate Sector 1914–47* (Delhi: Oxford University Press, 1979).

[18]   In the early decades of this century the managing agency system in India provided some role in promoting, underwriting, and financing new firms, but it fell into disrepute on account of interlocking industrial collusion and exclusivity, and was abolished after Independence.

[19]   The French poet Paul Valery is reported to have said: "If the state is strong it will crush us; if it is weak, we will perish."

[20]   In the theoretical literature Armendariz de Aghion, drawing upon the 1995 model of Dewatripont and Maskin, shows that in a private decentralized banking system banks tend to under-invest in and under-transmit expertise in long-term industrial finance. A public development bank can reduce these problems if

couraging the development of the nascent parts of financial markets, and nudging existing firms to upgrade their technology and to move into sectors that fall in line with an overall vision of strategic developmental goals. In this process, as Aoki, Murdock, and Okuno-Fujiwara have emphasized, the state has enhanced the market instead of supplanting it; it has induced private coordination by providing various kinds of cooperation-contingent rents.[21] In the early stages of industrialization, when private financial and other related institutions were underdeveloped and coordination was not self-enforcing, the East Asian state created opportunities for rents conditional on performance or outcome (in mobilization of savings, commercialization of inventions, export "contests," and so on) and facilitated institutional development by influencing the strategic incentives facing private agents through an alteration of the relative returns to cooperation in comparison with the adversarial equilibrium.

One should not, of course, underestimate the administrative difficulties of such aggregate coordination, and the issues of micro-management of capital may be much too intricate for the institutional capacity and information processing abilities of many a state in Africa, Latin America, South Asia, and even East Asia (think of the Philippines, for example).[22] One should also be wary, as the more recent East Asian experience warns us, about the moral hazard problems of too cosy a relationship between public banks and private businesses and the political pressures for bail-out that a state-supported financial system inevitably faces. Nevertheless, I think institutional economics will be richer if we admit the possibility of a more nuanced theory of the state, beyond the oversimplifications of either the Marxist theorist's class-driven state or the public choice theorist's rentier or predatory state. Some of the success stories of state-led industrialization in the history of the last century and a half (starting with the classic case of Meiji Japan) suggest that the impulses that shape major policies and actions by the state elite can sometimes be fueled not merely by motives of self-aggrandizement, but also by some larger organizational goals or nation-building mission.

Olson has modified the theory of the rent-maximizing or predatory state by pointing to the smaller distortionary effects of the "stationary bandit" as opposed to the "roving bandit" (i.e., the state as *organized* crime has more stake in the prosperity of its subjects than the state as petty, decentralized

conditions like the targeting of development bank intervention, co-financing arrangements, and/or coownership with private financial institutions are attached to government sponsorship: B. Armendariz de Aghion, "Development Banking," DEP no. 64, London School of Economics, 1995; M. Dewatripont and E. Maskin, "Credit Efficiency in Centralized and Decentralized Economies," *Review of Economic Studies* (October 1995).

[21] M. Aoki, K. Murdock, and M. Okuno-Fujiwara, "Beyond the East Asian Miracle: Introducing the Market Enhancing View," unpublished paper, Stanford University, 1995.

[22] As the example of Japan in recent years shows, when the technologies become more complex and the exploration of new technological opportunities becomes highly uncertain, the state loses some of its efficacy in guiding private-sector coordination, as is pointed out by Aoki et al., "Beyond the East Asian Miracle."

theft).[23] He shows that a self-interested ruler with an "encompassing" and stable interest in the domain over which his coercive power is exercised will be led to act in ways that are consistent with the interests of society and of those subject to that power. Formally speaking, Olson's ruler maximizes his own objective function subject to the reaction function of the ruled and so in the process the ruler internalizes the economic cost of his impositions in accordance with that reaction function. The ruler is thus a Stackelberg leader, even though Olson does not quite characterize him as such. In contrast, one can say that the weak or the "soft" state is a Stackelberg follower; it cannot commit to a particular policy and merely reacts to the independent actions of the private actors like special-interest groups. Thus, it is easy to see[24] that, compared with the "strong" state ("strength" defined as ability to credibly precommit), the "soft" state will have too much of undesirable interventions (creating distortions in the process of generating rent for the lobbying groups), and by the same logic, will have *too little* of the desirable interventions (as in the case of market failures or the kind of coordination failures alluded to above), since the state does not take into account or internalize the effects of its own policies. So the distinction between a "strong" state (as in much of East Asia, at least in the recent past) and a "soft" state (as in much of Africa or South Asia) is not in the *extent* of intervention, but in its *quality*.[25] This also means that the beneficial effects of a "strong" state go beyond the ideal of "strong but limited government" of the New Institutional Economics.

An important example of the strong state's ability to precommit like the Stackelberg leader arises in the case of the popular infant-industry argument for protection. At the time when such protection is initiated, by the very nature of this argument for temporary protection, it is granted for a short period until the industrial infant can stand up on its feet. But in most countries infant industry protection inevitably faces the time inconsistency problem: when the initial period of protection nears its completion, the political pressures for its renewal become inexorable, and in this way the infant industry soon degenerates into a geriatric protection lobby. In the recent history of the strong states of East Asia, however, there have been some remarkable instances of a government withdrawing protection from an industry after the lapse of a preannounced duration, letting the industry sink or swim in international competition.[26]

[23] M. Olson, "Dictatorship, Democracy, and Development," *American Political Science Review* (September 1993).

[24] For a simple but illuminating demonstration of this result, see D. Rodrik, "Political Economy and Development Policy," *European Economic Review*, 36 (April 1992).

[25] For a discussion of the issue of quality of intervention, see P. Bardhan, "Introduction to the Symposium on the State and Economic Development," *Journal of Economic Perspectives* (Summer 1990).

[26] For an example of how the government in Taiwan imposed an import ban on VCRs in 1982 to help out two of the main domestic electronic companies, and withdrew it after 18 months when they failed to shape up to meet international standards, see R. Wade, *Governing the Market: Economic Theory and the Role of the*

5 The Developmental State and Ability to Precommit

The problem is to figure out the factors that predispose a state or a political coalition to have an "encompassing interest" in the economic performance of the country as a whole, or, to put it differently, to figure out what helps in the making of a strong state. There are many path-dependent factors (deeply historical, cultural, geo-political) that determine the process of formation of a strong or a weak state. But there are some patterns, decipherable from a comparison of East Asia with South Asia, that may be important from the point of view of the political economy of what is called a developmental state.

Many political scientists have commented on the remarkable insulation of the technocratic elite in charge of policy-making in the successful East Asian states from the ravages of short-run pork-barrel politics (ignoring, for the time being, the policies with respect to some relatively small sectors like the protected rice farmers); the role played by powerful semi-autonomous technocratic organizations like the Economic Planning Bureau in South Korea and the Industrial Development Bureau in Taiwan have been cited. Of course, authoritarianism is neither necessary (e.g. many sectors in postwar Japan, Austria, or the Scandinavian countries) for such insulation, nor sufficient (e.g. many states in Africa and Latin America in recent history). Among the enabling conditions for this insulation, Evans emphasizes the Weberian characteristics of internal organization of the state, for example the highly selective meritocratic recruitment and long-term career rewards for members of the bureaucracy.[27] The post-Independence Indian case (where these Weberian characteristics are present to a reasonable degree) suggests that equally important are the mechanisms of promotion and transfer: on the one hand, the strong officers' unions in the Indian administrative services make sure that, once recruited, an officer is regularly promoted (more on the basis of seniority than performance), and on the other hand, powerful politicians who cannot sack you can make life unpleasant for you by getting you transferred to undesirable jobs and locations.

But insulation of the technocratic elite has its costs in terms of efficiency. Apart from the loss of localized information and accountability that this entails (to which we shall return later), bureaucratic insulation makes it difficult to attain flexibility in dealing with changes in technical and market conditions (and

Government in East Asian Industrialization (Princeton: Princeton University Press, 1990). Jeff Nugent has pointed out to me that with the recent advent of democracy some of these precommitments have become somewhat weaker, as for example in the case of the promised withdrawal of protection of small manufacturing enterprises against competition from the chaebols in South Korea.

[27] P. Evans, *Embedded Autonomy* (Princeton: Princeton University Press, 1995).

thus may discourage risk-taking) and also in correcting wrong decisions. This flexibility has been achieved in East Asia by the fostering of a dense network of ties between public officials and private entrepreneurs through deliberative councils (as in Japan or South Korea) or through the tightly knit party organization (as in Taiwan), allowing operational space for negotiating and renegotiating goals and policies and for coordinating decisions (and expectations) with remarkable speed. Such government–business relations (with the state retaining its privileged position as a senior partner in the relation) not only facilitate the sharing of information and risks, but also provide a framework for compromise and rent-sharing within the business elite. Evans has described this networked insulation of the top bureaucracy as the "embedded autonomy" of the state, which he regards as a key to the success of the East Asian state (at least up to the beginning of the 1990s).

But is such "embedded autonomy" of the state elite feasible in societies that are more heterogeneous and unequal than Japan, South Korea, or Taiwan? As we know from Olson, heterogeneity makes collective action problems more difficult.[28] The relevant collective action problem here is that of formulating cohesive developmental goals with clear priorities and avoiding prisoner's-dilemma-type deadlocks in the pursuit even of commonly agreed upon goals. Not merely do societal differences in rule obedience and organizational loyalty[29] matter in this context (palpable differences in this respect between Northeast and South Asia are commonly remarked upon), but also, it is important to keep in mind the different backgrounds of structural conflict in civil society. When wealth distribution is relatively egalitarian, as in large parts of East Asia (particularly through land reforms and the widespread expansion of education and basic health services), it is easier to enlist the support of most social groups (and to isolate the radical wings of the labor movement and the petty bourgeoisie) in making short-run sacrifices and coordinating growth-promoting policies.[30] There is some cross-country evidence[31] that inequality and other forms of polarization make it more difficult to build a consensus about policy changes in response to crises and result in instability of policy outcomes and insecurity of property and contractual rights.

When society is extremely heterogeneous and conflict-ridden, as in India, and no individual group is powerful enough to hijack the state by itself, the democratic process tends to install an elaborate system of checks and balances

[28] M. Olson, *The Logic of Collective Action: Public Goods and the Theory of Groups*, (Cambridge, Mass.: Harvard University Press, 1965).

[29] For a discussion of the multiple equilibria in their evolutionary process, see C. Clague, "Rule Obedience, Organizational Loyalty, and Economic Development," *Journal of Institutional and Theoretical Economics*, 1993.

[30] E. Campos and H. L. Root emphasize this point in *The Key to the East Asian Miracle: Making Shared Growth Credible* (Washington: Brookings Institution, 1996).

[31] See P. Keefer and S. Knack, "Polarization, Property Rights and the Links between Inequality and Growth," unpublished paper, 1995.

in the public sphere and meticulous rules of equity in sharing the spoils at least among the divided elite groups.[32] There may be what is called institutionalized suspicion in the internal organization of the state (in the Indian case, enhanced no doubt by the legacy of the institutional practices of the colonial rulers suspicious of the natives, and an even earlier legacy of the Moghal emperors suspicious of the potentially unruly subadars and mansabdars) and a carefully structured system of multiple veto powers. The tightly integrated working relationship of government with private business which the "embedded auto-nomy" of Evans involves is very difficult to contemplate in this context. Not merely is the cultural distance between the "gentleman [or lady] administrator" and the private capitalist considerable in India (though it is declining in recent years), but, much more important, in the Indian context of a plurality of contending heterogeneous groups a close liaison and harmonizing of the interests of the state with private business would raise an outcry of foul play and strong political resentment among the other interest groups (particularly among organized labor and farmers), the electoral repercussions of which the Indian politicians can afford to ignore much less than the typical East Asian politician. While cozy relations between the state and private capital remain inherently somewhat suspect in such political regimes in general, however, there is some interesting sectoral variability. In some sectors in the Indian economy a shared vision and some consensus building on encompassing development projects have not been absent, and it is very important to study the preconditions and modalities of such instances. The comparative study in Evans of the emerging relationships between the state and private industrialists in Korea, Brazil, and India in the new information technology sector (elec-tronics and telecommunications) is thus quite instructive.[33]

The general theory of bureaucracy suggests[34] that it is difficult to devise high-powered incentive contracts for civil servants, primarily because of what is called a "common agency" problem (i.e., the civil servant has to be the agent of multiple principals) or a multi-task problem (i.e., the civil servant has to pursue multiple goals, many of which are hard to measure). Under low-powered incentives for civil servants, their "capture" by interest groups is considered very likely, and this is usually taken into account in structuring bureaucratic organizations in the form of checks and balances in the allocation of control rights and some bit of multiple veto power systems even in less conflict-ridden

---

[32] For an analysis of the developmental gridlock in India as an intricate collective action problem in an implicit framework of non-cooperative Nash equilibria, see P. Bardhan, *The Political Economy of Development in India* (Oxford: Basil Blackwell, 1984).

[33] Evans, *Embedded Autonomy*.

[34] See J. Q. Wilson, *Bureaucracy: What Government Agencies Do and Why They Do It* (New York: Basic Books, 1989); J. Tirole, "The Internal Organization of Government," *Oxford Economic Papers* (1994); and A. Dixit, *The Making of Economic Policy: A Transaction Cost Politics Perspective* (Cambridge, Mass.: MIT Press, 1995).

societies than India. But these institutional devices create their own opportunities for a kind of inefficient corruption. A multiple veto power system
makes the centralized collection of bribes in exchange for guaranteed favors
very difficult. One high official in New Delhi is reported to have told a friend: "if
you want me to move a file faster, I am not sure I can help you; but if you want
me to stop a file I can do it immediately." This ability to "stop a file" at multiple
points (a system often originally installed to keep corrupt officials in check) may
result in increasing inefficiency as well as increasing the rate of bribes. In
general, centralized corruption (as in South Korea or Taiwan) has less adverse
consequences for efficiency than decentralized bribe-taking, since in the former
case the bribee will internalize some of the distortionary effects of corruption.
Shleifer and Vishny have used a similar argument in explaining the increase in
inefficient corruption in post-communist Russia compared with the earlier
regime of centralized bribe collection by the Communist Party.[35]

An important aspect of the quality of state intervention in East Asia has to do
with the use, by and large, of clear, well-defined, pre-announced rules of performance criteria. In South Korea, for example, the heavy involvement of
the state in directing investment through credit allocation has been largely
successful (at least until very recently) because of its strict adherence to the
criterion of export performance. Through this precommitment device, the
strong Korean state has used the vital disciplining function of foreign
competition to encourage quick learning and cost and quality consciousness
among domestic enterprises, something that is conspicuously absent in many
other interventionist regimes.

While it is easy to see that transparent and pre-announced rules rather
than discretion and credible commitment devices can be very important for
efficiency and long-term investment, particularly in states prone to "capture,"
one should also keep in mind, as Laffont and Tirole mention, that commitment
may allow the government in one period to bind governments in subsequent
periods to a rent-generating contract with a firm with which the politicians in
the former government have colluded, but which is not beneficial for the
country as a whole.[36] In a multi-period model, if state actors who behave like a
Stackelberg leader with a presumed encompassing interest have some chance
of being thrown out of office (in future elections or otherwise), commitment
may act as a rent-perpetuating device. While Laffont and Tirole correctly point
out that the concern of the incumbent government for re-election will reduce
the probability of collusion, elections after all are highly imperfect as disciplining devices.

[35] A. Shleifer and R. Vishny, "Corruption," *Quarterly Journal of Economics*, 108(3) (August 1993).

[36] J. J. Laffont and J. Tirole, *A Theory of Incentives in Procurement and Regulation* (Cambridge, Mass.: MIT
Press, 1994). In India this kind of argument was cited in the recent political controversy around the Enron
power project in Maharashtra.

Thus, the "strength" of a state in the sense of the ability to commit itself credibly to developmental goals is clearly not sufficient. It may not even be necessary: the remarkable economic success of Italy over three decades (until very recently), with a notoriously weak and corrupt government heavily involved in the economy, is an obvious counterexample. Nevertheless, the correlation between growth performance and state "strength" (in the sense defined above) is probably quite robust. It is, of course, possible that economies in their most successful phases have less political conflict (most groups are doing well without political exertion, and few groups are bribed) and that governments therefore have an appearance of "strength"; their commitments are not challenged or reversed by political action. This may give rise to a selection bias. This is an important issue, which needs to be examined with detailed historical data. The determined way in which the Korean state has handled various macroeconomic crises, say, in the 1970s (the two oil shocks, massive foreign debt, inflation, etc.), suggests to me that its "strength" was not just a reflection of the success of the economy.

In most situations the state is neither a Stackelberg leader nor a Stackelberg follower. Usually neither the state actors nor the private interest groups have the power to unilaterally define the parameters of their action. Both may be strategic actors with some power to influence the terms, and the outcome of the bargaining game will depend on their varying bargaining strengths in different situations. Under these circumstances, it is important to strengthen the accountability mechanisms on both sides, as Przeworski emphasizes.[37] On the one hand, credible commitment devices and rules (including constitutional safeguards) may be necessary to insulate some of the economic decision-making processes from the marauding lobbies of special-interest groups; on the other hand, institutional arrangements, such as an independent office of public accounting and auditing, an election commission with powers to limit (and enforce rules on) campaign contributions and to conduct fair elections, citizens' watchdog committees providing information and monitoring services, an office of local ombudsman with some control over the local bureaucracy, etc., can help in limiting the abuse of executive power and providing a system of punishments for undesirable government interventions in the economy and reward for desirable interventions. In a country like India, where most of the economy is still in the informal sector and is dispersed in far-flung villages, such accountability mechanisms have to be reinforced by informal institutions at the local community level, an issue to which we shall return in the last section of the paper.

---

[37] A. Przeworski, "Reforming the State: Political Accountability and Economic Intervention," unpublished paper, New York University, 1995.

6 Difficulties of Collective Action Block Spontaneous Emergence of Good Institutions

The history of evolution of institutional arrangements and of the structure of property rights often reflects the changing relative bargaining power of different social groups. North, unlike some other transaction cost theorists, comes close to this viewpoint traditionally associated with Marxist historians.[38] He points to the contrasting and path-dependent processes of change in bargaining power of the ruler versus the ruled in different countries, particularly in the context of the fiscal crisis of the state. Despite some of the similarities between England and Spain at the beginning of the sixteenth century, North traces the diverging subsequent evolution of economic institutions, and consequently of economic growth, in the two countries to the diverging development of their rulers' power vis-a-vis their constituents (represented by the English Parliament and the Castilian Cortes, respectively). He also finds a reflection of this difference in the institutional evolution of the English North American colonies compared with that of the Spanish colonies in South America, with similar economic consequences.

The relative bargaining power of different social groups alters with changes in material conditions and in ideology or cultural belief systems (which adapt only slowly to changes in material conditions). The major historical change in material conditions that is usually emphasized is in relative prices, which vary with population growth or decline and with improvements in production or military technology. This acts as a main motive force for institutional changes in history, primarily by inducing the development of property rights to the benefit of the owners of the more expensive factor of production. For example, demographic changes altering the relative price of labor to land led to the incentive to redefine property rights on land and to a rearrangement of labor relations. North, and Hayami and Ruttan, give several examples from European and recent Asian history respectively.[39] But from Brenner's analysis of the contrasting experiences of different parts of Europe on the transition from feudalism (those between western and eastern Europe and those between the English and the French cases even within western Europe), we know that changes in demography, market conditions, and relative prices are not sufficient to explain the contrasts.[40] Changes in relative prices may at most alter the costs and benefits of collective action for different social groups (creating

[38] North, *Institutions*.

[39] Ibid., and Y. Hayami and V. Ruttan, *Agricultural Development: An International Perspective* (Baltimore: Johns Hopkins University Press, 1985).

[40] R. Brenner, "Agrarian Class Structure and Economic Development in Pre-industrial Europe," *Past and Present* (February 1976).

new opportunities for political entrepreneurs), but they cannot predetermine the balance of class forces or the outcome of social conflicts. Brenner shows that much depends, for example, on the cohesiveness of the landlords and peasants as contending groups and on their ability to resist encroachments on each other's rights and to form coalitions with other groups in society. Hayami and Ruttan refer to the case of mid-nineteenth-century Thailand, where the expansion of international trade triggered a rise in rice prices which led to a major transformation of property rights: traditional rights in human property (corvee and slavery) were replaced by more precise private property rights in land.[41] But one should not forget that the expansion of grain trade in the sixteenth and seventeenth-century Poland (the rise in grain prices fueled particularly by expansion of Dutch demand) was quite compatible with the *relapse* into serfdom. There are other examples of institutional stagnation or retrogression following an expansion of trade in more recent colonial history.

The "old" institutional economists (including Marxists) often used to point out how a given institutional arrangement serving the interests of some powerful group or class acts as a long-lasting block to economic progress. In contrast, the property rights school as well as the transaction cost theorists often underestimate the tenacity of vested interests and the consequent persistence of dysfunctional institutions. There are two kinds of collective action problem involved here: one is the well-known free-rider problem about sharing the costs of bringing about change; the other is a bargaining problem where disputes about sharing the potential benefits from the change may lead to a breakdown of the necessary coordination.

The costs of collective action on the part of potential gainers of a socially beneficial institutional change may be too high. This is particularly the case, as we know from Olson, when the losses of the potential losers are concentrated and transparent, while the gains of the potential gainers are diffuse[42] (or uncertain for a given individual, even though not for the group, as suggested by Fernandez and Rodrik[43]). It is, of course, difficult for the potential gainers to credibly commit to compensate the losers ex post.

One can also formalize the obstruction by vested interests in terms of a simple bargaining model, where the institutional innovation may shift the bargaining frontier outward (thereby creating the potential for all parties to gain), but in the process the disagreement payoff of the weaker party may also go up (often owing to better options of "exit" and "voice"), and it is possible for the erstwhile stronger party to end up losing in the new bargaining equilibrium.

---

[41] Hayami and Ruttan, *Agricultural Development*.

[42] Olson, *The Logic of Collective Action*. As Machiavelli reminds us in *The Prince*, "the reformer has enemies in all those who profit by the old order, and only lukewarm defenders in all those who would profit by the new."

[43] R. Fernandez and D. Rodrik, "Resistance to Reform: Status Quo Bias in the Presence of Individual-Specific Uncertainty," *American Economic Review* (December 1991).

(How likely this is will, of course, depend on the nature of shift in the bargaining frontier and the extent of change in the disagreement payoffs). As Robinson has emphasized, it may not be rational, for example, for a dictator to carry out institutional changes that safeguard property rights, law enforcement, and other economically beneficial structures, even though they may fatten the cow that the dictator has the power to milk, if in the process his rent extraction machinery has a chance of being damaged or weakened.[44] He may not risk upsetting the current arrangement for the uncertain prospect of a share in a larger pie. This may be the situation even for long-lasting dictators. History is full of cases that may otherwise fit Olson's description of "stationary bandits" (in the recent past, Mobutu in Zaire, the Duvaliers in Haiti, Trujillo in the Dominican Republic, Somoza in Nicaragua, and so on), of dictators who have systematically plundered and wrecked their economies for excruciatingly long periods; largely because of the insecurity of their tenure and the uncertainty surrounding their succession, they never acquired what Olson would call an "encompassing" interest in the economy.

In general, given the enormity of the collective action problem and the differential capacity of different groups in mobilization and coordination, institutional arrangements are more often the outcome of strategic distributive conflicts, in which groups with disproportionate resources and power try to constrain the actions of others, than they are the outcome of a society's decentralized attempt to realign property rights and contracts in the light of new collective benefit–cost possibilities, as is the presumption in much of the New Institutional Economics.[45]

....

7 Social Fragmentation, Inequality, and Institutional Failure

The classic example of inefficient institutions persisting as the lopsided outcome of distributive struggles relates to the historical evolution of land rights in developing countries. In most of these countries, the empirical evidence suggests that economies of scale in farm production are insignificant (except in some plantation crops) and that the small family farm is often the most efficient unit of production. Yet the violent and tortuous history of land reform in many

---

[44] J. A. Robinson, "Theories of 'Bad Policy'," unpublished paper, 1995.
[45] For an earlier exposition of this point of view, see P. Bardhan, "The New Institutional Economics and Development Theory: a Brief Critical Assessment," *World Development* (September 1989); and Jack Knight, *Institutions and Social Conflict* (New York: Cambridge University Press, 1992).

countries suggests that there are numerous road blocks to creating a more efficient reallocation of land rights, erected by vested interests over generations. Why don't the large landlords voluntarily lease out or sell their land to small family farmers and grab much of the surplus arising from this efficient reallocation? Clearly there has been some leasing out of land, but problems of monitoring, insecurity of tenure, and the landlord's fear that the tenant will acquire occupancy rights on the land have limited efficiency gains and the extent of tenancy. The land sales market has been particularly thin (and in many poor countries the sales go the opposite way, from distressed small farmers to landlords and money-lenders). With low household savings and severely imperfect credit markets, the potentially more efficient small farmer is often unable to afford the going market price of land. Binswanger, Deininger and Feder explain it in terms of land as a preferred collateral (and also carrying all kinds of tax advantages and speculation opportunities for the wealthy), often having a price above the capitalized value of the agricultural income stream for even the more productive small farmer, rendering mortgaged sales uncommon (since mortgaged land cannot be used as collateral to raise working capital for the buyer).[46] Under these circumstances, and if the public finances are such that landlords cannot be fully compensated, land redistribution will not be voluntary.[47] Landlords resist land reforms also because the leveling effects reduce their political power and their ability to control and dominate even non-land transactions.

India has a long history of exactions from the tiller of the soil by the state and a whole array of revenue-collecting intermediaries. In this century land has gradually passed from absentee landlords to medium-sized cultivator–owners (more slowly in eastern India than elsewhere), but the distribution of operational holdings as well as ownership remain quite concentrated, in spite of the built-in egalitarian forces generated by inheritance practices of subdividing the family land. The overwhelming majority of the peasants are landless or are marginal farmers and insecure tenants. The labor cost advantage of the small farmer in productivity is outweighed by the severe constraints on his access to credit, marketing, technological information, and above all to a controlled supply of water, a crucial factor in a country where large parts are either semi-arid or floodprone. The dismal failure of the colonial and (to a smaller extent) of the post-colonial state in most parts of the country has largely been in the area

---

[46] H. P. Binswanger, K. Deininger, and Gershon Feder, "Power, Distortions, Revolt and Reform in Agricultural Land Relations," in J. R. Behrman and T. N. Srinivasan (eds.), *Handbook of Development Economics III* (Amsterdam: Elsevier, 1995).

[47] Mookherjee shows, in a complete contracting model with the presence of incentive-based informational rents and endogenous credit rationing arising from wealth constraints, that there are additional arguments why a voluntary transfer of land ownership will not take place in the market even when it is socially more efficient: D. Mookherjee, "Informational Rents and Property Rights in Land," unpublished paper, Boston University, 1994.

of providing public goods like irrigation and drainage, education and health, and infrastructural facilities like roads, power, and extension services, and in grappling with credit market imperfections. Added to this are the adverse consequences of the post-colonial state's price, trade, and regulatory policies for the farmers.

But along with this set of government failures in Indian rural development, one must recognize institutional failure at the local level. This failure, often ignored in the ideological state-versus-market debates, is that of local self-governing institutions and the resulting lack of accountability and legitimacy at the local level. Even when the state in the last four decades has spent vast sums of money on irrigation, education, health, and subsidized credit, the programs are usually administered by a distant, uncoordinated, and occasionally corrupt bureaucracy, insensitive to the needs of the local people; and often, very little reaches the intended beneficiaries of the programs. One reason why public investment in irrigation has been more effective in Korea than in India is, as Wade has indicated, that the local community organizations in the former country have been by and large more vigorous in working with (and putting pressure on) the irrigation bureaucracy.[48] This lack of community coordination in India is acute not just in water allocation from public canals and maintenance of field channels, but also in unregulated private groundwater pumping, leading often to salinity and the depletion of fragile aquifers.

As in water management, so in other local public projects, such as environmental protection, prevention of soil erosion, regulated use of forests and grazing land, and public health and sanitation, local community-level institutions that can play a vital role in providing an informal framework of coordination in design as well as implementation are largely missing in most parts of India. There is also enough evidence that the serious problem of absenteeism of teachers in village public schools and of doctors in rural public clinics would be significantly less if they were made accountable to the local community rather than to a centralized bureaucracy. Subsidized credit is administered through government and semi-government agencies who do not have enough local information about the borrower and so insist on collateral, which disqualifies many of the potentially productive poor; these agencies do not have access to the systems of peer monitoring and social sanctions that local community institutions can provide.

This local institutional failure is another example of the severity of collective action problems in India. I believe that extreme social fragmentation in India (brought to boil by the exigencies of pluralist politics) makes cooperation in community institution-building much more difficult than in socially homogeneous Korea, Taiwan, and Japan. There is also some scattered evidence that

---

[48] R. Wade, "State Effectiveness as a Function of State Organization and Social Capital," unpublished paper, Sussex University, 1994.

community-level institutions work better in enforcing common agreements and cooperative norms when the underlying property regime is not too skewed and the benefits generated are more equitably shared. Putnam's study of the regional variations in Italy[49] also suggests that "horizontal" social networks (i.e. those involving people of similar status and power) are more effective in generating trust and norms of reciprocity than "vertical" ones. One beneficial byproduct of land reform, underemphasized in the usual economic analysis, is that such reform, by changing the local political structure in the village, gives more "voice" to the poor and induces them to get involved in local self-governing institutions and management of local public goods. In Indian social and political history when in situations of extreme inequality local organizations have been captured by the powerful and the wealthy, instances of subordinate groups appealing to supra-local authorities for protection and relief have not been uncommon: the intervention by the long arm of the state even in remote corners of rural India have been in such cases by invitation and not always by arbitrary imposition.

In the economics literature the complex relationship between inequality of endowments and successful collective action is still an underresearched area (I am currently involved in a research project exploring the theoretical and empirical issues in the context of cooperation in the management of local commons). On the one hand there is the well-known suggestion of Olson[50] that in a heterogeneous group a dominant member enjoying a large part of the benefits of a collective good is likely to see to its provision even if he has to pay all of the cost himself (with the small players free-riding on the contribution of the large player); on the other hand, there are cases where the net benefits of coordination of each individual may be structured in such a way that in situations of marked inequality some individuals (particularly those with better exit options) may not participate and the resulting outcome may be more inefficient than in the case with greater equality; besides, the transaction and enforcement costs for some cooperative arrangements may go up with inequality.

In general, there need not always be a tradeoff between equality and efficiency, as is now recognized in the literature on imperfect information and transaction costs; the terms and conditions of contracts in various transactions that directly affect the efficiency of resource allocation crucially depend on who owns what and who is empowered to make which decisions. Institutional structures and opportunities for cooperative problem-solving are often forgone by societies that are sharply divided along economic lines. Barriers faced by the poor in the capital markets (through a lack of collateralizable assets, which borrowers need to improve the credibility of their commitment) and in the

---

[49] Putnam, *Making Democracy Work*.
[50] Olson, The Logic of Collective Action.

land market (where the landed oligarchy hogs the endowments of land and water) sharply reduce a society's potential for productive investment, innovation, and human resource development. Under the circumstances, if the state, even if motivated by considerations of improving its political support base, carries out redistributive reform, some of this reform may go toward increasing productivity, enhancing credibility of commitments, and creating socially more efficient property rights. Even the accountability mechanisms for checking the state abuse of power at the local level work better when the poor have a greater stake in the asset base of the local economy. By dismissing all state-mandated redistribution as mere unproductive rent-creation, some of the New Institutional economists foreclose a whole range of possibilities.

When talking about the institutional impediments in the Indian economy, particularly in the context of attempts at economic reform in recent years, the discussion usually veers around the impediments posed by various government failures: in over-regulating the private economy; in denying autonomy and sheltering the inefficiency of operations in the vast public sector; in jeopardizing the viability of the public financial institutions through a system of massive credit subsidies that have built-in disincentives to invest wisely or to repay promptly; in labor laws that make deployment and readjustment in organized sector employment in response to changing market and technical conditions extremely difficult; and generally in not being able to provide a tight legal framework for contract enforcement without which a market economy cannot function properly. All this is very important and is rightly emphasized in the literature, but in this paper I have focused on some other institutional failures that are important, some of them even outside the as yet small formal sector of the economy.

I started with the historical role of "collectivist" mechanisms of eastern mercantile economies (as opposed to the more formal western institutions) and with the critical coordination role the state can play in the leap from mercantile to industrial economy. The problem is to figure out the factors that can predispose a state to have an encompassing interest in the economic performance of its country and the conditions under which the state frequently fails. The institutional arrangements of a society are often the outcome of strategic distributive conflicts between different social groups, and inequality in the distribution of power and resources can sometimes block the rearrangement of these institutions in ways that are conducive to overall development. I have drawn particular attention to the inevitable collective action problems in this rearrangement, both at the level of the state (which underlie the difficulty of breaking out of the policy deadlock, of which inefficient interventionism is only a symptom) and at the local level (which make provision and management of crucial local public goods highly inefficient).

Index